Virtual Reality Systems

Virtual Reality Systems

edited by

R.A. Earnshaw
University of Leeds, UK

M.A. Gigante
Royal Melbourne Institute of Technology, Australia

H. Jones
Middlesex University, UK

ACADEMIC PRESS
Harcourt Brace & Company, Publishers
London   San Diego   New York   Boston
Sydney   Tokyo   Toronto

ACADEMIC PRESS LIMITED
24/28 Oval Road
LONDON NW1 7DX

United States Edition published by
ACADEMIC PRESS INC.
San Diego, CA 92101

A catalogue record for this book is available from the British Library

ISBN: 0-12-227748-1

Typeset by Photo·graphics, Honiton, Devon
Printed in Great Britain by The University Printing House, Cambridge

Contents

PART 1 – INTRODUCTION

PART 2 – SYSTEMS

PART 3 – TECHNIQUES

Foreword

Few developments in computer-related technologies have caused as much excitement in the general press as 'virtual reality'. In newspapers, in magazines, on television, everyone seems to be talking about this 'fantastic new technology', even if they're vague on precisely what it is. Even among the experts, the definitions vary. Here's one definition: a VR system is one that gives the user an experience of being 'immersed' in a synthesized environment. This definition would, of course, include the most common VR systems, those that use head-mounted displays. It would also include professional flight simulators, but probably would not include flight simulator programs on home computers. It's unfortunate that we call this field 'Virtual Reality', for the term can easily be misunderstood.

The simulations in current VR systems are far from reality and there's not much chance that they're going to get even close to reality in the foreseeable future. The term is reminiscent of 'electronic brain' for computer, naive and misleading at best, certainly irritating, and it invites hype from the general press. How about virtual environments or simulated environments? They don't have the sizzle, the MTV appeal, but then neither does 'computer'. I'm afraid, for better or for worse, we're stuck with 'virtual reality' as the name, at least for the general public.

It's important to know that VR didn't just come into being in the last few years. Many experts trace the beginning of VR to Ivan Sutherland's 1965 IFIP address, 'The ultimate display' and to the description of a prototype VR system in his 1968 paper, 'A head-mounted three-dimensional display'. Although digital flight simulators became widely utilized for pilot training in the 1970s, VR research was rather sparse until the late 1980s, by which time the needed technologies – real-time image generation, head-mounted display devices, and head tracking – became commercially available at affordable prices. This availability, plus a number of very capable promoters ignited the current craze. Not only is VR widely popular in research and in the press, but some predict that VR will become available widely to everyone in the not-so-distant future. Dr James Clark, Chairman of Silicon Graphics Computer Systems Inc., a leading supplier of 3D graphics-oriented workstations, in his ACM Siggraph '92 invited talk, predicted that soon the home 'telecomputer' (television plus computer) will have the power and functionality of 'VR graphics', and such a telecomputer will enable a whole new range of applications to be engaged in by the ordinary user.

With the fantastic possibilities and the promise of widescale availability, it should be no surprise that the media are in love with VR, occasionally seeming to promise more than the more conservative technical specialists would think is prudent. Papers such as the ones collected here are major influences in restricting the hype and in promoting the 'reality' in virtual reality.

'Systems' in the title and theme of the book is especially appropriate. For VR to be effective, a systems approach is essential – it is futile to develop more powerful graphics image generation systems without an appropriate display device (and the current colour LCDs in helmets leave much to be desired); it's difficult to walk about a simulated house without an effective way to walk (pointing a glove and 'flying' leave much to be desired). It's not clear how much of a force VR will be in the technological landscape of the future.

If the VR community of developers works hard (and is lucky), much of the fantastic vision and promise of VR may become a reality in the next two decades. If so, we'll look back on these years as the exciting pioneering era, just as we now look back on the first years of today's major technologies – the radio, the telephone, television, and the computer. And we'll bore our grandchildren with tales of how primitive our systems used to be, how we couldn't move more than a step or two in our virtual environments without losing head tracking, how we couldn't see much in the helmets because the pixels were the size of boulders. If we're not lucky, we'll be like the developers of failed technologies – probably forgotten. Of course we could have a middle ground – 50 years ago, some people predicted that by now we'd have a helicopter in every garage. They thought that flying through the air would be a much better way to commute than using roads. Despite the failure, so far, of that prediction, helicopters are enormously important to humankind in many roles, particularly search and rescue. Another example is space travel. In the 1960s there was much talk about travel to the moon soon being like international air travel. There's not much talk of that now.

Much of the excitement of this field may lie in the uncertainty about the future. We don't know which of the dreams of VR will be realized. As my colleague Gary Bishop says, 'it's not a done deal'. Today we can't even get a virtual cube to stand still in front of us – it swims and lags behind our head and body movements due to delays in tracking, image generation and displays subsystems. This 'swimming' irritates and gives headaches to users and destroys the experience of being in a virtual environment. It's not at all clear how easily we'll be able to overcome this and related system problems. It's ironic that after spending years trying to get objects to move rapidly we now find that it's harder to keep them still.

However this field develops, this volume will be valuable. It not only teaches us much about the current state of the art in VR systems, but it will serve, in future years, as a marker for where we were this year.

May we live long enough to be able to talk about these as 'the good old days' of VR.

Henry Fuchs
Federico Gil Professor of Computer Science
University of North Carolina at Chapel Hill
North Carolina

About the Editors

Dr Rae A. Earnshaw, University of Leeds, UK

Rae Earnshaw is Head of Computer Graphics at the University of Leeds. He has been a Visiting Professor at Illinois Institute of Technology, Chicago, USA, Northwestern Polytechnical University, China, and George Washington University, Washington, DC, USA. He was a Director of the NATO Advanced Study Institute on 'Fundamental Algorithms for Computer Graphics' held in Italy in 1985, a Co-Chair of the BCS/ACM International Summer Institute on 'State of the Art in Computer Graphics' held in Scotland in 1986, and a Director of the NATO Advanced Study Institute on 'Theoretical Foundations of Computer Graphics and CAD' held in Italy in 1987. He is a member of the ACM, IEEE, CGS, EG, and a Fellow of the British Computer Society.

Dr Earnshaw chairs the Scientific Visualization Group at the University of Leeds, is a member of the Editorial Board of *The Visual Computer*, Vice-President of the Computer Graphics Society, and Chair of the British Computer Society Computer Graphics and Displays Group.

His interests are in graphics algorithms, human–computer interface issues, scientific visualization, graphics standards, fifth generation graphics software, workstations and display technology, mathematics of computer graphics, CAD/CAM, graphics system building, and education issues.

Dr Earnshaw has authored and edited 15 books on graphics algorithms, computer graphics, and associated topics, and published a number of papers in these areas.

Michael Gigante, Royal Melbourne Institute of Technology, Australia

Michael Gigante is the founder and director of the Advanced Computer Graphics Centre at the Royal Melbourne Institute of Technology. He was previously a research engineer in the Department of Mechanical and Production Engineering at RMIT (1985–89). From 1982 to 1985 he was a design engineer at the Government Aircraft Factories where he designed and implemented software tools for the design and analysis of conventional and composite aircraft structures.

Michael Gigante received a BE from the University of Sydney and a BSc from the University of Melbourne. He is a member of ACM and the IEEE. He has served as a committee member of the Victoria branch of the Royal Aeronautical Society of the Australasian Computer Graphics Association, acted as adviser and consultant to both government and industrial organizations, and served as Technical

Program Chair of the International Conferences Ausgraph 88 and Ausgraph 90. He is a member of the editorial board of *Computers and Education*, an international journal published by Butterworth-Heinemann Ltd.

His research interests include image synthesis, virtual reality and real-time interaction techniques, spatial data structures, and computer graphics in education.

Huw Jones, Middlesex University, UK

Huw Jones was brought up in South Wales and graduated from University College Swansea with a BSc in Applied Mathematics in 1966. The following year he obtained a Diploma in Education from the same institution and, after a short period as a school teacher, has spent the rest of his working life as a lecturer in higher education in London. During this period, he obtained an MSc in statistics from Brunel University, became a Fellow of the Royal Statistical Society, a member of the European Society for Computer Graphics and of the British Computer Society, currently being vice-chair of that society's Computer Graphics and Displays Group Committee. He is currently a Principal Lecturer in Computer Graphics and Human–Computer Interaction in the School of Mathematics, Statistics and Computing at Middlesex University, where he follows his research interest in fractal geometry, and is head of the MSc in Computer Graphics and the BSc in Human–Computer Interaction Design courses. He is married to Judy, a Mathematics teacher, and has a son, Rhodri, and a daughter, Ceri.

Addresses of Editors

Dr R. A. Earnshaw
Head of Graphics
University of Leeds
Leeds LS2 9JT
United Kingdom
(Email: R.A.Earnshaw@uk.ac.leeds)

Mr M. A. Gigante
Advanced Computer Graphics Centre
Royal Melbourne Institute of Technology
723 Swanston Street
Melbourne 3053
Australia
(Email: mg@cgl.citri.edu.au)

Mr H. Jones
School of Mathematics, Statistics and Computing
Middlesex University
Bounds Green Road
London N11 2NQ
United Kingdon
(Email: huwl@uk.ac.mdx.cluster)

Contributors

Klaus Böhm, ZGDV – Zentrum für Graphische Datenverarbeitung, Wilhelminen-strasse 7, D-6100 Darmstadt, Germany
(E-mail: {boehm}@zgdvda.uucp)

D. A. Butler, Advanced Interfaces Group, Department of Computer Science, University of Manchester, Oxford Road, Manchester M13 9PL, UK

Kim Michael Fairchild, Institute of Systems Science, National University of Singapore, Heng Mui Keng Terrace, Kent Ridge, Singapore 0511
(E-mail: [fair]@iss.nus.sg)

Martin Friedmann, Vision and Modeling Group, The Media Laboratory, Massachusetts Institute of Technology, Cambridge, MA 02139, USA
(E-mail: {martin}@media-lab.media.mit.edu)

Charles Grimsdale, Managing Director, DIVISION Ltd., 19 Apex Court Woodlands, Almondsbury, Bristol BS12 4JT, UK.

Lee Beng Hai, Institute of Systems Science, National University of Singapore, Heng Mui Keng Terrace, Kent Ridge, Singapore 0511
(E-mail: [benghai]@iss.nus.sg)

Ng Hern, Institute of Systems Science, National University of Singapore, Heng Mui Keng Terrace, Kent Ridge, Singapore 0511
(E-mail: [nghern]@iss.nus.sg)

T. L. J. Howard, Advanced Interfaces Group, Department of Computer Science, University of Manchester, Oxford Road, Manchester M13 9PL, UK

R. J. Hubbold, Advanced Interfaces Group, Department of Computer Science, University of Manchester, Oxford Road, Manchester M13 9PL, UK

R. S. Kalawsky, Systems Technology R & D, British Aerospace plc, Brough, North Humberside, HU15 1EQ, UK

Ang Tin Leong, Institute of Systems Science, National University of Singapore, Heng Mui Keng Terrace, Kent Ridge, Singapore 0511

George L. Mallen, System Simulation Ltd, 250M Bedford Chambers, Covent Garden, London WC2E 8HA, UK

Craig McNaughton, Advanced Computer Graphics Centre, Royal Melbourne Institute of Technology, 723 Swanston Street, Melbourne 3053, Australia

A. D. Murta, Advanced Interfaces Group, Department of Computer Science, University of Manchester, Oxford Road, Manchester M13 9PL, UK

Michael J. Papper, Advanced Computer Graphics Centre, Royal Melbourne Institute of Technology, 723 Swanston Street, Melbourne 3053, Australia

Alex Pentland, Vision and Modeling Group, The Media Laboratory, Massachusetts Institute of Technology, Cambridge, MA 02139, USA
(E-mail:{sandy}@media-lab.media.mit.edu)

P. Quarendon, IBM UK Scientific Centre, St. Clement Street, Winchester SO23 9DR, UK
(E-mail: Internet pq@venta.vnet.ibm.com)

Warren Robinett, Computer Science Department, University of North Carolina, Chapel Hill, North Carolina, 27599-3175, USA

Jannick P. Rolland, Computer Science Department, University of North Carolina, Chapel Hill, North Carolina, 27599-3175, USA

T. W. Rowley, Technical Consultant, W-Industries Ltd, ITEC House, 26–28 Cherny Street, Leicester LE1 5WD, UK

Luis Serra, Institute of Systems Science, National University of Singapore, Heng Mui Keng Terrace, Kent Ridge, Singapore 0511
(E-mail: [luis]@iss.nus.sg)

D. N. Snowdon, Advanced Interfaces Group, Department of Computer Science, University of Manchester, Oxford Road, Manchester M13 9PL, UK

Thad Starner, Vision and Modeling Group, The Media Laboratory, Massachusetts Institute of Technology, Cambridge, MA 02139, USA
(E-mail: {testarne}@media-lab.media.mit.edu)

Robert J. Stone, UK Advanced Robotics Research Centre, University Road, Salford, M5 4PP, UK

Daniel Thalmann, Computer Graphics Laboratory, Swiss Federal Institute of Technology, CH-1015 Lausanne, Switzerland

Kaisa Väänänen, ZGDV–Zentrum für Graphische Datenverarbeitung, Wilhelminen-strasse 7, D-6100 Darmstadt, Germany
(E-mail: {kaisa}@zgvda.uucp)

John Vince, Rediffusion Simulation Ltd, Crawley, W. Sussex, RH10 2JY, UK

A. J. West, Advanced Interfaces Group, Department of Computer Science, University of Manchester, Oxford Road, Manchester M13 9PL, UK (E-mail: ajw@cs.man.ac.uk)

L. J. Whalley, Department of Mental Health, University of Aberdeen, Medical School Buildings, Foresterhill, Aberdeen, AB9 2ZD, UK

Acknowledgements

Many people have supplied information on their uses and applications of virtual reality systems. Many designers and implementors have supplied details of their systems, and also illustrations. Others have supplied details of aspects of virtual reality, as well as slides. We express our thanks and appreciation to all those who have contributed.

The Bibliography is an extended version of a reference list for virtual reality in the public domain. It is reproduced in its extended form with due acknowledgement to all those who contributed information to earlier versions.

This is to be included in the on-line bibliography stored at the sci.virtual-worlds archive site (milton.u.washington.edu). This bibliography has been built by a number of people who have volunteered their time and effort, and is in the public domain.

Some companies were unable to supply information or illustrations of their products, despite being invited to do so. They have therefore been omitted from the information on current vendor systems. The list of vendor systems does not therefore claim to cover all the systems in the market place at the time of writing.

Disclaimer

The views expressed by the contributors of information on products is believed to be accurate and given in good faith. However, authors and publisher do not hold themselves responsible for the views expressed in this volume in connection with vendor products or public domain products. In addition, the authors and publisher do not hold themselves responsible for the accuracy or otherwise of data extracted from vendor specifications.

Copyright Material

Some slides are reproduced by permission of their originators and these are noted in the text. Some materials are reproduced by permission of other publishers and societies. In particular those by Professor R. S. Kalawsky are reproduced by kind permission of Addison-Wesley Ltd, and those by W. Robinett and J. P. Rolland by kind permission of the Society of Photo-Optical Instrumentation Engineers (SPIE). Material by Professor M. Friedman *et al.* is reproduced by kind permission of the Association for Computing Machinery (ACM).

Cover Illustrations

The images on the cover come from the chapters by T. W. Rowley, M. Friedmann *et al.*, and D. Thalmann. They are reproduced with legends in the colour plate section.

Preface

This volume is based upon presentations made at an International Conference in London on the subject of 'Virtual Reality Systems'. Its objective was to bring together some of the leading practitioners and exponents in the field, and to explore some of the issues in virtual reality and its associated hardware and software technology.

Based on this initial conference, and subsequent exchanges between the editors and the authors, revised and updated papers were produced, and further international contributions have been added. These papers are contained in the present volume.

A comprehensive bibliography is provided at the end of the volume to enable readers to follow up particular areas of specialism.

We thank all those who contributed to this effort by way of planning and organization, and also all those who helped in the production of this volume.

R. A. Earnshaw
M.A. Gigante
H. Jones

August 1992

Introduction

The ideas underlying virtual reality systems are not new. The 'father' of computer graphics, Ivan Sutherland, first postulated the use of stereographic head-mounted displays in the 1960s [1]. Michael Frayn's novel *A Very Private Life* [2], first published in 1968, describes a heroine whose experience of life is through her upbringing within an immersive artificial environment. William Gibson's *Neuromancer* [3] was the first instance of a genre of science fiction writing, in which practitioners 'jack in', sometimes directly through brain-mounted electrodes, to the cyberspace 'matrix', an immersive artificial world of organizational data, visualized within brightly coloured geometric forms. 'Cyberspace. A consensual hallucination experienced daily by billions of legitimate operators, in every nation . . . A graphic representation of data abstracted from the banks of every computer in the human system.' Enclosed environments within the matrix are guarded from unwanted intruders by 'ice', protective software that is attacked illegally by special viruses.

In 1984, many of the situations described by Gibson existed only within the realms of science fiction, unreachable by science fact. Now, early in the 1990s, many of these features have been implemented; others will be realized within the very near future. We have seen the visionary speculations of earlier writers like Verne, Wells and Clarke achieved in reality within our lifetimes. It now appears certain that many of the scenarios described by Frayn, Gibson and others will soon be commonplace. The reason for this certainty is the rapid advance in computer technology, enabling massive increases in computer power at relatively decreasing cost. This is matched by improved software systems, enabling real-time animation of images and sound based on large data sets, major steps forward in human–computer interaction systems design and new initiatives in the creation of innovative input and output devices. All these features can now be made available some of the time; it will not be long before they are all readily available to relatively modest users.

The increasing belief that true 'virtual reality' systems will soon be widely used is only part of the reason for the mushrooming of interest in the area. There is a fascination with the nature of such systems, giving an immersive escape from the everyday environment or enabling researchers to 'step in' to the core of their research activities. Even with today's fairly crude methods of stereographic animation and visualization, useful innovative tasks can be performed using such systems. Leisure machines using these currently imperfect technologies attract users into their immersive environments. Demonstrations of virtual reality systems at conferences and trade shows attract long queues of delegates, whose amusement at the externally visible antics of the person currently strapped in to the system may be tempered by the thought that they will soon be giving such a performance. With this increasing interest, we read of worries of the possible harmful effects of virtual reality systems [4] similar to those that have accompanied potentially pervasive technological advances in the past. Some of these past worries were justified, so developers of the new technology should address these warnings seriously.

It was in the background of the burgeoning interest in these rapid and potentially powerful developments that the British Computer Society Computer Graphics and Displays Group decided to host an International Conference on Virtual Reality Systems at the University of London in 1992. The papers in this volume are based on presentations at this event, which describe the advances outlined above in the context of their historical development and concerns regarding potential abuses of the new technology. The following chapters are broadly clustered within the categories of introduction, systems, techniques, applications, interface and contextual issues, and ethical and societal issues and concerns.

To set the scene, Michael Gigante of the Royal Melbourne Institute of Technology, outlines the main components of the current generation of virtual reality systems, and discusses major worldwide developments of such systems.

Effective virtual reality systems require great power to drive their interactive and visual engines. Charles Grimsdale of Division Ltd describes how his company has harnessed the power of a transputer-based parallel architecture specifically designed for this purpose.

Terry Rowley describes the systems requirements for a commercial virtual reality product in the context of the complete hardware and software systems produced by W-Industries, largely sold for the leisure market, but with other potential uses.

Warren Robinett discusses the relationship of the perceived objects in 3D space (as viewed in a VR system, for example) to how they are expected to be – to ensure constancy and consistency of their shape, size, and relative positioning as the observer's head moves around. This involves modelling the geometry of the head-mounted display.

Roy Kalawsky leads a major research team in virtual reality systems at British Aerospace plc. His contributions describe the requirements for a comprehensive virtual reality laboratory system, and highlight the way in which limitations of current systems capability leads to user problems with stereographic displays.

The DataGlove is a common input device for virtual reality systems, often used only for pointing and selection tasks. Kaisa Väänänen and Klaus Böhm of the Zentrum für Graphische Datenverarbeitung at Darmstadt show how a repertoire of hand gestures can be used to generate a wider range of input commands.

The objects that comprise a virtual world need to 'behave' in as natural a way as possible to enable users to control them in pseudo-natural ways. Michael Gigante and Michael Papper present further work at the Royal Melbourne Institute of Technology in developing and testing a suitable subset of pseudo-physical constraints for model objects.

Some of the most highly developed immersive systems in use today are found in flight simulators, which give pilots real tactile cues from their immediate environment and simulate motion and visual cues to an often alarmingly realistic extent in the middle and far distance. John Vince of Rediffusion Simulation Ltd describes his company's convincing work in this arena.

An intrinsic element of virtual reality systems is the process of real-time animation. Daniel Thalmann of the Swiss Federal Institute of Technology at Lausanne turns this situation on its head by describing how virtual reality systems can be used in the development of animated video and film sequences to control and generate the 'actors' and the pseudo-camera movements of such sequences.

Kim Fairchild, Luis Serra and others of the National University of Singapore have created systems for the visualization of complex information sets. Their work shows how users can navigate the most complex data sets when virtual reality systems enable them to 'swim' through visual representations of the interrelationships between the data. The VizNet prototype described has many of the features of William Gibson's Cyberspace.

Telepresence enables real robotic devices to perform human-like tasks in situations that would be hazardous to human operators. Recent history has made it only too clear how valuable such devices could be for bomb disposal and in the aftermath of nuclear accidents. Robert Stone of the UK Advanced Robotics Research Centre describes how his company has developed virtual reality features that enable such telepresence activity, and shows how virtual reality systems are used in human factors research.

Adrian West and a team from the University of Manchester discuss potential applications areas of virtual reality systems, and show how the Manchester group is moving towards developing its own virtual reality system. They describe the conceptual models, software architecture and hardware platforms underlying their developments, showing how educationally-based research institutions can contribute to the subject's advance.

The Royal Melbourne Institute of Technology partnership of Michael Papper and Michael Gigante return to the theme of hand gestures interpreted by DataGloves. Their contribution considers how such gestures can be used to control a virtual robotic arm, following naturally from the previous discussion of how to capture such gestures.

One of the major chores for developers of virtual reality systems is to produce a rich environment for potential users. This involves modelling the appearance of objects within that environment, a painstaking process using current modelling systems. Peter Quarendon of the IBM UK Scientific Centre discusses a potential semi-automatic method for generating the appearance of objects. Although his method is not yet fully developed, it has potential value for systems developers.

George Mallen discusses images, reality and knowledge. His subtle probing of history and philosophy opens questions that are more vital than ever in the context of today's development of virtual reality systems. He describes the creation in 1970, by his company System Simulation Ltd, of an early interactive immersive environment that had many of the properties of more modern systems.

As a reminder of the potential problems of overenthusiastic acceptance of rapidly developing technology, Lawrence Whalley of the University of Aberdeen Medical School makes a plea for caution in the application of virtual reality systems to the treatment of psychiatric disorders. He discusses how seductive new techniques have been used without proper justification in the past, and asks for proper consideration of ethical issues to be made with regard to the potential proliferation of virtual reality systems.

Craig McNaughton of the Royal Melbourne Institute of Technology provides an overview of virtual reality software suppliers, and summarizes the most popular and readily available software toolkits.

Delegates at the British Computer Society Computer Graphics and Displays Group event were educated and prompted into lively discussion by the conference presentations. These presentations have been refined and expanded in the written contributions included in this volume. The materials have also been augmented by further international contributions. We present them to a wider audience in the hope and expectation that they will be similarly informed and stimulated.

Rae Earnshaw
Michael Gigante
Huw Jones

References

1   Sutherland, I.E. 1968. A head-mounted three dimensional display. *Proceedings Fall Joint Computer Conference*, Thompson Books, Washington, DC, 757–764.
2   Frayn, M. 1968. *A Very Private Life*, William Collins, Glasgow.
3   Gibson, W. 1984. *Neuromancer*, Victor Gollancz, New York.
4   Arthur, C. 1992. Did reality move for you?, *New Scientist*, **134** (1822): 22–27, 23 May.

Part 1
Introduction

1 Virtual Reality: Definitions, History and Applications

Michael A. Gigante
Royal Melbourne Institute of Technology
Advanced Computer Graphics Centre

1 Introduction

Virtual Reality (VR) has received an enormous amount of publicity over the past few years. Along with this publicity has arisen a great deal of conflicting terminology, some unrealistic expectations and a great deal of uninformed commentary. In this paper, I will attempt to provide an overview of developments in the area and attempt to lay down some realistic medium term goals. I will also lay to rest a number of misconceptions about VR and where it is today.

1.1 Terminology
First, let me provide a minimal definition; VR is characterized by

> The illusion of participation *in* a synthetic environment rather than external observation of such an environment. VR relies on three-dimensional (3D), stereoscopic, head-tracked displays, hand/body tracking and binaural sound. VR is an immersive, multi-sensory experience.

Under this broad definition, VR is also referred to as *Virtual Environments*, *Virtual Worlds* or *Microworlds*. Although these names are essentially equivalent, many research groups prefer to avoid the term VR because of the hype and the associated unrealistic expectations.

Telepresence represents one of the main areas of research in the VR community – that of VR-mediated remote presence and remote operation. The classic example of a telepresence environment is the teleoperation of a robot in a hazardous or remote environment. You can imagine coupling your visual system with remote cameras that track your head and eye movements so that you can see what you would see yourself *if you were in fact in that remote place*. Then also couple your hand and arm movements with those of a mobile robot arm in the same environment – you can now interact with that environment as if you were there! You can grasp objects, or perform maintenance or repairs from the safety of your office.

The term *Cyberspace* is often incorrectly used to describe VR. In fact, Cyberspace has two distinct meanings:

1. A global information and entertainment network as described in the science

VIRTUAL REALITY SYSTEMS
ISBN 0-12-227748-1

fiction novels of William Gibson. In Gibson's world, today's international computer networks have evolved into 'The Matrix'. From Gibson's short story *Burning Chrome*:

> The matrix is an abstract representation of the relationships between data systems. Legitimate programmers jack into their employer's sector of the matrix and find themselves surrounded by bright geometries representing the corporate data. Towers and fields of it ranged in the colourless non-space of the simulation matrix, the electronic consensus-hallucination that facilitates the handling and exchange of massive quantities of data. Legitimate programmers never see the walls of ICE (Intrusion Countermeasures Electronics) they work behind, the walls of shadow that screen their operations from others, from industrial espionage artists and hustlers.

A techno-criminal subculture, cyberpunks, break into corporate systems in the matrix, stealing data. In Gibson's world, drugs, brain implants, nerve splicing and microbionics are integral parts of that culture. The elite thieves, cowboys, jack into a custom cyberspace deck so that, with the help of ICE-breaking software (viruses), they can steal corporate or military secrets.

Even though Gibson's cowboys are clearly direct descendants of today's hackers (computer criminals), they are the heroes in his stories.

Clearly, the cyberspace that Gibson describes is merely a single possible application of VR. Gibson's cyberspace is to VR as the suburban brick home is to accommodation – one instance of a general, broad class of possibilities.

2. A trademark for AutoDesk's prototype of a VR CAD system. AutoDesk Inc., the developers of the popular PC CAD program Autocad, showed a prototype PC-based VR CAD system at Siggraph '89 in Boston. Their name for this program was Cyberspace. AutoDesk took out a trademark on the name and demonstrated the system worldwide.

As an interesting side note, Gibson, annoyed that AutoDesk trademarked a term he invented, retaliated by trademarking the name 'Eric Gullichsen', one of the AutoDesk team who built their Cyberspace!

Artificial Reality is a term defined by Myron Krueger to describe video-based, computer-mediated interactive media. The work was quite different to what we conventionally consider VR. His work, Videoplace, is essentially a two-dimensional outline of the user acquired by a video camera and projected onto a large screen. The user interacts with this projected image of him/herself. The computer system that processes the video image also adds sprite-like agents[1] that have a rule-based programmed behaviour, providing the user with an interesting environment to experiment. Videoplace is very engaging and quite clever; it inspired many of the people who now work in VR. It also inspired other video-based art work like 'The Very Nervous System' and 'Mandala'.

1.2 History

There are a few outstanding historical contributors to VR that deserve special mention.

---

[1] Sprites are graphical objects that can be moved around the screen, a sort of generalized cursor.

1.2.1 Morton Heilig

The first real example of a multi-sensural simulator was the *Sensorama* which was first shown in 1962. *Popular Photography* had this to say in a 1964 review:

> Watch out for a remarkable new process called Sensorama! It attempts to engulf the viewer in the stimuli of reality. Viewing of the colour stereo film is replete with binaural sound, scents, winds, vibration. The original scene is recreated with remarkable fidelity. At this time, the system comes closer to duplicating reality than any other system we have seen.

The viewer could take a motorcycle ride through New York, complete with fan-generated wind, the noise and smells of New York. Heilig's system had all the hallmarks of a VR system except that it was not interactive; the route was fixed and pre-recorded.

1.2.2 Ivan Sutherland

Ivan Sutherland is a pioneer in the field of computer graphics, probably contributing more than any other individual to its development. In 1965, he wrote about 'The ultimate display' [1] which included interactive graphics, force-feedback devices, as well as mentioning audio, smell and even taste!

In 1968 he described [2] a head-mounted display that tracked the viewer and updated a graphics display to correctly reflect the new viewing position. Sutherland's system used two displays which were visible from a pair of half-silvered mirrors. This provided the viewer with stereoscopic computer graphics images overlaid onto the real world!

1.2.3 Flight simulators

The development of flight simulators has made very significant contributions to the development of VR. Much of the technology needed for VR was developed ostensibly for military flight simulators. In fact, some of the most significant work in VR was done by Tom Furness at the US Air Force's Armstrong Medical Research laboratories [3].

Furness and his group developed an advanced fighter cockpit (Visually Coupled Airborne Systems Simulator (VCASS)) where the fighter pilot wore a head-mounted display that augmented the out-the-window view with graphics. These graphics included friend-or-foe identification, targeting information, threat information (e.g. ground-based missile sites) as well as optimal flight path information. The value of this work is clearly understandable. The fighter pilot is operating under extremely high stress levels (both cognitive and physical), yet has to assimilate and process masses of data. Furness' work addressed most of the major issues in VR, independent of whether or not the application is a military one. Furness now heads the VR lab (Human Interface Technology Lab) at the University of Washington.

In general, work in flight simulators also led to a far greater understanding of the technical requirements underlying VR – like VR, simulators are only effective if, from the participants' view, the experience is an accurate one. Some of the needs identified to make this possible include:

- rapid update rates (i.e. very fast tracking and redisplay, preferably at least 30 frames per second);

- short lag times (so there is no noticeable delay between movement and the production of the correct (new) visuals);
- secondary visual cues like shadows and textures;
- motion feedback and force feedback;
- techniques for the management and efficient display of complex worlds.

Needless to say, while the commercial flight simulators successfully address these issues, they cost millions of dollars each. For VR to be successful, we must achieve similar fidelity at a tiny fraction of the cost.

1.2.4 NASA Ames

In 1984, Dr Mike McGreevy and Jim Humphries at NASA Ames were the originators of the contemporary VR setup – VIVED (VIrtual Visual Environment Display) (Fig. 1.1). They evaluated the potential of the monochrome head-mounted display system for future astronauts.

Later [4], the VIEW (Virtual Interactive Environment Workstation) project developed a general-purpose, multi-sensory, personal simulator and telepresence device. The configuration included head and hand tracking, monochrome wide field-

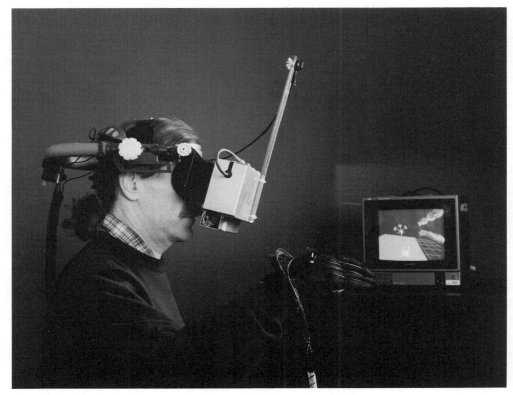

Figure 1.1 The VIVED system, designed and built in 1984 by Dr Mike McGreevy and Jim Humphries at the NASA Ames Research Center.

of-view stereo head-mounted displays, speech recognition, 3D audio output, and a tracked and instrumented glove (Fig. 1.2).

The company VPL, which manufactures the most popular glove (DataGlove) and head-mounted display (EyePhone), was a spinoff from the work at the VIEW lab. VPL now sells turnkey VR systems as well as 'computerized clothing'.

1.2.5 Other contributors

Andy Lippman at the MIT Machine Architecture Group (later to become the Media Lab) made an interactive video disk that allowed the user to wander the streets of Aspen, Colorado. Lippman drove around Aspen recording thousands of individual frames. He then stored these images on video disk and provided software to allow the user to navigate his/her own way around Aspen [5].

There are some contemporary contributions that also deserve a mention. Disney's

Figure 1.2 The VIEW system, developed at the NASA Ames Research Center under the direction of Dr Scott Fisher.

Star Tours provides a flight simulator-like ride for the general public. It also, through elaborate scene setting as the participants wait in line, establishes a well constructed 'total experience'.

The 'Private Eye' is a novel device that allows a PC user to attach a pen-size display device to a pair of glasses and see the display suspended out about 15 inches from his/her face. Like Sutherland's display, the Private Eye graphics are overlaid on top of the real world; it is only visible to the wearer. While this is primarily promoted as a mechanism for confidentiality, it is also useful in training and maintenance/repair applications.

There is one further group that have been a source of stimulation for those who have thought about VR – science fiction authors. It is interesting to see that many of these authors have written, in fiction, about issues that are only now being seriously discussed about VR. Arthur C. Clarke wrote about 'personalized television safaris', Robert Heinlein wrote about 'Waldoes' (teleoperated machines), John Brunner wrote about the use of VR in changing society's attitudes to race and religion, and Roger Zelazny wrote of the use of a VR-like device in psychotherapy.

2   VR Applications

One of the reasons that VR has attracted so much interest is that it offers enormous benefits to so many different applications areas.

2.1   Operations in hazardous or remote environments

There are still many examples of people working in hazardous or hardship environments that could benefit from the use of VR-mediated teleoperation. Workers in radioactive, toxic or space environments could be relocated to the safety of a VR environment where they could 'handle' any hazardous materials without any real danger. Furthermore, like the example of the advanced fighter cockpit, the operator's display can be augmented with important sensor information, warnings and suggested procedures – resulting in a lower cognitive load and hence less chance of error.

Naturally, telepresence needs further developments in haptic feedback to be truly useful, but it is also clear that, as a major industrial application, these developments will happen and we will see real industrial VR teleoperation applications inside five years.

2.2   Scientific visualization

Scientific Visualization (SciVis) provides 3D, dynamic computer graphics tools to assist scientists to interpret (qualitatively) masses of data. It also assists them to develop better models of system behaviour. There is considerable evidence that SciVis does improve the quality of scientific research when it is used effectively.

Many of the current efforts in SciVis are directed towards providing the investigator with immediate graphical feedback during the course of the computations and giving them the ability to 'steer' the solution process. Similarly, by closely coupling the computation and visualization processes, SciVis provides an exploratory, experimentation environment that allows the investigators to concentrate their (and the computer's) efforts on the important areas.

The best example of this is the NASA Virtual Wind Tunnel at the NASA Ames Research Center (Fig. 1.3). In this application, the scientist (computational fluid dynamicist) controls the computation of virtual smoke streams emanating from his or her fingertips. Using supercomputers to simulate the full Navier–Stokes equations (the underlying equations for general fluid flow), the smoke stream follows the computed airflow around a digital model of the aircraft. By moving around the aircraft, the scientist can discover areas of instability, separation of the flow from the aircraft's surface, and other interesting phenomena. The computation is performed in real-time by closely coupling the CFD solution on the supercomputer with the VR environment on graphics workstations. Since the computation is mostly a single streamline at a time, today's supercomputers can solve the problem interactively. The solution of the complete flow around an aircraft would require orders of magnitudes more computer power – by providing a well planned VR environment the NASA researchers have reduced the need for the complete solution.

Figure 1.3 The NASA Virtual Wind Tunnel, developed at the Ames Research Center.

2.3   Architectural visualization

Imagine being able to wander through your new house before it was even built –
you could get a feel for the space, experiment with different lighting schemes,
furnishings, or even the layout of the house itself, all without committing a single
cent to production costs!

Most architects have been using computer graphics for design for a number of
years, however the majority of the systems they use fall far short of being able to
provide any degree of realism and could not adequately simulate the furnishings
and subtle lighting effects that really make an environment comfortable.

Even if your architect can provide high quality renderings of your proposed
building, it still doesn't provide you with a sense of space. It is after all just a 2D
flat photograph-like image. It is like taking photographs of (say) the Grand Canyon
– when you look at those photographs later, they do not (and cannot) convey the
feeling of being there. The reasons have been explained earlier, most of the visual
cues necessary have been thrown away in producing a planar image.

A VR architectual environment *can* provide that feeling of space. Once better
head-tracked displays become available, I believe that such a VR design environment
will be a serious competitive advantage.

Figure 1.4 The UNC walkthrough project uses the Pixel-Planes 5 graphics workstation to
display complex textured models in real time to a VR user. The user's head and hand
movements are tracked with a custom optical ceiling tracker.

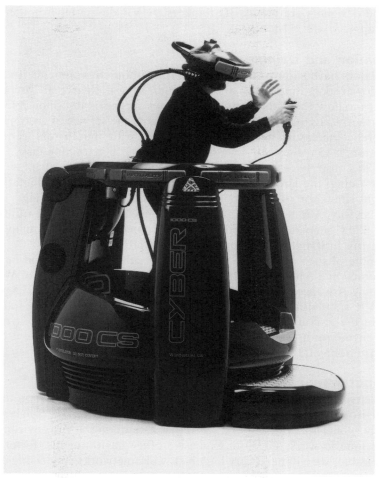

Figure 1.5 The Virtuality 1000CS from W-Industries.

2.4 Design

Many areas of design are inherently 3D. Take, for example, the design of a car shape, where the designer looks for sweeping curves and good aesthetics from every possible view.

Computer tools are essential for most designers now because of the increased flexibility they provide in the rest of the product development cycle (e.g. engineering analysis, manufacturing and testing). These days, the geometry the designer creates is the essential information that is shared by the rest of the project team. However, today's design tools are mouse or stylus/digitizer based and thereby force the designer to work with inherently 2D input devices. For many designers, this is difficult since it increases the cognitive load – forcing them to mentally reconstruct the 3D shape from 2D sections. Similarly, instead of just sweeping out a shape in space, elaborate constructions in multiple views are often necessary.

Most good designers are visual, 3D thinkers. A VR design environment can give them back appropriate 3D tools.

2.5   Education and training

Flight simulators have shown the benefits of simulation environments for training – they have lower operating costs and are safer to use than real aircraft. Flight simulators also allow the simulation of dangerous scenarios not allowable with real aircraft. Furthermore, they free aircraft to be used in the service of customers and/or freight, thereby increasing income. The difficulty with the current generation of flight simulators is that they are not readily used for other training tasks. While the technology has also been used for other (military) training such as tank and submarine training, the large amount of specialized physical instrumentation means that the flight simulator cannot be used the next day for tank training.

In a similar way, VR promises many more applications of similar utility. Unlike specialized flight simulators, a good VR environment can have many different applications run in it simply by running different programs.

One example of such a training system is the result of collaboration between the Human Interaction Technology Laboratory (HITL) at the University of Washington and the Boeing Advanced Technology Centre. The VSX (Virtual Space Xperimental craft) is a VR simulator of a tilt-rotor aircraft. It allows the user to interact with the design of the aircraft to some extent as well as using the flight controls to start the tiltable engine/rotors and take off. The current version requires the user to wear the VPL EyePhone and DataGlove.

2.6   Computer supported cooperative work

Shared VR environments will allow possibly remote workers to collaborate on tasks. The VR environment can also provide additional support for the collaboration.

Eventually, going to work may be as simple as entering a VR environment! No more travel time to work, no more expensive office environments, fewer cars. For this to be feasible, we will need very high bandwidth networks connecting our homes and offices and indeed our cities and countries.

2.7   Space exploration

The Virtual Planetary Exploration (VPE) laboratory at NASA Ames Research Center, run by Mike McGreevy, is investigating ways to help planetary geologists remotely analyse the surface of a planet. They are applying virtual reality techniques to roam planetary terrains. Their data are extremely complex height fields derived from Viking images of Mars.

2.8   Entertainment

The application of VR in entertainment could possibly be viewed as trivial, but the reality is that entertainment will probably drive the development of VR technology in the next few years. The reason is not that entertainment has more demanding technical requirements, if anything the converse is true, but rather entertainment requires mass production. The biggest limiting factor in VR research today is the sheer expense of the technology. It is expensive because the volumes are low.

With increasing volumes used in entertainment and the associated reduction in price, many more research organizations will be able to afford VR. More VR research will bring better VR and faster realization of its promise. Greater diversity will also mean new applications of VR will appear.

The UK company W-Industries has developed two networked, multi-player VR entertainment systems: one standing (Virtuality 1000CS) and one seated (Virtuality 1000CD). There are a number of successful installations already in use. There are currently five games available for the W-Industries systems. These systems are apparently based on Amiga 3000 computers with custom graphics accelerators. At the current time, only W-Industries is in a position to write applications for these systems.

3   Social Impact

There has been a great deal of speculation about the impact of VR on our lives. I have no doubt that the impact will indeed be felt, but I do not believe we can predict exactly how.

I have tried to show that while VR does provide a fundamentally different experience for the user, it can be viewed as yet another step in the development of computer graphics (CG) and human–computer interaction (HCI) techniques. In that sense it merely accounts for more perceptual and physiological phenomena that earlier generations of techniques decided to ignore (mostly because they didn't have any choice in the matter!).

So before we ask what impact VR will have on society, we must look behind us to the impact that computers, computer graphics and HCI have had on society as a whole.

Even 20 years ago, computers were locked away in secure computer rooms only accessible to the computing high priests. Today nearly every home has a computer. Few people would have predicted the rapid changes we have seen over that period – nearly every machine we use has at least a microprocessor. The social impact of computers is clearly enormous, with nearly every aspect of our everyday lives affected in some way.

We have yet to see the same impact of CG and HCI, although all the signs are there. In a pattern similar to the impact of computers in general, computer graphics has gone from a very specialized, almost elitist small group to being an everyday tool of scientists, engineers and designers. If the 1980s were the decade of the personal computer, the 1990s promise to be the decade of computer graphics, and perhaps the first decade of the next century will be the decade of VR.

So to answer the question 'How will VR impact society?', we should examine how computers have affected society thus far. I contend that despite the proliferation of computers, it has caused little change to society itself. While I concede that I am by no means the best person to make this judgement, it seems to me that society's attitudes to most social issues has developed independently of the impact of computing. Will this be true of VR? I find this a difficult call to make. Many commentators on VR argue that the change on society will be dramatic (which I agree with), and that change will include a major cultural shift. It is this latter point that I find difficult to grapple with. Certainly there is potential for change, whether or not it occurs probably depends on factors outside VR.

Probably the issue most discussed is the potential to provide participatory, interactive entertainment. Many people see VR as a replacement for television where, unlike the current system, the medium would not be designed for the lowest common denominator, and would be less corruptible than other media because the producer of the medium cannot impose a view upon the user.

Finally, many people are concerned about external control of a VR environment. At this point it is difficult for me to imagine that this is really possible. The close coupling between our kinaesthetic and visual senses which provides the power of the medium also means that the user becomes rather nauseous if that coupling is suddenly broken. I cannot believe the user would willingly stay in an environment which made them nauseous! Getting out of VR is simply a matter of removing the head-mounted display or using the *exit* gesture. While that is true, external control will not be a serious issue. We therefore should ensure that we always have the 'way out' of any VR environment.

4   Conclusion

VR is an interactive, participatory environment that could sustain many (remote) users sharing a single virtual space. It has the potential to provide additional power to its users through increased perceptual fidelity. It can also improve the performance of users by lowering the cognitive load in the completion of a task.

VR can improve the quality of life for workers in hazardous or uncomfortable environments and may eventually impact on the whole of society.

It is important to investigate the technological and social issues underlying VR now before we find ourselves overtaken by its spread through the global community.

Acknowledgements

This work is supported in part by a grant by the Victorian Education Foundation. Figures 1.1, 1.2 and 1.3 courtesy of NASA Ames Research Center. Figure 1.4 photographed by Bo Strain, courtesy of Department of Computer Science, University of North Carolina at Chapel Hill. Figure 1.5 courtesy of W Industries.

References

1   Sutherland, I. 1965. The ultimate display. *Proc. IFIP Congress*, 506–508.
2   Sutherland, I. 1968. A head-mounted three dimensional display. *Proc. Fall Joint Computer Conference*, 757–764.
3   Furness, T.A. 1986. The Super Cockpit and its human factors challenges. *Proc. Human Factors Society*, 30.
4   McGreevy, M., Humphries, J., Robinett, W. and Fisher, S. 1986. Virtual environment display system. *Proc. Workshop on Interactive 3D Computer Graphics*, 77–87.
5   Lippman, A. 1980. Movie-Maps: An application of the optical videodisc to computer graphics. *Computer Graphics (SIGGRAPH '80 Conference)* **14** (3).

2 Virtual Reality: Enabling Technologies

Michael A. Gigante
Royal Melbourne Institute of Technology
Advanced Computer Graphics Centre

1 Introduction

Virtual reality is reliant on the following technologies:

1. Real-time 3D computer graphics
2. Wide-angle stereoscopic displays
3. Viewer (head) tracking
4. Hand and gesture tracking
5. Binaural sound
6. Haptic feedback
7. Voice input/output

Of these, the first three are mandatory, the fourth is conventionally used but under some circumstances may not be necessary, and items five and six are becoming increasingly important to researchers in the field. The last item, while of immense utility, is probably not a key technology that characterizes VR.

It is important to describe how such a system differs from that of conventional computer systems. A VR system is not just a bigger, faster or better version of a conventional computer graphics (CG) system. In conventional CG systems, the user is like an external observer, looking in through a window at some synthetic environment. The combination described above transforms the user to a participant **in** the synthetic environment.

The most important contributors to this transformation are the wide field of view (greater than 120°), and the binocular and motion parallax achievable with a stereoscopic, head-tracked display. This transformation is a dramatic one and really separates a VR experience from other conventional graphics experience.

2 Real-Time 3D Computer Graphics

The generation of an image from a computer model, *image synthesis*, is well understood. Given sufficient time, we can generate a reasonably accurate portrayal of what that object would look like under given lighting conditions.

However, the constraint of *real time* means we have anything but time. The main lesson VR has learned from flight simulators is that update rate is extremely important. We do not want to reduce the number of image updates to less than 15 times per second. It is very desirable in fact to increase the rate to greater than 30 frames per second! This demand constrains both the quality we can expect and the geometric complexity of our virtual worlds.

Modern high performance CG workstations can render as many as 350,000 independent facets (polygons) per second when giving medium quality shaded images. This includes hidden surface removal and some lighting effects. Some quick calculations show that if we want 15 frames per second, we can interact with scenes of approximately 23,000 facets, less if we wish to use textures or calculate shadows.

In terms of 'interestingness', models of approximately 20,000 polygons are rather sparse indeed! If we can achieve scene complexities of a few hundred thousand textured polygons (with shadows), then we can really say we have arrived![1]

3 Wide-Angle Stereoscopic Displays

Most of us have stereoscopic, or binocular, vision – it is a natural consequence of having two coordinated eyes. Each eye sees the same world around us, but from a slightly different position. The resulting different images are then fused by the brain to give the impression of a single view, but with auxiliary depth information. We also have other visual cues like focus which augment our depth perception.

Binocular vision is also fundamental to VR. Without it we would not have sufficient depth cues to work in the synthetic environment.[2] It is achieved by placing independently driven displays in front of each eye. The image on each display is computed from a viewpoint appropriate for that eye. In the same way as your normal vision, the brain fuses these images together and derives depth information.

Kalawsky [1] has stated that the minimum features of a VR display system are greater than 110° for horizontal field of view, greater than 60° vertical field of view, and greater than 30° of stereo overlap.

In some systems, two separate computers are used to drive each display and in other systems, like ours, one computer generates two separate images, one for each display. In the first case, care must be taken to synchronize the two computers! In the latter case, the sustainable model complexity is halved.

The current generation of head mounted displays (HMD) use Sony Watchman™ liquid crystal displays (LCD). These displays use the same encoding as American television broadcast (NTSC). The fact that they use a so-called *composite* video standard means that a considerable amount of information in the original image is thrown away. Both the spatial and colour resolution of composite video is considerably worse than we are accustomed to in computer graphics. This means that no matter how beautiful and intricate the image on our high-resolution computer display, we will almost certainly be disappointed with the image we see in the HMD.

The quality of the image is further degraded by the limited effective resolution

---

[1] Given our current expectations. However, experience has shown that our expectations are *always* beyond the reach of the current technology!

[2] Most VR systems ignore focus (everything is in focus at infinity where the human eye is at its most relaxed position).

of the LCD screen. Although being driven by an NTSC signal of approximately 500 lines, the effective resolution of the most common LCD display is only about 140 resolvable lines. This will result in a blurred and indistinct image.

The problems are further exacerbated by the need to spread the physically small image over a very wide field of view. The effect of this is to magnify the graininess of the already 'chunky' display. The physical nature of a HMD also has several problems associated with it. The optical system used results in noticeable pin cushion distortion and inadequate field of view and stereo overlap. The adjustability of the displays also presents a problem, with the inter-ocular distance and focus distance being fixed for a display, and unable to compensate for differences between individual users' eyes.

One alternative to bulky HMDs is the use of boom-mounted displays. Fake Space Systems produce a wide-angle stereoscopic display that is mounted on a desk-side boom. This has the advantage of fast and accurate tracking of the display (as optical encoders can be used instead of the magnetic field sensors like the Polhemus) as well as comfort and convenience. The display boom is balanced so that the user doesn't need to support the display on his or her head. The boom is also very convenient if the user needs to go back to the 'real world' (for example, to debug their program, to answer the phone or to drink a coffee).

4 Head and Eye Tracking

The synthetic environment that the VR user (called a *cybernaut* by some) enters is defined with respect to a global zero-point (origin) and has built-in conventions for directions (axes). The objects in this environment are defined with respect to this global coordinate system, and like these objects, the user has a position and orientation with respect to the same coordinate system.

What the user can see in that world depends on the *viewing frustum* – the sub-volume of space defined by the user's position, head orientation and field of view. This is similar to a movie camera but differs from the human visual system in that we can also move our eyes independent of our head orientation.

The objects outside our field of view are still in the environment, it is just that they are not visible until such time as we are looking in their direction.

We need to be able to translate and rotate our virtual head so that the VR user can look around in their environment. In conventional computer graphics, these so-called *viewing transformations* were attached to a mouse, dials or other similar devices. While this is functionally satisfactory, it breaks the coupling between our visual system and our kinaesthetic senses (i.e. our middle ear).

With head tracking, the VR user's kinaesthetic senses and visual system can be re-coupled. As the VR user turns his or her head, the viewing frustum and hence the display is updated. We have thereby increased the perceptual fidelity of our system.

An added advantage of head tracking is that in addition to binocular parallax, we get motion parallax – i.e. as you move your head from side to side you see around the side of objects. This extra visual cue also improves your depth perception.

There has also been considerable work on eye tracking, although most of this work is not easily applicable to VR at the moment. Information from eye tracking could provide us with a better description of the viewing frustum and decreases the gap between our real world vision and our VR model of vision.

5   Hand and Gesture Tracking

The keyboard and mouse are the most conventional way we interact with computers now. While the keyboard is great for text-based systems, it is fairly useless for real-time 3D graphics. Similarly, the mouse, while providing an excellent way to interact with a 2D space, is extremely cumbersome in a 3D space like VR. In 3D space, you have six degrees of freedom – three for position (x, y, z) and three for orientation (the Euler angles θ, ϕ, γ). There is no intuitive way to map the 2D, planar motion of a mouse onto arbitrary motion in 3D space.

There have been a few conventional devices that have provided 6 degrees of freedom (DOF), notably the 3Space digitizer and the SpaceBall.

The 3Space digitizer was designed to provide a means of measuring points on a physical model and enter them into a CAD database. It is a pen-like stylus with a sensor attached which measures the position and orientation of the pen with respect to the control unit. The sensor, the Polhemus, uses perturbations in orthogonal magnetic fields (caused by an AC solenoid in the pen) to calculate the position and orientation. In theory, this provides the required information to track a position and orientation in 3D space, but there are several problems with the Polhemus sensor.

The working volume of the sensor is very small, being a hemisphere of approximately 30 inch radius from the transmitter. Its static accuracy in that hemisphere ranges from 0.13 inches if the sensor is less than 15 inches from the transmitter, to 0.25 inches if the sensor is up to 30 inches away. The orientation accuracy is about 0.85°. The usable resolution of the device is also fairly poor, ranging from 0.09 to 0.18 inches. Each sensor is capable of returning positional information at 60 Hz. However, if several sensors are being used in the same environment, they must be time sliced to avoid the magnetic fields interfering. For a typical setup of three sensors (two hand and one head tracker), this reduces the maximum update from 60 Hz to a barely acceptable 20 Hz.

As the sensors are based on magnetic field technology, the accuracy and repeatability are strongly affected by environmental considerations such as ferrous objects, electronic equipment and CRTs. In a 'typical environment', the magnetic fields will be highly distorted resulting in very non-linear measurements which must be corrected. Also, the noise in the returned data will be very significant and will need to be filtered.

Phase lag is the combination of latency (acquisition rate in the analogue domain) and update rate (number of samples per second of digitized data). Current Polhemus trackers have a total phase lag of up to 100 ms. This causes serious problems for real-time interaction. This is exacerbated by the graphics latency that is added after all the tracker phase lag. The problems of latency can be partly compensated by the use of good predictive filters [2].

In spite of the shortcomings, the Polhemus is the most popular sensor for VR today (Fig. 2.2).

The SpaceBall is a rigid sphere that fits comfortably under the palm of your hand,

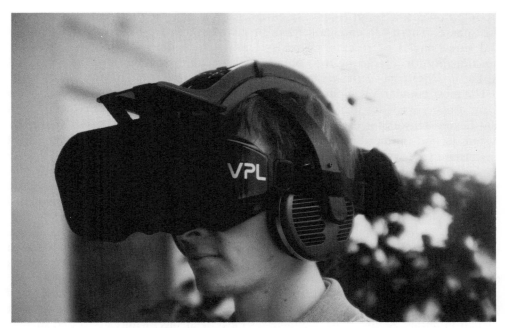

Figure 2.1 Low resolution head-mounted display. The model shown is the VPL EyePhone II.

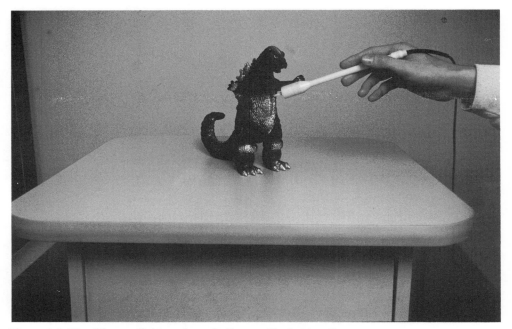

Figure 2.2 The 3Space digitizer from Polhemus Navigation Systems.

mounted on a low stand (Fig. 2.3). Strain gauges measure the force you apply to the sphere. There are enough sensors to measure translation in three dimensions and three angles of rotation. This is clearly sufficient to provide the necessary functionality for interacting with objects in 3D. The disadvantage of the SpaceBall is that it doesn't move (it is a tabletop device).

The most popular VR input device is an instrumented glove. The VPL DataGlove is the classic example; it has a Polhemus sensor attached to the back of the hand and flexure sensors for each finger and the thumb (Fig. 2.4). This setup allows the system to find the position and orientation of the hand (through the Polhemus) at any instant (the system queries the glove controller for its current data). The flexure sensors are used to also measure the joint angles of each finger and the thumb. When combined with recognition software, this data can be used for gesture-based input to the system. This is like using a form of sign language to enter commands into the computer!

There is also the opportunity to recognize gross motion gestures of the hand (say waving goodbye) also to be used for interaction. The GRANDMA system developed at Carnegie Mellon University has been used successfully to recognize gross motions of a mouse and should be readily extensible to a Polhemus.

There are some difficulties with the DataGlove, including a high noise level, slow sample rate, noticeable lag, and the need to re-calibrate the flexure sensors at regular intervals. Some of these difficulties have been successfully addressed by new competitors to the DataGlove such as the Cyberglove from Virtual Technologies (Fig. 2.5). The Cyberglove has a superior flexure measurement system that provides

Figure 2.3 The SpaceBall 6 DOF input device from Spatial Systems.

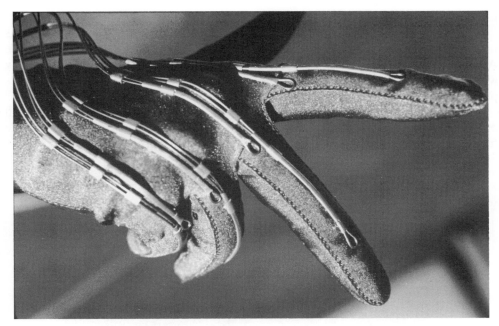

Figure 2.4 The VPL (10 sensor) DataGlove II.

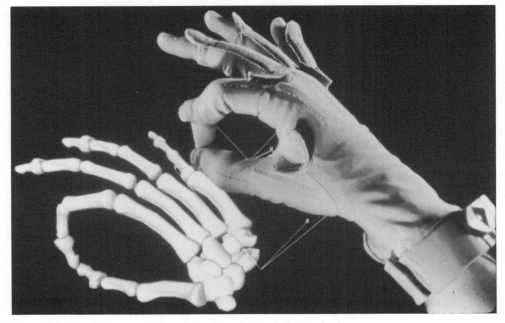

Figure 2.5 The 18 sensor Cyberglove from Virtual Technologies.

greater resolution and better repeatability. The addition of extra sensors also provides far more information about the user's hand.

One of the problems inherent in the Polhemus, its intolerance to metallic objects in its operating envelope, has been addressed by a newer sensor, The Bird, from Ascension Technologies, while problems with noise, slow sample rate and lag may well be addressed by a new model from Polhemus called FASTRACK. It claims a phase lag of only 4 ms and an update rate of up to 300 Hz.

Exos has developed an exoskeleton (Dextrous Hand Master™ that provides high precision joint/flexure measurement (Fig. 2.6). Exos has also incorporated a tactile feedback device (Touchmaster™) based on a low cost voice-coil oscillator.

Figure 2.6 The Dextrous Hand Master from Exos.

6 Binaural Sound

Humans are quite good at locating the direction of a sound source. In the horizontal plane, it is mostly a matter of phase delay – the time between the sound arriving at one ear and the other. Out of the horizontal plane, location of sound direction is a learned skill and is heavily dependent on the shape of your ear.

We can place small microphones in each ear and make a stereo recording that, when replayed, will also recreate the sensation of directionalized sound. However, any head motion during replay will also change the perceived direction of the sound. This is a serious problem if we wish to use binaural recorded sound in VR – we want the position of the sound source to be independent of the user's head movement!

We would like to attach recorded, live or computer generated sound (including synthesized speech) to an arbitrary object in the synthetic environment. To achieve this, Scott Foster, now at Crystal River Engineering, developed a device called the Convolvotron while he was at the NASA Ames VIEW Lab. The Convolvotron can process four independent point sound sources simultaneously, compensating for any head movement on the fly. More recently, Crystal River Engineering has developed a more sophisticated device, the Maxitron, that can handle more sound sources (up to 8) as well as simulating the acoustics (including reflection of sound) of a moderately sized room.

Focal Point produce a low cost ($<$ US$1500) 3D audio card for Macintoshes and PCs. It processes a single sound source in real time, providing affordable binaural sound.

Once again, by the inclusion of another perceptual cue that we are accustomed to in real-world life, the fidelity of the VR experience is improved. The use of sound is reported to be a surprisingly powerful cue – researchers in VR and in the simulation industry are beginning to use binaural sound more often. At the minimum, this technique can be used to provide additional feedback to the user for such activities as grasping objects and navigation.

7 Haptic Feedback

One of the problems with many VR systems is that there is no tactile feedback. The VR user can reach out and grasp a cup but will not feel the sensation of touching the cup; furthermore, unlike grasping a real cup in your physical hand, there is nothing to prevent your grasp continuing right through the surface of the cup!

There are therefore two issues to be addressed:

- *Tactile feedback*
  Providing a means to provide some feedback through the skin. Some examples of this might be an array of vibrating nodules under the surface of the glove. This may not be an accurate simulation of touch (consider the different touch sensation of silk, wood, metal, and rock), but it would at least provide *some* indication of surface contact. Other possibilities include inflatable bubbles in the glove, materials that can change from liquid to solid state under electric charge and memory metals.

Exos has incorporated a tactile feedback device (Touchmaster™) into their Dextrous Hand Master. It is based on a low cost voice-coil oscillator. The Teletact Glove provides low resolution tactile feedback through the use of 30 inflatable air pockets in the glove. These pockets can be individually inflated up to 12 psi for most pads and up to 30 psi for a large palm pad.

• *Force feedback*

Providing a means to enforce physical constraints, also simulating forces that can occur in teleoperation environments. Some devices have been built to provide force feedback:

— MIT force feedback joystick [3]
— Ceiling-mounted force feedback arm at the University of North Carolina (UNC)
— UNC mountain bike
— The steering wheel in Atari's *Hard Drivin'* and *Hard Racin'* arcade games.

An example of the use of force feedback is the drug design work at UNC, where researchers need to find receptor sites for a drug molecule. These receptor sites in large organic compounds are the right size, shape and valence necessary for the drug molecule to fit and be stable. At UNC, using a ceiling-mounted arm designed and built at the Argonne National Laboratories, the researcher can hold the drug molecule and try and place it into potential receptor sites (Plate I). Poor receptor sites generate a repulsion force in the arm giving immediate feedback. The combination of 3D head-mounted display of the compound and drug combined with force feedback provide a quality tool to help researchers effectively solve an otherwise complex problem.

8   Voice Input/Output

Speech synthesis is common today even at the personal computer level. Such facilities are of clear utility in a VR environment – online help can be the spoken word instead of text, command feedback can be computer generated text, etc. Some improvement in speech synthesis is still needed, particularly in the quality of speech. As someone recently commented, 'Current computer generated speech sounds like a drunken Swede!'. It is unlikely that, in the near future, we will be free of the American accent in such systems.

A considerable amount of work has also been done in the field of voice recognition systems, to the point where commercial systems are available off-the-shelf. However, the goal of person and accent independent continuous voice recognition is beyond the budget of current VR systems. This means that at the moment there is a training process to go through for each user. Also, the user must be careful to leave a noticeable gap between each word (as opposed to our normally unbroken speech). This is happily one technology that has major applications outside VR and is the subject of major research and development initiatives. Improved, more affordable systems are likely to continue to appear at regular intervals.

9   Future Trends

Much of the equipment available to VR researchers today suffers from inadequacies that need to be addressed before VR will become a prominent technology.

Superior position and orientation tracking technology are required. The major limitations on the current sensors are the small working volume and the slow update/high phase lag problem. Ideally, a room sized working volume should be available, freeing the user to interact with a large environment.

Two recent examples of new tracking technology are the UNC optical head tracker [4] and the latest Polhemus sensor, the FASTRACK.

Better screens are required for head-mounted displays. The current high end VPL EyePhone can only provide a resolution equal to that of an NTSC video signal. The next generation of HDTV[3] LCDs promise to improve the quality available for HMDs. Improvements in the optical systems will also provide a better visual display for the user, with increased field of view and greater stereo overlap. One possible technology that may assist in this area is the use of holographic optical elements (HOE).

Another important step for HMDs will be the development of see-through displays. These will enable computer generated graphics to be overlayed over a real-world situation. This has application both in providing additional information in much the same way as an aircraft heads-up display (HUD), and in producing computer generated scenery around a physical situation (an aircraft cockpit, for example) without the need for large projection systems.

Finally, graphics workstations will continue to increase in power and functionality, while lowering in price. The passage of several years may see an order of magnitude increase in hardware speeds, and the application of spatial data structures from other areas of graphics can promise a similar speed increase over the naive software techniques common today.

Acknowledgements

This work is supported in part by a grant by the Victorian Education Foundation. Figure 2.4, courtesy of VPL Research Inc.; Figure 2.5, courtesy of Virtex Technologies; Figure 2.6, courtesy of Exos Inc.

References

1   Kalawsky, S. 1991. From visually coupled systems to virtual reality: an aerospace perspective. *Proc. Computer Graphics '91*.
2   Starner, T., Pentland, A. and Friedman, M. 1992. Device synchronization using an optimal linear filter. *Symposium on Interactive 3D Graphics*, 57–62.
3   Ouy-Young, M. and Stelle Minsky, M. 1991. Feeling and seeing: issues in force display. *Symposium on Interactive 3D Computer Graphics*, 235–244.
4   Azuma, R., Bennet, R., Gottschalk, S., Fuchs, H. and Ward, M. 1992. A demonstrated optical tracker with scalable work area for head mounted displays. *Symposium on Interactive 3D Graphics*, 43–52.

---

[3] High Definition Television, providing over 1000 lines of vertical resolution.

Part 2
SYSTEMS

3 SuperVision – A Parallel Architecture for Virtual Reality

Charles Grimsdale
DIVISION Ltd

Abstract

For virtual reality to realize its potential requires a paradigm sufficiently flexible and scalable to meet an unlimited requirement for computation. DIVISION's contribution to this field has been the development of the underlying parallel model, and parallel processing hardware, to help realize this potential. This paper discusses the architecture of SuperVision, a next generation parallel virtual reality system, and the underlying concepts of dVS, the first dedicated operating system for virtual reality. The various levels of parallelism exploited within this system are presented and discussed.

1 A Parallel Approach

Given the real-time demands of advanced 3D computing systems, it is essential to define a model which will scale with increasing demands for resolution and environment complexity. Therefore we need to establish a unified model for such systems which can exploit the natural parallelism inherent within the problem of virtual environment simulation.

I present a simple model of four *levels* of parallelism:

Environment			
Entity	human	cat	rat
Element	visual	audio	behaviour
Primitive	render hand	render head	render torso

At the highest level, the so-called *Environment* level, we can simulate different environments independently. This may be particularly valuable whilst supporting multiple users active within one or more environments. For example two engineers working on a common design problem.

The environment can then be subdivided into a number of autonomous *entities*. These entities typically represent high level 3D objects, which encapsulate all of the state required to define visual attributes, audio attributes, behaviour, etc. of an object. Each entity can then be processed in parallel, enabling us to build very realistic environments in which large numbers of objects/entities participate. The

VIRTUAL REALITY SYSTEMS
ISBN 0-12-227748-1

VEOS operating system under development at the University of Washington exploits exactly this principle, with different entities in the virtual environment modelled in parallel [1].

Entities possess a range of attributes or *elements*, such as position, behaviour, constraints, visual, audio, tactile, force, collision, etc. If each of the elements of an object as described above is independent, then this also forms the foundation for a data parallel decomposition of entity control processing. We can consider processing the *visual* elements of the environment in parallel with the *audio* elements, we can acquire *speech* elements in parallel with *gesture* elements. So the problems of image generation, audio processing, collision detection, gesture recognition, etc., can all be performed in parallel. Several groups have looked at exploiting this level of data parallelism [2–4].

This level of parallelism is going to be essential to realize the performance required by many potential applications. A diagram representing a simple parallel architecture is illustrated in Fig. 3.1.

This model, in which different elements of the virtual environment are maintained by different autonomous processes or actors, running in parallel, forms the foundation of the dVS operating system developed by DIVISION.

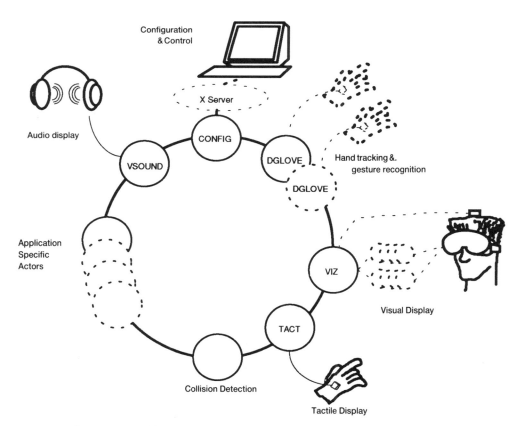

Figure 3.1 Example parallel system.

2 dVS Overview

dVS is a complete distributed virtual environment operating system based upon the general principles described above. This development was initiated on the recognition that we must realize more parallel models for virtual environment simulation to achieve the levels of performance, scalability and flexibility required of future virtual reality systems. The dVS software has been developed over the last two years, and was first released in August 1991. This software is now in everyday use in a wide range of application areas, and forms the core system software for DIVISION's *Vision* range of parallel virtual reality systems.

The key features of this software include: parallel process model; object-oriented API, hardware independence; scalability; open system; and support for multiple participants. It therefore offers a well-established foundation for creating very powerful virtual environment simulation scenarios.

dVS was designed to support a range of different parallel architectures, including loosely coupled networks, closely coupled shared memory multiprocessors, and distributed memory multiprocessors. First implementations were completed for the distributed memory parallel computers (ProVision and SuperVision) developed by DIVISION for virtual environment simulation.

dVS is a system architecture which supports a highly parallel model of computation designed to facilitate the building of advanced user interfaces. It combines the requirements of both distributed event simulation and real world control into a single, well-defined package for distributed virtual environment simulation. It encourages the application developer to consider the inherent parallelism within their problem domain, and enables the development of a parallel solution to match. This ensures that processing resources can be dedicated to different elements of the overall environment simulation as and where it is required.

The dVS architecture is completely open, allowing developers to create new specialized actors to address given application demands. However, it also greatly encourages the development of general purpose actors which can then be re-used in a wide range of applications, for example, a general purpose collision detection actor, or Newtonian mechanics actor. It also enables developers to incorporate existing simulation systems through the simple addition of dVS-compatible interface calls. An existing simulation code can then be used to control objects within the environment, for example, an existing flight dynamics package can be used to control the dynamics of an aircraft within the environment. This can be implemented as a separate actor, keeping the whole implementation very clean and maintainable.

The dVS software has been designed to support a single distributed virtual environment shared among a large number of participants. The consistency and temporal coherence of this shared environment is achieved at the operating system level, alleviating all responsibility from the programmer. Whilst it is possible to support networked systems with large transport delays, for example a wide area network, it must be appreciated that this can lead to coherence problems. This does not affect local performance for individual participants, but causes problems when participants attempt to interact. The networking problem has been addressed from the outset in dVS by providing a framework in which the environment database is distributed amongst multiple actors, which may be located on different machines, or even in different locations. To ensure that each participant's experience is truly interactive requires that we dedicate visual processing, collision detection and body tracking functions to the local participant. To overcome the problems created by transport delays, and low bandwidth connections between machines, dVS supports the notion that multiple actors can maintain the same element of the environment. So two actors located on different machines could both simulate the dynamics of an object, and confer at regular intervals to ensure approximate coherence of events. The frequency of such updates will vary according to communications bandwidth and latency of the transport.

dVS provides a consistent set of services to all actors. The application programming interface for dVS is called VL. This is an object-oriented virtual environment control interface which enables different actors to share elements of the virtual environment in a consistent way. VL is essentially a distributed database access library that enables different actors running in parallel to share data, and to maintain the consistency of this data.

Higher level functions are provided in the form of an object-based toolkit called VCTools. This toolkit provides functions to change the *visual* properties of objects, e.g. colour, texture, position, visibility; functions to change the *audio* properties of objects, e.g. frequency, sample type, envelope, position, etc.; functions to create cameras, lights, and to monitor collisions; and many other functions.

The VL and VCTools libraries are both written in C. An actor written in some high-level language can therefore communicate with other actors by making system calls through these libraries. It can also access any of the standard language runtime functions or operating system calls. So, for example, an actor can change the colour of selected objects in the virtual environment by making VCToolkit calls, and read data from a database using standard C runtime file I/O calls (fread()), and display information in an X window, whilst also communicating results to another UNIX process via a socket. The basic configuration of the various software layers is illustrated in Fig. 3.2.

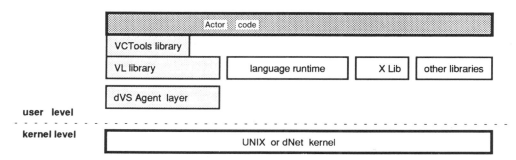

Figure 3.2 System services.

3   The Vision Range of Parallel Accelerators

DIVISION have developed the only dedicated parallel computing system for virtual reality. There are two basic models which address different application requirements. Both systems are based on a distributed memory architecture, and combine the unique I/O capability of the Inmos transputer and the floating point performance of the Intel i860. The basic architecture dedicates a single processing cluster (either transputer or i860) to each of the main tasks in the system. A separate cluster is dedicated to each of the main 3D peripherals, so for example a transputer is used to control the tracking system and gesture recognition for the VPL DataGlove. If the user needs to add a second DataGlove then the system can be upgraded with a second DataGlove control transputer. The main application tasks run on separate transputers, or i860 clusters, and truly parallel applications can be run on a multi-cluster system.

There are a number of clear advantages to using a dedicated parallel system of this type, and these include support for dedicated I/O control, guaranteed real-time response, and a high degree of flexibility and expandability.

3.1   SuperVision

SuperVision is a high performance parallel visualization system. It combines the flexibility of a multi-transputer architecture with the performance of the Intel i860 to provide dedicated stereo visualization.

The system is comprised of a control front end and a dedicated parallel graphics subsystem. The control front end is based upon the standard *PROvision* system, with multiple transputers providing data acquisition and control. The graphics subsystem employs multiple (1–32) i860 chips connected by a high performance scalable interconnect (200 Mbyte/s). Each i860 compute board has its own local memory, and is connected to every other via a dedicated point-to-point link. Each board can communicate concurrently, so that the bandwidth of the system scales linearly with the number of compute processors. Image generation is provided by the PAZ parallel renderer, running on multiple i860s. This means that a very flexible and expandable system can be constructed, with 1 to 32 i860s computing an image in parallel. The SuperVision system is software compatible with the lower cost *PROvision* system, running the dVS operating environment.

This represents a new generation of parallel visualization system. It is a highly scalable software solution which can therefore be programmed to satisfy a number of specialized requirements in areas such as telepresence, volume visualization and multi-channel image generation.

3.2   System overview

The SuperVision can be broadly subdivided into two functional blocks. The control front end is a dedicated parallel virtual environment simulation system based predominantly on Inmos transputers. The basic architecture is outlined in Fig. 3.3.

Different transputers are dedicated to specific acquisition and display processing tasks. This provides distributed processing of 3D position data, gesture data, etc., with guaranteed response times to local peripherals, and localized 3D transformation of this incoming data. Incoming hand and head positions and hand gestures can

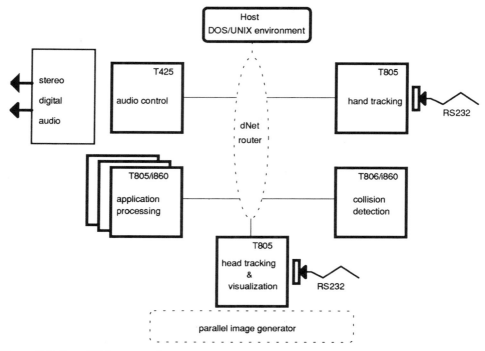

Figure 3.3 SuperVision overview.

then be distributed to other processes which require this information. A separate transputer provides control of a dedicated digital audio system called Vsound. This provides an independent stereo or quad audio display capability. Within the Vsound system a separate transputer with a 4 Mbyte sample store drives two/four 16 bit DACs, and up to eight independent samples can be replayed at 44.4 kHz, with localization in each of the four channels. This system can be further extended with a dedicated 3D audio processor called the Convolvotron™ [5]. This takes up to four independent audio inputs from the Vsound system and localizes these inputs in space.

A message-passing kernel called dNet provides a virtual routing system, which allows a process to communicate with any other, regardless of target processor. Intel i860s have been integrated into this system by providing each i860 with its own local I/O transputer. The dNet kernel running on the I/O transputer provides message-passing services to any process running on the i860. So application code can be developed for either transputer or i860 with a common dNet message-passing interface.

In this way floating point intensive problems can be addressed by the addition of dedicated i860s. So, for example, collision detection performance can be increased by replacing transputer with i860. Also, application processes can be developed for one or more i860s or transputers, as required.

Whilst the underlying architecture of the SuperVision system is essentially a distributed memory message-passing multiprocessor, a higher level of abstraction is provided by the dVS operating environment built upon this system. This enables sequential or parallel applications to gain access to the services provided by standard actors for visual processing, audio processing, collision detection, etc., without recourse to direct communication. As described above, the VL library provides a general purpose data management system in which actors communicate implicitly by virtue of sharing instances of an element (or data type). This greatly simplifies the task of application development, and ensures portability of application actors across a wide range of target machines.

The various levels of parallelism described above can be exploited within this system. Firstly, *environment* level parallelism is achieved by dedicating separate machines to different users, each exploring their own perspective upon a shared environment. A parallel application can be developed for this system in which different *entities* are processed in parallel by multiple application actors running on different processors. For example, in a complex animation the inverse kinematics of different objects could be processed by different actors. The different *elements* of an entity are automatically processed in parallel by the standard services (actors), for visualization, audio synthesis, collision detection, etc. Finally, the parallel image generator developed for the SuperVision system exploits *primitive* (as well as other) levels of parallelism to provide a scalable system for real-time image generation.

3.3 A unique architecture for stereo visualization

The SuperVision image generator is based upon two high-speed communication rings, each of which provides an interconnection between 1 to 16 compute cards. Each compute card combines a single 40 MHz Intel i860, with 4/8/16 MBytes of local memory. Each of the compute cards operates in parallel to compute a fraction of the 2D frame; the pixel data for a given frame is then combined for display in a remote frame store, which also sits on the communication ring. Other high performance acquisition systems, such as a 24-bit frame grabber, are supported so that live video images can be combined in real-time with computer generated images to produce a composite image (Fig. 3.4).

The communication system is a point-to-point link, with a worm hole router which will route data packets from any processor on the ring to any other. This is a general purpose communication system which has been designed to provide high bandwidth, low latency communication between large numbers of microprocessors, frame buffers and frame grabbers. Each processing cluster on the ring has a dedicated input and output port which run concurrently, so input and output transfers run in parallel. This communication system can be used for any data type, not exclusively pixel data. So, for example, live video from a frame grabber can be used as a dynamic texture within a computed frame, whilst object geometry updates are broadcast, and transformed polygon data are transferred between compute boards.

Therefore, this system forms the foundation of a highly parallel image generator, in which different distribution schemes can be adopted to optimize performance for different problems.

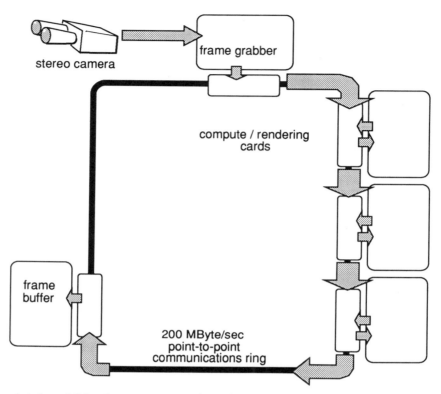

Figure 3.4 SuperVision image generator (mono).

4   The PAZ Renderer

PAZ is a high-level PHIGS-like renderer, which runs on all of the current DIVISION systems. It is a parallel renderer which has been developed to exploit the scalable performance of the SuperVision system. PAZ also provides direct support for multiple views, and so stereo images are easily generated and synchronized. PAZ has a high level, object-based application programming interface, under which the application manipulates OBJECT instances within one or more defined SCENES. The application maintains only OBJECT instance ID and OBJECT space transformation matrix, for each object. It does not typically modify OBJECT geometry which is defined when the OBJECT is created. Geometry updates are supported, but not essential, so the application interface is a low bandwidth interface, and is typically addressed from a remote processor.

The main aims of the PAZ design have been to *maximize*: hardware utilization; and multi-processor scalability, and *minimize*: rendering latency; clipping operations; application to PAZ bandwidth, whilst *ensuring*: generality; and portability.

A number of different approaches have been explored in our attempts to produce an efficient implementation of PAZ for the SuperVision system. The most consistently productive approach involves a combination of object space and 2D screen space subdivision in a multi-pass algorithm. This approach is very similar to that adopted for Pixel Planes 5 [6], and tends to perform well regardless of the number of objects and their average screen coverage. As always, a constant compromise must be made between complex load balancing, which typically consumes time and bandwidth, and maximizing data coherence on a given processor, thus minimizing communication and latency, to provide the best performance for any problem.

5 Conclusions

The SuperVision system represents a unique architecture for virtual environment simulation. It exploits several levels of parallelism to maximize functionality and performance. Highly parallel applications can be developed to provide what I referred to as *entity* level parallelism. The *elements* of these entities are then automatically processed in parallel by multiple actors, which form a standard core of this system. Finally, the graphics subsystem exploits what I have called *primitive* level parallelism to provide highly cost-effective and expandable image generation capability.

References

1 Bricken, W. 1990. *Virtual Environment Operating System: Preliminary Functional Architecture*. Human Interface Technology Lab. TR-HITL-M-90-2, University of Washington, Seattle.
2 Roskos, E. 1991. *Towards a Distributed, Object-Oriented Virtual Environment*. Report to the National Science Foundation, NSF Grant CCR89-09197.
3 Ling, D., Lewis, B. *et al*. 1991. *An Architecture for Virtual Worlds*. IBM internal Research Report RC 16446(#73023) 1/10/91, IBM Research Division TJ Watson Research Center, Yorktown Heights.
4 Grimsdale, C. 1991. dVS – Distributed virtual environment System. *Proc. Computer Graphics '91 Conference*, London, UK.
5 Wenzel, E.M., Wightman, F. and Foster, S. 1988. A virtual display system for conveying three-dimensional acoustic information. *Proc. Human Factors Society*, **32**: 86–90.
6 Fuchs, H.J., Poulton, J.E., Greer, T. *et al*. 1989. A heterogeneous multiprocessor graphics system using processor enhanced memories. *Computer Graphics: Proc. Siggraph '89*.

4 Virtual Reality Products

Terry W. Rowley
W-Industries, UK

Abstract

From the days of the first flight simulators, engineers have been striving to convince people that they are in some other world than the one they expect to be in by removing the real world sensory inputs and replacing them with manufactured ones. As the techniques have improved, the manufactured sensations and the way in which they are delivered are so convincing that they have become known as 'virtual reality'. Current virtual reality units use head-mounted displays for the main interfaces to the eyes and ears, and track head and hand movements for a control interface. There are many possible applications now being proposed as a result of the wide publicity received by the first VR products to be manufactured for the entertainment industry.

1 Introduction

Virtual reality (VR) systems are developed from training simulators, which were invented earlier this century. Since they began, engineers have been improving the techniques which convince the users that they are driving the real vehicle rather than a computer-based model. Environments have been copied with great attention to detail to convince an operator that the aircraft cockpit or ship's bridge which is being simulated is the real thing. Controls and instrumentation are copied exactly, or are actual examples of the real ones, to give the correct feel to the exercises to be performed. Motion systems have been developed with precise control over the motion cues given to a trainee, and expensive visual systems have been devised to give out-the-window views of terrain and sea.

The ability to produce sophisticated training simulators was the result of developments in a variety of technologies which include:

- computer-controlled hydraulics
- high-speed digital computers
- computer generated images for visual scenes
- sophisticated software for modelling terrain and features to be viewed
- powerful display techniques for full colour, bright visual displays with collimating optics.

The latest developments are in low-cost LCD colour monitors for the visual displays, which allow them to be mounted on the head.

Some of the most important developments are in the generation of the visual

VIRTUAL REALITY SYSTEMS
ISBN 0-12-227748-1

scene, which is an essential factor in a convincing environment. To provide the necessary detail film, slide and video techniques have been tried with varying amounts of success, but the most controllable methods have been those using video techniques. The first methods used in flight simulators were based upon large model boards, which carried a three-dimensional scale model of the terrain to be used in the exercise. These models were difficult and expensive to build and maintain, but enabled a computer controlled TV camera to be flown across the surface by the trainee operating the controls of the simulated aircraft. Optical systems for the TV camera had to work with extremely small apertures to get a reasonable depth of field, which led to the requirement for very high light levels and therefore a lot of heat. To prevent the model from being cooked, an air-conditioning unit was necessary, so that the costs of setting up the model and using it rose as the picture definition improved.

The ability to generate full colour TV images from a computer, where the model was entirely within its database, enabled the provision of the visual scene without the use of cameras and physical models. This step came about when the computational power of computers increased over a threshold and costs became competitive.

2   Virtual Reality

Definitions of VR vary widely and need to be considered before the techniques used can be discussed. Our perception of the outside world is controlled by our five senses, through which we have built a world model over the years by our own experience. We interact with the real world by interpreting sensory inputs using our own model, which is in detail, different from everyone else's. In practice, most features of these models are similar, so we interact with the real world in similar ways. If we have an inconsistent set of sensory inputs, they may cause disruption of the interpretation process and cause discomfort and disorientation. As long as the sensory inputs can be interpreted into a coherent result, this will be our picture of the current outside world, however fantastic it may appear, and will be our current reality. If the sensory inputs are being deliberately produced by a computer to represent some other environment, we call the current reality *virtual reality*.

The VR systems currently available are based upon training simulators which have been engineered to be low-cost systems rather than the flight and ship simulators, which were only available to applications where other training methods were more expensive, hazardous or impossible. Moon landings would have been impossible without simulators because there was no chance of a second attempt on the real trip.

A major factor in the cost of training simulators was the visual display system. This was required to provide a bright, fully coloured, wide angle picture using collimating optics or a large screen projection technique and was usually based upon the use of a number of high power TV projectors of the light-valve type. In VR systems the display is mounted on the head as part of a visor assembly, and consists of a pair of LCD screens equipped with filters and collimating optics, one for each eye, to make stereoscopic viewing possible. The display field of view can be traded with resolution, because the motion of the head is tracked using sensors in the visor, and more head movement can be used to compensate for narrower viewing angles.

Other aspects of the visor include earphones, for sound input, and a locking device to ensure that a good fit is obtained for a range of head sizes.

Reduction of the cost of the visual system goes hand-in-hand with the increase in power of microcomputers, which brings them to a point where they can produce moving images of high quality at low cost to drive the display system.

3   VR Hardware Requirements

The hardware needed for a VR system can be divided into three main subsystems:

1. Head-mounted display
2. Computer complex
3. Console.

The head-mounted display (HMD) is required to be an assembly which is light in weight and very rugged if it is to be used by several different users, who may drop it or bump into things while wearing it. The shell must ensure the safety of the user by covering all electrical circuits and not cause damage to a user who falls while wearing it. Its surface must be smooth, hygienic and easily cleaned of any organism which could cause infection. There must be a mechanism for ensuring a good fit to people with a range of head sizes so that it doesn't move about with respect to the user's head as the head is moved rapidly in any direction. The operational parts, which are the man/machine interface, must provide a good visual display, a sound input, communication with other people in the same virtual world and a means of tracking the position of the head and the direction of look.

The computer must provide a pair of images for the visual display which are sufficiently detailed and updated at a sufficiently high rate as the head is moved or elements of the visual scene move about to provide the illusion that the user is in a different world. The sounds produced from sound samples within the computer must generate a sound stage for the user which is coherent with the visual scene. The rate at which the head position and direction are tracked must be sufficiently high not to cause annoying lags in the picture position update. The computer needs a large store for the visual scene and sound samples to make sure that the experience is kept interesting, and experiences must be software-based to ensure that changing from one to another is simple and straightforward.

The console is to house all the computer equipment and power supplies. It carries the controls for interaction with the virtual world and is where the visor is connected. The transmitters for the tracking system may also be contained within the console, to ease installation of the system. The same health and safety requirements are necessary as for the visor and ruggedness of the shell and controls is essential for trouble free operation of the unit.

4   Example VR System

An example of a VR system custom designed and built for the entertainments industry is the W-Industries Virtuality™.

The head-mounted display (Fig. 4.1) consists of a visor in which there is a separate display for each eye consisting of LCD, filter and folded optical path with a collimating lens, giving a small exit pupil which can be adjusted to be in an optimum position by a knob at the top of the visor support. The sound input consists of four loudspeakers arranged with one in front of, and one behind each ear, to give surround sound. A tracker sensor is mounted above the optical system to provide signals for the tracker computer. All this is contained in a glass fibre reinforced plastic shell with a highly polished surface, to make cleaning easy, and a padded interior for comfort and positive grip with the clamping mechanism. The clamping device, which clamps under the bulge at the back of the head, has an ingenious lock which is operated by a hoop at the rear of the visor. This hoop is pulled down until the visor is clamped to the head, and pushed up to release the clamp, providing quick, safe entry and exit of the head.

The computer complex is contained in a box which can be slid out of the console on runners to provide easy access. The graphics computers which compute the imagery for each eye are separate from the main system computer in which the experience is loaded and run during use. They each have their own floating point co-processor to ensure that the calculations needed for the geometrical transformations are performed at high speed and operate concurrently with the

Figure 4.1 W-Industries head-mounted display.

system computer. A separate tracking computer is used to process the signals from the head and hand tracking sensors.

The computers are interfaced to the controls on the console, the tracking sensors, the video leads to the visor, the audio amplifiers, the local area network and a coin operation mechanism. An interface is also provided for a keyboard to be attached for engineering and maintenance work to be done.

The consoles provided for this application include one in which the user sits to work the controls (Plate II) and one in which the user stands (Fig. 4.2). Each has the same functional characteristics and can be described together. They are

Figure 4.2 CS entertainment unit.

constructed from units which will pass separately through small doorways and which can be transported in small vehicles, to be assembled quickly on site. They are made from glass reinforced plastic with a polished surface to make cleaning easy. They are designed to cover completely any electrical terminals or circuits, and have lockable doors to prevent any entry during use. Slides are provided to enable the computer to be withdrawn completely for maintenance or software updates.

Only one power lead is required to connect to the external supply, and the footprint is kept small to enable efficient use of working space. The appearance of the consoles has been designed to be attractive to potential users and operators.

5 Software Structure

The two main areas of software in the system are in the main system computer and in the graphics computers. The programs in the system computer run the VR experience using the database of the environment model, and calculate the viewer's position and direction of look by using inputs from the user controls. If necessary, the computer calculates the positions and actions of colleagues or opponents to substitute for the actions of real performers if they are not on the network. These computer generated players can be given rules of engagement with real players or other computer generated players so that the virtual world is properly populated. Sound samples are also operated by the system computer to get the planned sound effects synchronized with the action. If the experience involves the driving of vehicles, the dynamics of the vehicles and their response to the controls is also the province of the system computer.

Programs within the graphics computers, which are loaded from the disc store of the system computer on start up, are responsible for the generation of the images to display in the visor, using the model data in the database and the position of the observer from the system computer. The calculations performed in the graphics computer include the geometrical transformations of rotation and translation, hidden surface removal, surface shading, perspective projection and the colour computations needed to simulate poor visibility conditions.

Programs to calculate the position and pointing direction from the tracker signals are on ROM within the tracker computer system.

6 Software Tools

Many software tools have been written to make generation of model database and experiences quicker and more reliable. The generation of terrain models for flight simulator use is a good example of the way in which use of the computer can save a great deal of time and effort. If a piece of selected terrain is to be modelled, it requires either access to digitized map data, such as the DMA data, or the digitizing of map data. In either case, the data must be processed to turn it into the required format for use. If this terrain can be generic terrain of the necessary type but not precisely like any specific area, a fractal generation program can be used with settable parameters to generate terrain in the right format directly.

Programs to generate models of wanted features are used with photographs of different views of the object taken from known points. This technique will produce coherent three-dimensional models from a number of views. For the experiences where travel is limited to a small area such as track events or within a city boundary, the background of distant scenery can be painted on the sky using sampled video from a TV camera and a frame grabber.

Other software tools have been produced for turning a definition of a twisting curve into a railway track, a bobsleigh run or a rally track, and completing the terrain model around the track to inlay it into previously generated terrain.

7   Modelling Virtual Worlds

When a new experience is produced, the environment is modelled with the required characteristics. First the terrain model is produced, then features such as buildings, roads, trees and bushes are added, and a two-dimensional background if necessary. A storyboard is drawn up to define the action and progress of the experience, and models are generated of all the players. Special effects are defined and drawn up as a series of frames to be added to the action at the correct time. Sound effects are sampled and arranged to be played at the correct time in the same way. Finally, the whole experience is pulled together by the operations program, which includes all the dynamics and the responses to the player. Collisions between objects within the experience must be detected and the correct effect calculated, which may be complicated if the colliding surfaces are complex. It may be necessary to simplify this procedure by defining simpler surfaces for the collison detection than those used in the visuals.

8   Applications of VR

As the implementation of VR systems improves, more applications of these techniques are proposed. Consideration of new applications requires the analysis of resolution of the image, colour range, field of view, and use of stereo viewing for the visual scene. There may be similar considerations for the sound simulation if acoustic behaviour is an important factor. Present applications under consideration or proposed include:

- entertainment
- training of various kinds
- therapy for a number of physical and mental disorders
- promotion and sales
- information interface for libraries and other data stores.

Some features for each of these applications will be considered.

8.1   Entertainment

This application is the first for which VR systems were manufactured in quantity. The appearance of VR products on the leisure market caused great public interest and attracted the attention of the media. The resulting spate of documentaries and news programmes spread the interest in the technology to a much wider audience and raised the public profile of VR all over the world.

VR systems used in entertainment are used as single units in an arcade environment, or are networked together in groups for team experiences or competitive events such as motor racing. The first of these experiences was based upon flight simulation, and had a VTOL aircraft in which one sat and flew using the console controls to shoot down the opposition and score points. Some of the manoeuvres needed in refuelling to continue the experience were very difficult to learn and took a long time.

The characteristics of a good experience are one in which it is possible to do something interesting in a short time as a beginner, but also continues to be interesting after many goes as an expert.

From the operator's point of view, it must be possible to recover the cost of the machine from the cash input by the users in as short a time as possible, preferably in less than a year. The cost to the user must be small enough to be attractive for a reasonable length of time in the experience, but large enough to produce the pay-back to the operator. From this equation the maximum cost of the machine is fixed, and the application must be designed to this price.

Other design considerations for leisure VR machines are the environments in which they operate. They are expected to operate for long periods unattended and are subject to occasional bouts of violent misuse, making ruggedness and reliability essential characteristics of the design. Health and safety considerations are also essential because the equipment is in a public place and can be used by anyone. Any live parts of the equipment must be covered and safe, in spite of considerable forces applied to the covering material. Cables must be armoured and capable of standing up to very high tension and shear forces without breaking. Because the equipment needs to be in use for the maximum amount of time to accomplish the optimum pay-back, down time for repairs, servicing or upgrading to a new experience must be minimized.

Current equipment in this application is used for role playing games of the dungeons and dragons type. It consists of a number of units networked together in which a team of players stand to play out their roles. An example of this equipment is shown in Fig. 4.3. Each player is completely surrounded by the ring which makes the rim of the console to give support in case of giddiness or disorientation. The ring also houses the transmitter for the head and hand tracking sensors.

For these role playing games, the times for which the participants are using the equipment are much longer. It is common for a length of time to be purchased, for which a credit is programmed into a key and used by the player in the equipment rather than using a coin mechanism. If players are killed off by the computer controlled players in the game, the state of the game at this point can be saved by programming it into the key, and the game can be resumed at this point at a later time, perhaps after the team have had time to analyse their errors and plan a new strategy.

8.2 Training

Since VR developed from the techniques used in training simulators it seems natural that one of the applications of VR would be as a training simulator. A number of possible training roles have been suggested, but actual implementations have been very slow to happen.

The main areas in which the possibilities are being assessed are:

Figure 4.3 CS unit in use.

- military
- vehicle driving, ranging from HGV to private cars
- gliders and light aircraft
- machinery maintenance
- sports and games in which technique is important.

Military training is still extremely important even at a time of reduction in armed forces and a general desire to move to a more peaceful world. As budgets are reduced it is essential to have a cost-effective way of keeping the remaining forces at the peak of readiness to ensure security from any potential aggressors. The training scenarios cover a wide range of activities, and include the individuals as parts of a team on the battlefield and also the strategies of whole armies and the logistics of their support for extended campaigns in unknown territory.

At present, there are simulators capable of running training exercises over days or weeks, which involve large numbers of personnel, some of whom may be actually plodding around in the mud of a training area. The methods used for these exercises are being updated continually, and VR is a strong contender for a role in future training systems. An important aspect of VR systems is the ability to network large numbers of units together to enable competitive exercises to be carried out easily over short or long distances using satellite communications.

Vehicle driver training using simulators has been going on for many years, but the number of simulators which are cost effective for this task are very few. There is a great interest in the use of VR for this application because of its potentially low cost and simple installation. The costs of training HGV drivers and the adverse effect of the training vehicles on street traffic make a classroom trainer attractive, and a set of standards could be applied which would be accepted internationally. Studies are going ahead to discover an optimum teaching method for use in a driving simulator using VR to be applied throughout the EEC.

Flight simulation has been possible only for large commercial aircraft and military aeroplanes because of the large costs involved. The danger and the expense of learning to fly in such aircraft justifies the high cost of the simulator. VR systems hold out the possibility of learning to fly gliders and light aircraft at reasonable cost in a classroom, thus reducing the dangers inherent in more traditional methods.

Maintenance of machinery where there are many types and varieties is an increasing problem as the rate of growth of technology increases. An example of this is motor car engine maintenance. The manuals produced for each new model and each annual update provide a bewildering array of knowledge that may be required very infrequently. It has been suggested that a self-teaching program run on a VR system to remind the mechanic of the features of an engine just before working on that model would be the most efficient way of running a maintenance organization.

There are many sports and games which require techniques which are acquired and perfected only by hours of dedicated practice. An example of a training facility set up to enable this practice is the driving range, set up to encourage golfers to improve their performance off the tee. Some of this training activity can be performed using VR equipment, which could be installed in areas where space is limited, to encourage potential players who are able to practise only for short intervals and haven't the time to travel to the sporting parks.

8.3 Design and creation

Using computers to aid design and creation is now common practice, but most systems only replace the drawing board with a TV monitor, giving the same two-dimensional projection as the first drawings in the sand of our distant ancestors. The potential of VR systems is to be able to experience three-dimensional objects by walking round them and feeling them, if they are small enough, or walking inside them or amongst them if they are large like buildings. There is also the ability to shape things interactively using virtual tools, long before they exist in the real world.

Other aspects of the use of VR in designing and shaping objects is the ability to experience other attributes of the objects, not only the visual ones. Stress patterns can be expressed, flow of gases can be shown, the acoustics of buildings can be experienced, the effects of lighting, both natural and artificial, can be visualized, and many other aspects deemed to be of importance to the design expressed in some effective form to interact with the designer's perception.

Design centres at several universities and polytechnics are now setting up projects to explore the technology and its applications to design and the performing arts.

8.4 Therapy

Medical applications of VR are not limited to virtual surgery, which could be considered under training applications, but include therapy for physical and mental problems. Physical problems may be the result of injuries to limbs or to illness, which have caused temporary loss of control or weakness, which can be remedied by specific exercises. Many such cases can be motivated to do the exercises if they are made part of a game or sport with goals to be attained at several levels. The use of VR equipment allows the exercises to be tailored precisely to the goals and the patient, whether they are standing, sitting or lying down, and requires the minimum of supervision by expert staff.

There are mental and psychological conditions in which therapy includes role playing for the patient. The patient is encouraged to escape their current reality for a limited period by taking on a specific role and acting it out. The power of VR in this area is the control which can be applied to the virtual environment to assist the playing of the role.

8.5 Promotion of products

Advertising and promotion of products is a big business which depends upon getting the attention of people long enough to describe the product, and have enough impact for them to remember it. While VR systems are still a novelty, they are used for promotion and advertising by having a specific experience programmed, related to the product, taking the equipment to a crowded area such as a shopping precinct and encouraging people to try the experience and carry away a free sample of the product. This procedure also enables people to experience VR, often for the first time, which widens the appreciation of what VR is.

8.6 Information interface

As the knowledge base of the human race increases, it becomes increasingly difficult to extract the information required for a particular subject. New methods are required for browsing through the recorded data or getting to specific areas rapidly as required. Amongst the methods being explored is VR. Virtual libraries are set up in which one can browse along the shelves, dipping into books as required and finding related and cross-referenced books instantly. Related topics can be drawn to the attention of the researcher and the sources of the data recorded for future use if necessary. The aim is to make the interface as friendly and familiar as possible while retaining the power and tirelessness of the computer.

9 Future Developments

The public interest caused by the VR products which have been produced so far has stimulated a rapid growth in the industries developing the key enabling technologies for VR products. The current developments are mainly associated with the visual displays, where improvements of the resolution and brightness of the LCDs continues rapidly and the power of the graphics computers increases. An associated reduction of cost enables more sophisticated graphic displays with more detail and better rendering procedures. This technological and economic development will stimulate the expansion of the market, and will also initiate new applications in areas not yet considered as possible beneficiaries of this technology.

Among the imminent developments will be a home-based version which will allow users in the home to dial up recreational activities or educational or training experiences, which will be provided along a fibre optic cable from their local telecommunications centre. This will complement, or in some cases replace, the dependence upon TV programmes for entertainment, in which people are the passive onlookers, and allow interaction of the viewers with the current story or game. The home version of the present visor will be designed to be lighter and more user-friendly because it will not need to survive the worst rigours of the public arcade or theme park. Conferencing facilities using such a readily programmable system and linking it with several work centres, including homes, will be a natural extension to the home version, and may reduce the need for so much travel to and from work.

There have been suggestions of the ultimate in lightweight visors which use contact lenses capable of writing the complete colour display on to the retina using a laser, but this may be some way off still. Force feedback gloves and complete suits are being developed rapidly to provide the sensation of touch, which may give us a version of Aldous Huxley's 'feelies' soon.

In the near future it seems likely that the realization of interactive cinema will become possible, and will be much bigger than the present rather limited theme room containing a few VR units networked together. Dedicated buildings will be built with a number of adventure or quest type games playing simultaneously with tens or even hundreds of role playing participants and an equal number of spectators, using big TV screens displaying views of the most exciting action for them to enjoy the interplay of personalities within the experience. The cinema would be equipped with the normal array of bars and fast food outlets to make it an entertainment and leisure complex for the whole family, making it the high-tech equivalent of the bowling alley or fair ground.

5 A Computational Model for the Stereoscopic Optics of a Head-Mounted Display

Warren Robinett and Jannick P. Rolland
University of North Carolina

Abstract

For stereoscopic photography or telepresence, orthostereoscopy occurs when the perceived size, shape and relative position of objects in the three-dimensional scene being viewed match those of the physical objects in front of the camera. In virtual reality, the simulated scene has no physical counterpart, so orthostereoscopy must be defined in this case as constancy, as the head moves around, of the perceived size, shape and relative positions of the simulated objects.

Achieving this constancy requires that the computational model used to generate the graphics matches the physical geometry of the head-mounted display being used. This geometry includes the optics used to image the displays and the placement of the displays with respect to the eyes. The model may fail to match the geometry because model parameters are difficult to measure accurately, or because the model itself is in error. Two common modelling errors are ignoring the distortion caused by the optics and ignoring the variation in interpupillary distance across different users.

A computational model for the geometry of a head-mounted display is presented, and the parameters of this model for the VPL EyePhone are calculated.

1 Introduction

1.1 The problem: Computing the correct stereoscopic images in virtual reality

As you move through the world, images of the objects that surround you fall onto your retinas. As you move past a fixed object, seeing it from various angles, the size and shape of the images on your retinas change, yet you effortlessly and unconsciously perceive the object to have a stable position, shape and size. This innate perceptual ability, honed by your daily experience ever since infancy, is so fundamental and habitual that it seems almost absurd to talk about objects that could change their position or shape or size depending on how you moved your head.

Yet the current state of the art in virtual reality (VR) gives us simulated objects that change their position, size and shape as the head moves. The location of these objects appears to change as the head moves around, and their size and shape appear to change depending on whether they are being viewed directly in front of the user's head or off to the side.

In virtual reality, a head-mounted display (HMD) and a head tracker are used to rapidly measure head position and create an image for each eye appropriate to its instantaneous viewpoint. The HMD user can then see simulated objects from different points of view as the head moves. However, it is difficult to correctly calculate the images to be painted onto the display screens of the HMD. The user's eyes and brain (and vestibular system) are very sensitive to inconsistencies.

The computational problem of calculating the correct stereoscopic images in VR – getting the perceived objects to have the right position, size and shape – is the same problem that faces the designers of stereoscopic photography and telepresence systems. For these systems, orthostereoscopy occurs when the perceived size, shape, and relative position of objects in the three-dimensional scene being viewed match those of the physical objects in front of the camera. In virtual reality, the simulated scene has no physical counterpart, so orthostereoscopy must be defined in this case as constancy, as the head moves around, of the perceived size, shape and relative positions of the simulated objects. To calculate orthostereoscopic images, the display code must precisely model the geometry of the HMD system on which the images will be viewed. This includes the relative positions of the display screens, the optics, and the eyes. The relationship between the screen and the virtual image of it must also be modelled.

This paper addresses only the static image generation problem. To simulate objects that are spatially stable, temporal problems must also be solved, but those problems are outside the scope of this paper.

1.2 Prior work

Since Ivan Sutherland built the first HMD in 1968, several HMD systems have been built. The display code for each system defined an implicit model for the particular geometry of each HMD. The authors of the display code for each system structured the code as they judged appropriate, and it is difficult to know the precise details of their display code from what has been published. It appears that most HMD systems treated their optics simply as a magnifier, ignoring distortion introduced by the optics.

In Sutherland's HMD, tiny half-inch monochrome CRTs were the display devices, and the virtual images seen through the optics subtended an angle of 40° and appeared to be at a distance of 18 inches in front of the eyes [1,2]. Half-silvered mirrors superimposed the computer graphics onto the user's direct view of the real world. Later versions of the HMD were stereoscopic. The stereoscopic HMD had both a mechanical adjustment for interpupillary distance (IPD) and a software adjustment for the virtual eye separation. This HMD system was moved to the University of Utah, and essentially the same system was used by several students there [3,4].

In 1983, Mark Callahan at MIT built a see-through HMD similar to Sutherland's [5]. It used half-silvered mirrors mounted on eyeglass frames, 2 inch monochrome CRTs, and a bicycle helmet. An optical disk was used to rapidly display prerecorded images in response to head movements.

In 1985 at NASA Ames Research Center, Mike McGreevy and Jim Humphries built a non-see-through HMD from monochrome LCD pocket television displays, a motorcycle helmet, and the LEEP wide-angle stereoscopic optics [6]. This HMD was later improved by Scott Fisher, Warren Robinett, and others [7]. The display code for this system treated the LEEP optics as a simple magnifier. The LEEP optics system has very large exit pupils, and therefore no mechanical IDP adjustment.

At Wright-Patterson Air Force Base in the 1970s and 1980s, Tom Furness directed a program that developed prototype HMDs for use in military aircraft [8]. The system was called Visually Coupled Airborne Systems Simulator (VCASS), and several prototype see-through HMDs with custom-designed optics were developed there [9,10].

CAE Electronics of Quebec have developed a fibre optic helmet-mounted display system (FOHMD), intended for flight simulators [11,12]. Four light valves drive the HMD through fibre optic cables and pancake optics allow the user to see through to the flight simulator's control panel. There is a mechanical adjustment for IPD. The binocular field of view (FOV) is 135° horizontally by 64° vertically, and it also has a 25 × 19° high-resolution inset field.

Several prototype HMDs have been constructed at the University of North Carolina at Chapel Hill [13,14]. In 1985, a see-through HMD was made from colour LCD displays, half-silvered mirrors, magnifying lenses and a pilot's instrument training hood. The FOV was approximately 25° horizontally. A later model, built at the Air Force Institute of Technology (AFIT) with UNC collaboration, was made from colour LCDs, very strong reading glasses and a bicycle helmet. Its FOV is about 55° horizontally and it is not a see-through HMD. We are currently designing a see-through HMD for medical imaging applications. It will incorporate custom-designed optics.

In 1989, Eric Howlett, the inventor of the LEEP optics, put together a commercial HMD, the LEEPvideo System I. It used monochrome LCD displays, the LEEP optics, and a head-mounted apparatus designed by Howlett. Howlett subsequently introduced improved models that use colour LCDs and have a wider FOV [15].

Later in 1989, VPL Research of Redwood City, California, began selling the EyePhone [16]. It uses colour LCD displays and the LEEP optics. It attaches to the head with a rubber diving mask and fabric straps, and is not see-through.

In 1989, Reflection Technologies of Waltham, Massachusetts, produced a product called Private Eye, a single eye monochrome HMD [17]. It uses a vibrating mirror and an LED linear array to produce a two-dimensional (2D) image. The horizontal FOV is about 25°.

1.3 Remaining problems

Generating correct stereoscopic images for an HMD is a difficult task. The display code for each HMD system embodies an implicit computational model of the geometry of the HMD, and there are many sources of error that must be compensated for. In current practice, most of these models are inadequate because they ignore certain sources of error. Also, since these models are embodied only in the display code of the HMD systems, they are difficult to comprehend, and are not accessible to most people. It is difficult to compare the computational models of different HMD systems.

The display software often ignores the system optics. But because the optics actually do affect the images seen by the eyes, some of the parameters in the display software are tweaked to get the convergence and FOV of the HMD to be roughly correct. This type of measurement of the parameters of the HMD system by subjective calibration by the users is inaccurate compared with calculating the model parameters from the specifications of the optics and display screens.

Another problem is that most current HMD systems ignore the variation in IPD across different users. In this case, wide- and narrow-eyed users will have different size perceptions of the same simulated objects.

This paper presents an explicit computational model for generating orthostereoscopically correct images. Implementing display software that follows this model will produce stereoscopic images that are orthostereoscopic – simulated objects will be perceived as three-dimensional and will be undistorted and correctly sized.

We first survey the various sources of error that cause incorrect stereoscopic images to be generated. We then introduce a computational model of the geometry of an HMD that models the optics, the distance between the user's eyes, and the relative positions of the eyes, optics and display screens. This model allows correct orthostereoscopic images to be calculated. Finally, we calculate the model parameters for the VPL EyePhone.

2   Sources of Error

There is a very precise correlation between the movements of one's head and the images of an object that are formed on the retinas from moment to moment. This correlation can be described by simple geometry: the object's images are projected onto the retinas, and the retinal images depend only on the object's shape and the relative position of the two eyes with respect to the object. An HMD system attempts to mimic this geometry, painting images onto display screens in front of the eyes to fool the eyes and brain into perceiving three-dimensional (3D) objects. If the wrong images are painted onto the screens, the user is not able to perceive the simulated object correctly. The object will either be distorted, or there will be no perception of a 3D object at all.

The wrong images are painted onto the screens either because of errors and inaccuracies in the head tracking, or because of errors in the software that controls the image generation. While the tracking hardware can introduce significant error, it is the display software that is the subject of this paper.

We will introduce a computational model for a head-mounted display, and say that the display software implements this model. For the display software to generate the images required to give the HMD user the perception of undistorted objects, the software must take into account the physical geometry of each hardware component that affects the final image seen by the eyes. This geometry includes the display screens, the optics used to image the displays, and the placement of the displays with respect to the eyes. Before introducing the computational model, we discuss some common errors in the display code for HMDs.

2.1 Incorrect convergence

Both eyes are necessary for stereoscopic vision. When the eyes are focused on a distant object, the lines of sight are roughly parallel, and when focused on a near object, the lines of sight converge. The nearer the object, the greater the convergence.

A stereoscopic HMD has, for each eye, a display screen and an optical system through which the screen is viewed. If the optical axes were parallel for the two optical systems, and if the optical axis passed through the centre pixel of each screen, then by illuminating those two centre pixels, the user would see a stereoscopic image of a point of light at infinity. This would be more or less like looking at a single star in the night sky. However, many HMDs do not satisfy those two conditions: turning on the centre pixels would either produce a percept of a not-so-distant point of light in front of the user, or else be too divergent to fuse at all into a stereoscopic percept.

In addition to the horizontal alignment problem related to convergence and divergence, there can also be a vertical misalignment between the two eyes. This is called divergence.

Creating stereoscopic images with the correct convergence, when the optical axes are not parallel or the centres of the displays are offset from the optical axes, requires corrective transformations in the computational model. Neither of these properties is a mistake in the design of an HMD, they just make the computational model a little more complicated. In fact, many current HMDs have nonparallel optical axes and off-centre screens.

2.2 Accommodation not linked to convergence

The eyes converge on a nearby object by rotating inward; the lenses of the eyes simultaneously accommodate to the distance of the object to bring it into focus. Thus convergence and accommodation are normally linked. However, in an HMD system, each eye sees the virtual image of a display screen. With respect to focus, the entire virtual image appears at a fixed distance from the eye. (In a physical scene, different parts of the scene will be in focus at different accommodation depths.) Hence, the HMD user must learn to decouple accommodation and convergence. This problem cannot be overcome with any currently used display device. Until a display device with variable focus is developed, this problem must be accepted as a limitation of HMDs.

2.3 Incorrect field of view

The display for a single eye in an HMD has an FOV, which is the angle subtended by the virtual image of the display screen, as seen by the eye. There is a horizontal and a vertical FOV corresponding to the left-to-right and top-to-bottom angular sweep across the virtual image of the display. Let us call these angles the physical FOV. To be accurate in our definition of the FOV, we shall consider that a point in object space contributes to the physical FOV if the chief ray defined as the ray passing through that point and the centre of the exit pupil of the viewing system (here the pupil of the eye) is not obstructed. We are somewhat conservative therefore in our definition of the FOV since a point could be said to belong to the FOV as long as at least one ray reaches the image plane. This FOV is usually referred to in the optics literature as the total FOV.

An FOV is also specified in the display code. This computational FOV determines how far away the centre of projection is from the screen rectangle in the perspective transformation that is used to project the 3D virtual world onto the 2D screen. There is both a horizontal and vertical FOV in this case, also. These are specified in many graphics systems by giving the aspect ratio, the ratio of horizontal to vertical FOV angles, and then giving the vertical angle. Another term that is sometimes used instead of 'computational FOV' is 'geometric FOV'.

Unfortunately, the computational FOV angles may not match the physical FOV angles. As with convergence, the software designer may not know the optical specifications and may be forced to measure the FOV empirically. To get it right, the position of the centre of projection with respect to the screen should be exactly at the entrance pupil of the eye.

The optics, the position of the display relative to the optics, and the FOV used to compute the images jointly determine a point in the exit pupil of the optics where the pupil of the eye is expected to be. If the pupil of the eye is not at this expected point in space (too near or too far, to the left or right, too high or too low), the lines of sight to a simulated object will not be correct.

2.4 Failure to use off-centre projection when required

If the display screen is perpendicular to the optical axis and off-centre from the axis, then the eye is off-centre with respect to the screen, and the computational centre of projection should be off-centre too. This situation requires an off-centre perspective projection, in which the left, right, top and bottom edges of the screen rectangle are specified independently of one another, rather than having left–right and top–bottom be symmetrical as usual. An off-centre perspective projection transformation can be set up with the standard computer graphics hardware using the standard 4 × 4 homogeneous matrix representation of the transformation. Many people even in the computer graphics profession are unfamiliar with the off-centre perspective projection – it is never needed in normal computer graphics because, since the physical eye position is unknown, a convenient one directly in front of the screen may as well be assumed.

Another mistake is to simply rotate the whole scene left or right to produce images for the two eyes. In general, the computational model needs to include transformations that take into account the position and orientation of the screens with respect to the user's eyes. This is likely to be a combination of translation, rotation and off-centre perspective projection, and very unlikely to be just a pure rotation [18,19].

2.5 Interpupillary distance ignored

Among male and female adults, there is a fairly wide variation in the distance between the eyes, called the interpupillary distance (IPD). The range is roughly 53 to 73 mm, with the average IPD being about 63 mm. Children have even smaller IPDs.

The variation in IPD imposes a requirement on the HMD optics and display hardware. Either the exit pupil of the optics must be large enough to be used by the widest-eyed and the narrowest-eyed people, or else there must be a mechanical adjustment such as is found on binoculars. Both of these approaches have been used. For example, the LEEP optics, used in many current HMDs, has a very large exit pupil. The CAE fibre optic HMD used for flight simulation requires a mechanical adjustment for each new user.

The distance between the eyes is the baseline from which a person judges the distance to objects in the physical world. The convergence of the lines of sight from the eyes to a point of fixation can be measured as an angle. As Fig. 5.1 shows, a narrow-eyed and a wide-eyed person will have different convergence angles when looking at an object at the same distance, say, half a metre away.

These two people have different convergence angles yet both perceive the object to be half a metre away. Each person is calibrated to his or her own IPD.

With the mechanical IPD adjustment, the images get piped into the user's eyes and his or her physical IPD has no effect on the images seen. With no mechanical adjustment but a large exit pupil, if the virtual images are at optical infinity, then a lateral change in eye position has no effect on the angles at which an object appears – in other words, in this case, too, the user gets the same one-size-fits-all images regardless of the physical distance between the eyes. If the virtual images are not at optical infinity, the situation is more complicated, and people of varying IPD are still not going to see images matched to their own IPDs.

The solution to this problem is to measure the IPD for each user, and have the IPD as a user-specific constant in the computational model. If this is done correctly, then each user can see a simulated object half a metre away with a convergence matched to his or her own IPD.

2.6 Optical distortion ignored

The display screens in an HMD are too close to the eyes to focus on directly, so an optical system is interposed between the eye and the screen. The main purpose of the optics is to provide an image to the user at a comfortable distance of accommodation and with as large a magnification as possible without altering the image. The eye, looking into the optics, sees a virtual image of the display screen. The virtual image is distant enough from the eye to focus on easily, and large enough to cover a large swath of the user's FOV. But the optics also distort the image nonlinearly, causing lines that were straight on the display screen to appear as curved in the virtual image.

Optical aberrations are defects of the image. They may be described in terms of the amount by which a geometrically traced ray misses a specified location in the image plane formed by the optical system. The displacement of the ray is referred to as the transverse ray aberration.

Most often, the specified location for a ray in the image plane is that inferred from first-order laws of image formation [20,21]. Rays that do propagate not only

Figure 5.1 Eyes with narrow versus wide IPDs looking at an object from the same distance.

near the optical axis but also at shallow angles with respect to the optical axis are known as paraxial rays. Under the paraxial approximation, the formation of images is referred to as first-order, paraxial, or Gaussian optics. The most common aberrations are spherical aberration (SA), coma, astigmatism (AST), field curvature (FC), distortion and chromatic aberrations. It should be noted that while SA, coma, AST, FC and chromatic aberrations all affect the sharpness of the image points being formed, distortion distinguishes itself from the others, since it causes the image points to be displaced transversally in a nonlinear fashion across the FOV but does not alter the sharpness of the image.

Transversal aberrations can be expressed mathematically as a polynomial expansion of third-order and higher order terms in both the image height and the height of strike of the ray on a reference sphere centred on the ideal image point and passing through the exit pupil of the optical system. The ideal image point is often chosen to be the paraxial image point. The sum of the exponents of the aperture and field terms indicates the order of the aberration represented by that term. Depending on how open the optical system is and how large the angles of incidence of the rays on the different surfaces of the optical elements are, a system is best described by a third-order or a higher order approximation. The complexity of the optics used is usually such that the sharpness of the images formed through the optical system is good enough for the display resolution available on the market today. The distortion of the images, however, is often disturbing if it has not been corrected for optically. The first-order polynomial is linear and describes an ideal magnifier with no distortion, and since there are no even terms appearing in the expansion, the third-order polynomial is the simplest model of distortion.

Nonlinear field distortion causes straight lines on the screen to appear curved. This can be corrected for in the graphics system by predistorting the images written onto the screens. A straight line in the virtual image would be created by writing a curved line onto the screen, such that its curvature exactly balanced out the optical distortion. This would require that the inverse of the screen-to-virtual-image distortion function be stored in the graphics system, and that each pixel be remapped to a new location on the screen. This is computationally expensive.

Most current HMD systems just ignore the optical distortion, because they may not have access to the distortion function for the optics, and because of the performance penalty even if they did do the correction. This is not an unreasonable choice in the early stages of development of an HMD, because the system is usable even with the optical distortion.

However, one side-effect of nonlinear field distortion is that there is no single correct value for the FOV. Nonlinear distortion causes the magnification to vary across the FOV. If the computational FOV is set to match the physical FOV, then objects in the centre of the field will appear to be the wrong size. But if the computational FOV is set to make small central objects appear to be the right size, the objects in the peripheral field will be positioned wrong. The only way to avoid this unpleasant choice is to predistort the image to correct the optical distortion.

If the optics are designed specially for an HMD, then specific types of aberrations can be minimized. But if optics designed for another purpose are used, then you take what you can get. The LEEP optics, used in many current HMD systems, were designed for stereoscopic photography, and purposely incorporate substantial field distortion and chromatic aberrations.

Our experience has been that although the LEEP optics in the VPL EyePhone introduce distortion, we have been able to use it very effectively without correcting the image to compensate for the distortion. However, our experience with shading and radiosity models has also shown us that we are not able to appreciate what we are missing until we have seen it done right.

2.7 Transforming only polygon vertices in the presence of nonlinearities

Computer graphics has traditionally gained much efficiency by representing graphics primitives such as lines and polygons as collections of points, running only the points through the transformation pipeline, and then drawing the lines or polygons between the transformed points. This works only if all the transformations in the pipeline are linear. It is tempting to run only the polygon vertices through the predistortion function and let the very efficient hardware fill in the polygons. But then only the vertices would be in the right place – the polygon edges would still be curved by the optical distortion. Figure 5.2a shows a simple case of this. Edges of polygons that cross a large fraction of the screen would be most noticeably curved.

Another problem with this approach is that continuity would be lost. A vertex that touched an edge before predistortion and scan-conversion would not be guaranteed to do so in the final image. Gaps and holes would open up (Fig. 5.2b).

3   Optics Model for a Head-Mounted Display

The purpose of the optics model is to specify the computation necessary to create orthostereoscopically correct images for an HMD and indicate the parameters of that system that need to be measured and incorporated into the model.

3.1   Single-eye optics model

To achieve orthostereoscopy, the nonlinear optical distortion must be corrected by remapping all the pixels on the screen with a predistortion function. Linear graphics primitives such as lines and polygons are written into a virtual screen image buffer, and then all the pixels are shifted according to the predistortion function and written

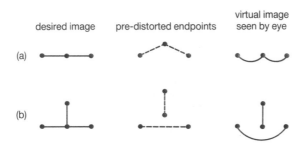

Figure 5.2 Problems with predistorting only vertices.

to the screen image buffer for display. The predistortion function is the inverse of the field distortion function for the optics, so that the virtual image seen by the eye matches the image in the virtual screen buffer. A straight line in the virtual image buffer is predistorted into a curved line on the display screen, which is distorted by the optics into a line that is seen as straight. Figure 5.3 shows the optics model for a single eye.

The mathematical representation of the optical distortion will depend on the nature of the optical system. For optics such as LEEP, a third-order polynomial approximation is adequate. We want to relate the radial position r_s of a pixel on the screen to the radial position r_v of the virtual image of that pixel. These two quantities are measured in millimetres with respect to the optical axis. Dividing r_s and r_v by the object field width w_s and the image field width w_v, respectively, we get the normalized position of the pixel on the screen

$$r_{sn} = r_s/w_s$$

and the normalized position of the virtual image of the pixel

$$r_{vn} = r_v/w_v$$

(The paraxial magnification of the system is thus $m_{sv} = w_v/w_s$.) The distortion is modelled with a third-order polynomial approximation

$$r_{vn} = r_{sn} + k_{vs}r_{sn}^3$$

in which the coefficient k_{vs} describes the amount of distortion present. This can be rearranged algebraically to

$$r_{vn} = (1 + k_{vs}r_{sn}^2)r_{sn}$$

and then expanded to rectangular coordinates using

$$r_{sn}^2 = x_{sn}^2 + y_{sn}^2$$
$$r_{vn}^2 = x_{vn}^2 + y_{vn}^2$$

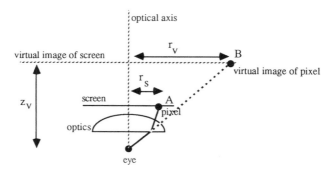

Figure 5.3 Single-eye optics model.

to give the position of the virtual image of the pixel

$$(x_{vn}, y_{vn}) = \{[1 + k_{vs}(x_{sn}^2 + y_{sn}^2)]x_{sn}, \ [1 + k_{vs}(x_{sn}^2 + y_{sn}^2)]y_{sn}\}$$

from the position (x_{sn}, y_{sn}) of the pixel on the screen. These positions are measured in the screen plane and virtual image plane, respectively, with respect to the optical axis.

The distance from the eye to the virtual image plane z_v is a constant. By combining the above equations, we have a function that gives the three-dimensional position of the virtual image of a pixel on the screen (x_v, y_v, z_v) in terms of its screen coordinates (x_s, y_s) and some constants. We will ignore z_v from here on since it is constant.

The expressions for x_{vn} and y_{vn} can be thought of as single-valued functions of two variables. If we name the distortion function D, then

$$(x_{vn}, y_{vn}) = D(x_{sn}, y_{sn})$$

and what we need to predistort the image on the screen is the inverse D^{-1}. There are various ways this inverse function could be represented in the computer. An exact closed-form expression is not feasible, but a polynomial approximation of the inverse is possible.

$$r_{sn} = r_{vn} + k_{sv}r_{vn}^3$$

$$(x_{sn}, y_{sn}) = D^{-1}(x_{vn}, y_{vn})$$

$$(x_{sn}, y_{sn}) = \{[1 + k_{sv}(x_{vn}^2 + y_{vn}^2)]x_{vn}, \ [1 + k_{sv}(x_{vn}^2 + y_{vn}^2)]y_{vn}\}$$

Note that these two functions D and D^{-1} are each third-order polynomial approximations and are not exact inverses of one another. The coefficients k_{sv} and k_{vs} will be opposite in sign.

Another possibility for representing D^{-1} on the computer is a two-dimensional table lookup for each of the output variables x_{sn} and y_{sn}. Using this approach, limits on table size would probably make it necessary to interpolate between table entries.

Distortion causes nonuniform magnification across the field, which causes the brightness also to vary across the field. This could be compensated for on a pixel-by-pixel basis with a brightness correction function $B(x_s, y_s)$, but limitations of space prevent us from going into this here.

3.2 Stereoscopic optics model

Figure 5.4 shows the stereoscopic optics model. One pixel is illuminated on each screen (points A1 and A2) and a line of sight is drawn from each eye to the virtual image of its corresponding pixel (points B1 and B2). These two lines of sight intersect at the three-dimensional point perceived by the user (point C). The IPD is the baseline from which the user makes distance judgments based on the convergence angles to perceived points.

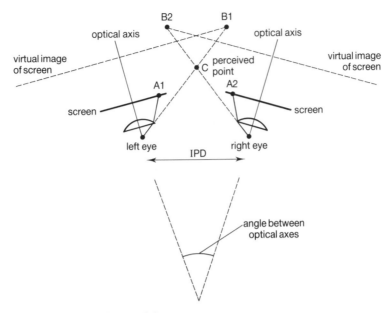

Figure 5.4 Stereoscopic optics model.

If the specifications for the optics are known, and the relative positions of the display screens, the optics and the eyes are also known, then it is possible to accurately calculate several important parameters needed in the computational model. The horizontal and vertical FOVs can be calculated by starting from the known positions of the left, right, top and bottom edges of the screen with respect to the optics and tracing the rays through the optics system back to the eye.

The screen centres may be offset from the optical axes by a certain distance. The two optical axes may be rotated with respect to one another. The screen centre offsets and axis divergence angles can be used to set the convergence properly with no need for subjective calibrations. From the known position and orientation of the virtual image of the screen relative to the eye, the eye-to-virtual-image transformation can be calculated to be the correct mix of translation, rotation, and off-centre perspective projection. Translation is needed because the eyes are in different positions in space, rotation is needed if the optical axes are not parallel, and the projection is off-centre if the screens are off-centre from the optical axes.

Table 5.1 shows the sequence of starting from the specifications of the optics and displays, measuring certain parameters of the HMD, and then calculating other parameters needed by the computational model. The left and right halves of the optical system are assumed to be symmetrical. The calculations are done for the right side, so the left edge of the screen is on the inside beside the nose and the right edge is on the outside.

Except for the IPD, which varies among users, every other parameter necessary to specify the head-to-eye, eye-to-virtual-image, and virtual-image-to-screen transformations for the left and right eyes can be derived from the specifications of the optics and the relative positions of the eyes, optics and screens. Calculating these

Table 5.1 Calculating parameters in the optics model.

Parameter	Symbol	Where it comes from
Screen resolution	$Res_H \times Res_V$	From display spec
Angle between optical axes	ϕ_{axes}	From optics spec or measure
Distance between optical axes (at front surface of optics)	d_{axes}	From optics spec or measure
Eye relief	d_{er}	Measure
Maximum field of view	ϕ_{max}	Calculate from d_{er} and optics spec
Object plane distance	d_{ob}	Measure
Distance from eye to virtual image plane	z_v	Calculate from d_{ob} and optics spec
Transversal magnification	m_{vs}	Calculate from d_{ob} and optics spec
Coefficient of optical distortion	k_{vs}	From optics spec
Maximum object field radius	w_s	From optics spec
Maximum virtual image field radius	w_v	$w_v = m_{vs}w_s$
Interpupillary distance of user	IPD	Measure user
Screen centre offset from optical axis	(Cx_s, Cy_s)	Measure
Position of left screen edge	(Lx_s, Ly_s)	Measure
Position of right screen edge	(Rx_s, Ry_s)	Measure
Position of top screen edge	(Tx_s, Ty_s)	Measure
Position of bottom screen edge	(Bx_s, By_s)	Measure
Object height (of point on screen)	r_s	$r_s = (x_s + y_s)^{1/2}$
Normalized object height	r_{sn}	$r_{sn} = r_s/w_s$
Normalized image height (third-order approximation of D)	r_{vn}	$r_{vn} = r_{sn} + k_{vs}r_{sn}^3$
Image height (of point in virtual image)	r_v	$r_v = r_{vn}w_v$
Angular position of point in virtual image	ϕ	$\phi = \tan^{-1}(r_v/z_v)$
Angular position of left edge (inner edge of screen)	ϕ_L	From formula for ϕ
Angular position of right edge (outer edge of screen)	ϕ_R	From formula for ϕ
Angular position of top edge	ϕ_T	From formula for ϕ
Angular position of bottom edge	ϕ_B	From formula for ϕ
Single eye vertical field of view	FOV_v	$FOV_v = \phi_T + \phi_B$
Single eye horizontal field of view	FOV_h	$FOV_h = \phi_L + \phi_R$
Overlapped field of view	FOV_{ov}	$FOV_{ov} = 2\,\phi_L - \phi_{axes}$
Binocular field of view	FOV_{bin}	$FOV_{bin} = 2\,\phi_R + \phi_{axes}$
Translation part of viewing transformation	M_{trans}	$(\pm IPD/2, 0, 0)$
Rotation part of viewing transformation	M_{rot}	$(\pm\phi_{axes}/2)$ around Y-axis
Perspective projection	$M_{perspec}$	Use FOV_v, FOV_h, and offset $[\pm Cx_s/(Rx_s-Lx_s),\ Cy_s/(Ty_s-By_s)]$

parameters is much more accurate than relying on subjective calibration procedures in which the parameters are adjusted until the image looks right. However, the subjective measurements provide a nice check against mistakes in the model, the measurements or the calculations.

We have defined a computational model for the graphics computation without reference to a particular HMD system. Having done that, we now turn to calculating the model parameters for a specific HMD, the VPL EyePhone.

4   Calculating the Model Parameters for the VPL EyePhone

4.1   Description of EyePhone components

We have used the optical specifications of the LEEP optics and size and positioning of the LCD screens inside the EyePhone to calculate the model parameters for the VPL EyePhone, Model 1 [16]. Model 2 of the EyePhone has identical optics, LCD displays, and positioning of the parts.

The LEEP optics [6] are wide-angle, stereoscopic viewing lenses. The system consists of three-lenses in front of each eye, encased in a moulded plastic mount, with a cut-out for the nose. It was designed for a single transparency in the object plane, upon which are two side-by-side stereoscopic photographs of a scene, each one a square approximately 64 mm on a side. For an eye relief distance of 29.4 mm, the FOVs for each eye are approximately +45 to −45° horizontally, and +45 to −45° vertically. The distance from the centre of the rearmost lens surface to the object plane is approximately 16 mm. The optical axes for the two eyes are parallel and are 64 mm apart. The two optical systems are bilaterally symmetrical with respect to each other, and each optical system is radially symmetrical around the optical axis, except for the cut-outs for the user's nose in the front lenses.

The construction of the EyePhone is rigid enough to keep the eyes, optics and display screens in a fixed relationship to one another, so it is possible to make accurate measurements of these relative positions.

The EyePhone uses the LEEP optics with two colour LCD display screens positioned in the LEEP object plane. The two displays are positioned symmetrically with respect to the left and right eye optical axes. Figure 5.5 is a diagram of the positions of the LCD screens in the object plane.

Six important points are labelled in Fig. 5.5. Only one side need be analysed since the LCDs and optics are symmetrical.

4.2   Calculation of EyePhone field of view

We use two different methods to compute the FOVs for the EyePhone. First, we use the optics model with the parameters specific to the EyePhone to calculate the angles at which the points in Fig. 5.5 are seen. Then, for comparison and validation, we compute these same angles by tracing rays through the LEEP optics. We do the ray tracing with Code V, a commercial optical analysis software package [22]. To do the ray tracing, we use the detailed optical specifications of the LEEP optics,

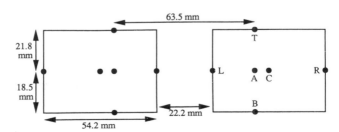

Figure 5.5 Position of the EyePhone's LCD displays in the LEEP object plane.

including the position, curvature, and index of refraction for each lens surface in the optical path.

First, we use the optics model. The dimensions given in Fig. 5.5 are sufficient to determine the coordinates of the points A, L, R, T and B in the LEEP object plane (with respect to the optical axis A). From these coordinates, the value of r_s for each point can be calculated. We feed the known positions of the edges of the LCD screens into the optics model to predict the positions of the screen edges in the virtual image, and from these positions calculate the FOVs for the EyePhone. We shall see that the chief rays corresponding to some of the object points on the LCDs are obstructed for $d_{er} = 29.4$ mm. In this case the FOV covers only part of the LCDs. The unseen part of the LCD is said to be vignetted. The model parameters for the LEEP optics as used in the EyePhone are

$$d_{er} = 29.4 \text{ mm}$$

$$w_s = 28.1 \text{ mm}$$

$$w_v = 271.5 \text{ mm}$$

$$z_v = 398.2 \text{ mm}$$

$$k_{vs} = 0.32$$

and the equations from the optics model

$$r_{sn} = r_s/w_s$$

$$r_{vn} = r_{sn} + k_{vs}r_{sn}^3$$

$$r_v = r_{vn}w_v$$

$$\phi = \tan^{-1}(r_v/z_v)$$

can be used to calculate the angle ϕ for each point, as shown in Table 5.2.

Table 5.2 EyePhone FOV Calculation, Assuming $d_{er} = 29.4$ mm.

Point	x_s (mm)	y_s (mm)	r_s (mm)	r_{sn}	r_{vn} third order	r_v (mm)	Angle ϕ from model (degrees)	Angle ϕ from ray tracing (degrees)
A Optical axis	0	0	0	0	0	0	0	0
R Right edge of screen	33.3	0	28.1 (33.3 vignetted)	1.000	1.32	358.5	42.0	45.0
L Left edge of screen	−20.9	0	20.9	0.744	0.876	237.9	30.9	30.3
T Top edge of screen	0	21.8	21.8	0.776	0.926	251.5	32.3	31.8
B Bottom edge of screen	0	−18.5	18.5	0.658	0.749	203.4	27.1	26.6
C Centre of screen	6.2	1.65						

The second method of computing the angles is ray tracing. Figure 5.6 shows a horizontal cross section of the right-eye LEEP optical system, with the rays from the points L, A and R traced back to the eye. The ray tracing was done for each of the points A, L, R, T, and B in Fig. 5.5.

Table 5.2 shows the angular positions of the virtual images of the edges of the LCD screen as predicted by the optics model, and as predicted by ray tracing. The comparison of the angles calculated by the two methods shows that the third-order approximation used in the optics model is adequate for the LEEP optics.

From these calculations, we can see that, for a single eye, the horizontal FOV is 75.3° (45.0+30.3) and the vertical FOV is 58.4° (31.8+26.6). These are the physical FOVs for the EyePhone − the physical angles at which the virtual images of the edges of the LCD screen are seen by the eye. To make the graphics calculation match the physical FOV, these angles must be incorporated into the calculation. Here at UNC, we are using the Pixel-Planes graphics engine [23] to generate images for the EyePhone. Like many graphics systems, the Pixel-Planes graphics software accepts an angle for the vertical FOV, here 58.4°, and an aspect ratio, here 1.289.

The graphics calculation must also take into account the fact that in the EyePhone, the centre of the LCD screen (point C) is off the optical axis (point A). How this off-centre perspective projection is specified to the graphics software varies somewhat among graphics systems. For the Pixel-Planes graphics software, off-centre projection is specified as a horizontal and vertical offset in pixels from the screen centre. For the horizontal offset, 512 pixels across a 54.2 mm screen gives 0.106 mm/pixel, so the 6.2 mm horizontal offset is 58.5 pixels. For the vertical offset, 512 pixels across a 40.3 mm screen height gives 0.079 mm/pixel, so the 1.65 mm vertical offset is 21.0 pixels.

These calculated values for FOV and screen-centre offset together with the IPD of the user is enough to specify precisely the perspective projection for the two eyes. Using these projections, the convergence and FOV are guaranteed to be correct, with no need for adjustment or calibration by the user. Our experience

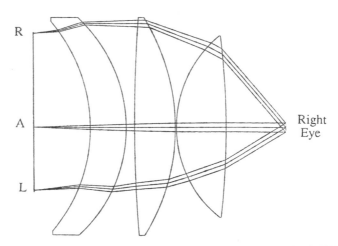

Figure 5.6 Tracing rays from the EyePhone's LCD screen through the LEEP optics.

with the EyePhone is that using the calculated parameters gives very solid stereo perception for all users who can see in stereo, with no need for tweaking these parameters. Getting this all to work depends on getting several subordinate things right – the specifications for the optics must be correct, the analysis of the optics must be correct, the measurements of the LCD positions and dimensions must be correct, and the graphics software for setting up the projections must be correct.

Before these calculations were done, the FOV and off-centre parameters had been tweaked, through a long process of trial and error, trying to get the image to look right. The most effective test was to try to get the image of a 5.75-cm red sphere to be the right size and stay on top of a physical 5.75-cm red 3-ball (from the game of pool) with a Polhemus sensor inside as the 3-ball was moved around. This 3-ball, which has two pushbuttons on it, is one of our manual input devices. The FOVs for a single eye which were finally arrived at through these subjective tests were a horizontal FOV of 80° and a vertical FOV of 60°. Since the EyePhone does not allow the user to see through to the real world, the subjective tests had to be done by repeatedly raising the EyePhone to see how the position of the physical 3-ball compared with the remembered position of the simulated 3-ball. We estimated the accuracy to be about 2°. For a see-through HMD, superimposing a 3D stereoscopic image onto a physical object of the same known shape is an extremely accurate test, because the eye can simultaneously compare the two scenes and detect tiny discrepancies. The acuity of the human eye is considered to be roughly one minute of arc.

Figure 5.7 shows that the horizontal FOVs for the two eyes in the EyePhone partially overlap. The region of overlap (60.6°) is wide enough for strong stereoscopic perception, and the binocular FOV (90.0°) is wide enough to provide a feeling of immersion within the scene. We believe, however, that a wider FOV will make the feeling of immersion stronger.

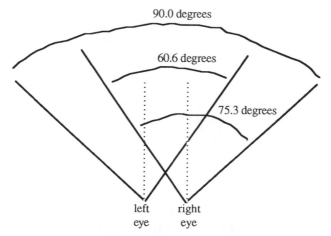

Figure 5.7 Binocular, overlapped, and single-eye FOVs for the EyePhone.

4.3   Correction of EyePhone optical distortion

To correct the image on the screen from optical distortion, the screen image must be predistorted as specified by the function D^{-1}. This would radially shift all the pixels in the image by some amount. This has not yet been implemented on the UNC HMD system, but we plan to use a pair of two-dimensional tables $T_X[x_v, y_v]$ and $T_Y[x_v, y_v]$ in this implementation.

We have a 512×512 pixel screen to cover, but a table size of 512×512 is impractical. We expect to use a reduced table size, such as 64×64, and interpolate bilinearly between table entries. The table values will be computed off-line using the formula for D^{-1}.

The optics projects object points of height r_s to image points of height r_v. This mapping is monotonic and so its inverse exists. We approximate the mapping with a third-degree polynomial D and approximate its inverse with another third-degree polynomial D^{-1}

$$r_{sn} = r_{vn} + k_{sv} r_{vn}^3$$

in which, for the LEEP optics, k_{sv} is -0.18.

Figure 5.8 shows the graph of the normalized virtual image position r_{vn} versus the normalized screen position r_{sn} for the LEEP optics. It shows that the third-degree polynomial approximation of the distortion function D is quite close to the more accurate graph of D calculated by ray tracing through the optics. The second graph compares the third-degree polynomial approximation of the inverse D^{-1} with the values calculated by ray tracing.

Figure 5.9 shows a grid which has been predistorted by the function D^{-1}. When viewed through the LEEP optics, the lines of the grid appear straight.

Although the predistortion function D^{-1}, also known as the virtual-image-to-screen transformation, has not yet been implemented on the UNC HMD system, we have looked through the LEEP optics at the predistorted grid printed on paper to verify that the grid lines do appear straight. The predistorted grid in Fig. 5.9 is full sized (79 mm square) and may be viewed through the LEEP optics. The lines will appear straight when the grid object is in close contact with the lens. Note that in the EyePhone, the LCD screen is separated by a gap of a few millimetres from the LEEP lens.

The straightforward method to correct computationally for the optical distortion would be to compute the image normally and then in a second step warp this 2D image using the predistortion function D^{-1}. This would require moving every pixel in the image to a new location and is thus quite expensive computationally. Since a straight line such as the edge of a polygon is mapped by D^{-1} to a gently curved line, and our graphics engine Pixel-Planes 5 has the ability to evaluate quadratics in parallel, we have considered the idea of approximating these curved lines with quadratic polynomials, but we have not yet evaluated this idea in detail.

Another approach that has been used [24] is to implement the distortion correction optically by displaying the undistorted image on a monitor and aiming a video camera with a LEEP inverse lens at the monitor.

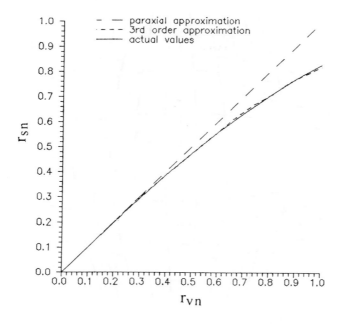

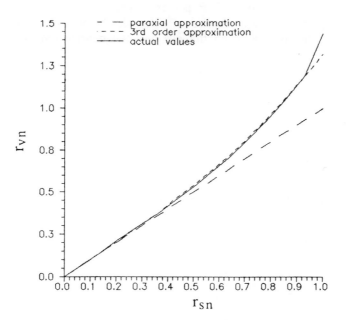

Figure 5.8 Graph of r_{vn} vs. r_{sn} for D ($k_{vs} = 0.32$) and ray tracing for the LEEP optics; graph of r_{sn} vs. r_{vn} for D^{-1} ($k_{sv} = -0.18$) and ray tracing.

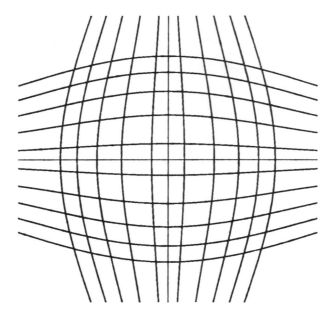

Figure 5.9 Grid predistorted for the LEEP optics.

4.4   Other EyePhone and LEEP parameters

The graph of Fig. 5.10 shows how the LEEP optics FOV varies with the eye relief distance d_{er}, the distance between the eye and the nearest lens surface. With the

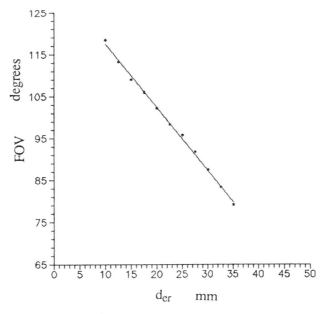

Figure 5.10 Graph of FOV vs. d_{er}.

nominal eye relief of 29.4 mm, the FOV for the LEEP optics is +45 to −45°. (The EyePhone's FOV is less than this because the EyePhone's LCD screen does not fill the LEEP object field.) If the eye was able to get closer, the FOV would increase, but an eye relief of 25–30 mm is necessary to allow people with spectacles to use the system.

When moving the eye closer to the lens, two factors contribute to an increase of the FOV: first, any point on the virtual image is seen over a larger angle, and second, more of the LCD screens can be perceived. Especially for the EyePhone, moving the eye closer to the lens does increase the FOV because some of the LCD display screen is vignetted for a pupil distance of 29.4 mm.

The virtual image of the screen is formed at some distance z_v from the eye, and the eye must accommodate to this distance. The graph of Fig. 5.11 shows that z_v is very sensitive to changes in the distance d_{ob} of the object plane to the LEEP optics. The EyePhone positions the LCD screen at d_{ob} = 16.4 mm from the nearest lens surface (measured along the optical axis). This value of d_{ob} results in an image distance of z_v = 398.2 mm and a magnification of m_{vs} = 9.66. As the object approaches the object focal point of the lens (d_{ob} = 20.7 mm) the image distance goes to infinity. However, such a positioning seems undesirable because of the conflict between convergence and accommodation.

The discussion of the resolution of the LCD display screens in the EyePhone is complicated by two competing ways of specifying resolution in a colour display − by colour pixels or by the RGB component cells of the pixels. The LCD used in

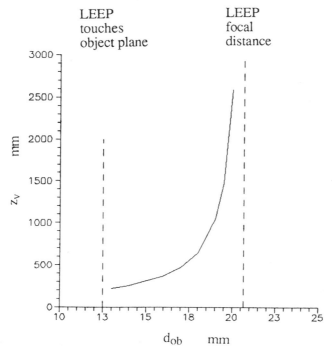

Figure 5.11 Graph of z_v vs. d_{ob}.

the EyePhone has a monochrome array of 360×240 individually controllable light-producing cells, with red, green, and blue filters overlaid to divide the cells into three equal-sized groups. A triad of one red, one green, and one blue cell makes up a colour pixel. There are 86,400 cells (360×240), and therefore 28,800 colour pixels. The resolution of the EyePhone in terms of colour pixels is thus approximately 207.8×138.6.

Table 5.3 lists all the parameters for the EyePhone with respect to the model developed in this paper. All the angles (ϕ and FOV parameters) were calculated from the other parameters as described above.

The LEEP optics are used in other HMDs besides the EyePhone, and a new model of EyePhone with a different LCD display is also being developed. Some of the parameters in Table 5.3 depend only on the LEEP optics (ϕ_{axes}, d_{axes}). Other parameters with specific values in the table describe the specific configuration in the EyePhone (Models 1 and 2) of the LCD screen's size and position in front of the LEEP optics.

The rubber diving mask of the EyePhone holds the face and eyes in a fairly constant position with respect to the LEEP optics, although some individuals have deeper set eyes than others. Decreasing d_{er} by moving the eyes closer to the LEEP lens would cause more of the object field to be seen and the value of w_s that was chosen to be the highest value of the field would then have to be increased

Table 5.3 Parameters for the VPL EyePhone, Models 1 and 2.

Parameter	Symbol	Value for EyePhone
Maximum object field radius	w_s	28.1 mm
Maximum virtual image field radius	w_v	271.55 mm
Transversal magnification	m_{sv}	9.66
Eye relief	d_{er}	29.4 mm (nominal)
Object plane distance (LCD screen to LEEP lens surface)	d_{ob}	16.4 mm
Distance from eye to virtual image plane	z_v	398.2 mm
Coefficient of optical distortion for D	k_{vs}	0.32
Coefficient of optical distortion for D^{-1}	k_{sv}	-0.18
Angle between optical axes	ϕ_{axes}	0°
Distance between optical axes (at front surface of optics)	d_{axes}	64 mm
Screen centre offset from optical axis	(Cx_s, Cy_s)	(6.4 mm, 1.6 mm)
Screen resolution	$Res_H \times Res_V$	208×139 pixels (colour triads)
Interpupillary distance of user	IPD	Varies across users
Angular position of virtual image of right edge of LCD	ϕ_R	45.0°
Angular position of virtual image of left edge of LCD	ϕ_L	30.3°
Angular position of virtual image of top edge of LCD	ϕ_T	31.8°
Angular position of virtual image of bottom edge of LCD	ϕ_B	26.6°
Single eye vertical field of view	FOV_v	58.4°
Single eye horizontal field of view	FOV_h	75.3°
Overlapped field of view	FOV_{ov}	60.6°
Binocular field of view	FOV_{bin}	90.0°

accordingly. If the same nominal eye relief used in this paper (29.4 mm) is assumed, then the distortion model can be applied to an HMD using the LEEP optics and a different screen using the coefficients calculated ($k_{vs} = 0.32$, $k_{sv} = -0.18$).

To determine the model parameters for other HMDs that use the LEEP optics, the distance d_{ob} from the LEEP optics to the display screen must first be known. This will determine the distance to the virtual image z_v and the magnification m_{sv}. An eye relief distance d_{er} must also be measured or assumed. This will determine the radius of the object and image fields w_s and w_v. The object and image fields describe what could be seen if the object field was completely filled, regardless of how completely the display screen does fill the object field. To compute the FOVs for the virtual image of the display screen, the positions of the edges of the display screen (points L, R, T and B) must be measured in the object plane with the optical axis as the origin. Cranking these measurements through the model will give the angular positions of the edge points (ϕ_R, ϕ_L, ϕ_T, ϕ_B), and thus the horizontal and vertical FOVs (FOV$_h$, FOV$_v$) for a single eye. To find the binocular field of view FOV$_{bin}$ for both eyes, the angles between the optical axes ϕ_{axes} must be taken into account. The position of the display screen's centre with respect to the optical axis must also be measured to properly set up the perspective projection.

5 Summary and Conclusions

The optics model presented in this paper, if implemented correctly, will generate undistorted orthostereoscopic images for the user's two eyes.

To calculate the display parameters needed by the model for the particular HMD being used, it is necessary to know or measure the specifications of the optics, and the relative positions of the eyes, optics, display screens and head position sensor. The construction of the HMD must be rigid enough that these values will not vary from day to day. If these parameters for the HMD are known, then several important derived parameters can be calculated – the FOVs, the screen-centre offset for the perspective projection, the angle between the optical axes, and the coefficients for the optical field distortion function. Calculating the values of these parameters is much more accurate than attempting to measure them subjectively with users.

Acknowledgements

This paper was originally published in *Stereoscopic Displays and Applications II*, John O. Merritt, Scott S. Fisher, Editors, Proc. SPIE 1457, 140–160 (1991). Reprinted with permission of The International Society for Optical Engineering (SPIE).

We would like to thank many people for their contributions to this work. Eric Howlett, designer of the LEEP optics, kindly provided the optical specifications. Mike Teitel of VPL provided needed measurements of the EyePhone. Jack Goldfeather helped with the mathematical representation of the distortion. Fred Brooks, Henry Fuchs and Steve Pizer helped to initiate and guide the HMD project at UNC, and various parts of the UNC HMD system were built by each of the team members: Ron Azuma, Bill Brown, Jim Chung, Drew Davidson, Erik Erikson, Rich Holloway, Jack Kite and Mark Ward. Fay Ward and Linda Houseman helped to hold it all together and Vern Chi, David Harrison, and John Hughes provided essential technical know how. The Pixel-Planes team provided us with the high-powered graphics engine needed to drive the HMD. This work builds upon earlier work by one of us (Robinett) at NASA Ames Research Center, and we would like to acknowledge the contributions of Scott Fisher, Jim Humphries, Doug Kerr, and Mike McGreevy. We would like to thank Fred Brooks for his critique of the paper, Julius Smith for his sketch of the ideal structure of a technical paper, and the anonymous reviewers for their suggestions. This research was supported in part by the Defense Advanced Project Research Agency, contract DAEA18-90-C-0044 and also by the Office of Naval Research, contract N00014-86-K-0680.

References

1   Sutherland, I.E. 1965. The ultimate display. *Proc. IFIPS Congress,* **2**: 506–508.
2   Sutherland, I.E. 1968. A head-mounted three-dimensional display. *Fall Joint Computer Conference, AFIPS Conference Proceedings,* **33**: 757–764.
3   Vickers, D.L. 1974. *Sorceror's Apprentice: head mounted display and wand.* PhD dissertation, Department of Computer Science, University of Utah, Salt Lake City.
4   Clark, J.H. 1976. Designing surfaces in 3-D. *Commun. ACM,* **19**(8): 454–460.
5   Callahan, M.A. 1983. *A 3-D display headset for personalized computing.* MS thesis, Department of Architecture, MIT.
6   Howlett, E.M. 1983. Wide angle color photography method and system. U.S. Patent Number 4,406,532.
7   Fisher, S.S., McGreevy, M., Humphries, J. and Robinett, W. 1986. Virtual environment display system. *Proc. Workshop on Interactive 3D Graphics,* 77–87.
8   Glines, C.V. 1986. Brain buckets. *Air Force Magazine,* **69**(8): 86–90.
9   Buchroeder, R.A., Seeley, G.W. and Vukobradatovich, D. 1981. *Design of a Catadioptric VCASS Helmet-Mounted Display.* Optical Sciences Center, University of Arizona, under contract to the U.S. Air Force Armstrong Aerospace Medical Research Laboratory, Wright-Patterson Air Force Base, Dayton, Ohio, AFAMRL-TR-81-133.
10   Kocian, D.F. 1988. *Design considerations for virtual panoramic display (VPD) helmet systems.* Armstrong Aerospace Medical Research Laboratory, Visual Display Systems Branch, Wright-Patterson Air Force Base, Dayton, Ohio 45433–6573.
11   CAE. 1986. *Introducing the visual display system that you wear.* CAE Electronics Ltd., C.P. 1800 Saint-Laurent, Quebec, Canada H4L 4X4.
12   Henderson, B.W. 1989. Simulators play key role in LHX contractor selection. *Aviation Week,* November 27.
13   Holloway, R.L. 1987. *Head-Mounted Display.* Technical Report TR87-015, Department of Computer Science, University of North Carolina at Chapel Hill.
14   Chung, J.C., Harris, M.R., Brooks, F.P., Jr., Fuchs, H., Kelley, M.T., Hughes, J., Ouh-Young, M., Cheung, C., Holloway, R.L. and Pique, M. 1989. Exploring virtual worlds with head-mounted displays. *Non-Holographic True 3-Dimensional Display Technologies, SPIE Proc. Vol. 1083.*
15   LEEP. 1990. *Cyberface II Applications Note.* LEEP Systems/Pop-Optix Labs, 241 Crescent St., Waltham, Massachusetts 02154.
16   VPL. 1989. *VPL EyePhone Operations Manual.* VPL Research, 656 Bair Island Rd., Suite 304, Redwood City, California 94063, p. B-4.

17 Mini screen is a real eye opener. *London Times*, May 28 1989.
18 Saunders, B.G. 1968. Stereoscopic drawing by computer – Is It Orthoscopic? *Applied Optics, 7*(8): 1499–1504.
19 Hodges, L.F. and McAllister, D.F. 1990. Rotation algorithm artifacts in stereoscopic images. *Optical Engineering, 29*(8).
20 Hecht, E. and Zajac, A. 1974. *Optics*. Addison-Wesley.
21 Longhurst, R.S. 1973. *Geometrical and Physical Optics*. Longman.
22 ORA. 1991. *Code V Reference Manual, Version 7.40*. Optical Research Associates, 550 North Rosemead Blvd., Pasadena, California 91107.
23 Eyles, J., Austin, J., Fuchs, H., Greer, T. and Poulton, J. 1988. Pixel-Planes 4: A summary. In A.A.M. Kuijik and W. Strasser, editors, *Advances in Computer Graphics Hardware II,* pp. 183–208. Eurographics Seminars, Berlin. Springer-Verlag.
24 Pang, X.D. and Durlach, N. 1990. Personal communication.

Biography

Warren Robinett is a designer of interactive computer graphics software and hardware. In 1978, he designed the Atari video game Adventure, the first graphical adventure game. In 1980, he was co-founder and chief software engineer at The Learning Company, a publisher of educational software. There he designed Rocky's Boots, a computer game which teaches digital logic design to 11-year-old children. Rocky's Boots won Software of the Year awards from three magazines in 1983. In 1986, Robinett worked as a research scientist at NASA Ames Research Center, where he designed the software for the Virtual Environment Workstation, NASA's pioneering Virtual Reality Project. In 1989, he came to the University of North Carolina as manager of the Head-Mounted Display Project, continuing to work in Virtual Reality.

6 A Comprehensive Virtual Environment Laboratory Facility

Roy S. Kalawsky[1]

Systems Technology R&D, British Aerospace

Abstract

Virtual reality has emerged from a concept known as a 'visually coupled system'. In essence it is a display or 'porthole' through a computer synthesized world that is updated with respect to head position [1,2]. Serious practitioners of this technology routinely describe these systems as *virtual environments*. The first virtual environment systems were essentially based on the concept of a visually coupled system. Recently, desktop VR systems have emerged which are based on computer aided design (CAD) tools with animation. Whether or not these systems are true virtual environment systems could be discussed at some length, but the purpose of this paper is to discuss the immersive virtual environment systems.

A virtual environment system involves a number of different scientific/engineering disciplines that have rarely been brought together before, and as a consequence the interface between these disciplines is not fully understood. Added to this is the problem that manufacturers do not understand the human factors element. Careful and critical examination of many systems reveals a clear lack of understanding by manufacturers when integrating VR technology to human factors [3].

To integrate effectively, a 'certain' level of technology and human factors must be available to, and fully understood by, manufacturers of these systems.

The labelling of 3D modelling on a computer screen as a virtual reality environment causes confusion, and although it could be discussed at length, the main object of this paper (as previously mentioned) is to discuss virtual environmental systems and the necessary research and development required to integrate a human operation into a virtual environment.

1 What is a Virtual Environment System?

A virtual environment system is an artificial, fully immersive surrounding that allows the user to interact with computer generated objects [4]. The interactive virtual environment can be a computer synthesized representation of a real world situation or an abstract form of a real world event. Taking it to the limit, a virtual environment

---

[1] Roy Kalawsky is visiting Professor of Virtual Environments and Advanced Display Technologies, The University of Hull, UK.

could be a completely synthetic representation of the world that can completely replace all the virtual and physical cues of the real world. These synthetic cues would be indistinguishable from the real world. Virtual objects would not only look, sound and feel like the real thing but they would move and behave in a real manner. Clearly, achieving this level of realism is beyond today's technology, and is likely to be for some considerable time [5].

However, if one can accept lower resolution cues and a restricted (confined) virtual world then there is tremendous potential for virtual environment systems. Whether or not one can accept a confined virtual world depends on the task to be undertaken, and of course the available technology. It is only too easy to disregard task requirements and 'cobble together' a virtual environment system that is little more than a curiosity. This may be acceptable for the entertainment business where the user is only immersed in the virtual environment for a relatively short time. The serious user of a virtual environment system will soon become intolerant of the technology unless the system has been carefully designed to meet the needs of the task. Figure 6.1 illustrates the conceptualization of a virtual environment system comprising visual, auditory and tactile world elements.

Figure 6.2 illustrates the basic functions and interfaces of a virtual man–machine system. The main component of the system is a virtual world generator whose function is to generate and maintain a computer representation of a world. Depending upon the application, the user interfaces to the virtual world through several interfaces ranging from speech recognizers through to virtual hand controllers. The user interfaces to the visual channel of the virtual world generator by means of a helmet-mounted display.

2   Justifications for a Virtual Environment Laboratory Facility

The availability of technologies that can be integrated into a virtual environment is increasing at a great pace [6]. There are discrete systems whose functional requirements and specifications are driven by perception of the market demand and

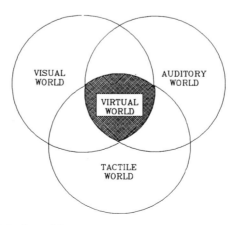

Figure 6.1 Integrated virtual world.

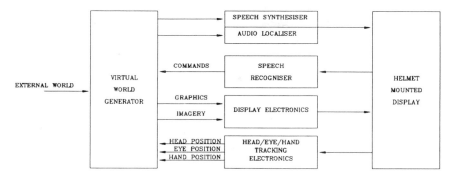

Figure 6.2 Virtual man–machine interface – immersive type.

a function of their manufacturing capability. Unfortunately, this 'bottom up' design approach is totally unacceptable from an integration point of view. It is not uncommon to realize that many manufacturers do not actually care how their system will be used. Their prime objective is to make a product that sells, for the maximum profit, and with a minimum of effort and risk. To the designer, higher up in the design lifecycle, this situation is intolerable. The risks are transferred to the designer and manufacturer of the integrated product. Manufacturers of the discrete enabling system do not seem to realize that if the integrated product fails, then their market will also collapse.

Successful manufacturers of products involving integration of a number of discrete enabling technologies use test rigs or comprehensive laboratory facilities [7]. These not only test the integration philosophy, but also drive the specification of the component technologies.

Virtual environments are no exception. Test rigs and laboratory facilities are used. A virtual environment system will generally have more variables than any other product. Therefore, it is vital to understand and control the effect of each variable within task and cost constraints. There is no doubt that virtual environments will play an important part in our lives in the future. The high profile this technology has achieved as a result of press coverage has resulted in many people and organizations jumping on the 'VR bandwagon' hoping to make a quick profit. Unfortunately, these initiatives are likely to fail unless they realize that they are dealing with a complex subject involving both human factors and engineering constraints. It is particularly important to capture the user's requirements and ensure that the product is actually matched to these requirements. Often with new technologies the customer may not know what his/her requirements are, or at least may not be able to specify them in a way that is understandable to the manufacturer. Rapid prototyping involving the customer and the manufacturer working together has emerged as an extremely effective way of encapsulating the end-user's requirements in engineering terms.

It has to be acknowledged that there are a number of VR technologies emerging that have been developed without consideration of the end application. These various products have been developed from manufacturers' perceptions of what is required. A cursory examination will reveal the limited extent to which human factors have been considered. Not unexpectedly, manufacturers are producing ambiguous specifications that are very inaccurate or, at worst, completely untrue. It is very disappointing that even though the fundamental technologies behind virtual environments have been around for many years we still cannot produce a set of consistent definitions. Perhaps this situation has arisen out of the multi-disciplinary nature of the subject. Manufacturers are working in areas that are completely new to them. This can be illustrated by an example – the majority of manufacturers of head-mounted displays for VR applications simply take the display resolution figure quoted by the LCD manufacturer and claim that their head-mounted display has this resolution. In doing so they make a fundamental error, since they are quoting the total number of individual dots (primary colours) on a display. This is not the conventional way of expressing resolution. What they should have quoted is the number of pixels on the display (composite of red, green and blue elements). Misquoting in this way gives a false impression of the actual display resolution. The resolution is really much lower than that specified.

3   Requirements of a Virtual Environment Laboratory

It is unlikely that a single virtual environment laboratory facility will meet the needs of all virtual environment products. It may even be necessary to employ a number of facilities throughout the lifecycle of a single product. To keep development costs to an acceptable level, migration of the concept from the prototype stage to the production line must be undertaken very carefully, in a seamless manner.

A few of the requirements include:

- rapid prototyping
- flexibility – reconfigurable
- investigation of human factors issues
- establishment of a series of system performance metrics
- validation of system design
- concept demonstration
- generation of specification and performance requirements
- assessment facility
- upgradable – technology independent
- technology independent.

3.1   Virtual environment laboratories

There are almost as many different configurations for a virtual environment laboratory facility as there are problems to be solved. Clearly, cost will be important and the facility must be tuned to address the key issues. Unfortunately, virtual environment technology has become available before we fully understand some of the very fundamental human factors issues of a complex man–machine interface. Therefore, it is very important to the whole virtual environment community that this fundamental and underlying research is conducted as rapidly and as thoroughly as possible. There is very little point in attempting some of the more exotic interfaces until this research has been conducted and we understand exactly what we are doing. The world is waking up to the importance of human factors design, especially in systems where human life is at stake. Future contracts will demand that validation of the underlying human factors issues be demonstrated. Aerospace companies know only too well the implications of safety critical systems to their design processes. Legislation in this field is very complex and very expensive.

The following section describes two virtual environment laboratory facilities. The first facility is perhaps an entry level system that will allow some of the more fundamental issues to be investigated, while the second is a complex facility that will be required to validate the integration of a number of VR technologies.

3.2 A simple virtual environment laboratory

It is relatively straightforward to assemble a simple facility with which to explore virtual environments, but before constructing a facility it is important to have a clear understanding of what research needs to be undertaken. Unless the facility is carefully integrated then the user will become very disappointed. Above all, one should be aware of the limitations of the available technology. The old adage 'you only get what you pay for' is very true in the VE field. In terms of computer graphics system performance, you can generally obtain the performance that you want, but at a price. However, in terms of the helmet-mounted displays and head tracking systems, there are technology limitations which restrict performance, irrespective of cost.

Very few people understand how a visually coupled system should be integrated, and consequently end up with a system that has unnecessary lags. These are immediately apparent to the end user, who finds them totally unacceptable. Many of these and other effects can be avoided by careful design. It is important to be aware that the human visual system is extremely good at detecting very small visual effects.

Figure 6.3 shows a relatively simple arrangement for conducting research into virtual environments. The facility will give stereo images that are visually coupled to the user's head line of sight. To keep costs down a video splitter is used to derive two channels of video information from a single graphics computer. Since the helmet-mounted displays available today have approximately a quarter of the resolution of the higher performance graphic systems, it is possible to generate a left and right eye view on the computer graphics system and to derive two separate video signals (lower resolution) via the splitter unit.

It is also possible to employ two separate graphic processors to drive the left and right eye channels, respectively. Whichever approach is used to produce the visuals, it is essential that maximum throughput rate is maintained as well as reducing lags to a minimum. Kalawsky examines the critical issues behind visually coupled systems in chapter 14. Unless the issues dealt with in this paper are adopted, then the resulting system will suffer from problems which will affect the overall performance.

The heart of the system is the virtual systems processor, a general purpose high-speed computer that interfaces to the external world and virtual environment peripherals such as datagloves, head trackers, etc. In practice, this processor would be within the same unit as the virtual display generator.

3.3   A comprehensive virtual environment laboratory

To understand all the implications of an integrated virtual environment system, it is necessary to have access to a facility where the end system can be rapidly prototyped to help identify key issues.

Features of a comprehensive virtual environment laboratory should include:

- *Visual world systems*
  Range of head-mounted displays (low, medium, and high resolution)
  Range of space tracking systems (different manufacturers and performance)
  Range of high performance graphics systems (software migratable across all platforms).
- *Auditory world systems*
  Sophisticated digital sound synthesis system
  3D audio localization
  Speech recognition system
  Speech synthesizer system.
- *Tactile world system*
  DataGlove
  Virtual environment joystick.
- *Virtual world development tools*

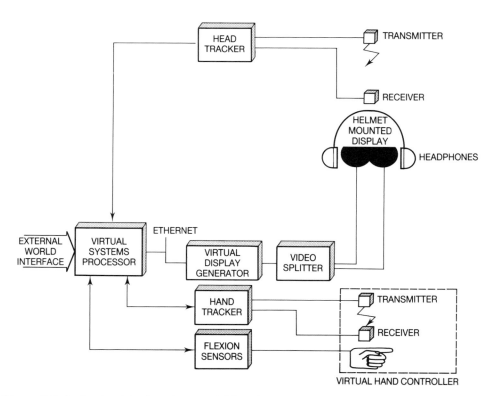

Figure 6.3 A simple virtual environment laboratory.

Multigen
VPL RB2 comprising Swivel, Body Electric, Isaac
Others.

Figure 6.4 shows the top level architecture of the British Aerospace Virtual
Environment Laboratory. It does not show the actual interface relationships between
the various equipments. For instance, the head tracker must be synchronized to the
position tracker used to determine hand position and orientation. If all such
interconnects were shown on this diagram it would be very complex. The facility
has been designed from the outset to allow evaluations to be undertaken on a range
of virtual environment technologies such as helmet-mounted displays. The facility
has been designed so that many of the current helmet-mounted displays can be
easily integrated with minimal interfacing. This also applies to the software that
must be executed in the graphics processors. Figure 6.5 shows the sort of
reconfiguration that can be accommodated with different helmet-mounted displays.
One should note that it is not just a case of re-routing video to the appropriate
display. Each display generally requires a different video standard that can range
from composite NTSC, RGB NTSC, PAL RGB through to different high resolution

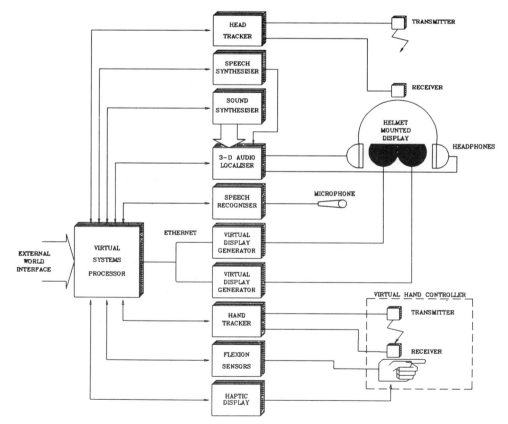

Figure 6.4 A comprehensive virtual environment facility.

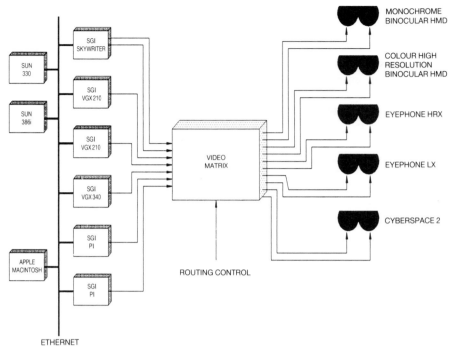

Figure 6.5 Virtual environment laboratory flexible video re-routing arrangement.

video standards. Achieving this level of compatibility calls for a video routing device that can handle these different video standards and corresponding video bandwidths. Furthermore, the graphics systems must be capable of being re-programmed to produce the appropriate video output. Finally, the application software must be designed to accommodate different spatial resolutions, fields of view and occasionally some peculiar transformations, to take into account optical distortions. Figures 6.6–6.8 show the British Aerospace systems in use.

Similar steps have to be taken when allowing other virtual environment devices such as space tracking systems to be integrated. To provide this level of flexibility it is necessary to define a consistent interface from the point of view of hardware and software. This can be a tall order when real-time performance must be maintained.

4   Systems Integration Issues

The virtual environment laboratory must be able to interface with a range of virtual environment peripherals as and when they become available. Unfortunately, no standard exists for the associated interfaces which means that the facility must be very flexible to accommodate a wide range of interfaces. It is rather odd that in a virtual environment system demand is placed on achieving real-time performance, yet the common interface is based on the RS232 serial interface. For example, a head tracking system is very time critical in terms of minimizing image lags. All

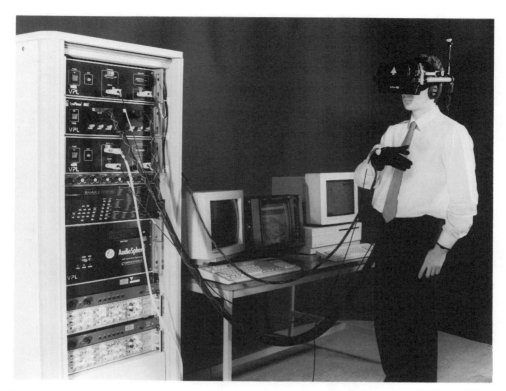

Figure 6.6

currently available head trackers employ the RS232 interface, which is certainly non-optimum as regards real-time performance. The system overhead of maintaining the serial interface from the host computer point of view can also be very high. Serial interfaces on host computers are not normally designed for real-time performance. Simply raising the serial interfaces band rate may increase data flow over the interface, but it can also lead to an increase in the number of interrupts the host has to service. Consequently, the servicing of interrupts can slow down the computation of graphics. This is a simple example that highlights the current trend in virtual environment systems.

Research must be undertaken to identify the architectural requirements of a virtual environment system and that includes a derivation of the specification of the interfaces [8].

Until equipment manufacturers recognize the need to harmonize their peripherals to the complete virtual environment system, we will have to try and accommodate their interfaces. To establish a research tool that will allow a whole range of virtual environment issues to be researched it will be necessary to provide interfaces such as serial, parallel and Ethernet. The video interface must not be overlooked either. For instance, the VPL low resolution EyePhone requires NTSC composite video signals, whilst the VPL high resolution EyePhone requires NTSC RGB video signals.

Figure 6.7

Other manufacturers' helmet-mounted displays can be based on different video standards such as the CC IR PAL format. Unless the graphics system can be reprogrammed to support a different video standard then it will not be possible to try different helmet-mounted displays. Obviously, for true flexibility it will be necessary to accommodate the full range of video standards.

Another important factor is that of performance. The usual approach to develop a complex system is to employ the lowest level of performance in the hope that it can meet the overall requirement. Unless the feasibility study has been thoroughly undertaken, then it is only possible to estimate the required performance.

In the majority of cases the actual performance is considerably higher than originally expected. This situation is often the case for computer graphic or visual systems. It is usually better to employ a computer with higher performance than originally expected. Whilst this may increase the research costs slightly, it is often

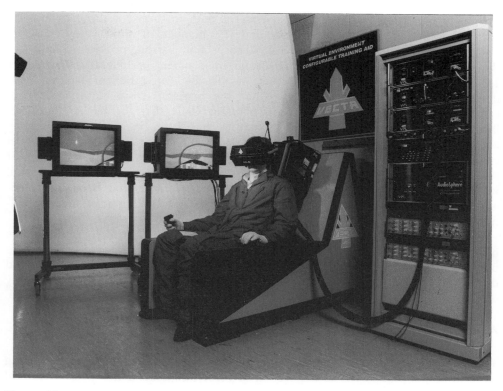

Figure 6.8

the best policy for two reasons. First, with a higher performance machine it is possible to degrade its performance to the point where it just meets the requirement. In the longer term, this approach is generally more economical. Secondly, and for a less obvious reason, computer systems are always increasing in performance. The high performance machines in research laboratories today are off-the-shelf tomorrow. Despite leaps and bounds in computer technology, you never seem to have enough processing power available. The successful business will match a machine's performance to the task, whilst ensuring that there is sufficient upgrade potential for the future.

5 Concluding Remarks

The virtual environment laboratory facility developed by British Aerospace is the result of many years of effort in building cockpit rigs and simulators [9]. Special techniques for achieving performance as close to real time as possible have been adopted to minimize the lags that are almost inevitable in visually coupled systems. The flexibility offered by the facility has been particularly important for rapid prototyping applications where variations in system performance are required to help evaluate or benchmark different systems. Many equipment manufacturers have expressed an interest in using this facility to evaluate their latest product. Some extremely important lessons have been learnt both in terms of the capability of current virtual environment products and the manner in which they must be integrated. This work has placed British Aerospace in a strong position to influence the specification and design of future virtual environment peripherals (see chapter 14). Work continues to be conducted in the associated human factors fields determining the critical parameters. Since the human factors requirements are extremely task dependent it has been of great value that the facility has been flexible. The virtual environment laboratory has been invaluable for rapidly constructing initial virtual environments for assessment. These initial virtual environments have been developed without writing any software at all. A range of tools allow the construction of virtual objects and their incorporation into a virtual world with minimal effort. Once the critical design criteria has been identified, application specific software is developed on the facility, taking advantage of real-time interfaces and programming techniques.

Rapid prototyping of virtual environment applications with potential end users has been a very effective process which has led to a greater understanding of the user's requirement. The end user has also had the advantage of being involved during the design stage where limitations in technology can be more accurately determined.

Acknowledgements

This paper is based with permission on an extract from a draft of a forthcoming book to be published by Addison-Wesley in 1993. Kalawsky: *The Science of Virtual Reality and Virtual Environments*, Addison-Wesley Ltd, 1993. Finally, kind permission to publish this article by British Aerospace is gratefully acknowledged.

References

1   Sutherland, I. 1965. The ultimate display. *Proc. IFIP Congress*, 506–508
2   Sutherland, I. 1968. A head-mounted three-dimensional display. *Proc. Fall Joint Computer Conference*, 757–764.
3   Kalawsky, R.S. 1992. Critical aspects of visually coupled systems. *BCS International Conference on Virtual Reality Systems*, 20–21 May, London, UK.
4   Furness, T.A. 1986. The Super Cockpit and its human factors challenges. *Proc. Human Factors Society – 30th Annual Meeting*.
5   Kalawsky, R.S. 1992. Beyond the Super Cockpit. *Proc. Virtual Reality 92*, London, UK.
6   Kalawsky, R.S. 1991. State of virtual reality in the UK. *IEE Colloquium on 'Real World Visualisation – Virtual World – Virtual Reality'*, London, UK.
7   Kalawsky, R.S. 1991. From visually coupled systems to virtual reality: an aerospace perspective. *Proc. Computer Graphics 91*, Blenheim Online.
8   Kalawsky, R.S. 1991. Reality of virtual reality? *IEE Colloquium on 'Real World Visualisation – Virtual World – Virtual Reality'*, London, UK.
9   Kalawsky, R.S. 1987. Pilot integration and the implications on the design of advanced cockpits. *Conference (425) the Man-Machine Interface in Tactical Aircraft Design and Combat Automation*, Agard, Stuttgart.

Biography

In 1978 Roy S. Kalawsky graduated from The University of Hull with a BSc in Electronic Engineering and commenced his aerospace career with British Aerospace. He was awarded an MSc by The University of Hull in 1984. In parallel with these developments at British Aerospace, Roy Kalawsky was rapidly becoming the UK expert in advanced cockpit technology. This led to close liaison with specialists from Wright-Patterson Airforce Base in the United States. He became a Chartered Engineer in 1986. In 1987 Professor Kalawsky was promoted to Project Leader Advanced Cockpits with responsibility for development of the UK's first Virtual Cockpit. The development of this research led to the formation of a significant company wide advanced cockpit research programme, for which he is still ultimately responsible. In 1989, in recognition of his international reputation for cockpit technology research, Roy Kalawsky was promoted to the position of Specialist, Cockpit Technology Research and Development. He also commenced with a more extensive research programme on Polarimetric Imagery for which he was conferred with a PhD in 1991 at The University of Hull. Roy Kalawsky is one of Europe's leading developers of advanced cockpit systems and has specialized in the evaluation of virtual reality as applied to this demanding environment. At British Aerospace Brough, he has established a centre of excellence in developing the United Kingdom's largest virtual environment laboratory, and in 1991 at the Paris Air Show he exhibited the world's first serious application of virtual reality. From an aerospace perspective, this work is likely to completely revolutionize the aerospace business from design through to manufacturing and post delivery support. Spin-off developments are seen to be far reaching and his work has been featured on the television and on the radio. In March 1992, The University of Hull invited Roy to take up the position of visiting Professor of Virtual Environments and Advanced Display Technologies, the first chair in VR in Europe and probably the world.

Part 3
Techniques

7 Gesture Driven Interaction as a Human Factor in Virtual Environments – An Approach with Neural Networks

Kaisa Väänänen and Klaus Böhm

ZGDV – Zentrum für Graphische Datenverarbeitung

Abstract

In this paper an approach to 3D interactions in a virtual environment using gestures recognized by neural networks is described. Our test environment, called GIVEN (Gesture driven Interactions in Virtual ENvironments), is introduced, and its gesture module architecture structure explained. Major attention is paid to the interaction in the 3D space in which hand gestures are submitted to the system by using a dataglove. In GIVEN, neural networks are used to recognize the gestures of the user or the 'visitor' of the virtual environment. We argue that this results in user-centred and intuitive methods of interacting and behaving in the environment and manipulating objects in it. In addition, a highly modular system architecture supports device independency, as well as application type and interaction type independency. The resulting environment is a user-friendly, re-usable and flexible system.

1 Gesture Interaction in Virtual Environments

1.1 Introduction to the field

The work presented in this paper is strongly related to the field of virtual worlds or virtual environments. However, the work is oriented to be more general in terms of its findings about interaction in new computer supported environments. In ZGDV (Center for Computer Graphics) our main topic of research lies in the design and validation of new 3D interaction methods (and, more generally, interactive multimedia techniques). In this field such subtopics as interaction metaphors and paradigms, as well as specific input techniques using new input devices, are considered [1–4].

Another subtopic of strong interest is the idea of using gestures in 3D (and 2D) interactions. This paper will explain one of our approaches in this direction: interaction using hand gestures recognized by neural networks when interacting in

VIRTUAL REALITY SYSTEMS
ISBN 0-12-227748-1

3D environments. The research (as well as the ideas and results presented in this paper) is a mixture of technical, system development oriented topics and human–computer interaction (HCI) topics in which the new implemented technical concepts are also tested from the human factors point of view.

1.2   Overview of 3D environment interactions

The human interaction in computer generated 3D environments requires a considerable amount of perceptual power from the user if the natural human communication methods are not taken into account. On the other hand, if the environment is well designed to follow some metaphor of interaction in space, and the objects in the environment have behaviour similar to objects in the real world, it can be very intuitive for the user to visit and experience these environments.

To make the use of graphical (or visual) 3D computer applications easy for both casual and professional users, the actions possible in the artificial environment must be similar to those respective actions in the real world. For example, grabbing an object should resemble the physiological action in reality. In addition, the objects in the environment should be highly responsive in their behaviour. This means that the actions of the users should be instantly followed by appropriate feedback (visual or audio) by the individual objects and the environment in total. This feedback should describe the event and the following state of the system, i.e. environment, as naturally as possible. For example, releasing an object should be followed by the natural fall of that object guided by the laws of gravitational force.

The input devices for 3D data are still not yet well designed and equipped for taking into account all the requirements of natural interaction methods. One move in this direction is the DataGlove, which can be used to submit hand positions and movements to the system to achieve objects and manipulations that are easy for any (non-handicapped) person to perform in a virtual environment, and which conform to the rules of many real-world interactions.

For other attempts to explore the tendencies of human–computer interaction and the nature of 3D interaction, see elsewhere [5–11].

1.3   What are gestures and how can they be used?

Gestures are body movements which are used to convey some kind of information from one person to another. Normally this information is easily understood by other humans (at least of the same cultural origin), but is not very exact in its nature (i.e. the gesture may have implicit connotations). In human–computer interaction, gestures can be used to convey information from the user to the computer system. In this case, however, the information must be exact (it should still be possible to make 'more or less'-type gestures, but the meaning of these gestures must be exactly defined because of the deterministic nature of the computer input).

The user uses some input device (e.g. DataGlove) to pass the information to the system. The system recognizes the gestures and attaches to them meanings relevant to the application. This approach has the advantage that the user can act in a way that is natural to him. Most of the gestures used in input methods thus far are hand gestures, or different hand positions (static gestures, which we will call postures) and sequences of these positions (dynamic gestures). Other possible gesture types are head positions, eye positions, and general body movements (such as shrugging one's shoulders) and positions (holding one's arms crossed over one's chest). In this work we are only exploring hand gestures, both static and dynamic.

2 A Testbed for Gesture Driven Interactions in Virtual Environment: GIVEN

2.1 Background and motivation
We have built a virtual environment system called GIVEN (Gesture driven Interactions in Virtual ENvironments), which serves as a testbed for the 3D interaction research ideas, especially in the field of gesture interaction.

The first version of GIVEN implements an environment of an office room. The objects in this room, such as a desk, a tea pot and a ball, can be manipulated (see Plate III). The user can move in the room by gesturing with his hand inside a DataGlove, and can also perform certain manipulations, resembling real-world actions, on the objects in the environment (see Plate IV).

Later, other environments will be constructed along the defined principles of GIVEN to obtain proof of the applicability of these principles to other types of interaction environments. These might include modelling environments for biology and architecture, as well as 2D modelling environments which require high interactive rates.

2.2 Concepts of GIVEN
GIVEN is designed and implemented according to conceptual issues, explained here briefly, but explained in more detail elsewhere [2]. On the whole, these concepts are intended to give GIVEN a toolkit-like structure, components of which can be re-used later to build other environments along the same guidelines:

- *Input device independence*   Ideally, it should be possible to exchange the input device with minimal effects on the functionality of the system. For example, we should be able to use a spaceball as the input (and gesturing) device instead of the DataGlove with minimum changes.
- *Application and object type independence*   Basic interaction techniques and concepts used in the first version of GIVEN can be used in several types of applications. Only the application and object-specific data and interactions need to be redefined.
- *Open (extendable) architecture*   One of our experiences is that a fixed set of predefined 3D interaction techniques with the toolkit is not sufficient for all applications. Therefore the toolkit must be open and expandable to allow the addition of new modules and extension of the old ones.
- *Object-orientedness*   The GIVEN world consists of visualized objects which can have various relationships to each other. They are hierarchically structured, which means that every object has a parent object (except the so-called root object).
- *Individual object behaviour*   Objects in GIVEN can have individual behaviour. In practice this means that under certain conditions and forces of interaction different objects behave (act) in a different way. For example, objects can decide themselves how certain gestures will affect them.
- *Gesture dialogue*   The study of the use of gestures in 3D interaction is one of

the main objectives in GIVEN. Gesture input or gesture dialogue is the only way of communicating with the environment. The ideas and concepts related to this will be explored in detail in section 3. (Also, see Lewis *et al.* [12] and Zimmerman *et al.* [13] for related ideas.)

2.3   Structure of GIVEN

GIVEN is constructed according to a toolkit approach. Interaction techniques need to be well defined and encapsulated to increase consistency and avoid the effort of building each environment based on new set of (possibly inferior) concepts. Different components affecting interaction between the human and interactional aspects of the system need to be modular. This will make it easy to change just certain aspects of the system, or to use defined techniques in other applications and system types. The system acts as a 3D interaction method package.

Figure 7.1 illustrates the components of the toolkit and their relations. The main components are briefly explained in the following.

The Event Handler receives user events from the Device Drivers and from the traditional input devices (e.g. to load/store data). The Cursor Manager controls the cursor actions according to the data it receives from the Event Handler. Navigation in the environment is controlled by the cursor actions.

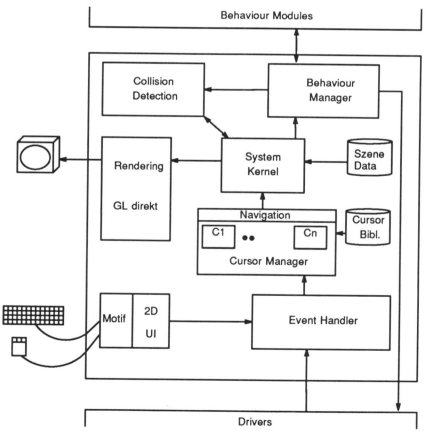

Figure 7.1 The GIVEN toolkit structure.

Renderer draws the current state of the world using a graphics language (which in the current version of the toolkit is Silicon Graphics' GL). The Collision Detection finds out if any objects collide in the world at any moment, e.g. the hand (represented by a virtual hand, i.e. the 'cursor') and a cup, or a falling ball and the floor. Finally, the System Kernel coordinates the actions between Cursor Manager, Renderer and Behaviour Manager.

The control of an interaction is as follows: the Event Handler gets events from a device driver that is triggered, e.g. by a DataGlove. The gesture information is contained by the event. The Cursor Manager interprets the gesture information and controls the navigation. Next, the System Kernel asks the Collision Detection if collisions are taking place in that state of the environment. Then, for objects that do collide it must be checked what kind of behaviour they should exhibit in that situation of the world. The same must be done for objects that have dynamic behaviour (active objects), e.g. a bird flying around. This is controlled by the Behaviour Manager. When the current behaviour of the colliding and active objects is known, as well as the position of the cursor and the related viewpoint, the current image can be rendered. All this happens in real time, which is a prerequisite of the system being a virtual reality environment. This way the recognized gesture is affecting the environment.

3   Gestures and Gesture Architecture

3.1   Principles and problems of gesture interaction

Gestures are the static positions and dynamic movements of a human's body parts, which normally cannot be detected by conventional computer sytems. Gestures are widely used in human communication, and thus for realistic, user-centred and creative interaction, humans must be able to use these non-verbal or unspecific cues. Because of the inherently vague nature of many of these gestures, it is very difficult to implement them in the interfaces of computer systems. There will always be a certain amount of uncomputability, and we can only aim at getting near to an understanding of the full range of natural and dynamic body gestures. Even with a very limited use of hand gestures, we need to develop highly sophisticated recognition methods and algorithms to achieve acceptable recognition rates of the gestures.

In the current version of GIVEN, these gestures are hand positions which are performed and input to the system by using the DataGlove. The program 'understands' different fist and finger positions (postures) received from the DataGlove as commands such as 'fly forward', 'fly faster', 'reverse', 'grab', 'release', and 'go to the starting point'. Later, different gestures for different manipulations of objects will be included in the gesture set. A gesture recognition editor allows the user to show new gestures interactively. The toolkit learns this new interaction via neural networks (see section 4 for detailed description of this approach).

Figure 7.2 illustrates some gestures that are used in the current version of GIVEN. The first two pictures (a) and (b) show the pair of gestures 'fly forward' and 'fly backward'. Picture (c) shows the 'release an object' gesture (the corresponding 'grab an object' gesture cannot be uniquely shown, because each object, according to the individual object behaviour principle, must decide by itself what is the way and appropriate gesture by which it can be grabbed). Picture (d) illustrates the 'reset' gesture used in GIVEN, which will bring the user back to the starting point in the

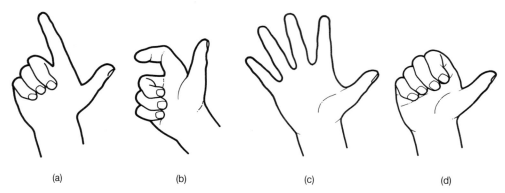

(a)   (b)   (c)   (d)

Figure 7.2 Some hand gestures used in GIVEN.

environment. The gestures are a set of well defined and easily understandable hand positions which have clear and obvious meanings in the respective actions in the virtual environment.

The gestures presented above were chosen partly according to *ad hoc* design decisions, i.e. they seemed to be obviously suited to certain actions. Partly they were selected and redefined through iteration of use, after experimenting with them during a long period of time and making slight alterations to them.

The gesture interactions have been used by us and some students during a six month period, and our experience shows among other things that:

- hand and arm get tired after a long continuous period of use
- it is difficult to make exact manipulations in the space
- force feedback (which is missing in our DataGlove) is essential for more 'reality' (especially for certain tasks such as grabbing an object)
- the environment interaction and object manipulation is considered easy and intuitive in most parts
- it helps to have metaphors related to each gesture, e.g. increasing the speed of navigation is related to 'pressing the gas pedal' in a car, i.e. the speed increases when the thumb is brought near to the palm; on the other hand, a gesture such as the 'reset' gesture (see above), which is represented as a tight fist posture, is less easily remembered (possibly because of the lack of a metaphor).

We are also experimenting with using 3D gestures for 2D input. Figure 7.3 illustrates one of these ideas: we have a sequence of gestures (hand positions), which conceptually form a 3D 'button click' on a 2D interface. The sequence is (1) index finger up, (2) index finger down (as pressing a mouse button), and (3) index finger up. This is metaphorically a button click on a button on the screen.

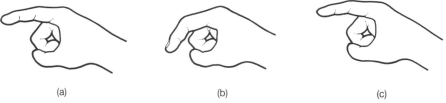

(a)   (b)   (c)

Figure 7.3 A conceptual 'mouse click' sequence of gestures.

3.2 Why (not) gestures?

As we have argued above, gestures appear to be a central component of human self-expression and information submission. To summarize the benefits of using gestures in the interaction between the expressive human and traditionally non-expressive computer, we suggest that gestures are needed because of:

- higher expression power of the user
- increase of 'reality' in computer generated environments
- easy mapping of certain (but not all) input tasks to respective user actions
- easy learnability and high usability.

At the same time, we do recognize that gestures are not appropriate for all kinds of interaction. If specific or accurate input data need to be given, difficulties may arise, because DataGlove is not an exact pointing device. The lack of force feedback in our DataGlove (the VPL Research DataGlove) introduces a certain lack of reality, because many real-world manipulations are done with the aid of feedback from the physical constraints of the objects. Also, the beginner in the environment may not immediately know what are the possible gestures, or might expect too much from the naturalness of the gestures.

3.3 Gesture module architecture

Our implementation of gesture recognition in GIVEN includes the modules for obtaining input information from the DataGlove, recognizing gestures with neural networks (for more details see section 4), and the connection to the GIVEN toolkit (see Fig. 7.1) to pass forward the information about the recognized gesture.

In Fig. 7.4 these modules and their relations are illustrated. The DataGlove detects the movements in hand and fingers of the user, and passes the information (about the angles of fingers and the position of the hand inside the DataGlove) to the Device Driver, which converts the glove information into the form that can be used by the NeuroGlove. The DataGlove Device Driver then passes the information to the NeuroGlove, which is the gesture recognition program using networks developed in our lab. NeuroGlove next uses its recognition methodology to find out (by pre-trained neural networks) which gesture (if any) is in question. It then passes the gesture information to the GIVEN (see also Fig. 7.4), which uses the information to find the current state of the world (affected by navigation or manipulation of objects) and finally renders a new scene (see the description in section 2).

These three modules (Device Driver, NeuroGlove and GIVEN toolkit; these are the darker boxes in Fig. 7.4) are actually three different programs that communicate with each other, and they follow the client-server architecture in their implementation.

The modular architecture guarantees that we can later easily substitute the DataGlove with another input device, e.g. the SpaceBall or other new input devices that allow gesturing. Also, different neural network types can be tried out for the gesture recognition without changes in the Device Driver or GIVEN.

This architecture works also over the network (e.g. Ethernet), in which case all the connections take place over the network. The modules can be running on different computers, e.g. in our environment the NeuroGlove on an HP workstation, the GloveBox with the Device Driver on a personal IRIS workstation, and the GIVEN Toolkit on a VGX SGI workstation. The advantage of this is that when

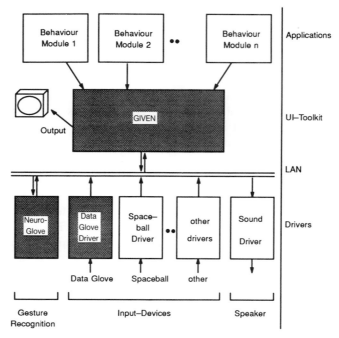

Figure 7.4 The overall GIVEN architecture.

one of the programs takes a lot of computing capacity (in this case the NeuroGlove program), it does not affect the real-time computation capacity of the actual GIVEN program, which naturally requires the largest computation power.

4   Neural Networks in Gesture Recognition

4.1   Background and idea

Based on our experiences with GIVEN, it is obvious that a toolkit for multimedia and 3D interaction cannot be restricted to a set of predefined interaction techniques. The toolkit must be extensible to new gestures for specific applications.

We are therefore experimenting with the use of neural networks for the recognition of gestures. In this approach the neural network is trained to recognize static and dynamic gestures without having to define them in an analytic way. This way the gestures can be defined quickly, and in an interactive way, and the system can easily adapt to different gestures used by different people. The user interactively demonstrates the hand position, the toolkit learns this gesture, and is then able to recognize it in different applications. Several hand positions are combined with operators like 'sequence, repeat, and, or' to describe complex gestures. For other experiments in this area, see Fels and Hinton [14] and Murakami and Taguchi [15].

4.2   Technical overview of NeuroGlove

The neural networks used for the gesture recognition in our system are backpropagation networks. (For implementation issues of the NeuroGlove program, see Ala-

Rantala [16].) The reason for using backpropagation networks is that they are the most powerful and convenient type of neural networks.

To describe how the gesture recognition modules using neural networks are 'built', we have to divide the 'gesture recognition' task into two separate tasks:

1. Recognition of static gestures (we call them hand postures).
2. Recognition of dynamic gestures.

The first task is much more straightforward than the second. In the first case, we only use the information about the angles of the fingers received from the DataGlove, and ignore the information about hand position and orientation. This means that in the case of static gestures we are not trying to recognize gestures which depend on the movement of the whole hand. This must, however, be done in the recognition of dynamic gestures. What we understand by dynamic gestures is the movement of the fingers in addition to the position of the hand in a sequence of time steps.

4.3 Recognition of static gestures

From the DataGlove the NeuroGlove program obtains ten inputs, two for each finger (angles of the two outer joints of the fingers). The inputs are preprocessed (PP), which for the static gestures simply means scaling the angle values by the factor of 90 (the maximum finger angle is 90°) to get input values for the neural network between 0 and 1 (between these values the networks work with the highest efficiency). After preprocessing, the scaled inputs are fed into the neural network, which does the recognition and sends the information to the GIVEN program for further use (see Fig. 7.5).

As already mentioned, we are using backpropagation networks. Usually, networks with three layers (input, hidden, output) perform adequately for posture recognition. The input layer has ten neurons, which correspond to the angles of all the fingers (two angles for each finger in the glove). The number of neurons in the hidden layer and the output layer depends on the number of postures (static gestures) we want to recognize, e.g. if we want to recognize 20 postures we have at least 20 neurons in the output layer. In this case we will also have 20 neurons in the hidden layer (see Fig. 7.6).

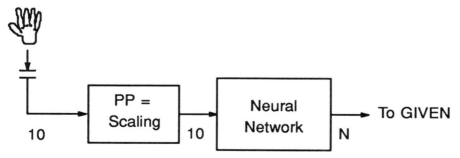

Figure 7.5 NeuroGlove recognition pipeline for static gestures.

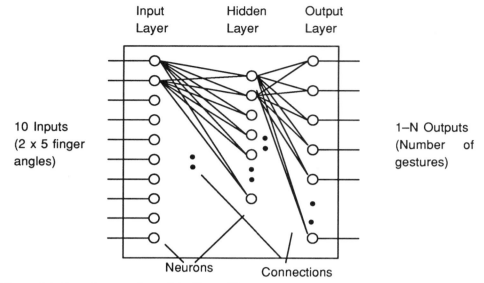

Figure 7.6 Neural network used in NeuroGlove.

4.4 Recognition of dynamic gestures

To recognize dynamic gestures there are two approaches, one of which is to use recurrent networks, and the second is to use 'normal' networks and have a complex preprocessing phase. We have implemented the second approach. This means that we are also using backpropagation networks for this case.

The problem with dynamic gestures is that there is a time dependency that must be taken into account in recognition. So the input for the neural network is not just hand information at one specific time, but the input for the neural network has to contain the information from, for example, five time steps. This sequence of steps with finger movement and hand position information forms a dynamic gesture (see Fig. 7.7). This implies that there will be more input information to be taken into account: 10 inputs from the finger angles as before, and in addition 6 inputs from the relative position of the hand (x, y, z-coordinates and roll, pitch and yaw).

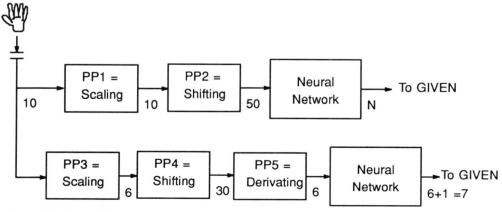

Figure 7.7 NeuroGlove recognition pipeline for dynamic gestures.

To capture the time-dependent information, we are using a 'time window'. This means that in the second preprocessor PP2 (the first preprocessor PP1 is, as in the static gesture recognition, a scaling function) we have a 'shift register' which has place for, for example, five sets of single-moment information. In the starting procedure we have to fill the shift register once, then every single time step we give the latest five information sets to the neural network. The next time we make a shift in the register (after a specified time sample delay), the oldest single-moment information is lost, and a new single-moment information is brought to the register.

This guarantees that the final movements are in the memory, and when an appropriate sequence is found by the neural network, it will pass the information to the GIVEN program.

The input information is actually divided into two sets, ten finger angles and six position informations. The six position informations have an additional preprocessing phase, PP5, in which the derivatives of the movement direction information are counted, to find the relative instead of the absolute movement.

The neural network is similar to that used in the static gestures, except that there are two of them working in parallel (for finger and hand position sequence data, see above) and the input and output amounts differ. The first network, which recognizes the finger angle sequences, has 50 inputs (five time steps times 10 angles) and N outputs (number of the dynamic gestures recognized), and the second network, which recognizes the hand position information, has six inputs (derivative values of the position data) and seven output values (six for position data and one for 'no movement' information). Together, these output sets define if and when certain gestures took place.

For one single time step 10 input-neurons are needed, and therefore for the example above with five time steps there are 50 input-neurons. The number of neurons in the output layer is equal to or more than the gestures to be recognized. We had good results with 50 neurons in the hidden layer, 50 neurons in the input layer, and 10 neurons in the output layer.

4.5   Why neural networks?

We are aware of other (classical) methods, such as maximum likelihood estimation, that can be used for classifying the type of data that are used to recognize gestures. However, we are convinced that there are good reasons to do gesture recognition with neural networks. Groß [17, p. 305] has argued for the superiority of neural networks as classificators as follows:

> Classical classification methods [18] often use Bayes rules and maximum likelihood estimation [19], and are restricted to the morphology of the clusters to be separated. To improve results, some approaches also include texture descriptions or a cluster analysis as preprocessing. Our approach aims at avoiding expensive preprocessing – often necessary to obtain reliable results – by introducing neural networks. Their capability lies in the fact that they are able to cluster arbitrary density functions in feature space, simply depending on the number of layers and neurons. Furthermore they are able to include texture and structure information of image objects [20].

In practice, we have found that neural networks in gesture recognition are better in comparison to classical recognition methods. Some of these reasons are 'convenience factors', mainly aiming at facilitating interaction and use of the system, such as:

- easy addition of new gestures (no need for re-training of already learned gestures)

- quick interactive training of the networks (not much preprocessing needed),

but other reasons are actually offering new technical possibilities, such as:

- possibility for gestures that are very close to each other.

5   Discussion and Future Work

5.1   Summary

In this paper we have presented our set of concepts for a computer supported virtual environment and especially the interactions within it. A test environment and its implementation called GIVEN have been described. GIVEN supports many of the theoretical concepts that are asserted about the methods of 3D interaction. It also acts as a testbed for further experiments about gestures and other interaction styles.

Furthermore, we have described our approach to gesture driven interactions, and justified the benefits of this approach. A technical description of the use of neural networks in this work has been given, and its advantages discussed. Below we summarize the benefits of using gestures in 3D interaction, and claim that it improves the usability of virtual environment systems in many application areas.

5.2   Benefits of using gestures

In this section the benefits of gesture interaction are listed, summarizing the reasons why we see gesture interaction as such a prominent way of inputting information, and why gesture driven interactions greatly increase the usability, re-usability and flexibility of 3D environment applications.

Gesture driven interaction improves usability because it:

- makes the techniques easily available for variety of users – professionals, naive users, occasional users, adults and children
- imposes easy manipulation and navigation (easy to learn and understand)
- is easy to adjust to new uses (neural networks; interactive adjustment)
- can be easily embedded to a variety of applications
- is device independent (at least the theoretical aspects)
- can be used for both 2D and 3D – even though the gesture methods are likely to be fairly different for both areas.

5.3   Application areas – where are gestures especially useful?

The approach taken here is especially useful in application areas where:

- there are complicated 3D interactions
- actions can be mapped into real-world actions (strong metaphors)
- there is a special 'reality' requirement.

These kinds of applications can be useful, for example, in the following areas:

- computer supported teaching (education) and self-learning
- CAD architecture and design
- virtual reality applications
- test and simulation systems
- planning systems
- scientific modelling (e.g. molecular modelling).

5.4 Future challenges

Our next step is to try other neural network types for the recognition of dynamic gestures, like recurrent networks. Another topic is to find 'good' translations for actions represented by these gestures. Dynamic gestures, where the whole hand movement is involved, are in our opinion the most intuitive and expressive, but can also in some cases be difficult to map on natural actions in a virtual environment or a computer modelling system.

One line of thought is that the gesture language cannot be the only possibility to communicate with a computer, because there are too many different actions which have to be activated for which no intuitive gestures exist. Either speech input could be combined with hand gestures, or another user interface inside the virtual world could be used. This interface could offer connection to keyboard or mouse interactions whenever it is more appropriate than pure hand gestures. Alternatively, to make gestures cover wider aspects of intuitive interaction a complete 'gesture language', like sign language for the deaf, could be developed. Even though this could make the use of gesture driven interfaces hard to learn, it might be suitable for certain applications. As a result, we think there is a need for new interaction metaphors where the gestures (or sequences of gestures) will be used. We will continue our work at ZGDV-lab in these directions.

Acknowledgements

We would like to thank Dr. Wolfgang Hübner for his comments on 3D interaction techniques, as well as his support in the process of writing this paper. Also, we thank Dr. Markus Groß and Frank Seibert for their invaluable advice with the theoretical background on neural networks. Furthermore, we want to thank Martti Ala-Rantala for his ideas and comments on the gesture recognition by neural networks, as well as his explanations on his implementation of the NeuroGlove program.

References

1 Astheimer, P., Frühauf, M., Göbel, M. and Karlsson, K. 1988. Visualisierung und Steuerung technischer Prozesse mit einer graphisch-interaktiven Benutzungs-oberfläche. In Valk, R., editor, *GI-18. Jahrestagung*. Springer-Verlag.
2 Böhm, K., Hübner, W. and Väänänen,K. 1992. GIVEN: Gesture Driven Interactions in Virtual Environments – a toolkit approach to 3D interactions. *Proc. Interfaces to Real and Virtual Worlds Conference*, Montpellier, France, March.
3 Ehmke, D. and Kreiter, M. 1989. PRODIA – Ein Dialogsystem zum Aufbau der Benutzungsoberflächen interaktiver Werkzeuge. *Software-Ergonomie '89* (meeting of the German chapter of the ACM and GI).
4 Hübner, W. 1990. *Entwurf Graphischer Benutzerschnittstellen – Ein objektorienti-ertes Interaktionsmodell zur Spezifikation graphischer Dialoge*. PhD dissertation. Springer-Verlag.
5 Chen, M., Mountford, S.J. and Sellen, A. 1988. A study of interactive 3D rotation using 2D control devices. *Proc. SIGGRAPH '88*, Atlanta, GA, August.
6 Encarnação, J.L. and Eckardt, D. 1989. *Entwicklungstendenzen in der Mensch-Maschine-Kommunikation* (meeting of INFINA '89).

7   Foley, J.D., Wallace, V.L. and Chan, P. 1984. The human factors of computer graphics interactive techniques. *IEEE Computer Graphics and Applications*, November.

8   Foley, J.D. 1987. Interfaces for advanced computing. *Scientific American*, October, 127–135.

9   Gold, M. 1990. *Multi-Dimensional Input Devices and Interaction Techniques for a Modeler-Animator*. Brown University Report, May.

10 Henderson, D.A. Jr. and Card, S.K. 1986. Rooms: the use of multiple virtual workspace to reduce space contention in a window-based graphical user interface. *ACM Trans. Graphics*, **5** (3).

11 Mackinlay, J.D., Card, S.K. and Robertson, G.G. 1990. A semantic analysis of the design space of input devices. *Human–Computer Interaction*, **5**.

12 Lewis, J.B., Koved, L. and Ling, D.T. 1991. Dialogue structures for virtual worlds. *CHI '91 Proc.*

13 Zimmerman, T.G., Lanier, J., Blanchard, C., Bryson, S. and Harvill, Y. 1987. A hand gesture interface device. *CHI '87 Proc.*

14 Fels, S.S. and Hinton, G.E. 1990. Building adaptive interfaces with neural networks: the Glove-Talk pilot study. *INTERACT '90 Proc.*

15 Murakami, K. and Taguchi, H. 1991. Gesture recognition using recurrent neural networks. *CHI '91 Proc.*

16 Ala-Rantala, M. 1992. *Konzeption und Entwicklung einer interaktiven Testumgebung zur Erkennung von Gesten mittels dem Dataglove und neuronalen Netzen*. Unpublished MSc thesis, Technical University of Darmstadt.

17 Groß, M. 1991. Advanced visualization systems – from parallel rendering to neural network imaging. In Ebner *et al.*, editors, *Digital Photogrammetric Systems*. Wichmann, Karlsruhe.

18 Duda, R. and Hart, P. 1973. *Pattern Classification and Scene Analysis*. John Wiley.

19 Benelli, G., Cappellini, V. and Re, E. 1986. Some digital techniques for processing and classification of SAR images. In Cappellini, V., editor, *Time-Varying Image Processing and Moving Object Recognition*. Springer-Verlag.

20 Groß, M. 1991. Physiological aspects of human vision and computer graphics. Tutorial, Eurographics '91.

Biographies

Kaisa Väänänen holds an MSc from the University of London, Queen Mary and Westfield College in Human–Computer Interaction (1990) and a Master of Technology degree from Helsinki University of Technology in Knowledge Engineering (1991). She has done research at Telecom Finland on cooperative work systems, and is currently a visiting researcher at ZGDV (Center for Computer Graphics) in Germany, where she is doing applied research in interactive multimedia techniques, including topics in interaction in virtual reality.

Klaus Böhm studied computer science at the Technical University of Darmstadt, and graduated in March 1991 with an MSc degree. He is currently working at the Zentrum für Graphische Datenverarbeitung in Darmstadt (Center for Computer Graphics) as a member of the scientific staff. His research areas include virtual reality, 3D interaction and multimedia interaction techniques.

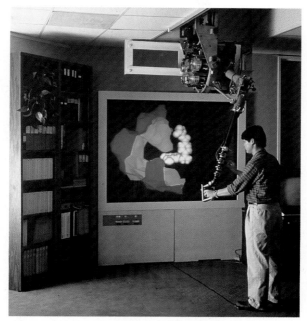

Plate I At UNC, the Argonne Force Feedback Arm is being used to position a molecule in a potential receptor site. (Courtesy of University of North Carolina, Department of Computer Science).

Plate II SD Entertainment Unit.

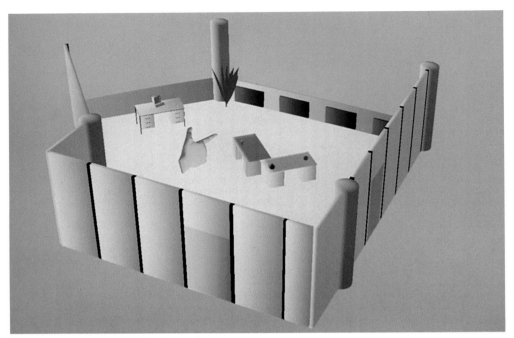

Plate III The GIVEN virtual environment.

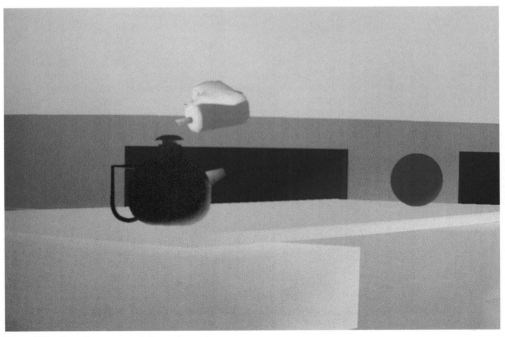

Plate IV Pouring sugar into a teapot.

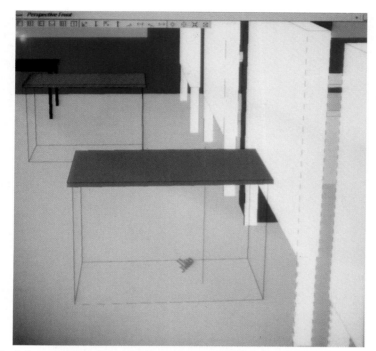

Plate V   A desk is moved until it collides with an anchored wall divider.

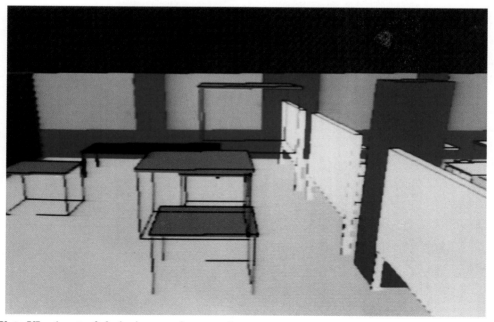

Plate VI   A set of desks is moved as a unit.

Plate VII Interactive drumming in Music World.

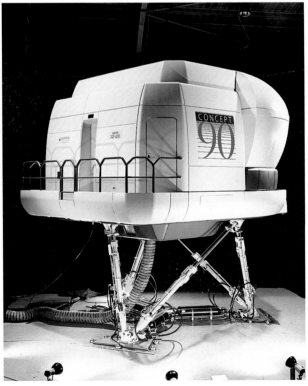

Plate VIII A Concept 90 Boeing 747-400 flight simulator manufactured by Rediffusion Simulation Ltd. (Reproduced with permission from Hughes Rediffusion Simulation Ltd).

Plate IX   A view inside a flight simulator showing the illuminated flight deck and a dusk/night scene incorporating calligraphic light points. (Reproduced with permission from Hughes Rediffusion Simulation Ltd).

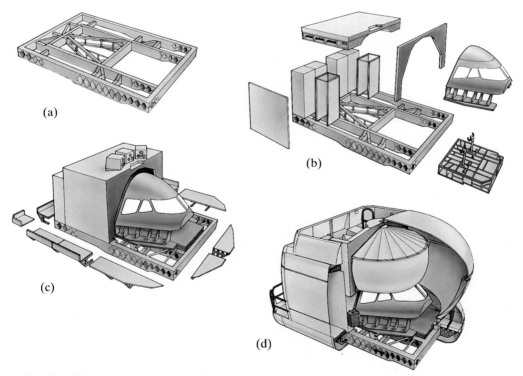

(a)

(b)

(c)

(d)

Plate X   This exploded diagram illustrates some of the major elements of a civilian flight simulator. (a) The motion platform. (b) The motion platform supports a low-weight cockpit and essential electrical interfaces to off-board computers and image generators. The module below the cockpit contains the flight controls. (c) This view shows the three colour calligraphic projectors which form a seamless computer-generated image on a back projection screen. (d) This final view shows the spherical back-projection screen in place, and part of the panoramic mirror that collimates the pilot's virtual image. (Reproduced with permission from Hughes Simulation Ltd).

Plate XI These three views show the high level of realism found in real-time image generators by using texture mapping. (Reproduced with permission from Hughes Rediffusion Simulation Ltd).

Plate XII This scene shows a pilot under instruction in a flight simulator. Behind the pilot the trainer controls the virtual environment through touch-operated computer terminals. (Reproduced with permission from Hughes Rediffusion Simulation Ltd).

Plate XIII   Inspection of an object using a physics-based camera.

Plate XIV   Dynamics-based motion.

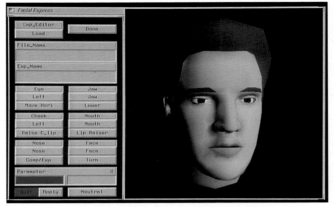

Plate XV The SMILE facial animation system.

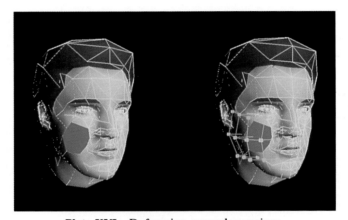

Plate XVI Deforming muscular regions.

Plate XVII Face shape obtained by 3D with hair rendering.

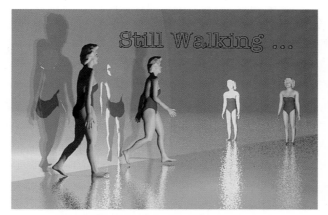

Plate XVIII   Individualized walking model.

Plate XIX   Walking along an arbitrary path.

Plate XX   Fashion show.

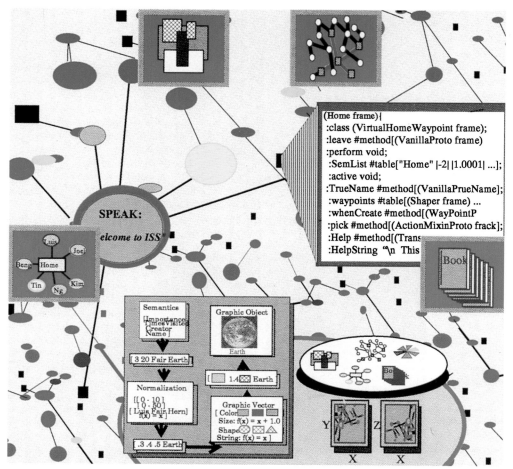

Plate XXI Visualization of an information visualization space.

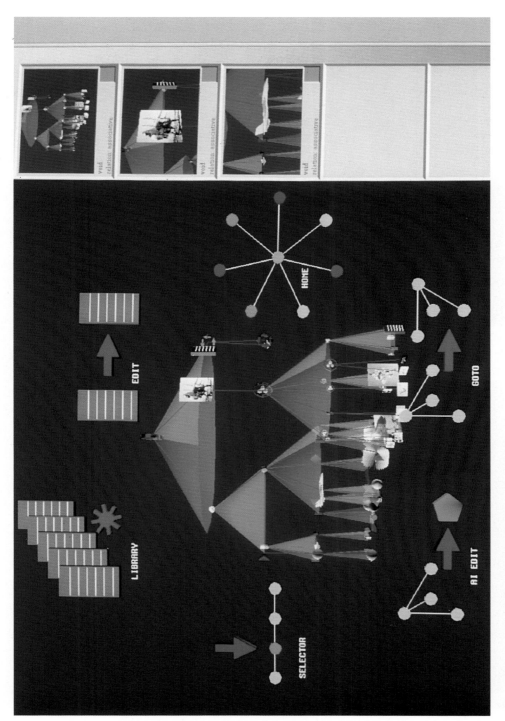

Plate XXII VizNet information management interface.

Plate XXIII

Plate XXIV

Plates XXIII and XXIV Cone Tree multimedia visualization of an aircraft.

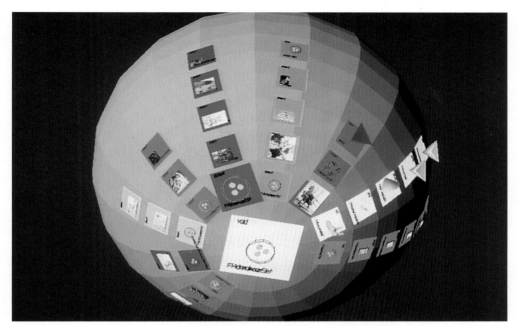

Plate XXV

Plate XXVI

Plates XXV and XXVI   The sphere information visualization.

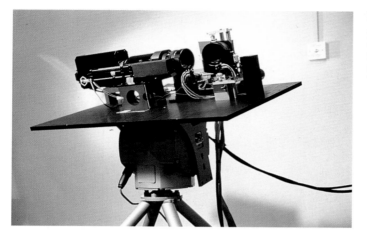

Plate XXVII The ARRC's Experimental Laser Rangefinding System (NEL Rangefinder) (equates to part of Figure 7 in original paper).

Plate XXVIII (a) The ARRC Reception Area.

Plate XXVIII (b) The ARRC Reception Area, Modelled Using the Dimension VR Toolkit (note the simple polygonal representation of the coffee machine, prior to including a texture map of the dispensing area using digitised pictures taken using a Canon Ion Camera).

Plate XXIX Teletact™ *Commander* Handgrip With Simple Tactile Feedback (equates to Figure 6 in original paper).

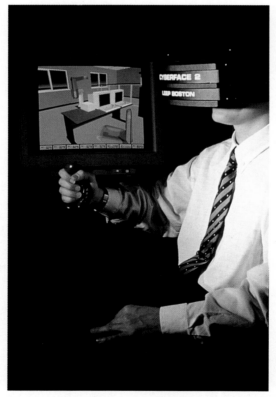

Plate XXX Operator Immersed in Part of the ARRC Manipulator Laboratory Area, Built Using the Dimension VR Toolkit and Ported onto the SuperVision VR Computer (Operator is using the LEEP Cyberface II Headset.

Plate XXXI   The ARRC Enhanced Cybermotion K2A Vehicle With Head-Slaved Stereoscopic Camera System (equates to Figure 4 in original paper).

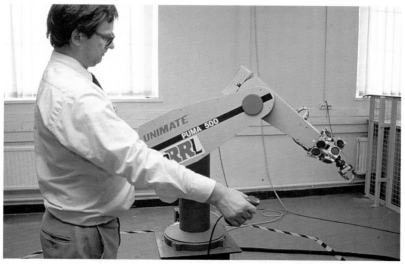

Plate XXXII   The ARRC Teletact Commander in Use With a Puma Robot and the Centre's Robust, Singularity-Free Controller.

8 Using Physical Constraints in a Virtual Environment

Michael J. Papper and Michael A. Gigante
*Royal Melbourne Institute of Technology,
Advanced Computer Graphics Centre*

Abstract

We describe a more intuitive virtual environment that provides naively realistic behaviour of objects by using simplified physical constraints. The major design goal of these constraints is to provide a degree of realism without sacrificing real-time updates. We describe the chosen constraints, and how they benefit interaction in a virtual environment.

1 Introduction

Most existing virtual environments do not attempt to model the physical behaviour of objects. The user is able to pass through objects, objects can pass through each other – that is these virtual environments ignore phenomena that we take for granted in the real world.

The implication of ignoring these phenomena is that the user must explicitly deal with placement and motion constraints that we take for granted in our normal interactions. One example is the placement of one object on top of another. In the current generation of computer aided design (CAD) systems the user must explicitly align the bottom of one object with the top of the other. The user may achieve this goal either by using an *align* command, or by iteratively adjusting the location of the objects. In either case, the need for explicit action has increased the burden on the user. A failure to take explicit action will either allow the objects to interpenetrate or make the top object to float above the surface of the object underneath.

In an attempt to increase the perceptual fidelity of our virtual environment, we have included some simplified versions of the real-world constraints.

Our *physical constraints* are rules that can be individually assigned to objects. The constraints are:

- *Gravity*: objects with gravity rest on other objects or at some ground level.
- *Friction*: all objects resting on top of selected objects move with the selected objects as a group
- *Pushing*: objects are solid, collisions among objects cause them to be pushed along in a compound rigid body motion

- *Anchor*: objects can be anchored in space so that they cannot be pushed by other objects.

This paper explores how these simplified physical constraints benefit interaction in a virtual environment. We look at how the physically based constraints aid interaction in a virtual environment.

We will describe how the system is used for space planning applications. Next we describe the physical constraints and explain how they benefit interaction in the virtual environment. Observations of users of this system indicate that our constraints represent reality *well enough* to be useful while not introducing excess computational overhead.

This work follows the work of the first author in successfully incorporating these constraints to a space planning application called Cubeworld. Cubeworld was originally developed as a conventional multi-window system at the Dynamic Graphics Project at the University of Toronto.

2 Overview of the System and the Problem

2.1 Goals and intents

There are two main goals we attempt to accomplish by including constraints in our virtual environment:

1. To make interaction in the virtual environment more realistic by the inclusion of collision detection and physical properties such as mass, gravity, friction.
2. To make interaction more intuitive for design problems.

These goals must not compromise the requirement for real-time interaction, so we have restricted ourselves to a set of simplified physical constraints. These provide enough realism to enhance the virtual environment without significantly reducing update rates.

The original work on Cubeworld was designed to explore how naive constraints can aid interaction; to this end, we decided to explore the realm of space planning to test our ideas. Space planning problems, as we've referred to them in this paper, involve arranging entities in a setting where the arrangement itself is the solution to the problem. The appearance of the arrangement to the user is used to determine (to a large extent) the quality of the design. Thus, visual information is the most important cue for creating and evaluating the class of design solutions studied. Other functional factors of an arrangement, such as noise, cost, or strength and stress on objects, are not considered as important as visual information, and are not dealt with in our system.

2.2 Examples of space planning problems

Room layout: constraints are used to aid in arranging objects. Furniture can be interactively manipulated (moved about) to reflect different aesthetic tastes and clearance requirements.

Urban design: may involve the layout of new buildings in an existing space. Different variations of a building and their effects on the surrounding landscape can be explored in an interactive fashion.

2.3 Methods for solving these design problems

This type of problem is typically solved using parametric-based or primitives-based CAD systems. A primitives-based CAD system uses a set of primitive entities and operations (move, scale, rotate) to model designs of physical objects. It also provides a *grouping* or *layering* mechanism to deal with abstract parts of designs. This allows a complex design to be created by building it out of primitive parts. One typical, general-purpose system is Autocad [1].

Parametric-based CAD systems have built-in knowledge of a specific set of parameterized objects. Design features are keyed as input parameters to objects, allowing users to create customized objects by substitution of specific values for the parameters [2]. The customized objects are used to construct designs.

The system's built-in knowledge of each object type aids in creating, assembling, drawing and modifying objects. For example, a room can be created from the wall, floor, window and door types. The system will know to place doors at the edges of the floor, and will centre windows in the walls. The windows will be created with the same thickness as the walls. An example of such a system is ArchiCAD [3].

Traditional CAD techniques do not address the problem of how users should go about the process of designing, just how to use a particular system to communicate designs. Danahy [4] suggests that a heuristic, trial and error approach be taken. He states that systems can be used to find design solutions by allowing users to make mistakes, encouraging users to explore the design space, and using an iterative approach to refine designs. This approach involves the evaluation of several possible design solutions which allow designers to explore promising designs while discarding unpromising ones.

Finally, most CAD systems are mouse and text-based, and do not use a virtual environment for object manipulation or scene viewing, and we wish to explore the utility of virtual environment technology for real design problems.

2.4 Caveats

We do not address the problem of creating models in this paper, but are concentrating on moving objects and viewing potential solutions (using a trial and error process). We have used the non-virtual version of Cubeworld to generate the initial models.

We have restricted our problem domain to axis aligned models to minimize the cost of collision detection. Recent work on hierarchical spatial data structures for dynamic simulation now allows real-time collision detection of complex, concave objects [5].

3 Constraints

The physical constraints are *gravity, friction, pushing* and *anchor*. Physical constraints are applied to individual objects. They restrict manipulation of an object to enforce real-world behaviour. This makes the object manipulation easy to learn, and is naturally suited to a virtual environment. They aid manipulation because the user does not have to worry about ensuring the objects obey physical rules, as the system enforces the rules for the user.

The following is a description of each physical constraint:

Pushing: the push constraint enforces the solidity of objects. When a manipulated object collides with another it pushes it. This constraint can be used to move several objects around the scene at once without leaving the move mode. For example, a set of tables can be moved simultaneously by moving one table and pushing the other tables ahead. Overriding the push constraint allows objects to pass through each other.

Anchor: the anchor constraint disables pushing against an object, i.e. an object that is anchored cannot be pushed by other objects. The anchored object can be directly moved, meaning that the user can explicitly select that object for moving. This constraint is used to simulate objects that are fixed in position.

A common example is an anchored wall – it prevents other objects from *pushing* the wall which prevents the other objects from exceeding the room boundaries.

The anchor constraint can also be used as an accelerator – a group of objects can be aligned simply by pushing the group against the anchored object.

Gravity: in this system gravity is a simplification of real-world gravity; however, it is still useful for interaction. It ensures that objects rest on other objects or at some defined *ground* level.

Objects that are directly manipulated are not subject to gravity until the manipulation is ended. If an object stacked on top of another is moved (off the other object) it will fall to the floor level. The gravity constraint ensures that objects rest on the floor, and not just above the floor or partly embedded in the floor.

An example is a 'phone resting on a table, which will remain resting on the table top after some local manipulation. This is important because if we later move the table, the *friction* constraint will ensure the telephone moves with the table. Without gravity, manipulating the 'phone position could result in it resting above the table and the friction constraint would no longer be enforced. In this case, the 'phone would not move with the table for some subsequent manipulation of the table.

Gravity can also be used with the push constraint to move a stack of objects vertically. Pushing ensures that the stack remains together during upward movements, and gravity ensures that the stack remains together for downward movements.

Friction: will cause objects resting on top of a manipulated object to move with the manipulated object. As an example, if a table is moved, any objects (such as computers, 'phones, etc.) on top of the table will also move. Friction is a one-way constraint – the objects resting on top of the table can be manipulated independently.

On a larger scale, this constraint is useful when moving a room to different positions (all objects in the room will move with the room).

4   Description of our System

Objects are modelled as collections of blocks [6] and are displayed in real time as they are manipulated. Constraints checking and satisfaction occurs as objects are manipulated.

The main interaction within our virtual environment is repositioning, or moving, objects. This is accomplished in two manners using a DataGlove to perform the operation. The first is to select an object with the hand (using an appropriate gesture) and the object will follow the hand through space. The second method is to use the same gesture, though activated when the hand has not selected any object, to create a *pusher cube* which can then be used to move other objects around. The pusher cube is treated by the system as any other object. Constraint checking can be switched off if desired to allow objects to be moved between rooms or to make large scale movements simpler.

Moving around the scene is accomplished by simply walking around; viewing is implicit in the nature of a virtual environment (that uses a head-mounted display). Because of the limited volume in which the user's real actions are recognized, we allow user settable motion scaling to simplify interaction with large environments. For instance, a giant step by the user may take him halfway across the virtual room or only a few centimetres.

Constraints influence the behaviour of entities as they are manipulated. We call this effect *constrained manipulation*. The constraints in our system encourage exploratory and iterative design because they aid the mechanics of manipulating objects. Thus they enforce design details (such as making sure objects rest on one another or do not share the same volume) which frees up a designer's cognitive load, and encourages an exploratory design style.

4.1 Example of a typical interaction

The designer's goal is to create a room, fill it with furniture, and explore different layouts of the furniture. To start, a room instance is created and instances of a desk, a chair and two wall-units are placed in the room. They immediately fall to the floor because of the gravity constraint. If a chair was accidently placed on the table, simply moving the chair off the table will cause it to fall to the floor because of the gravity constraint.

The next task is to place the objects in suitable positions (arranging furniture using the system is similar to moving furniture at home): objects that collide push one another until they hit walls or other anchored (stationary) objects. For instance, if all the chairs are tucked into the table and one chair is moved, the chair will push the table, and subsequently all the chairs, along the floor. The desk can be dragged until it contacts a wall, at which point the system stops the desk from moving (because of the anchor constraint). Next, the designer views the scene, and based on the current configuration decides to place the wall-units in the room side by side. The designer will continue in this manner until satisfied with the resulting layout of furniture.

4.2 Interacting in the Cubeworld virtual environment

In a virtual environment, interactive viewing is far simpler than in conventional systems. In addition, 3D selection is significantly simplified, although feedback is still necessary.

The drawback of interaction in our current application is the slow update rate and noticeable lag. This has caused slight nausea in at least one user. The problems of update rate and lag are primarily the result of the Polhemus tracker. We have recently seen significant improvements by using a different sampling scheme for the Polhemus. In our new setup, we have a separate process which reads the Polhemus and stores the raw data in a shared memory segment. On the application side, a predictive filter uses this raw data to rapidly return an estimate for the current position and orientation. While this improves the update rate considerably, it fails to improve the lag in certain situations such as rapid change in position or orientation.

The overall feedback from users is very positive for viewing (binocular, head-tracked display) and for moving through the scene (walking). However, the small working volume of the Polhemus is a major disadvantage.

5   Observations of Constraint Use during Manipulation

We have also observed users in the virtual version of our system. In general they use the constraints in the same manner as the non-virtual version.

The constraints seem to be of even greater benefit than in the non-virtual version of Cubeworld. This is most likely due to the poor interaction accuracy of the virtual environment. The slow update rates, poor quality display and the spatial inaccuracy of the 3D tracking devices all make exact positioning exceedingly difficult. In this environment, the simplified constraints reduce the load on the user by removing the need to attempt precise positioning.

We have performed experiments testing an unconstrained virtual environment against a constrained one. The task was to place objects in a design studio. The results indicate that time required to complete a task was significantly less when constraints were enabled. In addition, users have expressed the opinion that constraints are strongly preferred. Without the use of constraints, the resultant designs had physical inconsistencies such as objects which interpenetrated and objects which floated in space.

On the performance side, turning off the constraints had no significant impact on the interactivity of the system. This fulfils our requirement for no significant degradation of performance.

These experiments and the results parallel those from a non-virtual version of Cubeworld. Further details can be found in Papper [6].

Apart from those for whom constraints were disabled, users were told that there was an existing database of objects, and each object behaved somewhat similar to the article it represented. They were also told that the behaviour of the objects was due to the gravity, pushing, friction and anchor constraints. They were given the following information about the behaviour caused by each physical constraint:

- that objects were solid and had the friction constraint
- that if they collided during manipulation they would push each other
- that some objects (the room and the dividers) were anchored so they couldn't be pushed
- that all objects had gravity so they always rested on other objects or the floor.

They were also instructed on how to by-pass constraint checking during manipulation, and told that they could permanently add or remove constraints from objects.

The studio currently contains approximately 20 drafting tables, 20 work tables (about the same size as drafting tables), a few shorter, thinner cutting tables, six computer tables with computers on top, and a number of chairs and stools. For the experiment, the subjects were given a representation of the studio itself on the computer screen and pre-defined object types to represent each type of furniture available for the studio.

We will now describe how each constraint affected interaction. While describing the use of each constraint we consider beneficial and accidental situations: beneficial uses are those that aided the task of the subject (whether the subject was aware of the effect of the constraint or not); accidental situations are those that had to be corrected.

5.1 Pushing

Pushing was used beneficially to move a group of objects and was also used for feedback to decide whether or not objects were in contact. Accidental situations occurred when subjects pushed other objects out of position.

In general, subjects do not take advantage of the push constraint to move several objects at once; they tend to move objects individually. This could be caused by three possible factors:

1. The subjects are not familiar enough with the basics of the system to move objects any other way than in a straightforward manner.
2. The subjects are not familiar enough with the design to take advantage of moving groups of objects.
3. The subjects are not sure how a single object manipulation will affect the design, let alone the movement of many objects.

The subjects didn't think of pushing several objects as a natural operation. Even when the operation of pushing several objects was demonstrated, they forgot that objects could be manipulated in this manner. This possibly indicates that the operation was not a natural one.

Users did understand that objects should not and will not violate each others' space. This is deduced from observations of the use of *push* as a cue or special event to let them know when a moved object had contacted another object. Subjects recognized this cue, indicating that this type of behaviour of objects is natural (they recognize the cue even if they don't use pushing explicitly).

Users without constraints were forced to manipulate objects individually while those with constraints enabled did move objects in groups in some situations.

5.2 Anchor

Beneficial uses of the anchor constraint, accounting for the majority of its use, were to move an object against an anchored object such as a wall or occasionally a room divider. Plate V shows a typical use of anchor and pushing: the table (dark object) is moved until it collides with the anchored wall divider (in white).

Accidental uses of anchor occurred when subjects wanted to move an object inside the studio after accidentally creating it outside. In these situations, after realizing they couldn't push through the studio walls, subjects turned off constraints to move objects into the studio. In general these accidental situations did not hinder object manipulations.

Subjects took advantage of the anchor constraint without being fully aware of its use: even before moving any objects (they verbalized their intention to move something against a wall) they knew that certain objects (such as walls) would stop the movement of other objects (showing that they were not aware of anchor, but of the properties of walls). They were not sure if dividers and tables were anchored until they encountered an applicable situation. Eventually they came to understand that only certain objects were anchored. As subjects learned the system, they did not decelerate the movement of objects as they approached walls. Thus, the anchor constraint aids manipulation by determining the extent, or magnitude, of operations.

Users without constraints enabled attempted to place desks against each other and against the walls by visual inspection. This resulted in many inconsistencies.

In a virtual environment the user does not have auxiliary views such as top, front and side views. As a result, when trying to place objects by visual inspection, the users had to step back and move around the object to get multiple views in order to align objects correctly.

5.3 Gravity

Gravity was used beneficially to place objects on the floor that were originally (and unintentionally) created to rest on top of the walls of the studio. Most accidental situations occurred as objects fell off tables on to the floor and had to be placed back on the table (the *undo* command proved very useful in this circumstance).

Gravity was not immediately obvious to subjects, although once they realized its function, it was used to move objects to the floor. Sometimes they forgot that they could use gravity to make objects rest on the floor, even when they had done this action before. The gravity constraint is implicitly used during each operation, making sure that objects are always resting on other objects or the floor. Without this constraint objects may accidentally be positioned floating slightly above other objects.

For users without constraints enabled, the placement of objects on top of one another was once again by visual inspection with the resultant inconsistencies.

5.4 Friction

Friction was never used in an accidental situation. Subjects expected the effects of friction (even without being aware of the constraint). However, they still took a relatively long time to realize its effects. In fact, when subjects turned off constraint checking during a move operation (to move a desk through a divider for example), they were surprised when the computer on the desk no longer moved with the desk. These observations show that the function provided by friction seemed entirely natural to subjects.

Plate VI shows a set of desks moved as a unit in the design studio problem. The desks on top follow the bottom desk.

Users without constraints enabled were forced to move objects individually. This had an effect on the objects which the users chose to manipulate. None of the tables which had objects resting on them were selected to be re-arranged. This is in direct contrast to the other users who did not show a biased selection.

6 Discussion of Experimental Results

Physical constraints provide constrained manipulation, simulating various behaviours for objects. In our tests physical constraints simulated how objects would behave as articles in our physical environment. Constrained manipulation aids object manipulation in three important ways:

1. The manipulation of objects is easy to learn for beginners.

2. Constrained object manipulation is helpful for expert users.
3. Users don't have to fully concentrate on object manipulation tasks.

6.1   Constrained manipulation is easy to learn

Our test results indicate that the behaviour incorporated into the objects for the studio problem are easily learned. The observations of the subjects shows that they learn to move objects very quickly, taking advantage of constraints without being aware of them. This is shown by the high percentage of non-explicit situations observed during user testing. The low percentage of accident situations shows that users do not make many errors. Subjects intuitively understand object behaviour so they know how to manipulate objects effectively. For instance, users presented with the studio problem assumed that objects were stopped by walls and that objects resting on desks moved with the desks.

6.2   Constrained manipulation is useful

Constrained manipulation can provide efficient object manipulation without an extensive set of manipulation commands (only move, scale, and rotate commands are required). Experts[1] manipulate objects by using the constrained behaviour of objects in novel ways. For instance, they use an object having the anchor constraint to line up objects against it. The power of constrained manipulation is shown by examples of experts using the system:

- experts use push and friction to move sets of objects in one operation
- they line up objects by pushing them against an anchored object
- they use one object as a *pusher* block to move several objects in the same mode
- they use gravity alone with pushing, to move an unattached stack of objects up and down – while keeping the objects stacked on top of each other.

The constrained behaviour of objects doesn't change for beginner or expert users. Thus, physical constraints combine ease of learning (because it is a simulation users already know about) with power (by using the behaviour in novel ways).

To use physical constraints effectively users must discover novel ways to put constraints to use to aid manipulation. It is hypothesized that as users experiment with the system they will develop a useful set of techniques that use physical constraints for problem solving. They do not need to be taught specific techniques, but learn them on their own by experimenting.

6.3   Constrained manipulation may reduce cognitive load

Constrained manipulation has the potential of freeing users from tedious aspects of design. This may allow them to concentrate on more important aspects of design.

In a virtual environment, the provision of solid objects (acting under the *pushing* constraint) is the most important addition. These objects then conform to the users' natural expectations.

Anchor constraints provide a simple way to delimit pushing operations (which is especially useful with the current hand tracking technology). Anchor also prevents

---

[1] The following observations were gathered from observations of a long term user of the system.

the user from accidentally modifying parts of the space that are meant to be fixed (such as walls).

Gravity is used implicitly (and effectively) all the time by users of the system.

Friction was primarily used as a grouping mechanism. While it was used extensively, users were not explicitly aware of its use. The users made effective use of the friction constraint.

As a result of these experiments, we have shown that constraints make modelling in a virtual environment more feasible. The characteristics of current virtual reality systems (slow update rate, inaccuracy in tracking, low resolution displays) that make modelling more difficult than conventional systems are largely overcome by the addition of these simplified constraints. Without the constraints, it is exceedingly tedious to model accurately or to perform most direct manipulation tasks.

7   Implementation and Speed of Constraint Satisfaction

These constraints are hard-coded directly into the system; the main reason is for execution speed. Thus addition of new types of constraints, or changes to the existing constraints requires coding and re-compilation.

Observation of the system with constraint checking turned off indicates that they do not pose any significant overhead for computation. This is because most interactions involve few (less than 10) objects. Interactions requiring the solving of say 50 objects does show significant time delay (about 0.75 seconds). However, this type of situation rarely occurs. The order for the current constraint algorithm is m times n, where m is the number of objects colliding and n is the total number of objects. In the worst case this is an n^2 computation.

The computation for constraints can be broken into two sections, performed in succession. The first is constraint checking, the second constraint satisfaction.

7.1   Constraint checking

Constraint checking is performed for each manipulation to ensure the validity of the constraints. For each manipulation, each manipulated object is checked against all the objects in the system. Assume there are m manipulated objects (initially there is only 1 manipulated object) and n total objects. The push, friction, and gravity physical constraint checking algorithms are order $(m*n)$. The anchor constraint is of order (m). Constraint checking is fairly quick and does not slow manipulation. The difference in performance during manipulation with constraint checking on or off is not noticeable, even using the system limit of objects.[2]

7.2   Constraint satisfaction

Physical constraint satisfaction is invoked when the manipulation of a set of objects causes one or more objects to change in size or position. After these objects change state constraint checking proceeds, but with a larger m value; m increases for every constraint satisfaction performed. In the worst case m approaches n, for example when moving a string of objects. In this case the movement of one object colliding

---

[2] Actually, the drawing speed is a far greater slowdown for interactivity, especially as the number of objects increases.

with another object which collides with another – colliding with every object in the system. As *m* increases beyond 50 (for the Iris 4DVGX) the system performance is slowed noticeably, and at 100 the performance is very slow. Fortunately, this situation occurs rarely because the size of *m* is fairly small for most manipulation operations (i.e. much smaller than *n*).

7.3 Drawing

Drawing is the bottleneck for interactive performance in the current system. We have measured the time spent in constraint checking and satisfaction and compared it with the drawing time.

When the interaction involves movement of objects where no collision detection occurs (that is constraint checking but not satisfaction), constraints take approximately 10% of the drawing time for one view.

For the worst case, in which all the objects that are displayed are involved in constraint checking and satisfaction, constraints take approximately 25% of the drawing time for one view. One example of this scenario is pushing a set of stacked desks.

Most interaction does not involve a great deal of constraint satisfaction. The observed average case performance is close to the best case scenario.

8   Futures

We plan to improve the performance of the system for complex interactions by using a dynamic object hierarchy. Recent work in our lab has resulted in an *nlogn* dynamic collision detection algorithm [5]. The implementation of the dynamic bounding hierarchy allows general concave polyhedra, greatly improving the available range of object types.

We also plan to incorporate our new graphics display subsystem. We anticipate significantly improved update rates with the new graphics module.

References

1 Paker, D. and Rice, H. 1985. *Inside AutoCAD*. Thousand Oaks, CA: New Riders Publishing.
2 Gross, M.D. 1989. Relational modeling. *Proc. CAAD Futures Conference – Computer Aided Design Education*.
3 *Archicad Manual*, 1987. Graphisoft. (Distributed by CADraw Canada Inc., Mississauga.)
4 Danahy, J. 1988. Engaging intuitive visual thinking in urban design modeling: a real-time hypothesis. *Proc. ACADIA Workshop*, Michigan.
5 Webb, R. and Gigante, M.A. 1992. Using dynamic bounding volume hierarchies to improve efficiency of rigid body simulations. *Proc. CGI '92*, Tokyo, Japan.
6 Papper, M. 1990. *Using High-Level Constraints to Aid Space Planning Applications in Computer-Aided Design*. MSc Thesis, Department of Computer Science, University of Toronto.

Biography

Michael John Papper is a user interface specialist who has concentrated on real-time 3D computer graphics. He has a Masters degree in computer science from the University of Toronto, and a Bachelors degree in computer science from Queen's University in Kingston, Ontario. Michael spent two years as a Research Associate at the Advanced Computer Graphics Centre at the Royal Melbourne Institute of Technology in Melbourne, Australia. His work there includes a 3D scene editor, an educational software environment, and work on virtual environments.

9 Device Synchronization Using an Optimal Linear Filter

Martin Friedmann, Thad Starner
and Alex Pentland

Massachusetts Institute of Technology, MA, USA

Abstract

To be convincing and natural, interactive graphics applications must correctly synchronize user motion with rendered graphics and sound output. We present a solution to the synchronization problem that is based on optimal estimation methods and fixed-lag dataflow techniques. A method for discovering and correcting prediction errors using a generalized likelihood approach is also presented. And finally, MusicWorld, a simulated environment employing these ideas, is described.

1 Introduction

To be convincing and natural, interactive graphics applications must correctly synchronize user motion with rendered graphics and sound output. The exact synchronization of user motion and rendering is critical: lags greater than 100 ms in the rendering of hand motion can cause users to restrict themselves to slow, careful movements, while discrepancies between head motion and rendering can cause motion sickness [1,2]. In systems that generate sound, small delays in sound output can confuse even practised users. This paper proposes a suite of methods for accurately predicting sensor position in order to more closely synchronize processes in distributed virtual environments.

Problems in synchronization of user motion, rendering, and sound arise from three basic causes. The first cause is noise in the sensor measurements. The second cause is the length of the processing pipeline, that is, the delay introduced by the sensing device, the CPU time required to calculate the proper response, and the time spent rendering output images or generating appropriate sounds. The third cause is unexpected interruptions such as network contention or operating system activity. Because of these factors, using the raw output of position sensors leads to noticeable lags and other discrepancies in output synchronization.

Unfortunately, most interactive systems either use raw sensor positions, or they make an *ad hoc* attempt to compensate for the fixed delays and noise. A typical method for compensation averages current sensor measurements with previous measurements to obtain a smoothed estimate of position. The smoothed measurements are then differenced for a crude estimate of the user's instantaneous velocity. Finally, the smoothed position and instantaneous velocity estimates are combined to extrapolate the user's position at some fixed interval in the future.

Problems with this approach arise when the user either moves quickly, so that averaging sensor measurements produces a poor estimate of position, or when the user changes velocity, so that the predicted position overshoots or undershoots the user's actual position. As a consequence, users are forced to make only slow, deliberate motions in order to maintain the illusion of reality.

We present a solution to these problems based on the ability to more accurately predict future user positions using an optimal linear estimator and on the use of fixed-lag dataflow techniques that are well-known in hardware and operating system design. The ability to accurately predict future positions eases the need to shorten the processing pipeline because a fixed amount of 'lead time' can be allotted to each output process. For example, the positions fed to the rendering process can reflect sensor measurements one frame ahead of time so that when the image is rendered and displayed, the effect of synchrony is achieved. Consequently, unpredictable system and network interruptions are invisible to the user as long as they are shorter than the allotted lead time.

2   Optimal Estimation of Position and Velocity

At the core of our technique is the optimal linear estimation of future user position. To accomplish this it is necessary to consider the *dynamic* properties of the user's motion and of the data measurements. The Kalman filter [3] is the standard technique for obtaining optimal linear estimates of the state vectors of dynamic models and for predicting the state vectors at some later time. Outputs from the Kalman filter are the maximum likelihood estimates for Gaussian noises, and are the optimal (weighted) least-squares estimates for non-Gaussian noises [4].

In our particular application we have found that it is initially sufficient to treat only the translational components (the x, y and z coordinates) output by the Polhemus sensor, and to assume independent observation and acceleration noise. In this section, therefore, we will develop a Kalman filter that estimates the position and velocity of a Polhemus sensor for this simple noise model. Rotations will be addressed in the following section.

2.1   The Kalman filter
Let us define a dynamic process

$$\mathbf{X}_{k+1} = \mathbf{f}(\mathbf{X}_k, \Delta t) + \xi(t) \tag{1}$$

where the function $\mathbf{f}$ models the dynamic evolution of state vector $\mathbf{X}_k$ at time k, and let us define an observation process

$$\mathbf{Y}_k = \mathbf{h}(\mathbf{X}_k, \Delta t) + \eta(t) \tag{2}$$

where the sensor observations $\mathbf{Y}$ are a function $\mathbf{h}$ of the state vector and time. Both ξ and η are white noise processes having known spectral density matrices.

In our case the state vector $\mathbf{X}_k$ consists of the true position, velocity, and acceleration of the Polhemus sensor in each of the x, y, and z coordinates, and the observation vector $\mathbf{Y}_k$ consists of the Polhemus position readings for the x, y, and z coordinates. The function $\mathbf{f}$ will describe the dynamics of the user's movements in terms of the state vector, i.e. how the future position in x is related to current position, velocity, and acceleration in x, y, and z. The observation function $\mathbf{h}$ describes the Polhemus measurements in terms of the state vector, i.e. how the next Polhemus measurement is related to current position, velocity, and acceleration in x, y, and z.

Using Kalman's result, we can then obtain the optimal linear estimate $\hat{\mathbf{X}}_k$ of the state vector $\mathbf{X}_k$ by use of the following *Kalman filter*:

$$\hat{\mathbf{X}}_k = \mathbf{X}_k^* + \mathbf{K}_k\,(\mathbf{Y}_k - \mathbf{h}(\mathbf{X}_k^*, t)) \tag{3}$$

provided that the Kalman gain matrix $\mathbf{K}_k$ is chosen correctly [3]. At each time step k, the filter algorithm uses a state prediction $\mathbf{X}_k^*$, an error covariance matrix prediction $\mathbf{P}_k^*$, and a sensor measurement $\mathbf{Y}_k$ to determine an optimal linear state estimate $\hat{\mathbf{X}}_k$, error covariance matrix estimate $\hat{\mathbf{P}}_k$, and predictions $\mathbf{X}_{k+1}^*$, $\mathbf{P}_{k+1}^*$ for the next time step.

The prediction of the state vector $\mathbf{X}_{k+1}^*$ at the next time step is obtained by combining the optimal state estimate $\hat{\mathbf{X}}_k$ and equation (1):

$$\mathbf{X}_{k+1}^* = \hat{\mathbf{X}}_k + \mathbf{f}(\hat{\mathbf{X}}_k, \Delta t)\Delta t \tag{4}$$

In our graphics application this prediction equation is also used with larger times steps, to predict the user's future position. This prediction allows us to maintain synchrony with the user by giving us the lead time needed to complete rendering, sound generation, and so forth.

2.1.1   Calculating the Kalman gain factor

The Kalman gain matrix $\mathbf{K}_k$ minimizes the error covariance matrix $\mathbf{P}_k$ of the error $\mathbf{e}_k = \mathbf{X}_k - \hat{\mathbf{X}}_k$, and is given by

$$\mathbf{K}_k = \mathbf{P}_k^* \mathbf{H}_k^T \,(\mathbf{H}_k \mathbf{P}_k^* \mathbf{H}_k^T + \mathcal{R})^{-1} \tag{5}$$

where $\mathcal{R} = \mathbf{E}[\eta(t)\eta(t)^T]$ is the $n \times n$ observation noise spectral density matrix, and the matrix $\mathbf{H}_k$ is the local linear approximation to the observation function $\mathbf{h}$,

$$[\mathbf{H}_k]_{ij} = \partial \mathbf{h}_i / \partial x_j \tag{6}$$

evaluated at $\mathbf{X} = \mathbf{X}_k^*$.

Assuming that the noise characteristics are constant, then the optimizing error covariance matrix $\mathbf{P}_k$ is obtained by solving the *Riccati equation*

$$0 = \mathbf{P}_k^* = \mathbf{F}_k\mathbf{P}_k^* + \mathbf{P}_k^*\mathbf{F}_k^T - \mathbf{P}_k^*\mathbf{H}_k^T\mathcal{R}^{-1}\mathbf{H}_k\mathbf{P}_k^* + \mathcal{Q} \tag{7}$$

where $\mathcal{Q} = \mathbf{E}[\xi(t)\xi(t)^T]$ is the $n \times n$ spectral density matrix of the system excitation noise ξ, and $\mathbf{F}_k$ is the local linear approximation to the state evolution function $\mathbf{f}$,

$$[\mathbf{F}_k]_{ij} = \partial\mathbf{f}_i/\partial x_j \tag{8}$$

evaluated at $\mathbf{X} = \hat{\mathbf{X}}_k$.

More generally, the optimizing error covariance matrix will vary with time, and must also be estimated. The *estimate* covariance is given by

$$\hat{\mathbf{P}}_k = (\mathbf{I} - \mathbf{K}_k\mathbf{H}_k)\mathbf{P}_k^* \tag{9}$$

From this the predicted *error* covariance matrix can be obtained

$$\mathbf{P}_{k+1}^* = \mathbf{\Phi}_k\hat{\mathbf{P}}_k\mathbf{\Phi}_k^T + \mathcal{Q} \tag{10}$$

where $\mathbf{\Phi}_k$ is known as the state transition matrix

$$\mathbf{\Phi}_k = (\mathbf{I} + \mathbf{F}_k\Delta t) \tag{11}$$

2.2   Estimation of displacement and velocity

In our graphics application we use the Kalman filter described above for the estimation of the displacements P_x, P_y, and P_z, the velocities V_x, Y_y, and V_z, and the accelerations A_x, A_y, and A_z of Polhemus sensors. The state vector $\mathbf{X}$ of our dynamic system is therefore $(P_x, , V_x, A_x, P_y, V_y, A_y, P_z, V_z, A_z)^T$, and the state evolution function is

$$\mathbf{f}(\mathbf{X},\Delta t) = \begin{bmatrix} V_x + A_x\frac{\Delta t}{2} \\ A_x \\ 0 \\ V_y + A_y\frac{\Delta t}{2} \\ A_y \\ 0 \\ V_z + A_z\frac{\Delta t}{2} \\ A_z \\ 0 \end{bmatrix} \tag{12}$$

The observation vector $\mathbf{Y}$ will be the positions $\mathbf{Y} = (P_x', P_y', P_z')^T$ that are the output of the Polhemus sensor. Given a state vector $\mathbf{X}$ we predict the measurement using simple second order equations of motion:

$$\mathbf{h}(\mathbf{X},\Delta t) = \begin{bmatrix} P_x + V_x\Delta t + A_x\frac{\Delta t^2}{2} \\ P_y + V_y\Delta t + A_y\frac{\Delta t^2}{2} \\ P_z + V_z\Delta t + A_z\frac{\Delta t^2}{2} \end{bmatrix} \tag{13}$$

Calculating the partial derivatives of equations (6) and (8) we obtain

$$\mathbf{F} = \begin{bmatrix} 0 & 1 & \frac{\Delta t}{2} & & & & & & \\ & 0 & 1 & & & & & & \\ & & 0 & & & & & & \\ & & & 0 & 1 & \frac{\Delta t}{2} & & & \\ & & & & 0 & 1 & & & \\ & & & & & 0 & & & \\ & & & & & & 0 & 1 & \frac{\Delta t}{2} \\ & & & & & & & 0 & 1 \\ & & & & & & & & 0 \end{bmatrix} \qquad (14)$$

and

$$\mathbf{H} = \begin{bmatrix} 1 & \Delta t & \frac{\Delta t^2}{2} & & & & & & \\ & & & 1 & \Delta t & \frac{\Delta t^2}{2} & & & \\ & & & & & & 1 & \Delta t & \frac{\Delta t^2}{2} \end{bmatrix} \qquad (15)$$

Finally, given the state vector $\mathbf{X}_k$ at time k we can predict the Polhemus measurements at time $k + \Delta t$ by

$$\mathbf{Y}_{k+\Delta t} = \mathbf{h}(\mathbf{X}_k, \Delta t) \qquad (16)$$

and the predicted state vector at time $k + \Delta t$ is given by

$$\hat{\mathbf{X}}_{k+\Delta t} = \mathbf{X}_k^* + \mathbf{f}(\hat{\mathbf{X}}_k, \Delta t)\Delta t \qquad (17)$$

2.2.1 The noise model

We have experimentally developed a noise model for user motions. Although our noise model is not verifiably optimal, we find the results to be quite sufficient for a wide variety of head and hand tracking applications. The system excitation noise model ξ is designed to compensate for large velocity and acceleration changes; we have found

$$\xi(t)^T = [1 \ 20 \ 63 \ 1 \ 20 \ 63 \ 1 \ 20 \quad 63] \qquad (18)$$

(where $\mathfrak{Q} = \mathbf{E}[\xi(t)\xi(t)^T]$ provides a good model. In other words, we expect and allow for positions to have a standard deviation of 1 mm, velocities 20 mm/s and accelerations 63 mm/s². The observation noise is expected to be much lower than the system excitation noise. The spectral density matrix for observation noise is $\mathfrak{R} = \mathbf{E}[\eta(t)\eta(t)^T]$; we have found that

$$\eta(t)^T = [.25 \ .25 \ .25] \qquad (19)$$

provides a good model for the Polhemus sensor.

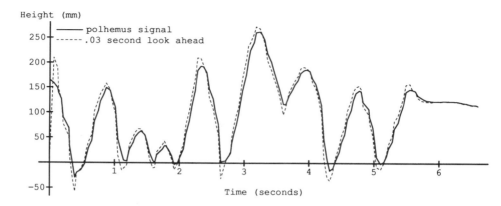

Figure 9.1 Output of a Polhemus sensor and the Kalman filter prediction of that output for a lead time of 1/30th of a second.

2.3 Experimental results and comparison

Figure 9.1 shows the raw output of a Polhemus sensor attached to a drumstick playing a musical flourish, together with the output of our Kalman filter predicting the Polhemus's position 1/30th of a second in the future.

As can be seen, the prediction is generally quite accurate. At points of high acceleration a certain amount of overshoot occurs; such problems are intrinsic to any prediction method but can be minimized with more complex models of the sensor noise and the dynamics of the user's movements.

Figure 9.2 shows a higher-resolution version of the same Polhemus signal with the Kalman filter output overlayed. Predictions for 1/30, 1/15, and 1/10 of a second in the future are shown. For comparison, Fig. 9.3 shows the performance of the prediction made from simple smoothed local position and velocity, as described in the introduction. Again, predictions for 1/30, 1/15, and 1/10 of a second in the future are shown. As can be seen, the Kalman filter provides a more reliable predictor of future user position than the commonly used method of simple smoothing plus velocity prediction.

3 Rotations

With the Polhemus sensor, the above scheme can be directly extended to filter and predict Euler angles as well as translations. However with some sensors it is only possible to read out instant-by-instant *incremental rotations*. In this case the absolute rotational state must be calculated by integration of these incremental rotations, and the Kalman filter formulation must be altered as follows [5]. (See also Liang *et al.* [6].)

Let ρ be the incremental rotation vector, and denote the rotational velocity and acceleration by ϑ and α. The rotational acceleration vector α is the derivative of ϑ which is, in turn, the derivative of ρ, but only when two of the components ρ are exactly zero (in some frame to which both ρ and ϑ are referenced). For sufficiently small rotations about at least two axes, ϑ is approximately the time derivative of ρ.

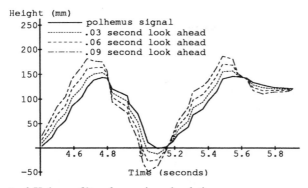

Figure 9.2 Output of Kalman filter for various lead times.

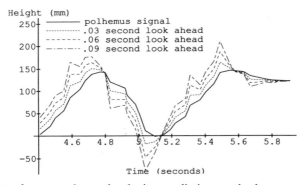

Figure 9.3 Output of commonly used velocity prediction method.

For 3D tracking one cannot generally assume small absolute rotations, so an additional representation of rotation, the unit quaternion $\overset{\circ}{\mathbf{q}}$ and its rotation submatrix **R**, is employed. Let

$$\overset{\circ}{\mathbf{q}} = \begin{pmatrix} q_0 \\ q_1 \\ q_2 \\ q_3 \end{pmatrix} \tag{20}$$

be the unit quaternion. Unit quaternions can be used to describe the rotations of a vector **v** through an angle ϕ about an axis $\hat{\mathbf{n}}$, where $\hat{\mathbf{n}}$ is a unit vector. The unit quaternion associated with such a rotation has *scalar part*

$$q_0 = \sin(\phi/2) \tag{21}$$

and vector part

$$\begin{pmatrix} q_1 \\ q_2 \\ q_3 \end{pmatrix} = \hat{\mathbf{n}} \cos{(\phi/2)} \tag{22}$$

Note that every quaternion defined this way is a unit quaternion.

By convention $\overset{\circ}{\mathbf{q}}$ is used to designate the rotation between the global and local coordinate frames. The definition is such that the orthonormal matrix

$$\mathbf{R} = \begin{bmatrix} q_0^2 + q_1^2 - q_2^2 - q_3^2 & 2(q_1q_2 - q_0q_3) & 2(q_1q_3 + q_0q_2) \\ 2(q_1q_2 + q_0q_3) & q_0^2 - q_1^2 + q_2^2 - q_3^2 & 2(q_2q_3 - q_0q_1) \\ 2(q_1q_3 - q_0q_2) & 2(q_2q_3 + q_0q_1) & q_0^2 - q_1^2 - q_2^2 + q_3^2 \end{bmatrix} \tag{23}$$

transforms vectors expressed in the local coordinate frame to the corresponding vectors in the global coordinate frame according to

$$\mathbf{v}_{\text{global}} = \mathbf{R}\mathbf{v}_{local} \tag{24}$$

In dealing with incremental rotations, the model typically assumes that accelerations are an unknown 'noise' input to the system, and that the time intervals are small so that the accelerations at one time step are close to those at the previous time step. The remaining states result from integrating the accelerations, with corrupting noise in the integration process.

The assumption that accelerations and velocities can be integrated to obtain the global rotational state is valid only when ρ_k is close to zero and ρ_{k+1} remains small. The latter condition is guaranteed with a sufficiently small time step (or sufficiently small rotational velocities). The condition $\rho_k = 0$ is established at each time step by defining ρ to be a correction to a nominal (absolute) rotation, which is maintained externally using a unit quaternion $\overset{\circ}{\mathbf{q}}$ that is updated at each time step.

4   Unpredictable Events

We have tested our Kalman filter synchronization approach using a simulated musical environment (described below) in which we track a drumstick and simulate the sounds of virtual drums. For smooth motions, the drumstick position is accurately predicted, so that sound, sight and motion are accurately synchronized, and the user experiences a strong sense of reality.

The main difficulties that arise with this approach derive from unexpectedly large accelerations, which produce overshoots and similar errors. It is important to note, however, that overshoots are *not* a problem as long as the drumstick is far from the drum. In these cases the overshoots simply exaggerate the user's motion, and the perception of synchrony persists. In fact, such overshoots seem generally to enhance, not degrade, the user's impression of reality.

The problem occurs when the predicted motion overshoots the true motion when the drumstick is near the drumhead, thus causing a false collision. In this case the system generates a sound when in fact no sound should occur. Such errors detract noticeably from the illusion of reality.

4.1 Correcting prediction errors

How can we preserve the impression of reality in the case of an overshoot causing an incorrect response? In the case of simple responses like sound generation, the answer is easy. When we detect that the user has changed direction unexpectedly – that is, that an overshoot has occurred – then we simply send an emergency message aborting the sound generation process. As long as we can detect that an overshoot has occurred before the sound is 'released', there will be no error.

This solution can be implemented quite generally, but it depends critically upon two things. The first is that we must be able to very quickly substitute the correct response for the incorrect response. The second is that we must be able to accurately detect that an overshoot has occurred.

In the case of sound generation due to an overshoot, it is easy to substitute the correct response for the incorrect, because the correct response is to do nothing. More generally, however, when we detect that our motion prediction was in error we may have to perform some quite complicated alternative response. To maintain synchronization, therefore, we must be able to detect possible trouble spots beforehand, and begin to compute all of the alternative responses sufficiently far ahead of time that they will be available at the critical instant.

The strategy, therefore, is to predict user motion just as before, but at critical junctures to compute several alternative responses rather than a single response. When the instant arrives that a response is called for, we can then choose among the available responses.

4.2 Detecting prediction errors

Given that we have computed alternative responses ahead of time, and that we can detect that a prediction error has occurred, then we can make the correct response. But how are we to detect which (possibly of many) alternative responses are to be executed?

The key insight to solving this detection problem is that *if* we have the correct dynamic model then we will always have an optimal linear estimate of the drumstick position, and there should be nothing much better that we can to do. The problem, then, is that in some cases our model of the event's dynamics does not match the true dynamics. For instance, we normally expect accelerations to be small and uncorrelated with position. However in some cases (for instance, when sharply changing the pace of a piece of music) a drummer will apply large accelerations that are exactly correlated with position.

The solution is to have *several* models of the drummer's dynamics running in parallel, one for each alternative response. Then at each instant we can observe the drumstick position and velocity, decide which model applies, and then make our response based on that model. This is known as the *multiple model* or *generalized likelihood* approach, and produces a generalized maximum likelihood estimate of the current and future values of the state variables [7]. Moreover, the cost of the Kalman filter calculations is sufficiently small to make the approach quite practical.

Intuitively, this solution breaks the drummer's overall behaviour down into several 'prototypical' behaviours. For instance, we might have dynamic models corresponding to a relaxed drummer, a very 'tight' drummer, and so forth. We then classify the drummer's behaviour by determining which model best fits the drummer's observed behaviour.

Mathematically, this is accomplished by setting up one Kalman filter for the dynamics of each model:

$$\hat{\mathbf{X}}_k^{(i)} = \mathbf{X}_k^{*(i)} + \mathbf{K}_k^{(i)} (\mathbf{Y}_k - \mathbf{h}^{(i)}(\mathbf{X}_k^{*(i)},t)) \tag{25}$$

where the superscript (i) denotes the ith Kalman filter. The *measurement innovations process* for the ith model (and associated Kalman filter) is then

$$\Gamma_k^{(i)} = \mathbf{Y}_k - \mathbf{h}^{(i)}(\mathbf{X}_k^{*(i)},t) \tag{26}$$

The measurement innovations process is zero-mean with covariance $\mathcal{R}$.

The ith measurement innovations process is, intuitively, the part of the observation data that is unexplained by the ith model. The model that explains the largest portion of the observations is, of course, the model most likely to be correct. Thus at each time step calculate the probability $P^{(i)}$ of the m-dimensional observations $\mathbf{Y}_k$ given the ith model's dynamics,

$$P^{(i)}(\mathbf{Y}_k) = \frac{1}{(2\pi)^{m/2}\mathrm{Det}(\mathcal{R})^{1/2}} \exp\left(-\frac{1}{2}\Gamma_k^{(i)T}\mathcal{R}^{-1}\Gamma_k^{(i)}\right) \tag{27}$$

and choose the model with the largest probability. This model is then used to estimate the current value of the state variables, to predict their future values, and to choose among alternative responses.

When optimizing predictions of measurements Δt in the future, equation (26) must be modified slightly to test the predictive accuracy of state estimates from Δt in the past

$$\Gamma_k^{(i)} = \mathbf{Y}_k - \mathbf{h}^{(i)}(\mathbf{X}_{k-\Delta t}^{*(i)} + \mathbf{f}^{(i)}(\hat{\mathbf{X}}_{k-\Delta t}^{(i)},\Delta t)\Delta t,t)) \tag{28}$$

by substituting equation (17).

5 MusicWorld

Our solution is demonstrated in a musical virtual reality, an application requiring synchronization of user, physical simulation, rendering, and computer generated sound. This system is called *MusicWorld*, and allows users to play a virtual set of drums, bells, or strings with two drumsticks controlled by Polhemus sensors. As the user moves a physical drumstick the corresponding rendered drumstick tracks accordingly. The instant the rendered drumstick strikes a drum surface, a sound generator produces the appropriate sound for that drum. The visual appearance of

Figure 9.4

MusicWorld is shown in Figure 9.4 and a higher quality rendition is included in the colour section (Plate VII.)

Figure 9.5 shows the processes and communication paths used to filter and query each Polhemus sensor. Since we cannot ensure that the application control process will query the Polhemus devices on a regular basis, and since we do not want the above Kalman loop to enter into the processing pipeline, we spawn two small processes to constantly query and filter the actual device. The application control process then, at any time, has the opportunity to make a fast query to the filter process for the most up to date, filtered, Polhemus position. Using shared memory between these two processes makes the final queries fully optimal.

MusicWorld is built on top of the ThingWorld system [8,9], which has one process to handle the problems of real-time physical simulation and contact detection and a second process to handle rendering. Sound generation is handled by a third process

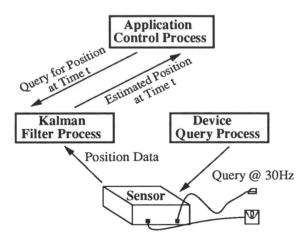

Figure 9.5 Communications used for control and filtering of Polhemus sensor.

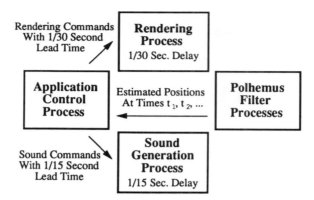

Figure 9.6 Communications and lead times for MusicWorld processes.

on a separate host, running CSound [10]. Figure 9.6 shows the communication network for MusicWorld, and the lead times employed.

The application control process queries the Kalman filter process for the predicted positions of each drumstick at 1/15 and 1/30 of a second. Two different predictions are used, one for each output device. The 1/15 of a second predictions are used for sound and are sent to ThingWorld to detect stick collisions with drums and other sound generating objects. When future collisions are detected, sound commands destined for 1/15 of a second in the future are sent to CSound. Regardless of collisions and sounds, the scene is always rendered using the positions predicted at 1/30 of a second in the future, corresponding to the fixed lag in our rendering pipeline. In general, it would be more optimal to constantly check and update the lead times actually needed for each output process, to ensure that dynamic changes in network speeds, or in the complexity of the scene (rendering speeds) do not destroy the effects of synchrony.

6   Summary

The unavoidable processing delays in computer systems mean that synchronization of graphics and sound with user motion requires prediction of the user's future position. We have shown how to construct the optimal linear filter for estimating future user position, and demonstrated that it gives better performance than the commonly used technique of position smoothing plus velocity prediction. The ability to produce accurate predictions can be used to minimize unexpected delays by using them in a system of multiple asynchronous processes with known, fixed lead times. Finally, we have shown that the combination of optimal filtering and careful construction of system communications can result in a well-synchronized, multi-modal virtual environment.

Acknowledgements

This research was made possible by ARO Grant No. DAAL03-87-K-0005. First thanks go to the ACM for this publication. Thanks are due to Barry Vercoe and

Mike Hawley for their help with CSOUND. Thanks! Special mention to Ali Azarbayejani, our newest member. And last but not least, shouts go out to the rest of the real-time programming posse: Irfan Essa, Bradley Horowitz and Stan Sclaroff.

References

1   Held, R. 1990. Correlation and decorrelation between visual displays and motor output. In *Motion sickness, visual displays, and armored vehicle design*, Aberdeen Proving Ground, Maryland, Ballistic Research Laboratory.
2   Oman, C.M. 1990. Motion sickness: a synthesis and evaluation of the sensory conflict theory. *Canadian J. Physiology and Pharmacology,* **68**, 264–303.
3   Kalman, R.E. and Bucy, R.S. 1991. New results in linear filtering and prediction theory. *Trans ASME (Journal of Basic Engineering),* **83D**: 95–108.
4   Friedland, B. 1986. *Control System Design.* McGraw-Hill.
5   Azarbayejani, A. 1991. *Model-Based Vision Navigation for a Free-Flying Robot.* Masters Thesis, MIT Department of Aeronautics and Astronomy.
6   Liang, J., Shaw, C. and Green, M. 1991. On temporal-spatial realism in the virtual reality environment. *Proc. ACM Symposium on User Interface Software and Technology.* Hilton Head, SC, 19–25.
7   Willsky, A.S. 1986. Detection of abrupt changes in dynamic systems. In M. Basseville and A. Benveniste, editors, *Detection of Abrupt Changes in Signals and Dynamical Systems*, Vol 77 of *Lecture Notes in Control and Information Sciences*. Springer-Verlag.
8   Pentland, A. and Williams, J. 1989. Good vibrations: Modal dynamics for graphics and animation. *Computer Graphics,* **23**(4): 215–222.
9   Pentland, A., Essa, I., Friedmann, M., Horowitz, B., Sclaroff, S. and Starner, T. 1990. The ThingWorld modelling system. In E.F. Deprettere, editor, *Algorithms and Parallel VLSI Architectures.* Elsevier.
10 Vercoe, B. and Ellis, D. 1990. Real-time CSOUND: Software synthesis with sensing and control. *ICMC Glasgow Proc.*, 209–211.

Biographies

Martin Friedmann received his BS in 1988 from the University of Michigan at Ann Arbor. His major interests then were in computer graphics and holography. He remained at Michigan's Center for Information Technology Integration working with Spencer Thomas on distributed 3D graphics systems until 1990, when he began work at the MIT Media Lab in the Vision and Modeling Group. His current research interests lie in interactive computer graphics, with emphasis on physically-based modeling, distributed systems and virtual environments. He is a member of the ACM.

Thad Starner received a BS in computer science and a BS in brain and cognitive science from the Massachusetts Institute of Technology in 1991. He is currently a United States Air Force Graduate Fellow studying in the Vision and Modeling Group at the MIT Media Laboratory. He has co-authored several papers in the fields of computer graphics, virtual environments, artificial intelligence and motion tracking. His current research involves face recognition, face tracking and large image database manipulation. Other technical interests include palmtop computers and personal networks, personalized news services, and simulator sickness.

Alex Paul Pentland received his PhD from the Massachusetts Institute of Technology in 1982, and began work at SRI International's Artificial Intelligence Center. He was appointed Industrial Lecturer in Stanford Universities' Computer Science Department in 1983, winning the Distinguished Lecturer award in 1986. In 1987 he was appointed Associate Professor of Computer, Information, and Design Technology at MIT's Media Laboratory, and was given the NEC Computer and Communications Career Development Chair in 1988. He has done research in artificial intelligence, machine vision, human vision and computer graphics. In 1984 he won the Best Paper prize from the American Association for Artificial Intelligence for his research into fractal texture models, and in 1991 he won the Best Paper prize from the IEEE for his research into face recognition. His last book was entitled *From Pixels to Predicates* (Ablex, Norwood, NJ), and he is currently working on *Dynamic Vision* (Bradford Books, MIT Press).

Part 4
Applications

10 Virtual Reality Techniques in Flight Simulation

John Vince

Hughes Rediffusion Simulation Ltd

Abstract

This paper examines the role of flight simulators for training civilian pilots, and identifies features of virtual reality that are central to the simulation industry.

1 Introduction

Virtual reality, or virtual environment systems, are, in general, systems where a user is interactively interfaced to a computer and engaged in a 3D visual task. The computer provides a virtual domain for supporting 3D models of objects or complete environments and, given suitable transducers, the user can interact with the system in real time. However, VR is not just concerned with this precise configuration of elements; it encompasses many variants where one or more features are removed, enhanced or substituted by something else.

Features such as immersion, real-time interaction, 3D graphics and force-feedback are well-known system concepts, but only recently have they been associated with low-cost VR systems. However, they have been used in one industry for over a decade, and that industry is flight simulation.

2 Flight Simulation

Flight simulators have been used by commercial airlines and the military for over twenty years, where they are used for training pilots in developing new skills in handling aircraft under unusual operating conditions, and discovering the flight characteristics of a new aircraft.

Modern military and civilian aircraft are extremely sophisticated electronic machines. Planes developed for military applications employ various technological aids that enable the pilot to deliver a lethal payload as quickly and as efficiently as possible. Planes developed for civilian applications are still required to be fast and efficient, but their delicate human cargo requires that safety considerations are paramount.

Both types of aircraft are expensive to construct: military craft employ sophisticated engines, accurate navigation systems, labour-intensive fabrication techniques, special materials, ruggedized computers and reliable communication systems; whereas civilian craft are necessarily large, employ multiple engines, and have systems for automatic landing and navigation. They also have the added expense introduced by elaborate safety standards.

Nowadays, with aircraft costing many tens of millions of dollars, it is unthinkable that would-be pilots should be allowed to train in such craft – hence the evolution of the flight simulator. Although this is also an expensive device, typically costing in excess of $10M, the modern flight simulator (see Plate VIII) has proven to be the most cost-effective method for training pilots without endangering their lives, damaging real aircraft or creating a hazard to the general public.

A flight simulator is also a sophisticated machine and employs a variety of technologies that include: hydraulics, electronics, real-time computing, optical projectors and real-time 3D image generation. They too, like aircraft, are expected to enjoy a long life, and must function at least 18 hours every day of their operating life.

The success of any training task can only be assessed by evaluating the skills acquired by the trainee after undertaking some training exercise, and in the case of pilot training, the only criterion can be whether the pilot is able to confidently and safely fly a real plane once trained. Indeed, pilots trained on a simulator having CAA Phase 3 approval are able to co-pilot a craft immediately after their simulation training. Achieving this level of competence demonstrates the effectiveness of the simulator as a training vehicle. However, this performance should not be too much of a surprise when one appreciates the lengths to which the simulation industry goes in reconstructing a duplicate of the real world (see Plate XII).

The usefulness of any simulation process relies upon the accuracy to which one system can be represented by another. This is true whether a discrete computer simulation language is being used to mimic a continuous physical system, or whether computer generated images are being used to predict what an object would look like if it were actually constructed. In the case of pilot training a flight simulator must be able to convince the pilot that he or she is actually inside a real plane. There can be no real place for features that destroy the simulator's credibility as an alternative reality, which implies that attention to detail is vital.

A flight simulator is the next-best place where a pilot can experience the sensations that are normally associated with a real plane. This means that the flight deck of some specific craft, such as an Airbus 320, Concorde, or a Boeing 767 is accurately reproduced to create the 'look' and 'feel' of the real thing. Furthermore, every instrument must function identically to their real-world counterparts (see Plates IX and X). This implies that fuel gauges must react to the rate at which imaginary engines consume fuel, which in turn must accurately reflect thrust and temperature characteristics.

One of the most difficult sensations to simulate is motion. In real life situations we obtain motion cues from the ear's vestibular system, visual data and the sensation of touch. Our ears are vital for maintaining balance and indicating spatial orientation. Visual cues provide overwhelming data relating our speed with other external objects, but they are not completely infallible. The scenario of sitting in a stationary train and believing one is in motion through the relative motion of another train, demonstrates how easy it is to simulate constant velocity movements. Finally, the wind blowing in one's hair or against one's face are additional cues that provide further evidence of motion. G-forces that manifest themselves in blood rushing to one's head or uncomfortable chest pressures are also valuable motion indicators. Civilian flight simulators attempt to reproduce these motion effects by accelerating the cockpit environment with the aid of powerful hydraulic rams, and military simulators employ further gadgets such as g-suits that simulate inertial forces.

The last component in a flight simulator is the visual system. This is responsible for creating and projecting the images of runways and airports needed for the various training exercises. Early simulators employed rigid models of airports built from card, wood and plastic, over which a camera was tracked using servo motors. These models were constructed to a scale of 2000:1, and although they provided extraordinary realism, they had some disadvantages and have now been replaced by computer image generators.

In this brief introductory description one can see the importance of immersing the pilot in a world that is a copy of the real world. Although this is not completely feasible, it is possible to achieve satisfactory levels of realism. One can also appreciate the importance of the real-time interaction associated with every simulated element, and one can also see the role of the complementary synthetic images.

The rest of this paper will examine in greater detail how a typical commercial flight simulator employs some of the features of virtual reality systems.

2 Immersion

Although the brain possesses incredible powers for filtering out unwanted information from the channels of sight and sound, it is tiresome to concentrate upon some activity that is being interrupted by irrelevant noise. We have probably all experienced the sensation of withdrawing from a television programme, having been engrossed in the images or an exciting story. Even in the medium of books, a gifted author can easily entice us into the pages, where we become immersed in the plot. This type of immersion is subconscious: we are never aware of moving from the real world into the imaginary world, but only returning to the real world because of some form of interruption.

Immersion is an important feature of virtual reality systems as it is central to the paradigm where the user becomes part of the simulated world, rather than the simulated world being a feature of the user's own world. In a flight simulator the immersion is achieved by a subtle mixture of real hardware and virtual imagery.

Real cockpits are constructed from arrays of instruments, joysticks, levers, switches, buttons, sliders, etc., that possess individual mechanical characteristics. Pilots are constrained to floor-mounted chairs, and during take-off and landing scenarios they are restrained by seat belts. It would be foolish to simulate this hardware at the virtual level as the pilot's interaction with this equipment is a vital part of flying. One has only to see a pilot attempting to land a fully-laden Boeing 747 in terrifying weather conditions to realize just how physical the landing manoeuvre is.

Although modern aircraft are equipped with automatic landing systems, and pilots are expected to make two or three automatic landings a year, the majority of landing approaches are made manually. Consequently, pilots do depend upon what they see through the cockpit windows, which in some weather conditions amounts to very little. This is where computer graphics complements the real cockpit environment to create the illusion of flying.

Unlike military pilots, civilian pilots do not wear any form of head-mounted display; the most they ever have to wear are headphones and a microphone for communication with air traffic controllers. Consequently, there seems little point in asking them to wear a head-mounted display system similar to those used in VR systems. The alternative is to mount a display system external to the cockpit.

Early display systems involved fixing two or more monitors to the cockpit windows, and to create an illusion of depth to the images they were viewed indirectly through suitable optics to collimate the image. Collimation creates the illusion that the image is located at infinity. In practice, the image may 'hang' approximately 15 m beyond the cockpit. One of the disadvantages of the monitor approach is that the pilot and the co-pilot cannot share each other's images, as the gaze of each pilot is directed towards their individual display. However, these problems were resolved by Rediffusion Simulation's WIDE system which comprises three elements: a group of projectors, a back-projection screen and a panoramic spherical mirror. Typically, three projectors form a seamless coloured image upon the back-projection screen, with each projector forming an image with 50° horizontal field of view. The translucent back-projection screen is mounted above the cockpit and out of view from the pilots; the image on the screen is then seen as a reflection in the panoramic mirror.

With the correct juxtaposition of the projectors, screen and the mirror, the pilot and co-pilot see a virtual image several metres beyond the physical domain of the cockpit. This also permits both pilot and co-pilot to share the same virtual image without the inconvenience of any extraneous hardware.

On a 3-channel system where the field of view is approximately 150°, the image is created to a definition of approximately 800 lines and the entire image contains in excess of 2 million pixels. The update and refresh rate is 50 Hz for day scenes, and 30 Hz for dusk/night scenes. The higher refresh rate is required for the bright daytime images to prevent flicker. By reducing the refresh rate for the dimmer night scenes extra time is made available to superimpose calligraphic light points upon the raster image. The light points are used to represent runway lights, stars, moving traffic and even particle systems for modelling snow.

3   Real-Time Computer Generated Images

In the early 1980s computer generated images (CGI) began to replace the rigid model boards used up to that time. The first systems could not compete with the fine detail that could be built into the physical models, but as computer graphics developed and processing power improved, image fidelity increased. Nowadays, a modern image generator can create coloured images with an update rate of 50 Hz, and a polygon count of 1000 polygons/image. Compared with some workstations this does not seem excessive, but the polygons are textured, and the image generators have other features such as: light points (displayed to a resolution of 4000 lines), transparency, weather effects (fog, rain, snow, lightning, clouds, horizon-glow), non-linear image mapping, collision detection, height-above terrain, and level-of-detail model management (see Plate XI).

One of the major problems associated with current VR systems is the low image update rate when a scene contains too many polygons. This is not peculiar to VR systems: any CGI system has update limitations, and subtle ways are needed to overcome them without dramatically increasing the cost of the image generator. In flight simulation, the virtual 3D world may encompass 100 square miles which means that some objects will appear very small when viewed in perspective. Consequently, certain features of the environment are modelled at two or three levels of detail, and the image generator selects the appropriate level to keep the polygon count at a minimum. Such strategies may have to become a feature of some VR systems.

4 Real-Time Interaction

Fortunately, pilots do not have to leave their cockpits and interact with the outside world whilst flying. Although it has been known for a pilot to be accidently sucked through a cockpit window due to some unusual malfunction, this does not have to be simulated! Nevertheless, there are times when the pilot's world must physically interact with the virtual 3D world. For example, when the aircraft actually makes contact with the virtual runway, the motion system must respond with a transient to simulate the undercarriage striking concrete obliquely at 200 knots.

Apart from the automatic level-of-detail model management described above, which is activated by the proximity of the pilot and the model features, the runway lights change their colour according to the approach angle of the plane. And when the pilot manoeuvres the plane to its final disembarkation point, he is guided by a marshall signalling commands through arm movements.

Another example of interaction between the aircraft and the virtual world is in the form of collision detection between the simulated plane and various features of the database. This is required to confirm that a manoeuvre has resulted in physical contact with another craft taxiing on the runway, or even the unlikely event of the aircraft striking a building.

In the more conventional VR system the user's head must be tracked to monitor the view direction, and currently there are still problems in obtaining a high sample rate and achieving a small transport delay. In a flight simulator it is not the pilot's head that must be tracked but the heading of the plane. These data are maintained in the computer system modelling the flight dynamics of the simulated craft, and are made available to the image generator at a rate of 30 Hz. And as the update rate of the image generator is in the order of 50 Hz, the heading samples are interpolated to derive intermediate values.

Once the image generator knows the heading of the plane, there is a delay of approximately 0.06 sec before the pilot actually sees the image corresponding to this position. This transport delay arises from the time required to 'walk' through the hierarchical database and retrieve the relevant geometry; apply the perspective transformation and clip surfaces to the viewing volume; and render the image into a frame store.

5   Force Feedback

Placing the simulator on a motion platform permits the pilot's virtual world to be subjected to some of the forces encountered when piloting a real plane. For example, on take-off the vibration introduced by the undercarriage riding over the runway can be simulated quite effectively. Even the dynamics of the plane's suspension can be included. When landing, the actual point of contact must be computed between the plane's undercarriage and the runway; and when this happens, the platform must be driven with sufficient force to mimic the powerful interaction that occurs at this point.

The attitude of the platform is also used to simulate the forces resulting from accelerating and decelerating. By tilting the platform backwards, the pilot feels pushed back into his seat and imagines being accelerated forward, whereas tilting the platform forward simulates a sensation of decelerating. However, one of the most difficult tasks for the motion software is to keep the platform in a central quiescent position from which it can move in response to the pilot's next manoeuvre.

Force feedback is also introduced into the flying controls which are generally connected via cables to the surfaces controlling the plane's flight characteristics.

6   Motion Sickness

Motion sickness is an uncomfortable sensation some people experience when travelling in boats, cars, trains, buses and planes. There does not appear to be a satisfactory explanation that accounts for every type of motion sickness experienced, but there are various techniques for reducing the symptoms that include taking drugs, stimulating a pressure point on the wrist, facing forward in the direction of motion, and gazing at the horizon.

When panoramic displays are used in visual systems, so powerful are the visual motion cues, physical motion cues are not necessary to show that one is moving through a virtual world. However, when the ear's vestibular system is not excited, and the brain is visually convinced that it is moving, motion sickness can quickly set in. This is a potential area for concern if panoramic head-mounted displays become a standard feature of VR systems.

7   Modelling Virtual Worlds

In a flight simulator the virtual worlds are based upon actual international airports, which are constructed from plans, maps, photographs and site visits. Although the airport is the central feature of the database, it is necessary to include surrounding detail up to a radius of approximately 10 miles. Creating such databases requires special software tools that can cope with features such as: scene complexity, level-of-detail management, textures, colour, animation sequences and hidden-surface removal strategies. At Hughes Rediffusion Simulation these tools were developed in-house and are implemented on an SGI workstation.

It may take several months to complete the database for an airport, during which time the modeller will require access to a simulator's visual display system to explore the accuracy of the model when viewed in real time. This will probably remain a time-consuming and a labour-intensive process, and must not be overlooked by potential users of VR technology.

8 The Future

The flight simulation industry has been using VR techniques for over a decade; not because the technology is exciting, but because it provides cost-effective solutions to real problems. During this period of time considerable effort has been expended in developing integrated systems for supporting virtual worlds that must be seen and interacted with. Many of the problems are non-trivial as today's designers of VR systems are discovering.

There is no doubt that VR will evolve to become an important method of interacting with computers, and considerable research and development is still needed to produce systems that will be able to solve real industrial problems. Fortunately, we are moving towards a period when massively parallel computers will become a reality, for such systems will be needed to undertake some of the applications identified having a VR solution. It would be foolish to assume that many of the projects predicted by the VR gurus will arrive this century, and it would be prudent to accept that like CAD systems, VR must follow a normal development path, no matter how exciting it appears today.

Biography

John Vince is a Research Consultant at Hughes Rediffusion Simulation where he advises on research activities into real-time 3D computer graphics. Before this appointment he was a Principal Lecturer at Middlesex Polytechnic, where he established the Computer Graphics Department. He has been associated with computer graphics/animation for 25 years, especially in its application to television. His research activities have been in the area of applied computer graphics to art and design, and his PICASO system was developed to promote the use of computer graphics within academia. He is the author of five books on computer graphics and computer animation. In 1990 was appointed Visiting Professor at Brighton Unversity. He is also Chairman of the National Centre for Computer Animation at Bournemouth University.

11 Using Virtual Reality Techniques in the Animation Process

Daniel Thalmann
Swiss Federal Institute of Technology

Abstract

This paper tries to find the various functions involved in an animation system and how virtual reality techniques and multimedia input could play a role. A classification of VR-based methods is proposed: real-time rotoscopy methods, real-time direct metaphors and real-time recognition-based metaphors. Several examples are presented: 3D shape creation, camera motion, body motion control, hand animation, and facial animation. The hardware and software architecture of our animation system is also described.

1 Introduction

The traditional main difficulty in the process of 3D animation is the lack of 3D interaction. Visual feedback, in a typical computer graphics application that requires items to be positioned or moved in 3D space, usually consists of a few orthogonal and perspective projection views of the same object in a multiple window format. This layout may be welcomed in a CAD system where, in particular, an engineer might want to create fairly smooth and regular shapes and then acquire some quantitative information about his design. But in 3D applications like 3D animation, where highly irregular shapes are created and altered in a purely visual and aesthetic fashion, like in sculpting or keyframe positioning, this window layout creates a virtually unsolvable puzzle for the brain, and makes it very difficult (if not impossible) for the user of such interfaces to fully understand his work and to decide where further alterations should be made. Moreover, good feedback of the motion is almost impossible, making the evaluation of the motion quality very difficult.

For a long time, we could observe virtual worlds only through the window of the workstation's screen with a very limited interaction possibility. Today, new technologies may immerse us in these computer generated worlds or at least communicate with them using specific devices. In particular, with the existence of graphics workstations able to display complex scenes containing several thousands of polygons at interactive speed, and with the advent of such new interactive devices as the SpaceBall, EyePhone and DataGlove, it is possible to create applications based on a full 3D interaction metaphor in which the specifications of deformations or motion are given in real time. These new concepts drastically change the way of designing animation sequences.

In this paper, we call *VR-based animation* techniques all techniques based on this new way of specifying animation. We also call *VR devices* all interactive devices allowing communication with virtual worlds. They include classic devices like head-mounted display systems, DataGloves as well as all 3D mice or SpaceBalls. We also consider as VR devices MIDI keyboards, force-feedback devices and multimedia capabilities like real-time video input devices and even audio input devices. In the next section, we present a summary of these various VR devices. More details may be found elsewhere (Balaguer and Mangili [1]; Brooks [2] and Fisher *et al*. [3]).

2   Survey of VR Devices

2.1   Position/orientation measurement

There are two main ways of recording positions and orientations: magnetic and ultrasonic. Magnetic tracking devices have been the most successful and the Polhemus 3Space IsoTrak, although not perfect, is the most common one. A source generates a low frequency magnetic field detected by a sensor. The second approach is generally based on a tripod consisting of three ultrasonic speakers set in a triangular position that emits ultrasonic sound signals from each of the three transmitters.

2.1.1   DataGlove

Hand measurement devices must sense both the flexing angles of the fingers and the position and orientation of the wrist in real time. Currently, the most common hand measurement device is the DataGlove™ from VPL Research. The DataGlove consists of a lightweight nylon glove with optical sensors mounted along the fingers. In its basic configuration, the sensors measure the bending angles of the joints of the thumb and the lower and middle knuckles of the other fingers, and the DataGlove can be extended to measure abduction angles between the fingers. Each sensor is a short length of fibre optic cable, with a light-emitting diode (LED) at one end and a phototransistor at the other end. When the cable is flexed, some of the LED's light is lost, so less light is received by the phototransistor. Attached to the back is a 3Space IsoTrak system to measure orientation and position of the gloved hand. This information, along with the ten flex angles for the knuckles is transmitted through a serial communication line to the host computer.

2.1.2   DataSuit

Much less popular than the DataGlove, this allows the positions of the body to be measured. A typical example of the use of the DataSuit is the Fuji TV film, *The Dream of Mr. M*. In this film, a 3D character approximately performs the same motion as the animator.

2.1.3   6D devices: 6D Mouse and SpaceBall

Some people have tried to extend the concept of the mouse to 3D. Ware and Jessome [4] describe a 6D mouse, called a bat, based on the Polhemus 3Space IsoTrak. Logitech's 2D/6D mouse is based on an ultrasonic position reference array, which is a tripod consisting of three ultrasonic speakers set in a triangular position which emits ultrasonic sound signals from each of the three transmitters. These are used to track the receiver position, orientation and movement.

To address this problem, Spatial Systems designed a 6 DOF interactive input device called the SpaceBall. This is essentially a 'force' sensitive device that relates the forces and torques applied to the ball mounted on top of the device. These force and torque vectors are sent to the computer in real time, where they are interpreted and may be composited into homogeneous transformation matrices that can be applied to objects. Buttons mounted on a small panel facing the user control the sensitivity of the SpaceBall and may be adjusted according to the scale or distance of the object currently being manipulated. Other buttons are used to filter the incoming forces to restrict or stop translations or rotations of the object.

2.2 MIDI keyboard

MIDI keyboards were first designed for music input, but provide a more general way of entering multi-dimensional data at the same time. In particular, it is a very good tool for controlling a large number of DOFs in a real-time animation system. A MIDI keyboard controller has 88 keys, any of which can be struck within a fraction of second. Each key transmits velocity of keystroke as well as pressure after the key is pressed.

2.3 Stereo and head-mounted displays

Binocular vision considerably enhances visual depth perception. Stereo displays like the StereoView option on Silicon Graphics workstations may provide high resolution stereo real-time interaction. StereoView consists of two items – specially designed eyewear and an infrar-emitter. The shutters alternately open and close every 120th of a second in conjunction with the alternating display of the left and right eye view on the display – presenting each eye with an effective 60 Hz refresh. The infrar emitter transmits the left/right signal from the IRIS workstation to the wireless eyewear so that the shuttering of the LCD is locked to the alternating left/right image display. As a result, each eye sees a unique image and the brain integrates these two views into a stereo picture.

The EyePhone is a head-mounted display system which presents the rich 3D cues of head-motion parallax and stereopsis. It is designed to take advantage of human binocular vision capabilities and presents the general following characteristics:

- headgear with two small LCD colour screens, each optically channeled to one eye, for binocular vision
- special optics in front of the screens, for wide field of view
- a tracking system (Polhemus 3Space Isotrack) for precise location of the user's head in real time.

2.4 Force transducers and force feedback

Robinett [5] describes how a force feedback subsystem, the Argonne Remote Manipulator (ARM) has been introduced into the Head-Mounted Display project at the University of North Carolina in Chapel Hill. The ARM provides force-feedback through a handgrip with all 6 degrees of freedom in translation and rotation.

Luciani [6] reports several force feedback gestual transducers, including a 16-slice-feedback touch and a two-thimbles, which is a specific morphology to manipulate flat objects. By sliding the fingers in the two rings, objects can be grasped, dragged, or compressed. Moreover, their reaction can be felt, for instance their resistance to deformation or displacement.

Minsky *et al.* [7] study the theoretical problem of force-feedback using a computer controlled joy-stick with simulation of the dynamics of a spring-mass system including its mechanical impedance.

The DataGlove THX™ is a pneumatic tactile feedback glove. The DataGlove TSR™ is lined with force sensitive resistors (FSRs) on its inner surfaces. When real objects are grasped, a distinct pattern of forces is generated over the FSRs. A stored proportional pressure pattern thus measured can be replayed on the DataGlove THX. The THX contains twenty pressure pads in the same positions as the input glove FSRs, as well as bend sensors. The DataGlove FBX™, announced by VPL Research in summer 1991, is a force feedback glove. It is fitted with micro-actuators producing force feedback to multiple fingers.

2.5   Real-time video input

Input video is now a standard tool for many workstations. However, it generally takes a long time (several seconds) to get a complete picture, which makes the tool useless for real-time interaction. For real-time interaction and animation purposes, images should be digitized at the traditional video frame rate. One of the possibilities for doing this is the Living Video Digitizer (LVD) or VideoLab from Silicon Graphics. With the LVD or VideoLab, images are digitized at a frequency of 25 Hz (PAL) or 30 Hz (NTSC) and may be analysed by the animation program.

2.6   Real-time audio input

Audio input may be also considered as a way of interactively controlling animation. However, it generally implies a real-time speech recognition and natural language processing.

3   The Animation Process

Three-dimensional animation scenes usually contain static objects grouped into a decor and animated objects that change over time according to motion laws. Moreover, scenes are viewed using virtual cameras and they may be lit by synthetic light sources. These cameras and lights may evolve over time as though manipulated by cameramen. To create all the entities and motions, coordinate and synchronize them, known collectively as choreography, it is necessary to know the appearance of the scene at this time and then computer graphics techniques allow us to build and display the scene according to viewing and lighting parameters. The problems to solve are how to express time dependence in the scene, and how to make it evolve over time. Scenes involving synthetic actors imply more complex problems to manage. Human-like synthetic actors have a very irregular shape which is hard to build especially for well-known personalities. Once the initial human shape has been created, this shape should change during the animation. This is a very complex problem to ensure the continuity and the realism of the deformed surfaces. The human animation is very complex and should be split into body motion control and facial animation. Basically, a synthetic actor is structured as an articulated body defined by a skeleton. Skeleton animation consists in animating joint angles. There are two main ways to do that: parametric keyframe animation and physics-based animation. An ultimate objective therefore is to model human facial anatomy exactly including its movements to satisfy both structural and functional aspects of simulation.

During the creating process, the animator should enter a lot of data into the computer. The input data may be of various types:

- *geometric*: 3D positions, 3D orientations, trajectories, shapes, deformations
- *kinematics*: velocities, accelerations, gestures
- *dynamics*: forces and torques in physics-based animation
- lights and colours
- sounds
- commands.

Table 11.1 shows VR devices with corresponding input data.

4 Classification of VR-based Methods for Animation

4.1 Real-time rotoscopy methods

Traditional *rotoscopy* in animation consists of recording the motion by a specific device for each frame and using this information to generate the image by computer. For example, a human walking motion may be recorded and then applied to a computer generated 3D character. This off-line approach will provide a very good motion, because it comes directly from reality. However, it does not bring any new concept to animation methodology, and for any new motion, it is necessary to record the reality again.

We call a *real-time rotoscopy method* a method consisting of recording input data

Table 11.1 VR devices with corresponding input data.

VR device	input data	application
DataGlove	positions, orientations, trajectories, gestures, commands,	hand animation
DataSuit	body positions, gestures	body animation
6D mouse	positions, orientations	shape creation, keyframe
SpaceBall	positions, orientations, forces	camera motion
MIDI keyboard	multi-dimensional data	facial animation
Stereo display	3D perception	camera motion, positioning
Head-mounted display (EyePhone)	camera positions and trajectories	camera motion
Force transducers	forces, torques	physics-based animation
Real-time video input	shapes	facial animation
Real-time audio input	sounds, speech	facial animation (speech)

from a VR device in real time allowing us to apply at the same time the same data to a graphics object on the screen. For example, when the animator opens the fingers 3 cm, the hands on the screen do exactly the same.

4.2   Real-time direct metaphors

We call a *real-time direct metaphor* a method consisting of recording input data from a VR device in real time allowing us to produce effects of different nature but corresponding to the input data. There is no analysis of the meaning of the input data. For example, when the animator presses the fourteenth key on a MIDI synthesizer, the synthetic actor's face on the screen opens his mouth according to the pressure on the key.

An example of traditional metaphor is puppet control. A puppet may be defined as a doll with jointed limbs moved by wires or strings. Similarly glove-puppets are dolls of which the body can be put on the hand like a glove, the arms and head being moved by the fingers of the operator. In both cases, human fingers are used to drive the motion of the puppet.

A strange situation that we have experimented with consists in driving a virtual hand using the DataGlove. The virtual hand moves the strings of a puppet. When we consider the motion of the virtual hand, it is a typical real-time rotoscopy method, but the animation of the puppet from the DataGlove is a typical real-time direct metaphor.

The relationship between the VR device and the animated motion is not as straightforward as one might think. Usually, some sort of mathematical function or 'filter' has to be placed between the raw 3D input device data and the resulting motion parameters.

4.3   Real-time recognition-based metaphors

We call a *real-time recognition-based metaphor* a method consisting of recording input data from a VR device in real time. The input data are analysed. Based on the meaning of the input data, a corresponding directive is executed. For example, when the animator opens the fingers 3 cm, the synthetic actor's face on the screen opens his mouth 3 cm. The system has recognized the gesture and interpreted the meaning.

4.4   The ball and mouse metaphor

In essence, *motion parallax* consists of the human brain's ability to render a three-dimensional mental picture of an object simply from the way it moves in relation to the eye. Rotations offer the best results because key positions located on the surface move in a larger variety of directions. Furthermore, in a perspective projection, depth perception is further accentuated by the speed at which features flow in the field of view – points located closer to the eyes move faster than those further away. In a 3D application, if motion parallax is to be used effectively, this implies the need for uninterrupted display of object movements and thus the requirement for hardware capable of very high frame rates. To acquire this depth perception and mobility in a 3D application, we make use of a SpaceBall.

When used in conjunction with a common 2D mouse such that the SpaceBall is held in one hand and the mouse in the other, full three-dimensional user interaction is achieved. The SpaceBall is used to move around the object being manipulated to examine it from various points of view, while the mouse carries out the picking and transformation work onto a magnifying image in order to see every small detail in real time (e.g. vertex creation, primitive selection, surface deformations, cloth panel position, muscle action). In this way, the user not only sees the object from every angle but he can also apply and correct transformations from every angle interactively. To improve our approach using stereo display we also use 'StereoView'.

5   3D Shape Creation

5.1   The sculpting approach

The operations conducted in traditional sculpture can be performed by computer for computer generated objects using a sculpting software [8,9] based on the ball and mouse metaphor. With this type of three-dimensional interaction, the operations performed while sculpting an object closely resemble traditional sculpting. The major operations performed using this software include creation of primitives, selection, local surface deformations and global deformations.

Typically, the sculpting process may be initiated in two ways: by loading and altering an existing shape or by simply starting one from scratch. For example, we will use a sphere as a starting point for the head of a person and use cylinders for limbs. We will then add or remove polygons according to the details needed and apply local deformations to alter the shape. When starting from scratch points are placed in 3D space and polygonized. However, it may be more tedious and time consuming.

To select parts of the objects, the mouse is used in conjunction with the SpaceBall to quickly mark out the desired primitives in and around the object. This amounts to pressing the mouse button and sweeping the mouse cursor on the screen while moving the object with the SpaceBall. All primitives (vertices, edges and polygons) can be selected. Mass picking may be done by moving the object away from the eye (assuming a perspective projection) and careful picking may be done by bringing the object closer.

5.2   Local and global deformations

These tools make it possible to produce local elevations or depressions on the surface, and to even out unwanted bumps once the work is nearing completion. Local deformations are applied while the SpaceBall device is used to move the object and examine the progression of the deformation from different angles, mouse movements on the screen are used to produce vertex movements in 3D space from the current viewpoint. The technique is intended to be a metaphor analogous to pinching, lifting and moving of a stretchable fabric material. Pushing the apex vertex inwards renders a believable effect of pressing a mould into clay. These tools also make it possible to produce global deformations on the whole object or some of the selected regions. For example, if the object has to grow in a certain direction, this can be obtained by scaling or shifting the object on the region of interest.

Pentland *et al.* [10] describe a modelling system, ThingWorld, based on virtual sculpting by modal forces. In the current system, the user specifies forces by use of slider controls, which vary the amount of pinching, squashing, bending, etc., force.

6   3D Paths for Camera Motion

6.1   Metaphors for camera control

One of the most important effects in computer generated films is the virtual camera motion. We may consider several real-time direct metaphors for controlling camera motion. We may separate these metaphors into kinematics-based metaphors and dynamics-based metaphors.

Ware and Osborne [11] describe three kinematics-based metaphors for moving through environments:

- *the eyeball in hand*: this technique involves the use of the Polhemus as a virtual video camera which can be moved about the virtual scene
- *the scene in hand*: the scene is made to move in correspondence with the bat. It is akin to having an invisible mechanical linkage which converts all hand translations and rotations into translations and rotations of the scene.
- *the flying vehicle control*: the bat is used as a control device for a virtual vehicle. The virtual environment is perceived from this vehicle.

Other kinematics-based metaphors have been tested in our laboratory:

- *the virtual sphere metaphor*: the virtual camera is considered as placed on the surface of a sphere centered on the interest point and with a variable radius. The Polhemus is used to control the sphere rotation and the translation is performed using a dial
- *a variant of the flying vehicle control* consists of positioning the camera on a plane with the normal controlled by the pen of the Polhemus placed on the animator's head
- *the airplane metaphor*: the camera is considered as always moving forward, the mouse allows rotations around horizontal axes, rotations around the vertical axis are performed using a dial. The velocity of the camera is controlled by another dial. The Polhemus is used to control the view direction. This metaphor allows the displacement of the camera in one direction while looking in another direction.

Mackinlay *et al*. [12] propose the key idea of having the animator indicate a point of interest (target) on a 3D object and using the distance to this target to move the viewpoint logarithmically by moving the same relative percentage of distance to the target on every animation cycle.

6.2   Kinematics and dynamics direct metaphors for camera control

For non-physically-based motion control, we developed ANIMATOR, a 3D interactive program allowing the creation of animation of several entities: objects, cameras and lights. For each entity, a 3D path may be interactively generated using the SpaceBall. The trajectory is generated using a spline. The animator may build the complete hierarchy of entities using only the mouse, then the animation is created by defining paths. These paths may be generated in 3D using the SpaceBall. Time information is defined by control points. The trajectory is then generated using B-splines.

Turner *et al*. [13] describe how naturalistic interaction and realistic-looking motion is achieved by using a physically-based model of the virtual camera's behaviour. In this approach an abstract physical model of the camera is created, using the laws of classical mechanics to simulate the virtual camera motion in real time in response to force data from the various 3D input devices. The behaviour of the model is determined by several physical parameters such as mass, moment of inertia, and various friction coefficients which can all be varied interactively, and by constraints on the camera's degrees of freedom which can be simulated by setting certain friction parameters to very high values. This allows us to explore a continuous range of physically-based metaphors for controlling the camera motion. A physically-based camera control model provides a powerful, general-purpose metaphor for controlling virtual cameras in interactive 3D environments. When used with force-calibrated input devices, the camera metaphor can be reproduced exactly on different hardware and software platforms, providing a predictable standard interactive 'feel'. Obviously, pressure-sensitive input devices are usually more appropriate because they provide a passive form of 'force-feedback'. In our case, the device that gave the best results is the SpaceBall. Plate XIII shows how to inspect an object.

6.3 A real-time rotoscopy method for camera control

For a car moving across a city, one good approach is the use of a SpaceBall to drive the camera. But, this type of approach is not necessarily appropriate for somebody walking in an apartment. The use of the EyePhone allows the animator to really live the scene which he enters. By recording the position/orientation of the sensor, we get the trajectory. For example, to pan across the virtual world the user just turns his head.

6.4 Coupling virtual real cameras

A related research is the dynamic coupling between a virtual camera and a real camera. For example, Fellous [14] explains how the position/orientation of a real camera may be sent to a workstation and used as the current position/orientation of the virtual camera. There is no direct application in pure computer animation, but this may solve the key problem for mixing real and synthetic images.

7 Skeleton Animation

One of the most important categories of figures in computer animation is the articulated figure. There are three ways of animating these linked figures:

1. By recreating the tools used by traditional animators.
2. By simulating the physical laws which govern motion in the real world.
3. By simulating the behavioural laws which govern the interaction between the objects.

The first approach corresponds to methods heavily relied upon by the animator: rotoscopy, parametric keyframe animation. The second way guarantees a realistic motion by using kinematics and dynamics (see Plate XIV). The problem with this type of animation is controlling the motion produced. The third type of animation is called behavioural animation and takes into account the relationship between each object and the other objects. Moreover, the control of animation may be performed at a task-level.

In summary, at a time *t*, the methods for calculating a 3D scene are as follows:

1. For a keyframe system: by interpolating the values of parameters at given key times.
2. In a dynamic-based system: by calculating the positions from the motion equations obtained with forces and torques.
3. For a behavioural animation system: by automatic planning of the motion of the figure on information about the environment (decor and other objects).

From an 3D input point of view, in a keyframe system positions may be entered using, for example, a SpaceBall and angles may be calculated by inverse kinematics. In a dynamic-based system, the natural types of input data are forces and torques. For behavioural animation, natural language is the most natural interface and an audio-input may improve the communication.

8   Hand Motion

Hand motion is a specific case of animation of articulated bodies. In this section, we present two very different uses of a DataGlove that we have experimented with in our laboratory.

8.1   A real-time rotoscopy method for hand animation

This gesture-oriented animation system [15] consists basically of two programs: GESTURE LAB, which enables an animator to record, playback and edit real hand movements using a DataGlove, and VOGE (VOice + GEsture), a program which accepts a monologue script consisting of phrases, emphasis and rhythm parameters, and gesture names to generate an animation sequence in which lip and hand movements are synchronized according to the specification. The output of VOGE is fed into the human animation system to obtain the final animation scene. The DataGlove is used in GESTURE LAB to measure the angles from the metacarpophalangeal joints. The user can select a previously recorded sequence to be played, and insert a part of this sequence in a new one, or perform a live recording using the DataGlove. There is a possibility of setting timers to have precise control over the duration and starting point of a playback or live performance. Even if the current version of GESTURE LAB only allows the recording of the performance of a hand, there is nothing to stop its extension for full body movement sampling using a DataSuit for example.

8.2   Hand gesture recognition

The purpose of hand gesture recognition is the association of meanings to the various configurations of the hand and its movements. A current approach in our laboratory is the use of a learning process to obtain this type of recognition. There are two stages in the process of recognition:

- the recognition of static hand configurations
- the recognition of movements considered as series of configurations over time.

For these recognition processes, an efficient way consists of using Kohonen neural networks, because of their efficiency in recognition tasks, their ability to learn to recognize and the possibility to take advantage of the parallelism. To classify postures (static configurations) MLP (Multi-Layer Perception) neural networks may be applied to provide a correspondence between the activations of the neurons of the Kohonen network and the types of gestures associated. However, the most important and difficult aspect is the recognition of gestures. Gestures are temporal sequences of hand configurations. Their recognition is a more complex task than posture recognition because it is necessary to take into account the motion history. Neural networks are also a natural way of solving this problem.

9 Facial Animation

9.1 A facial animation system

Computer simulation of human facial expressions requires an interactive ability to create arbitrary faces and to provide a controlled simulation of expressions on these faces. A complete simulation system should ensure synchronization of eye motion, expression of emotion and word flow of a sentence, as well as synchronization between several actors. A complete example is our SMILE facial animation system [16]. This system is based on a methodology for specifying facial animation based on a multi-layered approach. Each successive layer defines entities from a more abstract point of view, starting with muscle deformations, and working up through phonemes, words, sentences, expressions and emotions.

9.2 Direct control of muscular deformations

At the lowest level, to simulate the muscle action on the skin surface of the human face, we developed a 3D interactive system (see Plate XV) to define regions on the face mesh which correspond to the anatomical description of the facial region on which a muscle action is desired. Plate XVI shows an example. In this system, based on the ball and mouse metaphor, a parallelepiped control unit can be defined on the region of interest. The deformations which are obtained by actuating muscles to stretch, squash, expand and compress the inside volume of the facial geometry, are simulated by displacing the control point and by changing the weights of the control points of the control unit. The region inside the control unit deforms like a flexible volume, corresponding to the displacement and the weights of the control points. Displacing a control point is analogous to adding a muscle vector to the control unit. Specifying the displacement of the control point is, however, more intuitive and simpler to simulate the muscle vectors. In addition, the result matches the natural notion of muscles acting on that region. For example, a depressor muscle would need squashing the control point inside the control unit, and a pulling muscle would be interpreted as pulling the control points away from the control unit. To propagate the deformations of regions to the adjoining regions, linear interpolation can be used to decide the deformation of the boundary points. Higher order interpolation schemes can also be used, however, the movements in the face are rather small, higher ordered discontinuities arising may not affect so much the visual aspects.

For facial deformations, we use Rational Free Form Deformations (RFFD) [17], which is an extension of Free Form Deformation (FFD), a technique for deforming solid geometric models in a free form manner [18].

9.3   Facial animation control using a MIDI synthesizer or DataGlove

Direct manipulation of muscular deformations may also be performed in real time using multi-dimensional data input devices. The two best devices for this purpose are the MIDI keyboard and the DataGlove.

9.4   Video and speech input

Another approach consists of recording a real human face using a video input like the VideoLab or LVD and extracting from the image the information necessary to generate similar facial expressions on a synthetic face. This is a typical rotoscopy method. The problem with this approach is that the image analysis is not easy to perform in real time. We are experimenting on such an approach using snakes [19].

To specify sentences to be pronounced by a virtual actor, a direct speech input is certainly a good solution.

10   Physics-Based Animation and Force-Feedback Devices

10.1   Dynamic simulation

Kinematics-based systems are generally intuitive and lack dynamic integrity. The animation does not seem to respond to basic physical facts like gravity or inertia. Only modelling of objects that move under the influence of forces and torques can be realistic. Forces and torques cause linear and angular accelerations. The motion is obtained by the dynamic equations of motion. These equations are established using the forces, the torques, the constraints and the mass properties of objects.

A typical example is the motion of an articulated figure which is governed by forces and torques applied to limbs. There are three advantages of introducing dynamics into animation control:

- natural phenomena can be rendered with more reality
- dynamics free the animator from having to describe the motion in terms of the physical properties of the solid objects
- bodies can react automatically to internal and external environmental constraints: fields, collisions, forces and torques.

There are also serious disadvantages: the motion is too regular and it is time-consuming. But the main problem is a problem of user interface. Typically, a hierarchy is built first, then internal parameters are set until the desired effect is obtained. This is a severe limitation, because it means that systems are hard for the animator to control. Parameters (e.g. forces or torques) are sometimes very difficult to adjust, because they are not intuitive. For a car, it is easy to choose the parameters of a spring or of a shock absorber, it is more difficult to adjust those used to simulate the equivalent forces and torques produced by muscle contractions and tensions in an animated figure. The animator does not think in terms of forces or torques to apply to a limb or the body to perform a motion.

10.2   Using force-feedback systems in dynamic simulation

A solution to the above problem is to introduce a way of communicating forces and torques to the virtual object. However, force prescribed systems will be effective when forces transducers are intensively introduced in computer animation.

Consider, for example, the problem of modelling the deformations of human flesh due to contact with objects. Gourret *et al.* [20] propose a method based on finite element theory for calculating deformations when a hand grasps and presses a ball. The natural way of entering hand forces into the system is by using a force-feedback system.

Iwata [21] describes a force-feedback system with a 9 degree-of-freedom manipulator developed as a tactile input device with reaction force generator. A solid model handler has been developed for manipulating virtual objects using the manipulator. A virtual hand is displayed corresponding to the manipulator. The contact of the virtual hand with virtual objects is detected at 16 control points. The generated forces are calculated according to the solidity of the captured object.

11   A VR-Based Animation System

11.1   The animation system

We are currently developing in cooperation with MIRALab, University of Geneva, a complete three-dimensional animation system based on VR-animation. The main objective of the project is the animation of synthetic actors in their environment. In particular, the following animation applications are being developed:

- animation of articulated bodies based on mechanical laws
- vision-based behavioural animation
- hair rendering [22] and animation (see Plate XVII)
- object grasping
- facial animation
- personification in walking models (see Plates XVIII and XIX)
- synchronization in task-level animation
- deformation of flexible and elastic objects
- cloth animation [23] with detection of collision (see Plate XX).

In the current version, several applications provide a user interface based on VR devices:

- the sculpting program SURFMAN
- the muscle and expression editor in the SMILE facial animation system
- the program to create 3D paths for cameras, objects and light sources
- the hand gesture recording system in GESTURE LAB
- a communication program animator-actor (in development).

The first two programs are mainly based on the ball and mouse metaphor described earlier. SURFMAN may also take advantage of StereoView and the 3D Polhemus digitizer. Hand gestures are recorded using the DataGlove and 3D paths are mainly generated using the SpaceBall. We are developing a way of creating camera paths based on the EyePhone. The communication program animator-actor uses the Living Video Digitizer to capture the animator face and the DataGlove for gesture recognition.

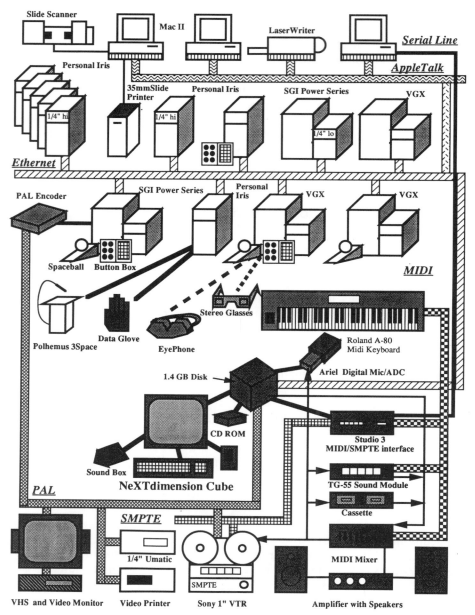

Figure 11.1 Swiss Federal Institute of Technology, Computer Graphics Laboratory system diagram.

11.2   Hardware and software

Our lab consists of a network of Silicon Graphics IRIS, a NeXT computer and VR devices including EyePhone, DataGloves, SpaceBalls, StereoView, a Polhemus digitizer, video input/output and a MIDI and audio equipment. As shown in Fig.

11.1, every piece of equipment is now connected to the network. Research is conducted in cooperation with the MIRALab group, at the University of Geneva, who possess about the same equipment. The software is based on the 5th Dimension toolkit [24] and a InterProcess Communication (IPC) library developed in the laboratory and built on top of the standard BSD Unix socket interprocess communication routines. The 5D toolkit implements a traditional 2D widget set integrated with a set of 3D graphical classes and non-conventional input device classes for encapsulating the behaviour of the various input devices. An interactive interface builder has been also developed. The IPC library allows all devices and processes in the laboratory to communicate with each other in real time.

12 Conclusion

For a few years, computer animation has tended to be more and more based on physics and dynamic simulation methods. With the advent of VR devices and superworkstations, brute force methods such as rotoscopy-like methods tend to come back. In the future, real-time complex animation systems will be developed taking advantage of VR devices and simulation methods. This development will be only possible by developing new approaches to real-time motion. In particular, developments should involve the following concepts: parallelism, neural nets, distributed animation, simplification of structures [25] and pseudo-physics.

Acknowledgements

The author would like to thank Russel Turner for the design of Fig. 11.1 and Arghyro Paouri and Agnes Daldegan for the design of several colour plates. The research was sponsored by Le Fonds National Suisse pour la Recherche Scientifique.

References

1 Balaguer, F. and Mangili, A. 1991. Virtual environments. In N. Magnenat-Thalmann and D. Thalmann, editors, *New Trends in Animation and Visualization*. John Wiley, 91–106.
2 Brooks, F.P., Jr. 1986. Walkthrough – A dynamic graphics system for simulating virtual buildings. *Proc. Workshop on Interactive 3-D Graphics*, 9–22.
3 Fisher, S.S., McGreevy, M., Humphries, J. and Robinett, W. 1986. Virtual environment display system. *Proc. Workshop on Interactive 3-D Graphics*, 77–87.
4 Ware, C. and Jessome, D.R. 1988. Using the bat: a six dimensional mouse for object placement. *Proc. Graphics Interface '88*, 119–124.
5 Robinett, W. 1991. Head-mounted display project. *Proc. Imagina '91*, 5.5–5.6.
6 Luciani, A. 1990. Physical models in animation: Towards a modular and instrumental approach, *Proc. 2nd Eurographics Workshop on Animation and Simulation*, Lausanne, Switzerland, G1–G20.
7 Minsky, M., Ouh-young, M., Steele, O., Brooks, F.P. Jr. and Behensky, M. 1990. Feeling and seeing: Issues in force display. *Proc. Workshop on Interactive 3-D Graphics*, 235–243.
8 LeBlanc, A., Turner, R. and Magnenat Thalmann, N. 1991. Rendering hair

using pixel blending and shadow buffers. *J. Visualization and Computer Animation*, **2** (3): 92–96.

9   Paouri, A., Magnenat Thalmann, N. and Thalmann, D. 1991. Creating realistic three-dimensional human shape characters for computer-generated films. *Proc. Computer Animation '91*, Geneva. Springer-Verlag, 89–100.

10 Pentland, A., Essa, I., Friedmann, M., Horowitz, B. and Sclaroff, S. 1990. The ThingWorld modeling system: Virtual sculpting by modal forces. *Proc. Workshop on Interactive 3-D Graphics*, 143–144.

11 Ware, C. and Osborne, S. 1990. Exploration and virtual camera control in virtual three dimensional environments. *Computer Graphics*, **24** (2): 175–183.

12 Mackinlay, J.D., Card, S.K. and Robertson, G. 1990. Rapid controlled movement through a virtual 3-D workspace. *Computer Graphics*, **24** (4): 171–176.

13 Turner, R., Balaguer, F., Gobbetti, E. and Thalmann, D. 1991. Physically-based interactive camera motion control using 3-D input devices. In Patrikalakis, N., editor, *Scientific Visualization of Physical Phenomena*. Springer-Verlag, 135–145.

14 Fellous, A. 1991. Synthetic TV. *Proc. Imagina '91*, 5.47–5.52.

15 Mato Mira, F. 1991. *ICSC World Laboratory LAND-5 Project*. Computer Graphics Lab, Swiss Federal Institute of Technology, Lausanne, Switzerland.

16 Kalra, P., Mangili, A., Magnenat-Thalmann, N. and Thalmann, D. 1991. SMILE: a multilayered facial animation system. *Proc. IFIP Conference on Modelling in Computer Graphics*, Springer-Verlag, 189–198.

17 Kalra, P., Mangili, A., Magnenat-Thalmann, N. and Thalmann, D. 1992. Simulation of facial muscle actions based on rational free form deformations. *Proc. Eurographics '92*, Cambridge, UK.

18 Sederberg, T.W. and Parry, S.R. 1986. Free-form deformation of solid geometric models. *Proc. SIGGRAPH '86, Computer Graphics*, **20** (4): 151–160.

19 Terzopoulos, D. and Waters, K. 1991. Techniques for facial modeling and animation. In Magnenat Thalmann, N. and Thalmann, D., editors, *Computer Animation '91*. Springer-Verlag, 59–74.

20 Gourret, J.P., Magnenat Thalmann, N. and Thalmann, D. 1989. Simulation of object and human skin deformations in a grasping task. *Proc. SIGGRAPH '89*.

21 Iwata, H. 1990. Artificial reality with force-feedback: Development of desktop virtual space with compact-master manipulator. *Proc. SIGGRAPH '90, Computer Graphics*, **24** (4): 165–170.

22 LeBlanc, A., Kalra, P., Magnenat-Thalmann, N. and Thalmann, D. 1991. Sculpting with the "Ball & Mouse" metaphor. *Proc. Graphics Interface '91*, Calgary, Canada.

23 Carignan, M., Yang, Y., Magnenat Thalmann, N. and Thalmann, D. 1992. Dressing animated synthetic actors with complex deformable clothes, *Proc. SIGGRAPH '92*.

24 Turner, R., Gobbetti, E., Balaguer, F., Mangili, A., Thalmann, D. and Magnenat Thalmann, N. 1990. An Object-Oriented Methodology Using Dynamic Variables for Animation and Scientific Visualization", *Proc. Computer Graphics International '90*. Springer-Verlag, Tokyo, 317–328.

25 Moccozet, L. and Magnenat Thalmann, N. 1991. Controlling the complexity of objects based on polygonal meshes. *Proc. Computer Graphics International '92*. Springer-Verlag, 763–779.

Biography

Daniel Thalmann is currently Professor, Head of the Computer Science Department, and Director of the Computer Graphics Laboratory at the Swiss Federal Institute of Technology in Lausanne, Switzerland. He is also Adjunct Professor at the University of Montreal, Canada. Since 1977, he has been Professor at the University of Montreal and codirector of the MIRALab research laboratory. He received his diploma in nuclear physics and PhD in computer science from the University of Geneva. He is coeditor-in-chief of the *Journal of Visualization and Computer Animation*, a member of the editorial board of the *Visual Computer* and *CADDM Journal* and cochairs the EUROGRAPHICS Working Group on Computer Simulation and Animation. Daniel Thalmann's research interests include 3D computer animation, virtual reality and image synthesis. He has published more than 100 papers in these areas, and is coauthor of several books, including *Computer Animation: Theory and Practice* and *Image Synthesis: Theory and Practice*. He is also codirector of several computer-generated films.

12 Dynamic FishEye Information Visualizations

Kim Michael Fairchild, Luis Serra,
Ng Hern, Lee Beng Hai and
Ang Tin Leong
Institute of Systems Science, National University of Singapore

Abstract

Recent advances in virtual reality technology suggest that encoding subsets of information using multimedia techniques and placing the resultant visualizations into a perceptual three-dimensional space increases the amount of information that people can meaningfully manage. For this approach to be successful, three basic problems must be addressed. First, how should individual pieces of information be encoded into visualizations? Secondly, assuming that reasonable visualizations exist for single pieces, how do these visualizations extend to large collections of these individual pieces? Thirdly, since all the pieces of information in large information bases cannot be shown to information professionals at one time, techniques must be available to allow user control of the subsets of the entire information presented at any one time. This paper describes theoretical solutions to these problems, as well as describing the *VizNet* prototype which demonstrates the solutions.

1 Introduction

Computers have made it possible to manipulate larger and larger amounts of information, but humans are cognitively ill-suited for understanding the resulting complexity. The information is all readily available, but users are unable to efficiently access individual items or maintain a global context of how the information fits together.

Recent advances in *virtual reality* technology suggest that encoding subsets of the information using multimedia techniques and placing the resultant visualizations into a perceptual three-dimensional space increases the amount of information that people can meaningfully manage [1,2].

Extending this work, an appropriate approach would be the creation of a visualization engine that could easily take just about any collection of abstract information and create a virtual reality-based visualization. This space, containing the visualized objects, would be available for one or more users to navigate while examining individual and clusters of objects in more detail. If a particular visualization is not appropriate for a particular user on a particular task, the user could immediately create a more suitable visualization.

For this approach to be successful, three basic problems must be addressed. First, how should individual pieces of information be encoded into visualizations? Secondly, assuming that reasonable visualizations exist for single pieces, how do these visualizations extend to large collections of these individual pieces? Thirdly, since all the pieces of information in large information bases cannot be shown to information professionals at one time, techniques must be available to allow user control of the subsets of the entire information presented at any one time.

This paper further describes the problems that must be addressed to exploit virtual reality technology for information management. It is organized in two parts: the first part describes the problems and solutions from a theoretical standpoint and the second part describes how the solutions have been implemented in the *VizNet* prototype.

2   Requirements

The central problem to be addressed is what can be done when there is just too much information to deal with. With some collections of information, the traditional node-link graph structure visualization can be used, but for modern real-world problems which require users to understand large collections of information, solutions must be found for managing the large amounts of complex information. This problem can be decomposed into three sub-problems: how to make meaningful visualizations of single objects; how to make meaningful visualizations of collections of objects; and how to allow the users to efficiently control the selection of the visualizations.

2.1   Visualization of a single complex object

Users are cognitively limited in their ability to understand multimedia encodings of the semantic information of objects. For example, the *x-y-z* position of an object might encode the object's creation date, importance, and complexity. The shape and colour might encode the type and creator of the object. Although a rich variety of additional encoding schemes are possible (i.e. sound, video, bitmaps, multiple shapes, texture, text), humans are cognitively ill-suited for readily understanding much more complex encodings [3].

Therefore, the requirement is for a model that can encode any type of semantic information into any of the available multimedia techniques. Since each object may have too much information to visualize in a single visualization, only subsets of the semantic information can be encoded at any one time. Since all or any part of the semantic information might be required for particular tasks, the visualization must be able to dynamically change to use different subsets of information.

2.2   Visualization of a large collection of complex objects

Even if appropriate visualizations can be found for individual elements, there are just too many pieces of information to be able to see all at once. The general solution to this problem is to develop models of *degrees of interest* (DOI) or *FishEye* views. FishEye views contain a mixture of objects with high and low levels of detail [4].

The DOI model associates two values with each object: *semantic distance* and *degree of interest*. The semantic distance is a measure of how far the viewpoint is away from the object. The degree of interest is a measure of how important an object is to the user.

The 'New Yorker's View of the World' is one of the most famous FishEye views. In this famous New Yorker cover, the mailbox in front of a New Yorker's house is shown in high detail, as well as some of the stores. Next the Hudson river and Brooklyn are shown in less detail. All the states between New York and California are skipped and the visualization ends with just labels demarcating Japan and China.

Perspective in our real world is another example of a limited FishEye view. It is limited in the sense that all objects have the same DOI value. As the euclidean distance to objects increases, their apparent size decreases. If the objects had different DOI values, similarly physically sized objects seen at the same distance would not necessarily appear the same size.

Therefore, the requirement is for a model that allows the automatic assignment of semantic distance and DOI to all objects in a visual scene. This results in some objects being shown with higher information content than other objects.

2.3   User definition of visualizations

Despite the promise of *natural interaction*, perhaps due to the immature state of VR devices, VR interfaces have yet to advance from the 'you can pick things up' and 'point the way you want to go' level of interactions.

In addition to overcoming these limitations in user interaction in VRs, development of VR space for information management requires two additional interaction methods. As described above, users must be able to both efficiently define the encodings of subsets of the individual object semantics to visualizations, and define the subsets of objects that should be shown in higher *information fidelity*.

3   Specifications

From these requirements come specifications that define a flexible object visualization model, a complexity management model, and a new interaction style suitable for virtual reality applications.

3.1   Visualizations of a single complex object

The problem is shown in Fig. 12.1. Complex objects such as information about a person contain a large collection of semantic properties. This information can be encoded using many of the multimedia primitives now available on modern computers, but the particular encodings used depend on the user and the tasks that user wishes to perform with the information.

A mechanism is needed to select a coherent subset of semantic properties and encode them into a multimedia shape. Each of the multimedia properties of the icon thus represents and reflects some combination of the semantic values of the original object.

For instance, if a visualization of the information is required in a typical hierarchical

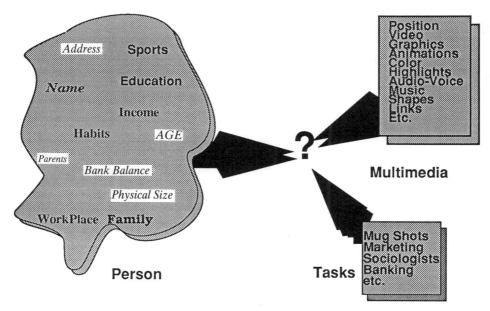

Figure 12.1 Visualization of a single complex object.

file system, the data available might include information on the size of the file, the person who created the file, the type (text, source code, executable, etc.), how often the file has been referenced by various people, where the file is located, etc. Semantic values obtainable from this data could be a measure of the file's importance to a particular person, its relationship to other files, a measure of completeness or usefulness, etc. A visualization of the file might associate colour with its importance (red meaning very important), completeness with the size of the icon, and usefulness might determine the position on the display.

Since preparing encoded representations of abstract information has traditionally been difficult and since users vary greatly in their needs for visualizations, the *AutoIcon* [5] model is used for allowing end-user control of the mapping between the semantic space of objects and a multimedia visualization. The AutoIcon model defines a representation and a user editing paradigm allows the mapping of semantic information into multimedia visualizations.

The AutoIcon components shown in Fig. 12.2 consist of four subparts: *semantics*, *normalization*, *graphic vector*, and *graphic object*. These parts in sequence produce a vector with the semantic values for a particular object, normalize these values, find the entry these values have in a vector of graphic shapes and then construct the encoded iconic shape.

The output from each component is a vector and the functions within each component are defined as a vector of vectors. The implementation of the AutoIcon model intentionally relies heavily on the manipulation of vectors. This allows the same functionality that focuses on vector manipulation to be useful for user editing of all the components of AutoIcons.

The user may apply different AutoIcons consecutively to collections of information

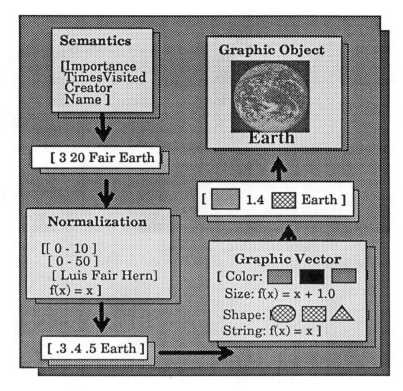

Figure 12.2 The automatic icon model.

to produce dramatically different views. For instance, changing the AutoIcon may produce views similar to the SemNet [6], Cone Tree [1], and Perspective Wall [7] views. The contents in Plate XXI demonstrate a view similar to a Cone Tree view.

3.2 Visualizations of large collections of complex objects

If objects are placed into a three-dimensional display as opposed to a two-dimensional display, the perceived complexity of the information is reduced. This can be further reduced by using a head-mounted display to create a virtual space.

This spatial metaphor allows users to see part of the information within a restricted viewing angle when looking in a particular direction from the viewpoint. The user is able to concentrate on the subset of objects within this viewing angle. Moreover, the perspective view makes objects nearer the viewpoint appear larger, helping the user to examine local neighbourhoods more effectively (Fig. 12.3a).

These local neighbourhoods will be understandable only if related elements are within the same neighbourhood. In other words, proximity in semantic space should correspond to proximity in the euclidean space. In general, however, it is not mathematically possible to achieve perfect correspondence between proximity in arbitrary graph structures and proximity in three-dimensional euclidean space, so AutoIcons provide for the initial placement of the objects in the virtual space and a DOI function provides for the distortion of the original space to reflect design

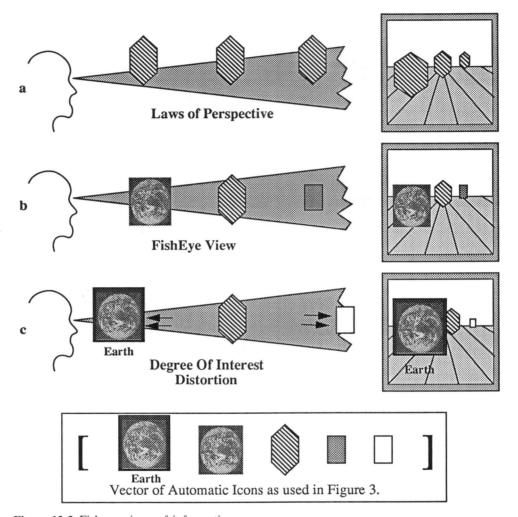

Figure 12.3 Fisheye views of information.

task requirements of the users. The DOI function provides a FishEye view (Fig. 12.3b), instead of just growing larger as an object gets closer to the user, the object increases in *information fidelity* as well. The total amount of information encoded into the iconic shape increases as the object becomes more important to the observer. When an object is currently not close to the observer's viewing location and when the object is not considered very important, only a small set of the semantic information about the object is encoded. But when this is not true, the object is either important or close to the viewing location, more of the semantic information is encoded in the iconic shape.

The DOI_{Index} value is used to index into a vector of AutoIcons to determine which AutoIcon to use for the visualizations. For instance, in the simple example (Fig. 12.3), the vector of AutoIcons has five members, the first AutoIcon produces a bitmap with a label and a colour coding, the second produces a bitmap, the third produces a textured shape, the fourth produces a square with colour information and the fifth merely shows that something is there.

Assuming a constant *a priori importance* (API) value for all three shapes and the semantic distance (SD) that corresponds to euclidean distance, a formula such as the following determines the AutoIcon used:

$$DOI_{Index} = Integer((SD + (0.5 - API) \times 2) \times VectorLength)$$

Where the API and Semantic Distance (SD) are normalized (0..1). Vector Length is the length of the AutoIcon Vector.

For example, if an object is of SD = 0.5 and API = 0.5 (the default values), then the middle index of the AutoIcon vector is used. If the API = 1.0, no matter what the semantic distance from the observer, the lowest index (i.e. 0, typically the highest information fidelity) will be used.

An improvement of FishEye views can be achieved by distorting the positions of the object in a space (Fig. 12.3c). Objects with a high degree of interest move towards the user while objects with a low degree of interest move away from the user.

The amount of distortion or movement can be given by this simple formula:

$$Distortion = (DOI - 0.5) \times DegreeOfDistortion$$

3.3   User definition of visualizations

There are two important interaction tasks that need to be accomplished by the users. First, the user must be able to *navigate* within the virtual space to dynamically define areas of interest. Several navigation methods were described and evaluated in Fairchild *et al.* [6] and are listed in Table 12.1. Many such methods exist but none are generally useful so new ones must be developed.

The second task is to allow end-users to develop their task specific visualizations efficiently.

Earlier information management prototypes like SemNet and Cone Tree views concentrated on finding appropriate positions for objects and then providing tools for moving the viewpoint.[1]

As described in the previous section, the problems of complexity management require the definition of multiple encodings of information. It might be possible that for a given task domain all the required encodings could be pre-defined by programmers, but to allow the system to be more flexible and extendable, methods must exist for allowing end-user definition of new visualizations.

In general, this would provide the users with an interactive style where they still could have control over the positioning of objects in space and allow them to move the viewing location dynamically in the space. Additionally, the models used for

---

[1] Actually, the Cone Tree approach keeps the viewer location static but rotates the objects to bring them towards the viewing location.

Table 12.1 Survey of navigation techniques

Name	Method	Evaluation
Relative	Sequence of small steps	This is method we use in reality, this was found to be the WORST movement method
Absolute	Pointing on a map where we want to go	Very fast method, but not very accurate
Teleportation	Once a position can be named, go to it	Very fast, but need to have been there before
Hyperspace	Follow the links between objects	Useful when the relationships between object is important for the task domain
Transformation	Instead of moving the viewpoint, move the objects desired to the viewpoint	Potentially very powerful, especially to query for reformation, not well understood yet

encoding the semantic information into the icon shapes can either be switched to entirely new models or iteratively modified from the current model.

What is needed is a new navigation paradigm that allows end-users to efficiently describe automatic icons as described above. This interface paradigm that shows promise for modifying automatic icons as well as accomplishing other user interaction tasks in VR systems is called *gesture sequence navigation*.

3.3.1   Gesture sequence navigation

Gesture sequence navigation, based on sequences of a small set of gestures, takes advantage of the human ability to respond rapidly to recognized stimuli. Gestures, specific to each user, allow users to rapidly traverse a semantic network. When the user arrives at a leaf node of the network a stored function is evaluated. This function, depending on the task domain, might do anything from copying a VR object, moving the viewpoint, to changing a visualization.

The initial production and learning of the gesture sequences is supported by automatically generating visualizations (stimuli) that describe the current user location in the network and what the next possible input gestures would accomplish.

After the gesture sequences have been learned, the visualizations are no longer needed. This reserves scarce VR display space solely for VR objects.

Gesture sequence navigation consists of four parts (shown in Fig. 12.4); *response*, *stimulus*, *semantic paths* and *user tasks*.

1.   *Limited Set of Gestures (response)*
The interface only requires the user to input a limited number of gestures. Many input devices can be used to make gestures. The only requirement is that the devices distinguish between some small number of user actions. These devices could include a limited key keyboard, a Polhemus six-degree-of-freedom positioning device, an

eyetracker [8], a tongue controller [9], or a DataGlove [10]. The devices essentially make an *n-way button choice* [11].

2. *Representation of Gestures Sequences (semantic paths)*

Sequences of gestures are represented as a semantic network. The user effectively navigates between connected nodes on this network by performing a gesture sequence. To create new gestures or to make existing gestures easier to perform (by shortening them for instance), the user modifies the network itself using gesture sequences. In essence, the input language is regular and the network is a virtual finite state machine parsing it.

3. *Dynamic Visualization of Gesture State (stimulus)*

Visualizations represent the current state and results of gestures. Since visualizations are the stimuli for the user response, the user may customize and create new visualizations to enhance the recognizability of the stimuli. Additionally, since users are notoriously poor customizers [12], the system is set up to modify the visualizations systematically as it is used. For instance, paths the user has followed before are annotated with appropriate graphics.

4. *Reflexive User Customized System (user tasks)*

To support the user customization of the gesture system, significant parts of the system itself may be modified using gesture input. These include editing the semantic

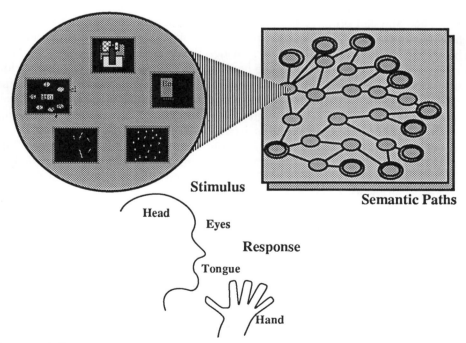

Figure 12.4 Gesture sequence navigation.

network of gestures, adding actions to nodes, creating visualizations of information, and in general, interactively extending the system.

3.3.2   Types of Gestures

There are three types of gestures that can be used to produce user input: absolute, dynamic, and coordinated gestures.

Absolute gestures are the easiest to learn for novices. They rely solely on the input device being in a certain state. For instance, a particular key on a keyboard was pressed or a foot was positioned in a certain spot. This type of gesture could easily be produced by disabled users with devices such as tongue controllers.

Dynamic gestures are tracked in time. For instance, using a two-dimensional mouse, a new node would be selected just because the user has moved towards it for a 'significant' amount of time. As a user learns a sequence of position gestures to get to a desired place, the sequence of position gestures becomes chunked into a single dynamic gesture.

Coordinated gestures use multiple sensors and it is the interaction between the states of the individual sensors over time that define the gesture input. The DataGlove is a device that has been used in this way to recognize the American Sign Language [13] for the deaf.

The user typically moves through a sequence of nodes or *WayPoints*[2] using gestures until a desired object or function is found. A real-time three-dimensional animation shows the movement between WayPoints which aids in the learning of the gesture sequences or *chunked* user inputs [14]. The stimulus to the user takes the form of a visualization of each node which shows the current status of the gesture and where the user will be after the next gesture. When the user has *chunked* the sequence and can produce the required individual gestures in quick succession, the animation speeds up until intermediate WayPoints may no longer be perceivable.

The visualization of the WayPoint provides the stimulus for the users to know where they are in the gesture sequence and where they will be next with the various gesture options. The WayPoint visualization (examples are shown arranged around the edge of Plate XXII) consists of the visualization of several subparts: the links or *branchpoints* to the next WayPoints, the contents of the WayPoint, and any action that will execute when the user arrives at the WayPoint.

The branchpoints in the current WayPoint present information as to what WayPoint or context the user will be in if that branch is taken. The branchpoints are visualized by taking a subset of the semantic information about that WayPoint and encoding it into an iconic form.

4   Combining the Theoretical Solutions

These specifications and their resultant theoretical requirements led to the development of a scenario of use and a general architecture for visualizing information from any application domain. These in turn have led to the ongoing development

---

[2] WayPoint. Originally a term in aviation, a WayPoint is the point on an aviation map that serves as a navigational aid.

of the *VizNet* prototype. In the following two subsections the scenario, architecture and prototype are presented.

4.1   A scenario: a visualization of a visualization system

The solutions to the three requirements described before are shown together in the sample *visualization of a visualization* scene shown in Plate XXI.

There are three distinct regions in this figure that can be easily distinguished from each other by their behaviour when the viewpoint moves.

At the bottom of the plate is an oval containing several tools. This is the *Virtual Toolbelt*, an object that contains tools for manipulating the visualizations and interacting with the space. This toolbelt is attached to the user's waist. As the user moves through the space the toolbelt moves as well.

Around the outside of the plate, shown in blue boxes, are the stimuli for the Gesture Sequence Navigation based interface. These stimuli are fixed in space. In a stereo view of the virtual space they would seem to be two-dimensional overlays on the three-dimensional space. Their appearance changes as users make gesture sequence input. When the user is not making a gesture sequence the stimulus does not appear, thus saving VR display space for other objects.

Finally, the rest of the objects comprise the visualizations of the information. The objects are shown at several degrees of interest. The printout of text on the right side of the plate shows the information in its highest fidelity. It is connected to the red-highlighted round shape on the left side which shows somewhat less information. This object in turn is connected to several other objects that are merely larger versions of the unconnected shapes in the background.

As the user moves through the space, the objects change into other higher or lower resolution visualizations. Objects that have been defined by the user to have higher DOI, distort from their assigned positions and follow the user viewpoint.

4.2   An information visualization architecture

In this subsection the theoretical solutions for addressing the requirements are integrated in a common architecture. In Fig. 12.5, a data flow view of the architecture is presented.

According to the requirements, end-users must be able to adapt the visualization system to new application needs. This requires the system to be able to visualize arbitrary information. For instance, if a corporation wishes to visualize employee records, mechanisms must be in place to allow smooth extension of the system to interact with employee records.

To accomplish this extension, the information is decoupled from the visualization system by a layer called *Surrogate Object Classes*. This is an extendable class hierarchy that implements an access protocol for different application information types. For each type of information that the system visualizes, a class exists in the surrogate object class hierarchy. When a visualization of a new type of information is required, either an existing class *similar* to the new type is modified or a completely new class is written and added to the hierarchy.

Using the appropriate surrogate class, for each application object an *instance of Composite Object* is instantiated. These instances consist of a triple, the original application object, the surrogate object, and an *automatic icon* for generating the

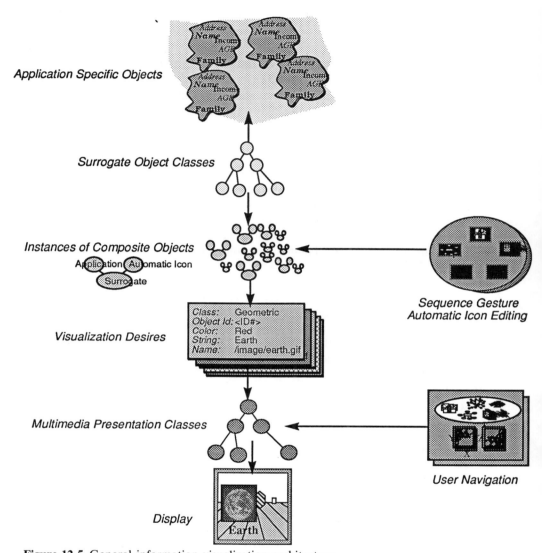

Figure 12.5 General information visualization architecture.

encoded presentation of the object. The particular automatic icon used is determined by the semantic distance of the object from observer and is selected from the automatic icon DOI vector. The automatic icon may also be modified by the user in real time.

The automatic icon is used for generating a table of slots and values for each composite object. These are called *visualization desires* and are sent to a particular class in the *multimedia presentation class* hierarchy. At a minimum these *desires* contain fields for the class in the multimedia presentation class hierarchy and the identification of the composite surrogate object. In the example shown in Fig. 12.5, the values for a string, colour and name are supplied as well.

Each multimedia presentation class implements a particular type of multimedia object; this might be live video, animation, voice, a combination, or anything else a designer has defined. The slot and value pairs are treated as suggestions and might be evaluated differently by different classes. Super classes in the hierarchy define default values for any slots not supplied by the visualization desires.

The users interact with the architecture in two ways: by modifying the values of the automatic icons and by navigating to different viewing positions in the virtual space.

5   VizNet Implementation

5.1   Context

VizNet has been implemented using the tools provided by a multimedia authoring environment called KICK [15]. KICK is a frame-based multimedia toolkit based on the Starship language [16], which includes, among other media objects, modelling and rendering tools for 3D graphics. VizNet has used these tools to construct its visualizations. At the same time, the internal structures of KICK have been used as testing data for VizNet. The internal structure of KICK is made up of multimedia information nodes linked together into hierarchies (class, part-of, etc.), and associations and thus provides an ideal domain to demonstrate the solutions presented in this paper. Each node is modelled as a frame. Frames also model complex links between nodes. Using the internal structures of KICK as test data accomplishes two goals: (1) the solutions we are proposing have a testing ground well understood by the developers; and (2) tools are created to support KICK which in turn support VizNet.

Using the AutoIcon model discussed above, VizNet has been used to produce visualizations of its internal structures. We discuss two of them here: the *Cone Tree* and the *Sphere Representation*. Representations like Cone Tree are suitable for visualizing hierarchical structures, while the Sphere Representation is used to visualize a set of relationships associated with a single object.

5.2   Methodology

VizNet constructs a visualization by traversing the frame structure to be inspected and simultaneously constructing a 3D structure of visualization nodes, in which each node corresponds to one of the frames in the knowledge base. These nodes are then positioned in space to form tree structures, spheres, etc.

Each visualization node in the network includes the following attributes: a link to the piece of information to be represented, detail level at which to display the node, its position in the tree structures (its parent and children), its position and orientation in space, and its appearance (shape and degree of complexity depending on the DOI).

There are altogether five different detail levels with which to display each icon. Level 0 means that the icon is not displayed. Level 1 displays a single polygon for fast display. Level 2 gives a low resolution display of the icon. Level 3 increases the resolution of the icon to its maximum. Finally, level 4 displays the entire content of the object that the node represents. The user can edit the object content at this point. The detail level of each icon can be modified by the user explicitly changing the detail level of the icon itself.

We have implemented a version of the generalized FishEye views, which modifies the detail levels of all icons in the network according to the node selected. Once a node of interest is selected, the degree of interest for all the nodes in the tree is calculated. The degree of interest of a node is calculated according to its level in the tree and its distance from the focal element. The detail level of each node is then modified according to its degree of interest. Thus, nodes with a higher degree of interest would be displayed with greater detail; nodes with degree of interest falling below a certain threshold will not be displayed.

The kind of graphical object to be attached to an icon is automatically generated according to the nature and attributes of the object. Typical examples are the solid, the image and the text media of the multimedia environment of KICK. Three-dimensional objects are mapped onto graphical objects which take the shape of the actual 3D objects; images are mapped onto 3D spatial images; and text is mapped onto a text object. As mentioned above, the size and resolution of each graphical object can be modified by its detail level. The icons for the 3D object are displayed at different levels of detail, which assign more or less polygons to the final image. The image icons are displayed with different numbers of '3D pixels', thus increasing their resolution according to the interest expressed by the user.

Plate XXII shows the VizNet interface. The interface is made up of a main window and a set of secondary windows on the right. The main window shows the gesture sequence WayPoints 'floating' over and surrounding a Cone Tree visualization. The secondary windows on the right-hand-side of Plate XXII are *bookmarks* of previous visualizations that have been saved for later retrieval. The WayPoints provide navigational tools and editing tools to allow modification of the visualization and the AutoIcons themselves (for instance, the 'AI EDIT' WayPoint, bottom-left, triggers the auto icon editor to change the particular visualization being selected; the 'HOME' WayPoint takes the user to a starting point of the navigation; the 'GOTO' takes the user to a specific visualization; the 'EDIT' lets the user edit the selected information; and so on).

Plates XXIII and XXIV show the Cone Tree of Plate XXII in more detail. The Cone Tree represents hierarchical information relative to the multimedia organization of an aircraft. This hierarchy includes the actual 3D structure of the aircraft (visible on the set of cones hanging from the left of the main cone), text (seen on the right-hand-side of the top cone) and images related to it (hanging from the set of cones on the right). Plate XXIV is a close up of the cone that holds the 3D structure of the aircraft (the fuselage can be seen at the top) and also shows the set of images at the bottom. Notice that the cones are transparent to allow the user to see through from any angle. The size of the icons is an indication of the degree of interest that they hold for that particular visualization.

For instance, if one image is displayed in higher resolution than another this implies that it is more relevant to the selection of the user. If the size of the image is also bigger, that reinforces the point. This can be seen in the image cone of Plate XXIV in which, although the image icons are at almost the same distance, some are much bigger than others. Also, some are displayed in coarse resolution while others give quite fine detail.

The user can navigate around the Cone Tree freely, to reach any part he finds of interest. The user can rotate the cone to bring the node into view, and select a node. After the selection of a node, visualizations of the object with higher level of detail can be chosen, or the *Sphere* representation may be brought into view (see below).

5.3 Associative relations

Associative relationships are visualized by means of the Sphere structure. The Sphere is used for the visualization of all relationships associated with an object of interest (OOI). The Sphere structure can be considered as a 3D version of the 2D Perspective wall [7] in that objects highly related to the node of interest are displayed nearer to it while objects less related are displayed further away.

In terms of layout structures, the sphere resembles that of an onion, whereby spheres are embedded beneath spheres. This is essential for representing different levels of information. For example, objects directly related to the *object of interest* (OOI) are displayed in the outermost sphere. Subsequent objects which are related to the OOI through other objects are considered as lower level objects and are displayed on the inner spheres. These lower level spheres have darker hemispheres surrounding them, thus giving a visual cue as to how deep within the spheres the user is.

For each sphere layer, objects highly related to the OOI are displayed nearer to the OOI while objects less related are displayed further away. These latter objects drop off at the side of the sphere and thus appear less visible. This provides a natural fisheye view for the display.

Plates XXV and XXVI show a *sphere representation* that visualizes the associated links that emanate from a 'set' of images related to the aircraft (sets are represented by an icon with three circles surrounded by a wire-frame fence). In the 'centre' of the sphere lies the piece of information under inspection (the set) and around it, arranged radially, are other related items, such as other sets, the fuselage 3D structure, text, etc. Plate XXVI is a close-up that reveals the nature of the associations. There are five sets of images and a link to a 3D structure. Again, the icons are shown in different degrees of interest.

In terms of manipulation, the sphere resembles the trackball. The user can slide and rotate the sphere, and thus bring the node he is interested in into clear view. In addition, if he 'walks' over a node that is linked to lower level nodes, he will 'fall' into the inner sphere. Likewise, if he walks over a node that is linked to higher level nodes, he will be 'transported' up to the outer sphere.

6 Summary

Three problems in using virtual reality technology to satisfy needs of information professionals were identified: *visualization of a single complex object, visualization of a large collection of complex objects*, and *user definition of visualizations*. Three theoretical solutions were proposed: a model for flexibly encoding the mapping from the semantic space of information objects to the multimedia space of visualizations, a model for managing information complexity using distorted FishEye views, and a new interface paradigm called *gesture sequence navigation* useful for controlling the above two models.

How these solutions can be combined into a single visualization system was demonstrated by showing and describing a sample visualization and by presenting a general dataflow architecture.

Example frames produced by the prototype, *VizNet*, demonstrated how the solutions can be used for visualizing the information of the prototype system itself. The developers are turning their attentions to further evaluating the solutions on the real-world problems such as visualizations of *discrete event systems* (i.e. international telephone systems) and supporting information understanding in general design environments.

References

1   Robertson, G.G., Mackinlay, J.D. and Card, S.K. 1991. Cone Trees: Animated 3D visualizations of hierarchical information. *Proc. ACM-SIGCHI'91 Human Factors in Computing Systems*, 189–194.
2   Fairchild, K.M. and Poltrock, S. 1987. Soaring through Knowledge Space: SemNet 2.1 [Videotape]. ACM-SIG-CHI'87 Human Factors in Computing Systems and in MCC Technical Report No. HI-104-86 Rev 1, Austin, TX.
3   Miller, G. 1956. The Magical Number 7 Plus Or Minus 2: Some limits in our capacity for processing information. *Psychological Review*, **63** (2): 81–97.
4   Furnas, G.W. 1986. Generalized fisheye views. *Proc. CHI'86 Human Factors in Computing Systems*, 16–23.
5   Fairchild, K.M., Meredith, L.G. and Wexelblat, A. 1989. A Formal Structure for Automatic Icons. *Interacting with Computers*, June 89 and in MCC Technical Report No. STP-311-88.
6   Fairchild, K.M., Poltrock, S.E. and Furnas, G.W. 1988. SemNet: Three-dimensional graphic representations of large knowledge bases. *Cognitive Science and its Applications for Human-Computer Interaction*. Lawrence Erlbaum Associates.
7   Mackinlay, J.D., Robertson, G.G. and Card, S.K. 1991. The Perspective Wall: Detail and context smoothly integrated. *Proc. ACM-SIGCHI'91 Human Factors in Computing Systems*, 173–179.
8   Jacob, R.J. 1990. What you look at is what you get: Eye movement-based interaction techniques. *Proc. ACM-SIGCHI'90 Human Factors in Computing Systems*, 11–18.
9   Fortune, D., Ortiz, J.E. and Barline, R. 1991. Adaptation of Tonguetouch Keypad and Zofcom System to Educational Applications. *Proc. Sixth Annual Conference on Technology and Persons with Disabilities*, 249–252.
10 Zimmerman, T., Lanier, J., Blanchard, C., Bryson, S. and Harvill, Y. 1987. A hand gesture interface device. *Proc. ACM-SIGCHI'87 +GI Conference Proceedings*, 192.
11 Foley, J.D., Van Dam, A., Feiner, S.K. and Hughes, J.F. 1990. *Computer Graphics, Principles and Practice, 2nd edition*. Addison-Wesley.
12 Mackay, W.E. 1991. Triggers and barriers to customizing software. *ACM-SIGCHI'91 Human Factors in Computing Systems*, 153–160.
13 Kramer, J. 1989. The talking glove in action. *Commun. ACM*, **515**, April.
14 Wickens, C.D. 1987. Information processing, decision-making, and cognition. *Handbook of Human Factors*. John Wiley.
15 Serra, L., Chua, T.S. and Teh, W.S. 1991. A model for integrating multimedia information around 3D graphics hierarchies. *The Visual Computer*, **7** (5–6): 326–343.
16 Loo, P.L. 1991. *The Starship Manual (Version 2.0)*, ISS TR#91-54-0.

Biographies

Kim Fairchild is a member of Research Staff at the Institute of System Science (ISS) at the National University of Singapore. He has a BA in psychology, an MS in computer science, and is a PhD candidate in computer science. Previously he was a member of technical staff at both the Human Interface program and Software Technology programs at the Microelectronics and Computer Technology Corporation (MCC) and at Honeywell's Systems Research Center. He has extensive experience in information visualization, man-in-the-loop systems, and virtual reality technology.

Luis Serra graduated in Electronics Engineering in 1982 from the Universitat Politecnica de Barcelona, Spain. At the University of Bradford, UK, he obtained an MSc (1983) and a PhD in multiprocessor systems for real-time 3D graphics (1987). He is currently an Associate, Research Staff at the Institute of Systems Science (ISS) at the National University of Singapore, where he leads project KICK, a research platform for multimedia. His research interests include 3D graphics, knowledge representation and video technology.

Ng Hern is a software engineer at ISS. He has a BS in computer science and is developing VizNet as part of his Honors project at the National University of Singapore.

Lee Beng Hai is a software engineer at ISS. He has a BS in computer science. He has developed Gesture Sequence software.

Ang Tin Leong is a software engineer at ISS. He has a BS in computer science. He has developed software for information visualization.

Part 5
Human–Computer Interface

13 Virtual Reality: A Tool for Telepresence and Human Factors Research

Robert J. Stone
UK Advanced Robotics Research Centre

Abstract

The UK Advanced Robotics Research Centre's (ARRC) Virtual Reality (VR) and Telepresence Project started in 1988, since when the company's experimental testbed, which is the most advanced of its kind in Europe, has been used to evaluate the interaction between human operators and semi-autonomous robots. Equipped with head-mounted or area projection stereoscopic displays, and intuitive input devices such as gloves, 3D 'mice', speech recognition and synthesis, operators are tested controlling either a robot vehicle (Cybermotion K2A) and/or an enhanced Puma Robot Arm. Virtual models of architectural and hazardous environments are constructed using a range of VR toolkits, although the ARRC was the first to demonstrate the feasibility of converting objects and surfaces, derived using a scanning laser rangefinding system, into 3D virtual images, suitable for display on a stereo headset. This will improve the performance and safety aspects of deploying future robots into environments where conventional TV feedback to a human is inadequate (due to smoke, fire, turbid water, etc.), except at close range. For close-in task performance, the ARRC has also developed a head-slaved stereoscopic camera system, capable of pan/tilt carriage speeds of the order of 1800°/s. To permit the switching between, or merging of VR imagery and real video, the centre uses a multi-transputer/i860 engine to coordinate these and other real-time aspects of the testbed. The company has also pioneered the use of tactile feedback for VR and telepresence applications, in both glove and 3D 'mouse' form. Complex virtual models have been built and demonstrated, including a model of the Robotics Centre, complete with an animated Puma Robot, which can be driven from a symbolic control panel and can demonstrate 'teach-and-repeat' behaviour. The centre specializes in the porting of models from CAD systems onto more dynamic platforms supporting VR, thereby permitting 'immersion' and intuitive interaction on the part of the human operator.

1 Introduction: Human Factors and Telerobotics

We (*the teleoperation community – Author's addition*) have demonstrated simple human-supervised, computer-aided teleoperation in a number of ways, but our understanding of human-computer cooperation is very primitive, hardly commensurate with the label 'telerobot' we so easily allow ourselves to employ.

Tom Sheridan 1987, 1989

Most researchers are now beginning to accept a range of definitions put forward by Sheridan when considering the systems aspects of controlling remote robotic vehicles and manipulators for handling and inspection tasks in hazardous environments [1, 2]. Until quite recently, the terms teleoperation, telepresence, robotics, telerobotics and supervisory control had been used interchangeably. The human factors issues have been considered even less than the systems covered by these definitions. The first edition of the journal *Presence*, dealing with telepresence and virtual reality issues and first published in 1992, contains what some believe will be the definitive statements on these terms (and their man–machine interface, or MMI counterparts), compiled by Sheridan himself, Nat Durlach, also of MIT, and contributions from the Journal's Editorial Board. The following, then, are definitions put forward by Sheridan in the references given above.

Teleoperation is the extension of a person's sensing and manipulation capability to a remote location. A *teleoperator* includes at the minimum artificial sensors, arms and hands, a vehicle for carrying these, and communication channels to and from the human operator. The term teleoperation refers most commonly to direct and continuous control of the teleoperator, but can also be used generally to encompass *telerobotics* (see below).

Telepresence is the **ideal** of sensing sufficient information about the teleoperator and task environment, and communicating this to the human operator in a sufficiently natural way, that the operator feels physically present at the remote site.

Robotics is the science and art of performing, by means of an automatic apparatus or device, functions normally ascribed to human beings, or operating with what appears to be almost human intelligence (adapted from *Webster's Third International Dictionary*).

Telerobotics is a form of teleoperation in which a human operator acts as a supervisor, intermittently communicating to a computer information about goals, constraints, plans, contingencies, assumptions, suggestions and orders relative to a limited task, getting back information about accomplishments, difficulties, concerns, and, as requested, raw sensory data – while the subordinate telerobot executes the task based on information received from the human operator plus its own artificial sensing and intelligence.

Supervisory Control is mostly synonymous with telerobotics, referring to the analogy of a human supervisor directing and monitoring the activities of a human subordinate. The term 'supervisory control' is used commonly to refer to human supervision of any semi-autonomous system (including an aircraft, chemical plant, power plant), while 'telerobot' commonly refers to a device having arms for manipulating or processing discrete objects in its environment.

1.1 The search for a 'natural' man–machine interface

This paper is generally concerned with the use of virtual reality technologies for achieving 'natural' MMIs for teleoperation, telepresence and telerobotics but what, exactly, does this mean? In fact, there is no such thing as a natural man–machine interface, simply due to the fact that an interface between a human and a mechanical or electrical system will never be natural – there will always be some form of 'connection' between the complicated human sensory and motor systems and the more primitive substrate of the system under control. Certainly there are international initiatives striving to achieve the ultimate in what may loosely be called 'natural interface' design. At the Human Interface Technology Laboratory of the University of Washington State, for example, part of their Virtual Reality and Human Interface Programme is considering the use of direct laser scanning of images onto the retina of the human eye to achieve a resolution approaching that of the human visual system. A similar, but militarily classified project, exists in the UK. Work has also been under way for some 10 years now, attempting to link brain electrical potentials (electroencephalography) with cognitive and motor behaviour. It is now possible utilize specific brain waves to select menu items on variable resolution displays, and, to some extent, quantify the workload and 'mental resource' a human can bring to bear on a given task. Research in the States, using a system known as Biomuse, is addressing how to use electrical potentials generated from brain and muscle activity to control real systems, including robots.

Given this physical barrier between the human's sensori-motor[1] capabilities and that of the system with which he is 'interfacing', there are those who feel that the preferred term for this form of research, therefore, should not be 'natural', but **intuitive**. An intuitive interface between man and machine is one which requires little training (particularly in complex operational procedures or computing languages) and proffers a working style most like that used by the human being to interact with environments and objects in his day-to-day life. In other words, the human interacts with elements of his task by looking, holding, manipulating, speaking, listening, and moving, using as many of his natural *skills* as are appropriate, or can reasonably be expected to be applied to a task.

However, does 'intuitive' imply that remote handling and inspection will only be achieved successfully and safely if the robot and MMI systems are so closely matched that every sensory and motor feature of the human is duplicated in the physical make-up of the robot (i.e. anthropomorphism?). The answer to this is no. Anthropomorphic man–machine systems, such as the American Naval Ocean Systems Center's *Green Man* Exoskeleton-Slave Project and the MMIs which appear to dominate the Japanese approach to teleoperation have met with limited success. The reason for this (particularly in the case of Japanese research) is a lack of attention to what information and control facilities the operator actually needs to complete a specific task. Some tasks (e.g. inspection of large, cluttered areas) may be well suited to using head-mounted displays, others (e.g. fixed area inspection) may only require conventional 2D camera and display devices. Some tasks (e.g. unbolting) may well benefit from using glove interactive devices, others (e.g. valve wheel operation) may not demand such complexity. The diversity of tasks faced by industries demand attention to both the requirements of the task and the information processing and control requirements of the human operator.

---

[1] The term 'sensori-motor' (a.k.a. 'perceptual-motor') is used by psychologists and ergonomists to describe the integrated human system for *sensing* (visual, auditory, tactile, etc.), *processing* (from the time the stimulus is sensed to its receipt in the brain, and from the brain to the receipt of low level commands at the muscle subsystems), and control (i.e. how the body moves or responds on receipt of commands).

Why should the designers of telerobotic systems even consider R & D programmes which move towards the intuitive interface? In the first instance, there is the issue of equipment or facility design. Many of the installations in place today – for example, those in the nuclear industry under consideration for decommissioning – were originally designed with **human intervention** in mind – rod handling, valve operation, object insertion, module coupling, tool operation, and so on. This means two things. Firstly, a single, so-called advanced telerobot, capable of limited learning and extrapolation by means of artificial intelligence (knowledge-based systems, neural networks, etc.), would not, by present day standards, be capable of effectively carrying out a remote task autonomously. This situation is not set to change for the foreseeable future – **the human still has an indispensable rôle to play** as supervisor (for those remote systems with some onboard intelligence) and as a direct controller – the 'manual intervener' (i.e. when remote failure occurs, or when the situation facing the robot is outside its scope of 'competence'). The transition from supervisory control of a telerobot to telepresence in the case of systems failure or uncertainty was not addressed adequately in Sheridan's definitions. Secondly, the deployment of a primitive robot platform (vehicle and/or manipulator) currently places undue mental and physical workload on the remote human operator, since the designer – consciously or unconsciously – appears to expect the human to adapt to working remotely with the most inappropriate man–machine interface facilities possible (e.g. batteries of joysticks and complex multi-screen displays). Of course, humans eventually adapt very well to most man–machine interfaces. Driving a car is an example here. Nevertheless, adaptation (or training) takes time and money, and does *not* guarantee constant efficient and safe performance. Under conditions of fatigue and stress, even the most proficient human operator can, in a split second, misinterpret a display or control condition, or revert to a previously dominant stereotype,[2] with possibly serious circumstances.

A related and (unfortunately) unavoidable issue is that of operational cost. Existing MMIs for teleoperated systems do little to save money for those who have commissioned their use. Why? Again the reason is a human factors one. By paying lip service to the actual nature of human perceptual and motor characteristics, and their integration, the MMIs 'bolted-on' to a remote system at the last minute require substantial training programmes, are inefficient operationally (for the reasons given above), could be inherently unsafe (due to the stereotype issue also listed above) and are likely not to be accepted by the 'hard-line' operator in the first place. Equipment developers are often to blame for these problems. A costly stereo television system or multi-axis controller might sound an attractive proposition when the experimental results show an $n\%$ improvement in performance under controlled conditions, but when this percentage relates to an advantage of just tens of seconds in the real world, one must question the expense of the initial outlay.

There is no doubt in the author's mind that a 'natural' or intuitive MMI will result in operational savings. But this will only occur when the designers of MMI

---

[2] The term 'stereotype' refers to an over-learned response or action to a particular situation. For instance, in the UK the light switch stereotype is press down for on; in the US it is the opposite. Often, under conditions of stress or high workload, operators will revert to previously well-established stereotypes, rather than invoking those in which they have been trained for a specific application. In the aircraft industry, this has occasionally proved fatal.

equipment recognize that the human sensory and motor factors are integrated and that specific attention to human stereo vision, *or* eye movements, *or* head movement, *or* tactile feedback, *or* force feedback, *or* 6-degree-of-freedom hand/wrist control will simply not succeed. One often finds statements in reports, by establishments with a commercial background, which read something like: '. . . stereo vision provides superior remote handling performance over conventional viewing techniques and force feedback . . .'. These should be treated with scepticism. These facilities should simply *not* be considered in isolation in the first place. When handling an object in the real world, vision, cognition,[3] motor 'preparation' (subconscious adaptation of the human motor system to prepare for handling a heavy or light load), tactile feedback, kinaesthesis[4] and closed-loop muscular adaptation all play an integrated rôle in effective materials handling. This is what a programme of research into natural or intuitive MMI, for telepresence – such as that under way at the UK's Advanced Robotics Research Centre (ARRC) – must address.

Virtual reality (VR) and associated technologies is a relatively recent development which, it seems, has given a new lease of life to those engaged in addressing the human factors aspects of telepresence for hazardous environments. VR has, in amongst the hype and rhetoric surrounding the field, spawned a substantial industry with an almost obsessive dedication to developing and supplying low-cost and reliable 'natural' MMIs. With the number of VR proposals evident in the recent call for ESPRIT III involvement, this trend is likely to continue for the foreseeable future, leading to many devices, only some of which will be useable by those involved in robotics and teleoperation developments.

2   The UK *VERDEX* Project

Recent papers by the author [3,4] described the early stages of a project, coordinated by the ARRC, to investigate the use of VR as a tool for the design of advanced human–computer interfaces for the remote control of robots, deployed in hazardous environments, such as subsea, nuclear installations, disaster events and space. During 1992, the *VERDEX* (Virtual Environment Remote Driving EXperiment) testbed has been upgraded to expand the centre's capabilities in VR generally (for new applications), and to focus on incorporating the results from some of the other demonstrator programmes under way at the centre. The ARRC has amassed considerable experience in the design, development, building and experimental testing of VR equipment and software and has developed excellent contacts with other leading R & D establishments, both within Europe and further abroad.

Much of the *VERDEX* Team's experience has arisen as a result of the Company's Core Research Programme, which has now been in place for nearly four years. The *VERDEX* Project started in 1988, since when the company's experimental testbed, which is now the most advanced of its kind in Europe, has been used to evaluate the interaction between human operators and semi-autonomous robots, as well as

---

[3] The term 'cognition' pertains generally to 'mental processes', or to modes of knowing, including perceiving, remembering, imagining, conceiving, judging and reasoning.
[4] The term 'kinaesthesis' relates to internal body mechanisms which help an individual to sense orientation. Specifically, it is provided by the sensation of forces exerted by muscles and of the position of the joints.

new software and interactive control/display products emerging from the VR 'market'. Equipped with head-mounted and projection stereoscopic displays, and intuitive input devices, such as gloves, 3D 'mice', speech recognition and synthesis, investigations are carried out into the control of either a robot vehicle (Cybermotion K2A) and/or an enhanced Robot Arm (Puma 560).

Virtual models of architectural and hazardous environments have been constructed using a range of CAD and VR toolkits, although in 1991 researchers at the ARRC were the first to demonstrate the feasibility of converting objects and surfaces, derived using a scanning laser rangefinding system, into 3D virtual images, suitable for display on a stereo headset. This achievement will serve to improve the performance and safety aspects of deploying future robots into environments where conventional TV feedback to a human is inadequate (due to smoke, fire, turbid water, etc.), except at close range.

For close-range task performance, the ARRC, together with Overview Ltd. (of North London, UK), has also developed a head-slaved stereoscopic camera system, capable of pan/tilt carriage speeds of the order of 1800°/s. To permit the switching between, or merging of VR imagery and real video, a multi-transputer/i860 engine has been developed to coordinate these and other real-time aspects of the testbed. This system, the first of its kind in the world, is called *SuperVision*, developed from the centre's original *Vision* Computer by Division Limited of Chipping Sodbury, UK. Together with Airmuscle Limited of Cranfield, UK, the ARRC has also pioneered the use of tactile feedback for VR and telepresence applications, in both glove and 3D 'mouse' form. The ARRC–Airmuscle Teletact™ Glove[5] is now being marketed by VPL Inc. of Redwood City, California, as the DataGlove THX.

With regard to virtual world modelling, quite complex virtual models have been built and demonstrated, including a model of the Robotics Centre, complete with an animated Puma Robot, which can be teleoperated in virtual space from an iconic control panel and can demonstrate 'teach-and-repeat' sequences. The ARRC has begun to specialize in the porting of models from CAD systems (e.g. AutoCAD, IGRIP) and other forms of modelling or simulation packages onto more dynamic platforms supporting virtual visualization, thereby permitting 'immersion' and intuitive interaction on the part of the human operator.

To summarize, the centre's VR testbed facilities fall into four categories, illustrated schematically in Fig. 13.1:

1. The 'Immersion' testbed (Main Laboratory), consisting primarily of a seated workstation, VPL, LEEP, Polhemus, Ascension and ARRC-developed VR equipment, and the *SuperVision* i860/T800 Graphics/Video Engine (see Fig. 13.2).
2. Desktop VR Modelling Systems & CAD, based around a number of CAD and VR Toolkits (e.g. Dimension VR Toolkit – see Fig. 13.3, Sense8 WorldToolKit, AutoCAD V.12), running on 486PC Systems and IGRIP, running on a Silicon Graphics Workstation. All desktop models are portable onto the *SuperVision* architecture.
3. 3D Graphics/Video Production and Projection Suite, based on an LCD (field

---

[5] The name TELETACT is a registered Trade Mark of Airmuscle Limited (UK; Trade Mark No. 1403130), manufactured under licence from Advanced Robotics Research Limited.

sequential) 3D workstation and Sharp LCD Video Projection System, giving a capability for projecting 3D virtual graphics or video from *SuperVision* onto a wall or large screen (for multi-observer viewing) and recording events in 3D onto a single VHS tape.

4. Interface links with other ARRC sensing and control projects, specifically the laser rangefinding and image processing system laboratory, the mobile vehicle laboratory and the Puma Robot collision avoidance testbed (see Fig. 13.4 and Plate XXXI).

The remainder of this paper will outline some of the more recent developments and goals in research and development at the centre, particularly in the areas of tactile feedback, virtual world construction using range image sensors and commercial toolkits, multi-person interaction and new computing architectures.

2.1 Teletact™ Developments

As described by Stone [3], the Teletact™ Virtual Tactile Feedback System was designed to investigate one of the key problems with interacting with objects in a virtual environment – the lack of tactile and force feedback. Its primary use, however, has not been in the tactile modelling of virtual objects, but as a vital additional cue to stereopsis for assessing the 'immersee's' proximity to features in the virtual world.

There is little doubt that virtual image quality has improved over the past year, as a result of powerful VR toolkits emerging onto the scene. However, VR researchers are still confronted with the fact that the stereoscopic qualities of these images are poor. This is due to a combination of factors. Blame particularly falls on the contrast-degrading nature of headset optics (although in the opinion of the author, LEEP still remains superior to Fresnel implementations of VR headset optics) which, together with the low resolution LCD displays, do not enhance the immersed user's skill in moving through the world in a collision free manner. These issues, combined with the absence of touch when grasping a virtual object, drove the ambitions of the early part of the Teletact Project. Another ambition, as yet unfulfilled, was to develop a glove capable of receiving force and tactile data from a remote robot gripper, for 'display' to the human in an intuitive form.

Teletact I, then, was described by Stone [3] as a 2-glove prototype, designed and built in conjunction with Airmuscle Limited of Cranfield (Patent Pending, UK Patent Reference GB91/01637). The prototype was a 2-glove system, the *Datacq* Input Glove possessing 20 force sensitive resistors (FSR), distributed across the underside of the hand, the Teletact Feedback Glove possessing 20 correspondingly located air pockets.

Since that time, three developments have taken the Teletact Concept a stage further. Firstly, an agreement between VPL Research Inc., Airmuscle Limited and the ARRC, prior to VPL's recent demise, was reached to distribute the UK Teletact Tactile Feedback Glove as an integral part of a DataGlove THX System, primarily in the USA and Japan. The UK–US agreement was announced by VPL at the Virtual Reality 'Gallery' of Siggraph 1991, held in Las Vegas at the end of July. An agreement was reached recently with Division Limited, with regard to European distributorship.

Secondly, a collaborative project is currently under discussion with Rutgers

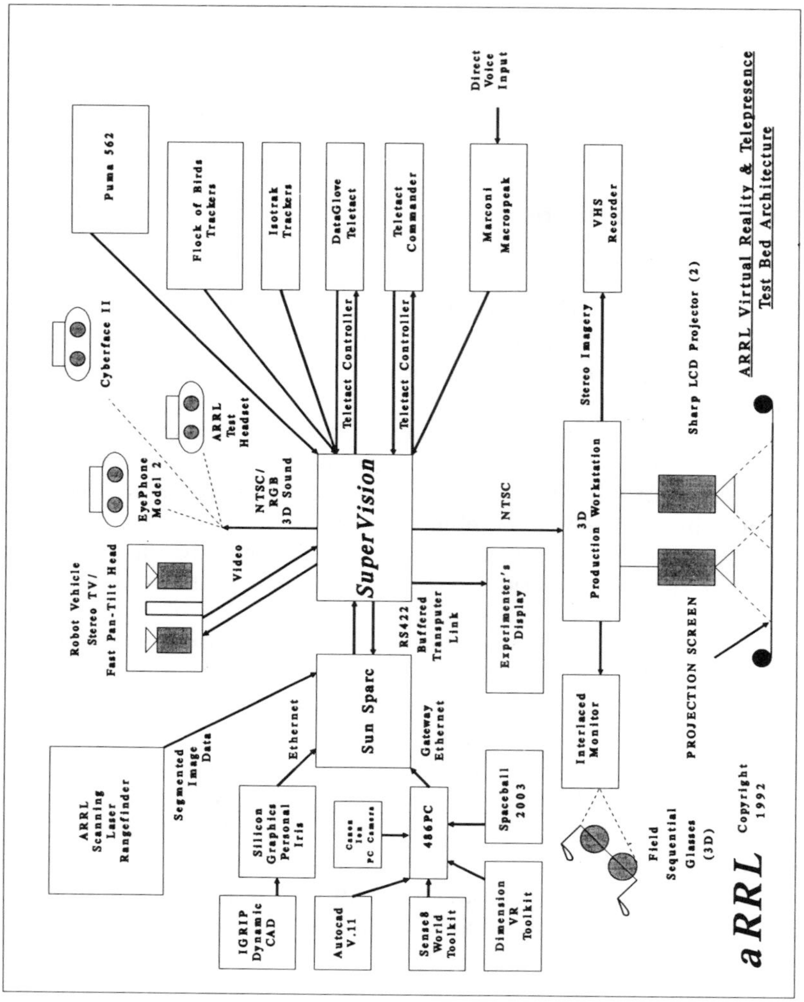

Figure 13.1 The ARRC VR Architecture.

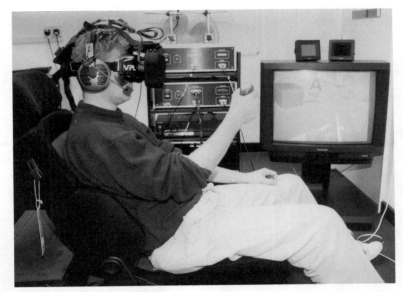

Figure 13.2 ARRC VR 'Immersion' testbed.

Figure 13.3 Dimension VR toolkit in use.

University in New Jersey, USA. This project plans to use multiple gloves for the purposes of post-operative hand performance measurement and rehabilitation. If successful, the project will bring together the UK Teletact/*Datacq* system, the VPL DataGlove and the Rutgers force feedback system. The Rutgers University Robotics Laboratory has been carrying out an R & D Programme to develop a pneumatic micro-piston tactile and *force* feedback system, also for use with input gloves. Work underlying this device was originally conducted at Bell Laboratories [5], resulting

(a)

(b)

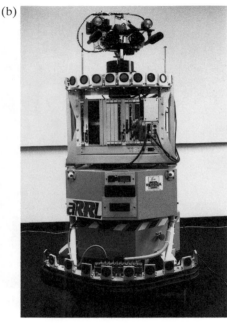

Figure 13.4 (a) ARRC enhanced Puma robot; (b) Cybermotion K2A vehicle with head-slaved stereoscopic TV system.

in a 1-degree-of-freedom master controller for the Utah Hand. This portable master with force feedback (referred to as PDMFF by the Rutgers Team) possessed one position sensor in parallel with the piston, and was compact enough to be held in the palm with only two fingers. Forces exerted on objects by the robot hand were determined by observing the difference between flexion and extension tensions in the tendons of the robot thumb. This value was then used directly to drive the value of the single piston pressure.

Research was continued at Rutgers by integrating three such PDMFF actuators with a DataGlove 'master', such that the position sensor could be replaced with the output of the DataGlove's fibre optic sensors. Currently, the three actuators have a forcing effect on the thumb, index and middle finger (attached using Velcro strips), although there are plans to provide actuators for all digits. To allow for abduction–adduction of the three digits, the actuators are co-mounted on an L-shaped base, using spherical joints through which the air tubes pass. Cylindrical joints attach the piston shaft to the fingertip Velcro strip [6] (US Patent No. 5,004, 391). Qualitative demonstrations, using virtual models of a hand grasping a spring, have confirmed the potential of the Rutgers System and further tests are planned. VPL Inc also plans to market the Rutgers device under the name of DataGlove FBX.

Finally, March 1992 saw the successful completion of the *Teletact II Prototype*. Teletact II is essentially similar in concept to Teletact I, albeit with a higher density of pneumatic air pockets – 30 in all (29 small + 1 large), particularly around the middle fingertip, index fingertip and thumb tip regions, as shown schematically in

Fig. 13.5a. The density of small pockets is greatest for the index fingertip, pockets 6–9 in Fig. 13.5a being arranged in a 2 × 2 matrix. Sequential inflation and deflation of these pockets is intended to convey virtual or robot-grasped object slip to the wearer. Additional pockets have been placed on the back of the hand (to cue inadvertent back-hand collisions to the wearer) and on the edges of the middle and index fingers to improve the sense of grasp for small tubular objects (e.g. holding a pencil). As with Teletact I, the pressure rating of 12 psi remains the same for each of these pockets, again under proportional control. Again, The micro-capillary PTFE tubes are housed in a single umbilical.

In addition to the 29 small pockets, Teletact II possesses a large palmar pocket (no. 30 in Fig. 13.5, pressure rated to 30 psi). The aim of including this larger pocket is, through interaction with the surrounding pockets (20, 21, 22, 23, 26, 27 and 28 in Fig. 13.5), to provide a simulated palmar *force* feedback. Thus, unlike Teletact I, the wearer will be able to exert grip forces and receive reactive stimuli, rather than being able to close the gloved hand completely.

2.2   The Teletact™ *Commander*

One of the problems found by the ARRC with current glove technology is reliability, both from physical and calibration points of view. To program certain glove controllers to record the current wearer's hand characteristics and preferred gesture patterns has, on occasions, taken up to 25 minutes (ageing or badly fitting gloves also contribute to the problems). Even then there is no guarantee that the calibration will hold firm during and between sessions. The result of this is that the glove can become non-intuitive and highly frustrating to use. Fingers can exhibit sporadic movement or even take on physically impossible shapes. To overcome this, a simple multifunction hand controller was designed by ARRC Researchers which, together with the Polhemus or Bird sensor, now provides a comfortable and reliable means of interacting with the virtual world.

Called the Teletact *Commander*, the controller is a general purpose hybrid pointing device which uses more reliable controls (momentary and centre-biased toggle switches) than that available with low-cost domestic PC joysticks, plus *simple tactile feedback*. The *Commander* is a resin or plastic hand grip, sculpted to fit a range of hand sizes (Fig. 13.6 and Plates XXXII and XXIX). The controls are mounted in areas of the grip accessible by three of the fingers and the thumb (in the scalloped finger region and across the top of the grip, within the thumb's arc of rotation). A single multi-wire/tube conduit leaves the base of the grip, and the Polhemus or Ascension tracking sensor fits into a sculptured recess within the resin body of the grip itself. For other developmental contracts undertaken by the Centre, Ascension Technology Inc. has supplied the Bird Sensor unpotted. This eases mounting of the device within the grip, since the Bird sensor shell is much larger than its Polhemus counterpart.

To achieve simple tactile feedback, the Teletact *Commander* uses air pocket technology similar to that supplied with the Tactile Feedback Glove. To reduce the cost involved in using a compressor such as that delivered with the Teletact, a low-cost airbrush compressor may be used. Hearing aid speaker diaphragms were investigated for tactile cueing but, despite their impressive vibro-tactile performance when tested off-line (i.e. away from the ARRC testbed), their electro-magnetic

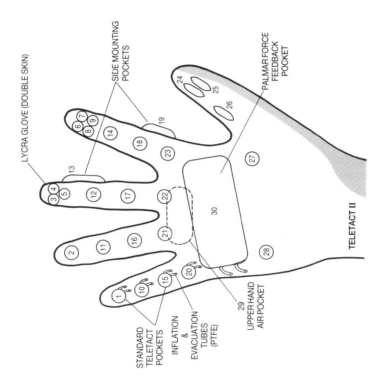

Figure 13.5 (a) Schematic of the Teletact II prototype; (b) Teletact I.

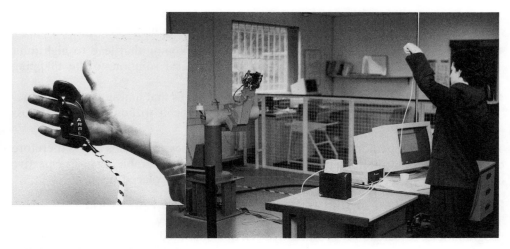

Figure 13.6 Teletact *Commander*.

characteristics were found to be highly disruptive to the performance of the Polhemus IsoTrak. Piezo-electric transducers were not found to be suitable for vibro-tactile transmission through the resin housing of the Teletact *Commander*'s main structure.

For the small number of air pockets currently in use with the Teletact *Commander* (three to five), there are two types and locations of air pockets used. The first – a Teletact circular pocket of 14 mm diameter fits into the finger recesses of the scalloped grip moulding. The second – a lozenge-shaped pocket (40 mm long by 12 mm wide/end circle diameter) – lies on the back of the grip, and imparts pressure to the base of the thumb and the ball of the hand, or directly to the palm of the hand. The air pockets and PTFE microcapillary supply tubes can simply be attached to the surface of the device or, alternatively, a single layer diaphragm can be glued over a sculpted recess on its surface. The advantage of the latter is that the PTFE feed tubes can be fed through the inside of the grip into the air pocket recess, rather than over its surface (thereby avoiding damage through snagging).

The Teletact *Commander* has been demonstrated to good effect throughout the past year, not only in navigating and interacting with virtual worlds, but also in providing 6-degree-of-freedom teleoperation control of Puma 500 and 700 Series Robot Arms. A key breakthrough in this respect is that of a robust teleoperation controller for industrial robots, which has been developed at the ARRC as part of a generic manipulator controller project. The control methods adopted and modular design of the software allow for porting onto most industrial manipulators. A prototype software package has been written and tested using a Unimation Puma 560 manipulator. The basic functionality of the controller is to accept Cartesian space teleoperation commands from the MMI (i.e. the ARRC's *Commander*) and convert them to joint positions suitable for supplying as set points to the manipulator joint servo controllers every 28 ms control interval. The joint positions supplied result in the manipulator performing the commands with high dynamic accuracy whilst maintaining the arm within its physical capacity. In addition the controller will facilitate joint space teleoperation.

There are traditionally two problems associated with Cartesian teleoperation control that have in the past prevented robust control on many manipulators:

- Singularities exist in the Cartesian to joint space mapping that lead to high joint accelerations in their proximity and no mathematical solution to the mapping function at a singularity.
- The non-linear Cartesian to joint space mapping means that limiting joint velocities and accelerations for a given Cartesian input is difficult without resulting in loss of Cartesian control.

The ARRC's teleoperation controller addresses both these problems and is therefore capable of keeping the manipulator in a controlled and operable state irrespective of its position in the workspace or the dynamic demands placed upon it.

2.3   Sensor-based virtual representations of the real world

The 'building' of virtual worlds using sensory data is a key element in the ARRC's programme of research. VR has already been demonstrated as an extremely powerful tool for permitting the visualization of, and interaction with, data from *non-visual* sensors [4]. The image database used by such systems is in essence a polygonal format, based on planar surfaces which fit together to create objects (in effect, a CAD package). Smooth shading and texture, which are extremely important effects for enhancing visual realism, are generated by Gouraud shading and radiosity algorithms respectively. Creating a polygonal or CAD-like world is performed by digitization of scale drawings and is the accepted technique. It is, however, called into question when these data are to be used to rehearse some critical remote operation; there is generally no guarantee that this information is correct. Factors such as modification, structural failure and unknown or changing environmental features prevent this approach from being used.

An alternative approach is to look actively at the environment using an appropriate vision system and produce – *from this* – a CAD representation. This approach has been used for many years in stereo photogrammetry. However, establishing correspondences between pairs of photographs is an extremely labour-intensive operation and hence is costly. Imagine then the applications potential of a system which could map the inherent 3-dimensionality of the real world directly into a virtual world. In parallel with the *VERDEX* Project, another part of the Core Research Programme has been seeking to lay the foundations for such a system.

2.3.1   Overview

A visual image is an extremely rich source of information. It is a partial record of the state of a scene from a particular viewpoint. Consider moving into the infra-red band and acquiring an image of the same scene. This image will contain information which is related to its visual counterpart but contains many thousands of differing parameters which could all be interpreted and added to some global database on the scene (virtual reality can be applied to an infra-red world too). Consider also the problems of obscuration, or partial obscuration of objects in the scenery by other objects. This requires multiple viewpoints to be captured and fused together to build the CAD representation. Capturing an image in three dimensions must also be considered. At this point one begins to appreciate the basic problems to be solved.

Much work has already been done on resolving such problems [4]. Using a scanning laser rangefinder (Fig. 13.7 and Plate XXVII), researchers at the ARRC have chosen to map only planar worlds for the present to prove the mapping methodology. The problem has been split into the following operations: image acquisition, image analysis and world modelling.

2.3.2 Image acquisition

A prime requirement for the vision system is that it can produce enough 3D information to produce a useful representation of the environment in which it is operating. Two possible candidates for an appropriate imaging system are stereo cameras or active laser systems. Work at the ARRC has focused on the laser-based approach since such systems are capable of producing extremely dense range information in comparison to the stereo systems. Laser-based systems do, however, have the disadvantage that they are comparatively slower than their stereo counterparts. This is due to the need to scan the laser across the scene. Many varieties of laser vision system are feasible, although the approaches to range measurement fall into two basic categories – time-of-flight or triangulation. Triangulation-based systems are usually better for short range work (up to 5 m) whilst time-of-flight systems can be used up to 100 m, but are generally not very reliable at short ranges due to timing difficulties. Range ambiguity can also be a problem when using time-of-flight systems. Scale is an important problem when attempting to produce a map of an environment. The resolution of the imaging

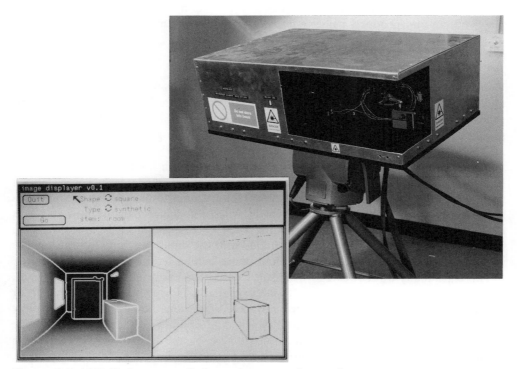

Figure 13.7 ARRC's laser rangefinder and segmented room image.

system must be high enough to measure surface detail which is appropriate to the scale of the map being produced.

2.3.3   Image analysis

The analysis stage is concerned with processing single range images into a segmented format. The segmentation algorithm attempts to convert the pixel based image into a collection of related surfaces. At present we have concerned ourselves with planar worlds and hence the surfaces in each incoming range image are segmented into planar regions. This process is extremely compute intensive and has been parallelized to reduce the processing time to 2 seconds, matching the frame rate of the laser imager.

Data from this stage of operation have already been ported onto the early Division *Vision* System used during 1991 at the centre. To down-load the output of the rangefinder system to the *Vision* computer, a 3-stage process was involved. Firstly the text file output of the rangefinder was converted to an appropriate three dimensional coordinate system. Next, complex polygon information was 'cracked' into simpler polygons. Finally, a file was produced which described the simplified polygons in an appropriate format for the *Vision* system. An early version of the ARRC's Unix filter segregated the image to allow the component objects to be moved around in the virtual world. However, since the rangefinder image was taken from a single viewpoint in early work, it was difficult to interpret the images from some angles. Work started in 1992 addressing the fusion of sensory data to overcome this problem and produce a near-complete virtual world model.

2.3.4   World modelling

Vision-related sensor fusion is one of the primary areas which has been covered under the ARRC Research Programme. The objective is to be able to move a robot vehicle around a hazardous environment and, using the laser imager, to be able to produce a planar surface map of the surroundings. Such a goal requires the creation of a 'surface world', which must be 'grown' from many segmented range images. An interpretation tree is currently being developed which holds the surface world. Each time the vision system presents a new segmented image from some defined viewpoint, then, taking into account the 3D transformations, the system matches those planes in the new image to discover which information in the new image is already held in the database. By finding such correspondences between existing features this allows new features to be added into the database. Initially, the surface world model will be empty and so the first image can be fed directly into the model.

There are many ways of categorizing surfaces such as surface area, surface normal, angles between surfaces, or surface boundary length. However, due to occlusion or partial occlusion of surfaces by other surfaces, these constraints are often partially wrong. Techniques have been devised which take account of these problems. The first port of a real world model, as 'constructed' by the laser imager occurred in September 1992, as part of a major demonstration to the ARRC's main sponsor, the Department of Trade & Industry.

3 Multi-Person Interaction

Multi-observer viewing of VR or stereoscopic display systems can be problematic technically and, in the case of networked VR systems, expensive. Many commercial non-immersive systems – using polarized screens or field-sequential stereo (shuttered LCD spectacles) – have been configured to allow a small number of observers to perceive the 3D imagery, but the visual 'cone' of the 3D effect from the display unit outwards is still quite narrow. In VR, it has also been difficult to convey the compelling effect of being immersed in a 3D world to those not equipped with a stereo headset. Whilst it is possible to network commercial VR computing systems, so that participants with headsets can share the same virtual 'experience', this results in a very costly method of achieving multi-user interaction. There is, however, an alternative which does not involve total immersion as experienced by a headset user but can provide a functional interface usable by a group of 'active' observers. Such a system has recently been installed at ARRC and is based on a 3D video production and playback system, marketed commercially by a UK Company, 3D Video Plus [7].

There are two methods of projecting the stereo output from a VR computing system (such as the ARRC's *Supervision*), or from the ARRC head-slaved stereo camera unit [3,4]. One method of display is to route the stereo images via the 3D workstation to a colour display, modified to provide field sequential viewing. Each signal from the stereo source is stored on the workstation's frame store and redisplayed together 1/50th second later, to produce a full 50 Hz stereo view. Of course, this then negates the use of fast (25 Hz) switching LCD goggles, which are often fraught with problems of perceivable and highly distracting flicker, and do not, as mentioned above, effectively support multi-user viewing.

The second method of display, and one which exploits the 50 Hz image regeneration rate (or can receive the twin composite NTSC video outputs from the VR computer directly), uses a pair of (in the centre's case) Sharp XG-200 high resolution LCD projectors, equipped with polarizing filters, allowing the stereo imagery to be projected onto a wall or large screen. This has the added advantage that a good proportion of the observers' fields of view can be covered by the display, achieving a reasonable immersion effect. Currently, the ARRC's 3D projection system is set up away from the main VR Laboratory. Demonstrations of interactive 'fly-throughs' are held using a voice-actuated radio communications link between the laboratory and room concerned.

Furthermore, interaction with a screen-projected virtual world or even a video image with supplemental graphics could easily be provided for the observers, using (for example) a number of 3D mouse systems or grip controllers, such as the ARRC's Teletact *Commander* (see above). Observers would then be able to designate objects of interest (by controlling a 3D cursor, highlighting objects using colour coding), thus directing the attention and motion paths of the immersed operator (who would be in a better position to control the walk/fly-throughs of the virtual world). This 'single-immersee–multi-observer' concept is currently being evaluated by ARRC. A hand controller is being constructed which contains a Helium-Neon laser diode and a Polhemus IsoTrak sensor and a 2-detent trigger control. Pressing to the first detent governs the firing of a real laser beam at the stereo projection screen (thus giving the user an immediate cue to his direction of point). Pressing to the second detent will send position and rotation coordinates from the Isotrak to the VR computers (see below), eliciting the firing of a 'virtual' laser beam. The first detected clash between the virtual beam and object polygon will colour code the object appropriately. Finally, the 3D video system installed at ARRC is also capable of recording stereo imagery from the 3D workstation onto a single VHS tape, thereby permitting 'canned' walk/fly-throughs of a virtual model.

4   Computing Developments: From *Vision* to *Supervision* and Desktop Systems

From the outset, the functional architecture of the ARRC *VERDEX* testbed was described as demanding a sophisticated computing system to permit coordination of head and hand tracking, finger flex registration, Teletact Glove control, *Datacq* Glove signal recording, Teletact Glove and Teletact *Commander* control, speech recognition and synthesis, camera control and vehicle control in real time. In addition, generation of the stereo virtual graphics and hand, *plus* integration with the stereo video feedback had to occur in parallel with these processes. At that time, existing VR solutions were inadequate for the centre's requirements, with the exception of one system, *Vision*, developed by Division Limited [8], which took the form of a distributed client-server or actor-director architecture using parallel processing. Division's proposal for a 36-transputer system capable of handling all of the above requirements was by far the most appropriate solution to coordinating the elements of the *VERDEX* Architecture. However, limitations in the early system (imposed by the centre's demanding requirements) were discovered, primarily with regard to model size, video lag and rendering speed. A number of new requirements were, thus, defined. In summary, these were:

1. To increase the polygon complexity of the world that can be handled by the *Vision* System (from 700–10,000 polygons, 1000–16,000 vertices, and from 100–1000 objects). This enhancement was to permit the handling of complex processed range images – segmented planar and occupancy data in polygon form (see above) – either in isolation (single laser scan) or as fused world model data from spatially disparate sensor readings (multiple laser scans).
2. To increase speed of rendering from 20,000 to around 60,000 polygons per second per eye. The simple model of the ARRC's laboratory area generated using the IGRIP CAD Package was close to the maximum capability of the *Vision* Computer (20,000 polygons per second per eye). It was not possible, for example, to include complex models of industrial robots, built using IGRIP. Future 'virtual' control of telerobot arms would also require a large polygonal modelling capability.
3. To provide a frame rate of 25 Hz (PAL max; from the existing 10 Hz).
4. To improve the system's video capture and display performance (from 10 Hz to 25 Hz, full colour (24 bit)).
5. To remove image generation lag (from 0.5 s to virtually zero (i.e. < 0.05 s) to minimize perceptual disruption). This, in conjunction with the Ascension *Bird* Tracking System, would dramatically improve head-graphics slaving characteristics.

In August of 1991, Division was once again contracted to enhance the ARRC VR Computing System. Division's solution was based on a next generation virtual reality system called *SuperVision*, based on a scalable communications architecture called a *High Speed Link* (HSL; 200 Mbytes per second), which has been designed to support parallel vision applications of the sort required by the ARRC. The High Speed Link is a point-to-point connection (rather than a bus) between high performance processors, such as the Intel i860, which enables complex multiprocessor systems to be built up without communications bottlenecks. Stereo visualization is provided by employing two HSL subsystems, each possessing two i860s for image generation. These are then controlled by the existing *Vision* T800 Architecture, which is also responsible for coordination of the peripherals used in the ARRC's system (DataGlove, Teletact, Macrospeak, etc.).

Besides the interfacing of CAD packages such as IGRIP with the *Vision/SuperVision* computers, another system currently in use at the ARRC is a Virtual Reality Toolkit, developed by Dimension International (UK) for use with a 486-PC and SPEA Graphics Card. This system permits the efficient construction of whole virtual worlds, through which the user move using (primarily) a Spaceball 6 degree-of-freedom joystick. To make full use of the VR Toolkit, researchers at the ARRC have recently ported Dimension files onto the *SuperVision* architecture with great success, thereby enabling the display of stereo imagery to the wearer of a headset such as the VPL EyePhone, and the interaction with virtual objects using a DataGlove, Teletact *Commander*, or other appropriate input device. Textures can be mapped onto selected polygons where appropriate. Digitized pictures from a Canon Ion PC Camera have received similar treatment, as soon will Sense8's WorldToolKit and AutoCAD V.12. The next section discusses the general issue of 'conversion' further.

5 Standards for VR?

Since the UK's first VR Conference in 1991 [9], the number of VR software packages available – Vream, WorldToolKit, VR Toolkit, Photo VR, Mandala, Virtus Walkthrough (to name a few) – has increased enormously, yielding a bewildering array of data formats and standards. This profusion of systems has succeeded in confusing many of the industrialists who visited the ARRC seeking a VR solution to their own visualization problems. While each of these systems may excel in a specialized area, it has become necessary to produce *conversion software* allowing models to be exchanged between their very different file formats and world generation techniques, thus enabling those who have already generated complex computerized models to experience them in the VR systems of their choice. Providing the ability to show the same model on a variety of systems allows the prospective user to judge not only the performance they require, but the level of immersion which suits their application.

While some file standards such as AutoDesk's DXF are supported on many platforms, the amount of information lost during conversions of these third party packages is considerable. Attributes such as animation and dynamics are rarely transferred. Also, worlds transferred in this manner are rarely optimized for the internal renderer of a specific VR engine and so give a false impression of the system's true capabilities.

These problems of compatibility, together with the fear of investing large amounts of capital in the production of models or simulations (which in a year's time could be inaccessible on an obsolete system) have dissuaded many from entering the field. In an effort to allay these fears and to demonstrate the abilities of a variety of visualization systems, a fully furnished virtual model of the ARRC building has been constructed complete with interactive animations of the research equipment it contains. The model's initial design was realized using Dimension International's VR Toolkit, using their standard 486PC, Spea Card and Spaceball hardware architecture (Plates XXVIII(a) and (b). Despite the relatively low power of this system it has attracted considerable interest from several large companies not currently involved in the field, as it displayed functionalities they had not known to be achievable. The conversion of the data to the ARRC's more powerful rendering engine (*SuperVision*) was quickly achieved, thus enabling the world to be compared directly on desktop and immersive VR systems with vastly differing input/output devices (Plate XXX).

Although the world has been successfully converted, the problem of how to pass animation and dynamics between the formats has not, at the time of writing, been resolved. The current approach being investigated is that of driving the animations from a dedicated external source (such as the IGRIP Dynamic CAD Package) which can accurately calculate the effects of actions in the world and pass the results to the renderer. Thus any platform could benefit from accurately simulated dynamics, which could be calculated in real time, or in the case of a complex problem, be the result of a large mainframe simulation package.

6   The Future: Nanopresence?

The concept of telepresence need not be restricted to hazardous environments which were originally designed for intervention by humans. It can also be readily extended to providing the human with an experience of presence in 3D worlds which are *invisible* to the naked eye. Successful developments in the new and exciting field of *nanotechnology* may well depend on providing researchers with the means of visualizing materials at an atomic level. In pursuit of this aim, the ARRC, together with the University of Salford, has demonstrated that VR can be used to allow virtual 'flight' over materials at such a level. To do this, a device known as a scanning tunnelling microscope (STM) has been employed.

An STM consists of a fine needle stylus whose height z above a conducting surface is controlled by a piezoelectric drive that can also deliver independent motion in the orthogonal axes x and y. A small voltage is applied between the tip and the surface to be scanned which causes a small quantum mechanical current to flow when the tip is positioned within a few atomic diameters of the surface. The tip is then scanned over the surface, whilst the z drive is controlled to maintain a constant tunnelling current between the tip and the surface. By converting the output of the STM into polygonal form, an operator can now 'fly' over the surface of, for example, a 15,000 Ångstrom-square sample of platinum that has been bombarded with helium ions and diamond polished (Fig. 13.8). These exciting new developments in

Figure 13.8 A virtual Reality representation of the atomic surface of a virtual image of Platinum derived using scanning tunnelling microscope data. The actual (real) surface size of this sample is 15.5 × 15.5kÅ; the equivalent virtual model size is 40,000 polygons, optimised for the Division *SuperVision* System into 140 tri-strips.

nanopresence have already demonstrated to microscopy engineers that it is possible to visualize new surface features, previously undetectable using conventional display techniques. The next step in this work has very similar aims to ARRC's telepresence initiative – to link the 'flight' of the human immersed in the microscopic virtual world directly to the motions of the real STM stylus.

The implications of using VR for nanopresence for non-destructive testing and inspection of materials in the offshore, aerospace and medical industry are enormous, as is its use in assisting the human in the assembly of future micro-devices, such as motors, pumps and actuators.

7 Conclusions

Research and development activities at the UK's Advanced Robotics Research Centre have, over the past two years or so, concentrated on the concept of using VR technology as a tool to achieve telepresence. Throughout this time, much effort has been devoted to 'troubleshooting' – addressing the fundamental limitations of VR hardware and software and attempting to devise low-cost and practical solutions. In the main, this philosophy, although not planned, has been successful in spawning projects and products such as the Teletact Glove. The ARRC is about to enter a new era in its history, with a number of new contract opportunities. Many of these are not, interestingly, related to advanced robotics. Nevertheless the skills and experience of researchers at the ARRC, together with the centre's VR laboratory facilities, place it in an unrivalled position to respond to these new challenges. Certainly research in the field of advanced robotics will continue, particularly in the areas of using VR for real-time sensing (e.g. laser imaging) and control (e.g. of mobile and manipulative robots). Whatever the future holds, the ARRC's small team of human factors, electronics, CAD and software specialists have done much to bring UK VR research to the forefront of international attention.

It is the feeling of the author that, of the many applications being suggested as appropriate targets for VR technologies, telerobotics and telepresence should be at the top of the list. Virtual reality is a *tool* for achieving telepresence, and telepresence is the means of demonstrating that VR will not remain just a crude game, or a useless stand-alone demonstration of a technology seeking an application. For once, researchers have a means of successfully integrating *real* intelligence in the robot sensor–robot control loop . . . that of the human being.

References

1   Sheridan, T.B. 1987. Telerobotics. *Plenary Presentation, 10th IFAC World Congress on Automatic Control*, Munich, Germany, July.
2   Sheridan, T.B. 1989. Telerobotics. *Automatica*, **25** (4): 487–507.
3   Stone, R.J. 1991. Applications focus: Telepresence. *Proc. Virtual Reality (Impact and Applications); Real World Applications of Virtual Reality (Day 2)*, June.
4   Stone, R.J. and Dalton, G.D. 1991. Virtual reality and telepresence: Creating visual worlds from non-visual sensors. *Proc. ORIA '91; Telerobotics in Hostile Environments*, Marseille, France, December.
5   Burdea, G. and Speeter, T. 1989. Portable dextrous force feedback master for robot telemanipulation. *Proc. NASA Conference on Space Telerobotics, 2*. Pasadena, CA, 153–161.
6   Burdea, G., 1991. Portable Dextrous Force Feedback Master for Robot Telemanipulation. US Patent, No. 5,004,391.
7   Fox, B. 1991. 3-D video doubles up on tape. *New Scientist* (1772), 8 June.
8   Grimsdale, C. 1991. *dVs*: Distributed Virtual Environment System. *Proc. Computer Graphics*, London, UK, 163–170.
9   Feldman, T. (Ed.). 1991. Virtual Reality '91: Impacts and Applications. *Proc. First Annual Conference on Virtual Reality*, London, UK, June.

Biography

Robert Stone is the Technical Manager of the UK Advanced Robotics Research Centre in Salford, UK, with prime responsibility for Virtual Reality and Telepresence Projects. He is a Chartered Psychologist with an MSc in Ergonomics, and has recently been appointed as Honorary Senior Research Fellow of Salford University, where he is also studying for a PhD. A member of the Editorial Board of the Journal *Presence*, Bob has lectured widely on the subject of VR at such venues as Cambridge, Salford and Dublin Universities, and at international functions such as MIMAD (Madrid), Imagina (Monte Carlo), MICAD (Paris), Informatique '92 (Montpellier) and advanced robotics and VR conferences in California, Tokyo, Marseille and Pisa.

14 Critical Aspects of Visually Coupled Systems

Roy S. Kalawsky[1]

Systems Technology R&D, British Aerospace

Abstract

A Visually Coupled System (VCS) forms the heart of all immersive virtual environment systems (frequently known as virtual reality systems). A VCS comprises space trackers, helmet-mounted displays, sensors and display generators [1,2]. In this paper a VCS is described along with its components, interfaces and performance requirements. Integration of the VCS components requires very careful selection and matching of a range of technologies from hardware interface and software integration points of view. Moreover, it is important to examine the task requirements and ensure that these are considered in the design [3,4].

1 Visually Coupled Systems

A generic VCS (Fig. 14.1) comprises a head tracking system, helmet-mounted display, computer graphics system and a steerable sensor system [5,6].

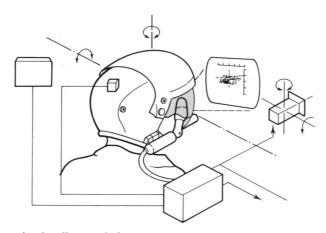

Figure 14.1 Generic visually coupled system.

---

[1] Roy Kalawsky is visiting Professor of Virtual Environments and Advanced Display Technologies, The University of Hull.

Head tracker: the head tracker determines the position (x,y,z) and orientation (azimuth, elevation and roll) of the user's helmet relative to a fixed position in space.

Helmet-mounted display: the helmet-mounted display provides the user with a monocular, biocular or binocular image in the user's line of sight. Depending upon the application, the image may be collimated at infinity or focused to a point in the near field. Display information is derived from either a computer graphics system or the steerable sensor system.

A visually coupled system is produced when head line of sight data are used to compute visuals for the helmet-mounted display from either the computer graphics system or the steerable sensor.

Figure 14.2 shows the actual components that must be considered in the design of a VCS.

2   Head Tracker Issues

Head tracking systems are frequently taken for granted [7], and little attention is given to the parameters that affect system performance. Unless the head tracker is carefully integrated with the VCS then unacceptable lags will become evident in the images presented to the user. Whilst the head tracker is not the only source of lags within a VCS, it is important to understand its contribution to the overall lag.

At one time update rate was thought to be the only critical parameter of a space tracking system. More recently, another term was introduced called *phase lag*. Whilst phase lag performance provides an explanation for tracker performance there are other inter-related parameters that must be considered. These parameters include, static accuracy, dynamic accuracy, latency and update rate.

When designing a VCS it is important to understand the consequence of each of these parameters, their interdependencies and how one parameter may be offset

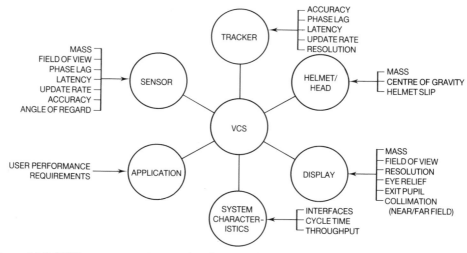

Figure 14.2 VCS component integration issues.

against another to achieve optimum performance. To optimize a head tracker for a particular task, trade-offs must be made. Unfortunately, few people understand how to answer the trade-off question from a scientific viewpoint.

Five performance criteria will now be defined to avoid mis-interpretation of performance specifications. To assist this definition, Fig. 14.3 shows where the main timing delays occur in a generic tracking system.

2.1 Static accuracy

Static accuracy is the ability of a tracker to determine the coordinates of a helmet in space. This figure is the maximum deviation on a single sample with no averaging or deviation applied. This value is the most empirical measurement (raw data value) and therefore objective. When quoting accuracy it is essential to state how the accuracy was measured and what type of confidence window was applied.

The factors contributing to the static accuracy include:

- receiver sensitivity
- transmitter signal to noise ratio
- analogue to digital convertor resolution
- analogue component noise tolerance levels
- rounding error during algorithm computation
- environmental effects
- algorithm errors
- installation errors
- operator error.

These factors contribute differently to the error of the overall system. Some parameters have a greater effect on static accuracy than others. Unfortunately, it is not possible to sum the individual errors for an overall system error. Neither is it possible to look at the maximum error and attribute overall system performance to that single component.

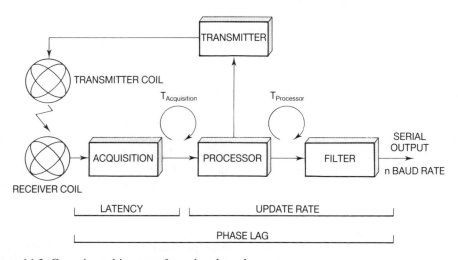

Figure 14.3 Generic architecture for a head tracker system.

2.2   Dynamic accuracy

Dynamic accuracy relates to the system accuracy as the tracker's sensor is moved. Dynamic accuracy is an additional attribute to the static accuracy. The following factors contribute to the system's dynamic accuracy:

- processor type
- system architecture
- time dependent system components.

Dynamic accuracy is extremely dependent on static accuracy. If a long integration period is used, the trade-off between static and dynamic accuracy is reasonably straightforward. For a large number of acquisitions over a long integration period the dynamic accuracy can be quite good.

If a time limit is imposed, as it will be, for fast tracking systems then dynamic accuracy suffers. The less time there is to acquire data and solve the coordinate position, the fewer acquisitions can take place.

2.3   Phase lag

Phase lag is perhaps the most important parameter of a space tracking system and is the ability of the system to determine an object's position within a given period of time after a change in object position. In a visually coupled system real-time generation of scene images is very important. A phase lag in the tracker system can lead to unacceptable lags in the visuals presented to the user. This leads to a symptom known as simulator sickness.

Main contributors to phase lag include:

- architecture
- processor type
- algorithm.

System architecture is very important and all elements must be chosen for real-time performance. This is especially true in the acquisition stage where real-time data collection is critical. The processor must be able to calculate the position and orientation data fast enough to keep the overall phase lag figure low.

Clearly, the type of algorithm used is of particular importance. An iterative solution will mean that the processor has to calculate position and orientation many times. If the algorithm is properly designed then each iteration will yield a more accurate solution. Unfortunately, each iteration increases the amount of phase delay. A second approach is to use a deterministic solution and orientations are calculated for each set of coordinates.

All time dependent components affect phase lag performance. If any of the components are improved then phase lag will be reduced. However, there is a trade off between static/dynamic accuracy and phase lag. In applying a tracker to a visually coupled system it is important to understand the requirements of the end application and these relate to the trade-off.

2.4   Update rate

Update rate is the tracker's ability to output position and orientation data to the output port. Many users place high update rate at the top of their requirement list.

Unfortunately, they do not understand the relationship of this parameter to the other parameters.

To some extent, update rate is dependent upon the factors that contribute to phase lag. Update rate is not a function of the acquisition process and consequently it does not reflect overall system performance. The system processor can have a significant bearing on the update performance in the sense that it must manipulate the algorithm and calculate the position/orientation value before outputting the data on the output port. Some tracker systems use old data when new information is unavailable because of slow internal processing systems. If the tracker stores position/orientation data in an array (that is not updated at the same rate as updating the output port), the resulting update rate and static accuracy can be high but phase lag and dynamic accuracy performance can become generally very poor.

2.5 Latency

There appear to be several definitions of latency. Some manufacturers use the definition of update rate given above to describe latency. Gaertner provides a good definition of latency which has been adopted in this paper.

Latency is the rate at which the acquisition portion of the system can acquire new data. As such it deals with signals in the analogue domain and is an evaluation of the receiver to perform in real time. There are two aspects to this, the first being how accurate the receiver assembly is, and secondly, how quickly the receiver can sense a change in the transmitter. Summing update rate with latency results in the phase lag response.

3 Helmet-Mounted Display Issues

There are many parameters of a display system that must be considered for a virtual environment system [4]. This paper will only deal with those parameters that specifically apply to the performance of a visually coupled system. These have an inherent timing relationship. However, before dealing with these issues, the question of display resolution will be raised. This is not directly related to the time criticality issues of a visually coupled system. Unfortunately, a large number of manufacturers are abusing the basic definition of resolution in such a way that a completely erroneous figure is given. Their quoted resolution figure is considerably higher than the actual value. It must be pointed out that this situation primarily applies to head-mounted displays that are based on liquid crystal displays. LCD manufacturers rightly or wrongly specify resolution based on the number of discrete LCD elements. These LCD elements are given either red, green or blue colour attributes. A single colour pixel being composed of a red, green and blue element (Fig. 14.4).

Manufacturers of LCD based devices simply transfer the LCD manufacturer's resolution figure to an overall display resolution figure. In the television and computer graphics industry, a colour pixel is a composite of the individual primary elements. Initial examination of a manufacturer's display specification often suggests an adequate resolution, but on closer examination all is revealed. For instance, a quoted resolution of 360 × 240 pixels is very different from an actual resolution of 208 × 139 pixels. Most displays are required to operate over very large fields of view. A display device with low resolution results in extremely disappointing displays

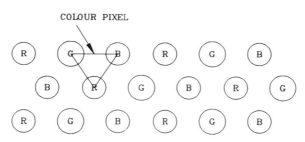

Figure 14.4 Arrangement of colour elements in a typical LCD.

when 'magnified' over a wide field of view. It is not uncommon to be able to see the individual primary colour elements. Certain manufacturers attempt to get round this problem by employing either diffuser screens or spatial filters over the LCD device. This has the effect of suppressing the edge information from individual primary colour elements. Whilst this reduces pixel structure it does tend to produce poor displays that take on a blurred appearance. Whether this is acceptable to the user or not depends on the application/task.

HMD parameters that have a bearing on the performance of a visually coupled system include:

- FOV
- Resolution
- Eye Relief
- Exit Pupil
- Collimation
- Update Rate.

4   Image/Graphic Generator Issues

The design and implementation of the graphics system can have a critical bearing on the performance of a visually coupled system. There is no doubt that the problems of lag in an interactive computer graphics system are complex. The problems of tracker induced lags have been discussed. However, the overall system lag can be a function of the way a computer graphics system has been constructed. Real-time interaction with a virtual environment places a high demand on the technologies involved. Unfortunately, few manufacturers are able, or willing to quote transmission delays through their systems. It is relatively straightforward to quantify transmission delays through a single processor system but with multiprocessor architectures the matter becomes extremely involved. In some instances it may not be possible to work out the exact transmission delay through a multiprocessor system. Instead, timings can only be calculated with a degree of uncertainty or tolerance.

From a complete system point of view two types of lag can be defined, these are transmission lag and position lag.

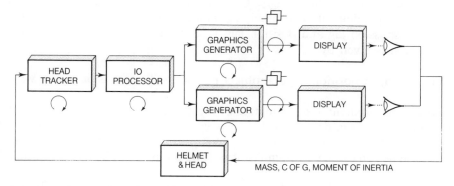

Figure 14.5 Simplified visually coupled system architecture.

4.1 Transmission lag

Transmission lag is defined as the time delay between a user interaction (e.g. head or hand position tracker) and a corresponding movement on the display.

Noise or uncertainty in the computation process within the tracker or graphics generator will cause a jitter in the output response.

4.2 Position lag

Position lag is induced by velocity and is defined in two parts:

- difference between the distance moved from a known position (at a given velocity)
- actual distance moved in the virtual image.

Position lag is also a function of the velocity of the tracker's sensor and any filtering

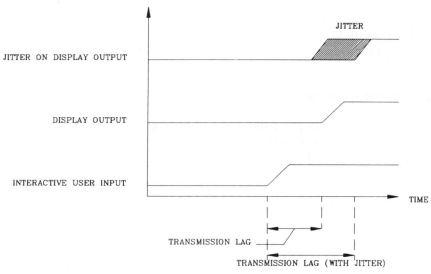

Figure 14.6 Transmission lag within a VCS.

applied to the output of the tracker. Unfortunately, transmission lag and position lag are not independent of each other. A simple expression describing the overall effect of transmission lag and position lag on a virtual object as a function of real object position is given by:

Virtual object position = Real object position − Transmission lag × Velocity.

In practice, measurement and calculation of these parameters is extremely involved.

To reduce the system dependent lags in a visually coupled system it is important to be able to measure the individual lags comprising the overall transmission lag. Architectural design can have a significant bearing on the overall system transmission lag.

Figure 14.5 shows an idealized visually coupled system architecture. The tracker is assumed to be interfaced to a dedicated input–output (IO) processor whose task is to convert tracker data into data appropriate for a graphics/rendering computer. Two identical graphics channels are used, one per eye. Information generated by the IO processor is supplied simultaneously to the graphics generators. In theory, this approach removes the synchronization problems between the left and right eye channels. The individual timing delays through this architectual arrangement are given in the figure. A visually coupled system is a closed loop system involving a helmet-mounted display that is mounted on the user's head. Parameters such as mass, moment of inertia and centre of gravity all affect the feedback path response. This in turn has a bearing on the overall performance of a user in a visually coupled system.

Departure from the idealized VCS can cause problems such as synchronization difficulties between the left and right eye channels. This manifests itself as an apparent update rate difference between the two channels. Even the idealized VCS can suffer from this defect if one of the channels contains more displayed information (e.g. a greater number of polygons). To reduce or eliminate this effect it is necessary to ensure that graphic drawing operations are completely written into corresponding frame buffers before the buffers are swopped onto the display generation electronics. This buffer swop must be synchronized between the two channels so that it occurs simultaneously.

5   Concluding Remarks

Visually coupled systems are at the heart of all immersive virtual reality systems today. It is very surprising that very few virtual reality researchers are aware of the type and exact nature of the lags within their systems. The overall transmission lag

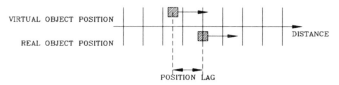

Figure 14.7 Position lag within a VCS.

may be estimated to a first order, but there are no standard techniques to measure this parameter or the consistent delays. To optimize the overall performance of a VCS it is very important to be able to understand where the delays occur and what their overall magnitude is.

When these data are available it will be easier to put design effort into those parts of the system where maximum delays or lags occur that affect the performance of a VCS.

Experience to date [8] (see also chapter 6) highlights that VCS lags are one of the most important parameters (second only to display resolution) of immersive virtual reality systems. User performance can be entirely limited by system lag. Having agreed on a series of system induced lags it now remains to develop techniques to measure and quantify the actual lags for a range of VCS components.

This paper suggests that the performance of visually coupled systems should be studied in terms of perceptual data and motion dynamics. There is not, as yet, a sufficient understanding to simulate the stimulus structure of the perceptual environment. Optimization of the VCS illusion can only be achieved if the performance of the technology is matched to the human perceptual system, a system that has evolved to perceive the natural environment. Failure to match the requirements of the perceptual system may appear as flaws in the illusion of a virtual environment. The available psychophysical research is a useful guide for current research. However, using these findings to determine the specific performance requirements of a VCS is dubious because of over-generalization. Current research represents examples of the perceptual research necessary to quantify the performance required for a VCS. Meanwhile, a gap exists between perceptual understanding and technical practice. The development of VCS technology in the absence of pertinent perceptual research is not surprising.

However, the gap of understanding is not a barrier to current development. The effects of inadequate performance are mitigated by the adaptability of the human perceptual system. For this reason, perceptual imperfections may be acceptable, since slight, and sometimes gross, distortions can cause the user to unconsciously adjust the visual or proprioceptive processes. This is the case with current virtual reality systems, that, despite perceptual distortions, produce an adequate illusion for a considerable number of users. In some cases however, mismatches are beyond the tolerances of the perceptual system, causing the virtual environment illusion to collapse. More seriously, perceptual conflicts may contribute to simulation sickness.

To create a perceptually rich virtual environment illusion, we must understand the performance requirements of the human perceptual system. Only then can rational trade-offs be made. This applies not only to discrete technologies such as position-tracking, but to the entire visually coupled system.

Acknowledgements

The author wishes to acknowledge the technical input provided by Chris Gaertner of Gaertner Research Inc., and Bob McFarlane, GEC-Ferranti. This paper is based with permission on an extract from a draft of a forthcoming book to be published by Addison-Wesley Publishers in 1993 (*The Science of Virtual Reality and Virtual*

Environments, Addison-Wesley, 1993). Finally, kind permission to publish this article by British Aerospace is gratefully acknowledged.

References

1   Sutherland, I. 1965. The ultimate display. *Proc. IFIP Congress*, 506–508.
2   Sutherland, I. 1968. A head-mounted three-dimensional display. *Proc. Fall Joint Computer Conference*, 757–764.
3   Kalawsky, R.S. 1991. Reality of virtual reality. *IEE Colloquium on 'Real World Visualisation – Virtual World – Virtual Reality*, London, UK.
4   Kalawsky, R.S. 1992. Beyond the Super Cockpit. *Proc. Virtual Reality 92*, London, UK.
5   Furness, T.A. 1986. The Super Cockpit and its human factors challenges. *Proc. Human Factors Society – 30th Annual Meeting*.
6   Kalawsky, R.S. 1987. Pilot integration and the implications on the design of advanced cockpits. *Conference (425) The Man-Machine Interface in Tactical Aircraft Design and Combat Automation*, Agard, Stuttgart.
7   Kalawsky, R.S. 1991. From visually coupled systems to virtual reality: An aerospace perspective. *Proc. Computer Graphics 91*.
8   Kalawsky, R.S. 1992. A comprehensive virtual environment laboratory. *BCS International Conference on Virtual Reality Systems*, 20–21 May, London, UK.

15 AVIARY – A Generic Virtual Reality Interface for Real Applications

A.J. West,[1] T.L.J. Howard, R.J. Hubbold,
A.D. Murta, D.N. Snowdon and D.A. Butler
*Advanced Interfaces Group, Department of
Computer Science, University of Manchester*

Abstract

This paper introduces the work of the Advanced Interfaces Group at the University of Manchester, which is applying recent innovations in the field of human–computer interaction to important real-world applications, whose present human–computer interfaces are difficult and unnatural. We begin with an analysis of the problems of existing interfaces, and present an overview of our proposed solution – AVIARY, the generic, hierarchical, extensible virtual world model. We describe a users' conceptual model for AVIARY, implementation strategies for software and hardware, and the application of the model to specific real-world problems.

1 Introduction

Our motivation for the work described in this paper is that we perceive many of the interfaces to today's complex computer applications to be difficult and unnatural to use. With any computer system it is necessary for users to be trained in using the system if they are to become adept at manipulating information via the system's interface. Indeed, a central problem of designing good user interfaces is that humans are very adaptable, and will often learn to cope with poor interfaces. Historically, the power of the computer to assist with complex tasks has made it so valuable a machine, that the issue of whether the interface is good or bad has almost seemed to be of secondary importance.

For straightforward tasks, such as word processing, the past decade has seen a major improvement in user interfaces based on direct manipulation, as exemplified by the popular 'desktop' paradigm. However, systems are becoming ever more complex, and there is evidence that paradigms such as this do not extend readily

---

[1] Author for correspondence, ajw@cs.man.ac.uk

VIRTUAL REALITY SYSTEMS
ISBN 0-12-227748-1

into these more complicated areas. We offer two particular examples which illustrate this situation.

The first concerns the problems of three-dimensional design. 3D graphics has been researched and used for thirty years – see, for example Tim Johnson's paper of 1963 [1] – and efforts have continued to improve the interfaces for 3D display and direct manipulation [2,3]. Much of this has been hampered by the central problem of interacting with a supposedly 3D world through a flat display screen. An exception to this was the pioneering work by Sutherland on head-mounted displays [4], which was technologically too far ahead of its time to find general acceptance. During the same period there have been very big improvements in the computer's capabilities for storing and manipulating precise geometric descriptions of 3D designs, of which solid modelling systems are but one example. It is evident that the user interfaces to these systems have not kept pace with the advances in modelling. User interface toolkits, based on the X windows system, for example, may give the interface a professional and modern look, but are not fundamentally different from very early CAD systems. Thus, there remain significant problems with the interfaces to 3D systems.

The second example is that of information management, a task which is becoming more complicated. The desktop paradigm begins to break down when we need to simultaneously track large amounts of information. One aspect of this is that the cognitive load on the operator increases. For example, consider a real-time application such as financial dealing, in which there is an enormous amount of information to be visualized and comprehended. Here, change may be frequent, and it is vital that important changes are quickly recognized and acknowledged. Limitations of screen size and flat display surfaces are contributory factors to the difficulty of designing interfaces for such complex systems. In the real world, however, humans have a remarkable ability to remember where objects are in 3D space – well, most of the time! In everyday life we are surrounded by very complex environments and we rely on our spatial memory and perceptual capabilities to keep track of things. For example, we can reach out and grasp a telephone almost without looking at it because we remember where the phone is positioned. These issues have been explored in spatial data management research [5,6], and more recently researchers have begun to consider whether it is possible to transfer some of the cognitive load to the perceptual domain [7].

We may conclude, therefore, that humans have 3D perceptual and spatial skills which are largely ignored in today's user interfaces, partly because of technological limitations, and partly because some of the ideas are untested in real world applications. Recent developments in the technologies of Virtual Reality (VR) have led to major interest in exploring these user interface issues.

2 Work on VR at Manchester

Much of the work on VR currently centres on development of the base technology, which is still too crude to find general acceptance for most real world tasks. There is also a widening interest in developing specific applications of VR although many of these are based on fairly specialized environments. Examples include flight simulations and arcade games.

Our own research focuses on developing a general framework for advanced interfaces, known as AVIARY, which we shall describe in this paper. We believe that it is essential to study how we can apply our ideas to real problems, because it is only by doing this that we will discover those ideas which work, and those which do not. An important objective of AVIARY is that it should support a broad range of quite different types of VR environment, and to test this we have selected a number of trial applications. We plan to develop our ideas for these in collaboration with companies and other potential users to ensure a correct understanding of the real problems.

The initial applications we are pursuing are air traffic control, computer-aided design, data visualization and medicine, and we now examine each of these very briefly to give a flavour of how VR might be used to improve their interfaces.

2.1 Air traffic control

Traditionally, air traffic controllers use two-dimensional displays which show aircraft positions and directions, with flight codes and heights displayed as text. These displays are effectively enhanced radar pictures which depict a time-varying 3D situation in a 2D projection. While there may be good historical reasons for this approach it is clear that other forms of presentation can be devised. Indeed, it is striking how the current displays illustrate a recurring feature of user interfaces generally – namely their evolutionary development. In this application, the information to be displayed is multidimensional. Aircraft have a position in 3D space, a direction and speed, flight code, and an intended flight path. There is pressure for controllers in the UK to handle an increasing number of flights. If air traffic does grow substantially it is hard to see how this can be done without improvements to methods currently employed.

How might 3D interfaces be developed for this problem? We are studying methods for displaying flight information in 3D. One idea we are pursuing is to show aircraft positions and flight paths using envelopes in 3D space; these are like 3D tubes through which the aircraft fly. The controller can check that the necessary constraints for horizontal and vertical separation of aircraft are satisfied. In practice the computer applies the checks and indicates any potential violations. The controller can re-route an aircraft by directly manipulating its flight 'tube', with the computer again checking for violations. With a full VR environment, one could envisage the controller surrounded by aircraft in three dimensions, and able to directly manipulate flight paths by pushing and pulling at the envelopes. The different control zones have complex shapes in 3D space, so there is considerable scope for investigating alternative display techniques.

In practice, such a scenario is unlikely – a controller needs to work in an environment in which he or she can see and converse with other colleagues, and is unlikely to wear a VR headset. This is likely to be true of many applications, notwithstanding research into methods which allow a user to move around in a model. However, we believe that large screen, full field of view 3D displays, and suitable input devices which support novel interaction techniques have much to offer with problems of this type.

2.2   Computer-aided design

CAD systems for 3D design have been developed for 25 years. Indeed, CAD is becoming pervasive, and is routinely used for designing microchips, product packaging, cars and aircraft, to name but a few areas. Thus far, a few CAD applications of VR have been highlighted, especially computer-aided architectural design [8,9]. In one novel application, a Japanese company has developed a system which allows a purchaser of a kitchen design to experience what the design will be like by moving around inside it, opening cupboard doors and so on.

Fun though this may be, the potential for improving interfaces to CAD systems themselves, as opposed to allowing people to experience the end product, is enormous. Many CAD interfaces, such as solid modellers, are rooted in the modelling techniques used in physical construction. Much of the research in such systems has been concerned with rule checking – making sure that what has been constructed is logically correct and does not violate a variety of design rules. Clearly, such issues are of major practical importance for the engineer or designer if these systems are to be useful for real work. CAD interfaces, like many others, have tended to use standard interface toolkits for interaction, and construction techniques with which engineers are familiar, such as 2D projections for representing three dimensions. Because such practical issues are so important, little attention has been paid to other issues concerning the way we design and manipulate objects in three-dimensional space.

There is a fundamental problem here, which is that human beings have very real difficulties in visualizing three-dimensional situations [10]. One of the major potential benefits of VR is that it opens up genuinely new ways to build and interact with designs which are not limited by flat display surfaces. For example, imagine a system in which it is possible to sketch in 3D [11].

As an example of how VR could improve such interfaces we consider chemical plant design, using a piping design program. A number of these systems exist, such as PDMS [12]. Complex networks are assembled from a library of parts, interconnected by varying lengths of piping. With a VR system, one could literally *construct* such a design, using voice input to call down appropriate parts, and plugging them into their correct positions and orientations with a DataGlove. Design rules could be applied to each connection, and tolerances, accurate positioning, and lengths of piping could be checked.

2.3   Visualization

Supercomputers are increasingly being used for large scale simulation. Applications include computational fluid dynamics (CFD), finite element analysis, earth sciences, theoretical chemistry, pharmaceutical design, and astrophysics. The numerical models used in these applications are multidimensional and frequently time-varying [13,14]. Attempting to present such information in two dimensions can be very difficult. 3D rotation is often used to convey geometrical shape, and animation is used to show time-dependent behaviour [15]. With the addition of colour, a variety of symbols and other display techniques, the overall effect becomes too difficult to comprehend, and the result is a cognitive processing overload. Again, with VR we believe that the potential exists to remove part of the cognitive load and replace it with perceptual processing. Within the Department of Computer Science at the University of

Manchester we are already studying visualization problems in relation to simulations carried out on parallel computers. We plan to explore the application of VR to some of these problems.

2.4   Medical applications

The concept of virtual surgery has already been suggested as an application of VR. One can envisage the benefits of using a combination of video camera and computer-generated imagery within surgical procedures – for example keyhole surgery. Another major area which we hope to pursue is that of student training. There is a shortage of cadavers for medical students to practise on. Using slides and videos may give students a good appreciation of what a surgical procedure looks like, but cannot convey what it feels like to actually carry it out. Experience from flight and battle simulators has already shown that it is possible to create a very realistic response to emergencies – and it is this degree of 'realism' which it would be especially helpful to capture, without harm to real patients.

Such a simulation can also record what a student actually did – whether correct or incorrect – for subsequent analysis and rehearsal. It would be possible to practise just those parts of a procedure which required improvement – just like rehearsing a passage of music – instead of having to start all over again. A virtual body can be reused (abused?) as often as required in order to perfect a technique, unlike a cadaver which can only be dissected once. Models for these procedures will be captured using CT and NMR scanners.

2.5   Towards a new model for human–computer interaction

Exactly as with graphics systems a few years ago, it is apparent that many applications have common requirements, some of which include the following:

- The ability to structure and name objects and parts.
- The control of display methods, such as wireframe, shaded representations, volume rendering, sound, tactile feedback, and so on.
- Attaching constraints and other, possibly time-varying, application-dependent behaviour to objects.
- Navigation of the viewer around a scene.
- Interaction, in application-specific ways.
- Interaction between multiple users, such as a medical student and teacher in a simulated operation.

Some of these are affected by the practicality of introducing VR into the workplace. In pilot training, for example, a completely enclosed environment may be acceptable. Equally, for some training tasks in which the user must move around, navigation techniques which permit a reasonable range of movement will prove appropriate [16]. But in other situations, users need to work in a normal office environment in which they can communicate with colleagues, drink coffee, read papers on their desk, and so on. Thus, it will be important to explore input devices and novel interaction techniques which can be employed with more traditional 2D workstations and with large-screen, full field of view stereo displays [17,18].

It is pointless to support only those features needed for one application area, unless it is a large and very lucrative one. Many existing VR systems are intimately related to particular hardware and software. If we wish to design a system which is capable of supporting a wide range of applications, we require a model which can be implemented on a range of underlying hardware and software. This is especially important when we consider that current VR hardware is in its early stages of development, and in the years to come we can anticipate continuing advances in technology.

In the remainder of this paper we describe such a model. First, we develop a general framework – or in user interface parlance, a users' conceptual model.

3   The Generic World Model

Having looked at the motivation behind the AVIARY project, we now turn to the development of a model which will satisfy the requirements of advanced human–computer interfaces. We are dealing with a complex model, in that we are concerned with the nature of a *reality*, albeit one which is greatly simplified compared to the reality of the physical world we inhabit. It is therefore important that we begin by having a consistent understanding of the nature of the proposed reality. From this we will go on to examine in more detail the implementation of its various aspects in the software model, and then describe how these are realized on the hardware implementation.

In the following discussion we use the term 'world' to refer to a collection of properties and the laws which operate on them. Here, for example, mass and energy could be attributes, and gravitation or conservation would be laws. 'Objects' are then defined which possess these properties and whose behaviour is constrained by the laws. The term 'virtual environment' refers to the experience presented to the user by the system.

3.1   A conceptual model of reality

If we are to construct a consistent model of a reality, it is essential to develop a coherent philosophy in order to understand the part played by each component of the system, and the nature of their interactions. At this level of exposition, there are essentially four aspects of the reality with which we are concerned. These are as follows:

- The world and its nature.
- Objects which exist in the world.
- Applications which interface to the world through an association with objects in that world.
- Users which interact with applications.

We must define what is meant by each of these, how they interact, and how they should be interpreted in relation to the reality. By so doing, we are defining a conceptual model, which forms the basis of the implementation, and lends coherency to the world. This coherency is important. The powerful perceptual mechanisms of the users that we are trying to engage rely on there being some regularity, or underlying consistency, to their experience. It is important that the users' conceptual model we develop has this characteristic if it is to be comprehensible.

The task of developing such an infrastructure is in itself an exciting and challenging problem. Historically, much effort has been expended by philosophers developing systems to explain the nature of the reality we experience in our day-to-day lives. Many systems have been developed, and it might be argued that none has been entirely satisfactory. Some of these ideas are useful when designing the rather specialized (and more limited) realities that are the subject of this paper. At this stage we are not primarily concerned with implementation issues, although of course, that harsher kind of reality must also be borne in mind.

3.2 The requirements of reality

We begin by considering the requirements of reality. The purpose of the AVIARY project is to provide a VR interface to real applications. If our system is to have general application, then the range of features to be supported must be wide. These range from 3D objects with gravity, inertia and collision detection, to notions such as temperature and abstract vector spaces.

It immediately becomes apparent that supporting even a small subset of these requirements 'well', is beyond the scope of current accessible technology. By 'well' here, we note that, for VR, the emphasis must be on maintaining seamless interaction rates, which implies keeping the closed loop feedback times low enough for perception of the world to be convincing. Although we know from our everyday experience that individual interactions may take significant time [7], our overall perception of the world is smooth and immediate. Given this constraint, we conclude that any current VR model cannot simultaneously provide all the facilities desired for the range of applications we wish to support. This is a fact, and is unsurprising. From these considerations we can identify several requirements of the model, which are in some cases conflicting. These are as follows:

- The closed loop feedback time must be small – we must have perceptual continuity if we are to maintain realism.
- A large number of different facilities are required to support the range of applications envisaged.
- The system itself should minimally constrain the nature of the world models that can be generated.
- The system should provide a means of lending consistency to the worlds that are supported.

3.3 A simple model

A straightforward approach is to provide an infrastructure for a basic model of a world, and to require this to be tailored to suit particular requirements. There are two ways in which this tailoring may be done. Firstly, the application writer may extend the VR system's model of the world with the facilities required by the application. Gravitation for example, could be added to the basic world model. While this is useful for limited development, it is not satisfactory as a basis for the general support of advanced interfaces to the range of applications we envisage. If the system's support for applications extends significantly beyond rendering and event handling, then this begins to determine the form of worlds that can be supported. To decide that 'solid' objects are fundamental to a world, for example, precludes some obvious methods for representing vector spaces required in data visualization.

The second way in which a simple VR model may be matched to particular requirements is to extend the application itself to provide the additional functionality. Gravitation could for example be handled by the application taking on the task of computing its effects. If, in this case, the VR system's support extends no further than managing rendering and events, then a lot of work is left for the application to perform. In addition to compounding the problems of code re-use, different applications may present widely differing world models to the user unnecessarily. The coherency of the world presented to the user would be left as a problem for the applications interface writers, if it were not in some way intrinsically supported by the system. This appears to conflict with the wish that the system should not constrain the kinds of worlds that can be created.

3.4 Parallel worlds

For the interface requirements of the broad range of applications we have been considering, there is much that is in common, but also much that is mutually exclusive, either logically, or for reasons of efficiency as indicated above. The conflicting properties of commonality and diversity may be catered for by postulating that there are many possible worlds, each with its own particular set of laws, and that an application should choose the most appropriate world to map onto.

It is important to consider the relationships which exist between worlds, since it is likely that they cluster into groups with very closely related properties, dependent on the nature of the applications they are intended to support. For example, we would expect to make particular use of worlds with a three-dimensional nature, which contain solid objects that may collide with one another. For some worlds of this kind, supporting mechanical simulations, for example, it would be appropriate

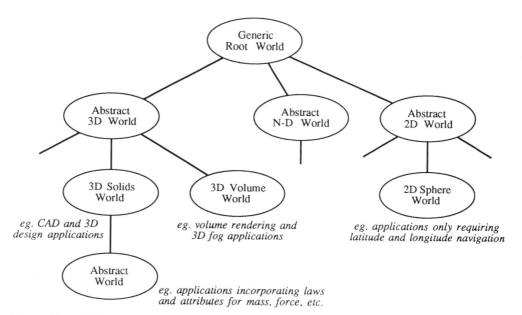

Figure 15.1 A hierarchy of virtual worlds.

to include gravity. For other applications, however, such as data visualization, gravity might not be appropriate.

From a consideration of the kinds of worlds appropriate to particular applications, we are led to propose a model of totality – the set of all possible worlds – which is structured as a hierarchy. This is illustrated in Fig. 15.1. At the top of the hierarchy are the laws and attributes that apply to all possible worlds. The basic support for time, space and causality would be appropriate here [19]. Beneath this we have a number of abstract worlds, which differ according to their fundamental spatial dimensionality. Below these are the broad classes of worlds that cover the most diverse world models (vector space, volume and 3D solid for example). Yet further down the hierarchy are worlds which have successive refinements of these laws. For example some worlds might have gravity, and others may not. Each world may therefore be viewed as a 'refinement' of its parent in the hierarchy, which inherits the properties of the parent and augments or amends them as appropriate.

What is the interpretation of the different levels of the hierarchy in our conceptual model of reality? As there is no constraint on what alterations a child world should make to the properties inherited from its parent, there is no absolute significance to the level of a world in the hierarchy. Furthermore, if we were to treat the highest level as the most abstract, with only the leaf nodes of the hierarchy as fully concrete worlds capable of being inhabited by objects, this would lead to a practical limitation. One can clearly envisage instances where the most appropriate world for an application is not one of the specialized nodes near the leaves, but one of the more general specifications nearer the top. If for example, we wished to construct a world to demonstrate relativistic effects, then a simple world near the top of the hierarchy would provide the most appropriate starting point, as more specialized worlds further down the hierarchy may have too restricted a view of spatial laws to support relativistic effects easily.

3.5 Worlds and objects

A world may contain objects which are governed by the laws of that world. The laws merely express relationships between objects; they have little to say about the objects themselves. An object, on the other hand, is a concrete entity – an instance of something upon which the laws act. Therefore the definition of a world must include a specification of the fundamental (minimum set of) attributes of all objects that may exist within it, and constraints on the values and relationships between these attributes. An object, as an instance, then specifies actual values for these attributes.

A conventional world for example, with gravity, inertia and collision detection would define mass, extent, location, velocity etc. as fundamental attributes of objects within it. A bouncing ball in this world must therefore possess these attributes. An application associated with the ball may define additional attributes, such as price, age, or the nature of the material from which the ball is made, which define the relationship of the object to the application.

At this point we should stress that we are conscious of the dangers of interpreting this model too literally with respect to the real physical world we inhabit. Clearly, the overhead of continually computing universal laws applying to all objects in a world would be immense. Rather, what is intended is that the system should provide methods for operating and interacting with items in the virtual world, and that operations which are essentially due to the nature of the world model rather than the application, should be automatically enacted and constraint checked by the virtual world system. In this way the system provides the default behaviour of objects and removes much of the burden of world dependent simulation from the applications.

Suppose, for example, that a simple 3D world has basic Newtonian mechanics defined, but only perfectly elastic behaviour on collision is supported. This defines the default behaviour of objects in this world. If we wish a particular object such as a bouncing ball to behave in a more complex way, perhaps non-elastically, or with deformation, or a jet motor, then some modification of the default behaviour of this object must be made. This new behaviour need only be invoked in situations where it applies. For a non-elastic model this would be on collision for example. When the new behaviour is not applicable, the object can be left in the hands of the world model.

3.6 An interpretation of applications and users

If objects act merely in passive accord with the laws of the world, then they are rather lifeless, or at least soul-less. We correspond the fact that objects are driven by forces beyond the mechanics of world laws to the notion of volition, or free will. This offers an explanation for the unusually structured or patterned behaviour of the world, that cannot be explained in terms of the world's laws alone.

We may distinguish two kinds of volitional behaviour: external and internal. When it originates from an application or user, then its source is external to the world model. We also permit objects to have behaviour directly, in which case its source is internal. The latter form enables the creation of autonomous world objects; this has practical implications discussed in the software implementation section which follows. Further, the two kinds of volition may be interrelated: the internal behaviour may be dynamically modified by the external sources. This volitional behaviour may appear at the level of individual objects, as in the case of an aeroplane 'icon' showing the position of a real world aeroplane, or it may be a more complex relationship between many objects, as in the representation of a vector space. In all cases however, it is essentially motivated by forces beyond the mundane laws of the world.

The operation of a single application in a world is conceptually straightforward. We are however particularly concerned to allow multiple applications to co-exist within the same world. In this case, if several applications are to interface with the same world model, then clearly their manifestations will be of that world, and must be compatible with it by conforming to its laws. In such a scheme, each application controls its own objects, which, as they affect and are affected by the world, may in turn affect, or be affected by other applications.

To use a trivial example, if two bouncing balls are driven by separate applications, and the balls collide, then one application is affecting another, purely through its representation in the world. Any interactions that take place via the world in this way will be consistent with the operation of the world. Interactions may certainly take place between applications directly without involving the world, in which case they occur beyond the realm of experience. This is illustrated in Fig. 15.2. From

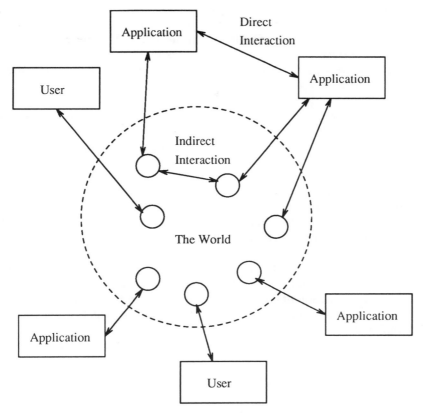

Figure 15.2 Direct and indirect interactions between applications.

the point of view of an inhabitant of the world, there can be no direct knowledge of ultimate reality (the applications), only of an indirect perception of it (the phenomena of the virtual world environment). If actions in the world, for example, cause files to be transferred between applications, then the mechanics of the actual transfer are direct communications between the applications involved, and are not experienced in the world unless explicitly manifested by the applications.

3.7 Users

How do users fit into this model? Given we have worlds with objects and applications driving them, what additional features are required to support users? To answer this question we must ask in what way users are special, and in what ways they differ from other aspects of the world.

A user may be an object in the sense of having an objective manifestation either to him/herself in the case of looking at one's body, or to other users if they exist. A user also has the qualities of an application in that they imbue the objects they control with volition beyond the background physical laws of the world. The fact that a user may perceive the world (whether visually, aurally, or with tactile feedback, and so on) and may interact with it, does not fundamentally distinguish a user from an application, which also 'perceives' the world, albeit in a rather different fashion. In the same way that an application needs to be able to interface with the world, a user requires suitable perceptual and effectual apparatus. For a human user the interface can be quite complex, as it involves a rendering task and needs a great deal of support. This is nonetheless viewed as merely the interface associated with the user application, and is not intrinsically central to the world model.

There will, of course, be more to be said on the subject of the perceptual apparatus available to the user when we come to address the implementation. At this level of exposition, however, we are led to treat users in the same way as applications.

3.8   Model summary

Our conceptual model comprises a hierarchy of extensible alternate worlds. A world defines a set of attributes, which all things that exist within the world must have, and laws which act on those attributes. Objects are concrete instances of things in the world. They have actual values for their attributes, and obey the laws of the world. Applications interact with the world through the objects, which may be regarded as the manifestation of the application within the world. Users are not considered as being fundamentally distinct from applications. Multiple applications and users are supported. This is the conceptual model to which users relate, and which the implementation supports.

4   Software Implementation

Any implementation of the AVIARY model should be fast, without compromising the philosophical model which underpins the system. The implementation therefore requires a large amount of computational power in order to provide the level of support needed in VR application development. Advantage may be taken of the natural parallelism present within the model.

To allow for the use of parallel hardware, the implementation is segmented into loosely connected processes which can execute concurrently. This is illustrated in Fig. 15.3. So as not to place too many restrictions on the nature of any particular kind of parallel hardware, the implementation assumes little about its capabilities. Specifically, there is no requirement for shared memory. The only interactions between processes occur explicitly via a communication system, which given a message will deliver it to a specified process. This strategy should allow the software to map onto a variety of hardware architectures. The components of the implementation are as follows:

- Input processes which monitor external hardware, such as a user's DataGlove or a speech recognition system, and produce input for interested processes.
- Output processes which respond to the state of the virtual environment and produce output to some external system. For example, an output process may monitor the state of the world from a given viewpoint and produce a graphical display on a user's headset, or may provide 3D audio output.
- A process, the Virtual Environment Manager (VEM), which maintains the consistency of the distributed database of virtual objects.

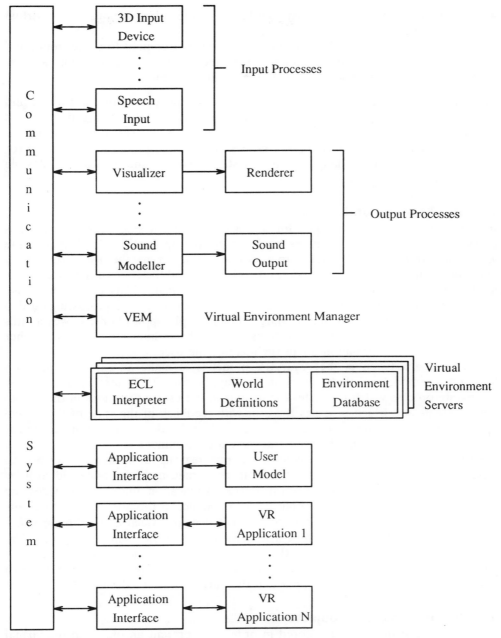

Figure 15.3 The software architecture.

- One or more server processes which contain an interpreter for a language, called the Environment Control Language (ECL), which is used to describe the virtual worlds and objects, class definitions for the virtual world and a distributed database which contains the objects present in the virtual environment.

- One or more applications which translate user input into actions in the virtual environment.
- One or more applications which use the virtual environment to gather input and to represent their output. A module is supplied which provides functions such as connecting the application to the communication system.

The remainder of this section describes issues affecting applications and users, and the reasons for their explicit separation; how worlds and objects are defined and the means of enforcing the universal laws; the mechanism by which the environment is distributed across loosely connected processors; and the use of an interpreted (or incrementally compiled) language to construct worlds and provide a flexible communications protocol.

4.1 Applications and users

In VR systems which cater only for a single user and a single application, it is possible to have the user's actions modelled by the application. In this case, the application directly reads input from devices attached to the user, such as a DataGlove and a headset, and updates its own state and the state of the user, which might be represented, for example, by a displayed hand. This approach is also suitable for supporting multiple users, although it is likely that the processing burden placed on the application would be large. For multiple applications, however, this approach is impractical, since applications must now communicate with one another in order to share information about the state of the user.

The approach taken in the AVIARY model is to make an explicit separation between the modelling of the user, and the application. Each user is modelled by a separate process which translates the actions of the user into actions in the virtual environment, and which provides the user with feedback of the state of the virtual environment. Communication between user and application is now indirect, and is achieved by manipulating objects in the virtual environment.

Although users and applications have different reasons for existence, they are no different as far as the rest of the system in concerned and are connected to it by identical interfaces. A module known as the 'Application Interface' provides the necessary facilities to allow an application to connect to the VR system, to access a particular world and manipulate objects in that world. Each application specifies which types of information it wishes to receive from which input processes. The applications receive messages from the input processes when an event in which they have registered interest occurs. Each application is then responsible for its own event processing based on this input and the current state of the world.

4.2 Worlds and their objects

The information that must be stored in order to represent an object in the virtual environment will vary, according to what the object itself is intended to represent. For example, an object which is visible will need to contain graphical information which can be used to render an image of that object. It may also need to store a bounding volume which could be used to help implement collision checking, and it may require additional data to describe its tactile properties, and so on. Clearly the nature of objects also depends on the world in which they exist: if the world models momentum (so that realistic collision effects may be achieved), then the objects will need to have particular masses. Because of these considerations it is not acceptable to simply provide a fixed number of object types and rely on the application writer to store any extra information.

As we saw in section 3.4, the conceptual model defines a hierarchy of worlds which provide the basic properties and laws governing objects in the worlds. The worlds are implemented as abstract classes – that is, they have no instances. Laws are encoded as program code in the methods of the world classes. For example a method 'move' for a Newtonian world would move the world object after first checking that the new position would not cause the object to occupy the same space as another object. Objects in the world are defined using sub-classes of the world classes. For example, a 'pipe' object might be defined using a sub-class of the 'CAD' class which would thus have a position, and be subject to the laws operating in the world of 3D solids. In addition, the 'pipe' class would define those attributes that describe real pipes such as length, inner and outer radii, material properties, and a graphical description. Creating a new pipe in the world is realized by creating an instance of the 'pipe' class.

The representation of objects can also be designated as 'active' or 'passive'. A passive object contains only data, and is operated on by applications. An active object has code as well as data associated with it, and can execute this code concurrently with the application which created it. The standard object-oriented notion of an 'object' actually falls somewhere between these two categories, in that the object will have code (in the form of methods) associated with it but will execute this code serially and in the same context as the application which invokes the method. With an active object it is possible for the object to reside in a different process from the application. This allows an application to create objects in a virtual environment which will then respond to stimuli in the environment without intervention by the application itself. In this way, the application writer can easily express the parallelism inherent in the environment. For example, in the real world a person is not limited to moving one item at a time, and as it is moved the object may touch several other objects, which may need to respond.

4.3   Distributing the virtual environment

Introducing parallelism into the implementation also creates problems, the most significant of which is the possibility of several concurrent processes requiring simultaneous access to the same data. A common situation might be that the application wishes to manipulate an object, at the same time that a renderer process needs to interrogate the object in order to display it. Storing the contents of the virtual environment in a single centralized database would result in a large amount of inefficiency due to the volume of communication needed between the database and the processes requiring access to the state of the environment. One solution is to allow multiple copies of each object to exist. However, this requires that consistency be maintained between the copies of each object, a situation which has much in common with the cache coherency problems experienced by shared memory multi-processors. To cope with this, the VEM maintains information regarding the allocation of all copies of objects to specific processors. When an object is modified in some way, an appropriate message is sent to the VEM which distributes the update to the relevant processors. In some machines the hardware and operating system manage this coherency, so this becomes trivial.

A further problem caused by the distributed nature of the system is that of synchronization. For example, several balls are arranged in a line on a flat surface so that each ball is touching its neighbour. An impulse is applied to a ball at the end of the line. An optimistic system might start the first ball moving and transmit a collision event to the next ball in line, and this would then propagate down the line of balls. If the ball at the other end is resting against an immovable obstruction, then an 'undo' message would have to be propagated back down the line restoring the balls to their original state as no movement could occur. A cautious system might propagate a message down the line to see if there was the possibility of movement before setting the balls in motion. In this case the cautious algorithm degrades performance in every case, while the optimistic algorithm will make mistakes and will subsequently need to correct them. The distributed nature of the implementation may make this problem worse, due to the inefficiency of inter-process communication. This type of problem occurs in distributed discrete event simulation, and is particularly difficult to solve for parallel machines. However, approaches to it do exist, such as the 'Time Warp' mechanism [20], and this is a central aspect of our research.

4.4   The environment control language

To get the necessary speed the core functions of the system should be written in an efficient compiled language. We would also like to be able to write the definitions for both the worlds, and the objects within them, in a language which provides support for object-oriented constructs. To ease prototyping it would be convenient if we could alter methods associated with worlds and objects at run-time. Also, we would not want to have to re-compile portions of the core system in order to change the definitions of worlds and their objects.

As stated earlier, the only communication between processes is by messages. Therefore, every time a new feature or class is added to the system, the interface which maps messages to 'procedure calls' must be extended. Also, if objects are to be passed between processors then the receiver needs some method of determining the type of an object at run-time. For these reasons, the implementation makes use of two languages: the Implementation Language (IL), and the Environment Control Language (ECL). The IL is the language which is used to code the VR system itself. The ECL is the language in which virtual worlds and objects are encoded. It is an interpreted (or incrementally compiled) language specially designed to support operations required by worlds and objects in the virtual environment. Since the ECL interpreter provides the interface which translates messages into actions, no explicit interface needs to be written when new classes are added. In fact, fragments of ECL code can actually be used as a message protocol, and this provides great flexibility since we are no longer constrained to having a fixed repertoire of message types. This also provides a mechanism for distributing code updates, as a code fragment which redefines one of an object's methods can be sent as an ordinary communication.

Using an interpreted language would seem to sacrifice performance in order to gain flexibility. However, this need not be so. Common functions are coded in the

IL and made available as primitive operations. ECL code then serves to 'glue' together these efficient building blocks which implement computationally expensive operations. This is an approach which has been used successfully in several areas. For example, the NeWS windowing system [21] is based on extensions to the interpreted language POSTSCRIPT [22], and systems such as GNU Emacs [23], WINTERP [24] and MusE [25] use versions of LISP combined with efficient primitive operations.

The ECL interpreter with its class hierarchy of worlds and objects and the environment database is packaged into a component of the system called the Virtual Environment Server. This component may be replicated as many times as required, in order to exploit parallelism. Its purpose is to provide a resource for storing the state of the world in the database and for executing the methods associated with each object in the virtual environment.

This section has presented an overview of our proposed implementation of our conceptual model for VR. The implementation is segmented into processes with explicit communication using code fragments of an interpreted language to provide a flexible communications protocol and the state of the system is contained in a distributed spatially oriented database.

5   A Hardware Platform for the AVIARY Model

The main focus of the AVIARY project is to develop a software environment based upon a consistent philosophical model, which will support the use of advanced interaction techniques within application domains. In this regard, the hardware on which the virtual world model is based, although essential in the realization of our goals, is not regarded as a primary research area. Although we have plans to implement our generic VR environment on a specific hardware architecture, the AVIARY model itself is platform-independent, and may be mapped onto any system with sufficiently high input/output and processing capabilities.

This section describes the computer system on which we initially intend to implement the AVIARY model. We have chosen a high performance, general purpose multicomputer – the ParSiFal 'T-Rack' – as the central processing resource.

5.1   The T-Rack
The T-Rack was designed and built in the Department of Computer Science at the University of Manchester as part of the Alvey sponsored ParSiFal (Parallel Simulation Facility) project [26]. It is a distributed memory machine, based upon the Inmos transputer [27]. The architecture of the T-Rack is shown in Fig. 15.4. The T-Rack contains 64 T800 transputer processors (numbered T1 to T64), on which user applications – in this case the AVIARY software – may be implemented. These are collectively known as the 'worker' transputer nodes. All inter-node communications within the T-Rack are performed via transputer links. Two links from each worker node are used to form a processor chain, known as the 'necklace'. The ends of the necklace are connected to a host interface transputer (TH), through which all code loading, and host-related input/output is performed.

The worker transputer links which do not form part of the necklace are attached to a large programmable switching network. This may be used to install additional

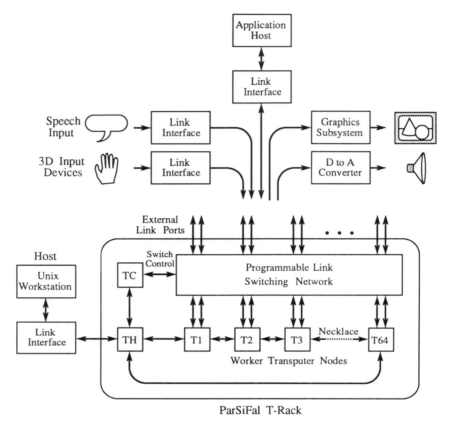

Figure 15.4 An overview of the hardware architecture.

connections between worker node pairs. Alternatively, some (or all) of the 128 off-necklace links may be routed through the switch for connection to external devices. The arrangement of communication routes within the switch network is managed by a control transputer (TC).

The Advanced Interfaces Group has a second T-Rack, which may be connected to the first rack via switched transputer links, should additional processing or input/output capabilities be required by the AVIARY implementation itself, or in support of the user applications interfaced to it.

5.2   Concurrency
One of the obvious benefits of using a parallel computer system such as the T-Rack, is the ability to take advantage of the inherently concurrent nature of the virtual world model. Concurrency is exhibited by the model at a number of levels, since there is support for multiple users interacting with multiple applications. Additionally, it can accept input from a number of active sources, and simultaneously drive several output devices. A virtual world may also contain within it many concurrently active objects, which respond to stimuli from external applications, users or other objects.

Consideration of the behavioural requirements of the virtual world model suggests an initial decomposition into two basic activities. The first is internal state maintenance, as performed by the Virtual Environment Manager and Virtual Environment Server processes of section 4.3. These allow objects to respond to stimuli, while checking that their behaviour is consistent with the universal laws which have been imposed. The second requirement is to interface with the real world. This involves commmunicating with users and external applications. This decomposition will be reflected in the way the AVIARY model is mapped onto the T-Rack worker processors. Some proportion of the processing nodes will be assigned the task of internal state maintenance (using a distributed state representation), and others will perform interface tasks. The precise number of transputers used for each of these basic activities need not be fixed, and will depend upon the complexity of the world being modelled, or the configuration of peripheral devices which are to be connected.

5.3   Connectivity and consistency

The communication of state information is a central issue in the implementation of the AVIARY model. As well as the inter-processor exchanges required to maintain internal consistency and propagate causality within the virtual world, the state of external peripherals such as 3D locators must be read and acted upon. At the same time, the state of the system as a whole must be presented to output devices so that it may be observed by users. The costs and complexity of communication within distributed systems must not be underestimated.

Within the T-Rack, transputer links provide the sole means of conveying state information between processors. The programmable link switching network of the T-Rack offers considerable flexibility in the installation of communication paths between different parts of the system. Thus networks may be constructed in which peripherals (connected to the T-Rack's external link ports) communicate with the state maintenance nodes via intermediate transputers which perform dedicated device interface activities.

The strategy of connecting peripherals to the T-Rack via the external link ports has two practical benefits. First, it is possible to attach a large number of external devices to the rack. In the current configuration up to 128 link ports may be made available for the attachment of peripherals. Second, the construction of transputer link interfaces which allow the connection of arbitrary hardware subsystems is relatively straightforward.

Maintaining consistency within a distributed state representation can be a problem in real-time applications such as VR. For example, the forwarding of state data across several nodes within a transputer network may result in the information being out of date by the time it reaches its destination. Problems such as this are alleviated by the ability of the T-Rack to dynamically re-arrange link connections at run-time, under the control of the distributed user application. This feature enables state data to be passed directly between arbitrary nodes in the network, wherever synchronism and latency are important issues [28].

5.4 Peripherals

Our virtual world model defines three fundamental types of peripheral: input devices (accepting data from users), output devices (supplying data to users) and external processing resources (supporting interaction with external applications).

Input devices will typically include spatial locators, such as DataGloves [29] and other 3D sensors [30–32]. Speech input provides another useful means of interaction [33]. In this realm, we hope to draw upon our previous research experience in using speech-based control within graphical environments [34].

Output to users may be presented through a variety of different media. For example, graphical representations of the virtual world may be generated for output to head-mounted, or other stereoscopic displays. Although individual transputer links do not have sufficient bandwidth to convey full screen pixel data at real-time rates, several such links may be used in parallel to write into a shared frame buffer [35]. An alternative solution is to use an off-board rendering subsystem, to which high-level graphical primitives are passed. We have opted for this second strategy, because it reduces the number of external link ports needed to support graphical output, and allows special purpose hardware to be used for low-level rendering operations. This approach is similar to that of Division's ProVision system [36].

A custom graphics subsystem for the T-Rack is currently under development; its structure is illustrated in Fig. 15.5. The hardware, as shown, provides stereoscopic output for a single user, and must therefore be duplicated if multiple users are to be supported. A display list is used to drive the rendering activities. It contains three types of information: geometrical object descriptions (each defined within a local coordinate system), transformations which specify the position and orientation of the objects in the virtual world, and a pair of user viewing transformations (one for each eye). The display list is updated by the T-Rack as the user navigates within the world, and as objects change position. Thus, for the majority of interactions, the traffic between the T-Rack and the graphics subsystem is limited to relatively low bandwidth transformation editing operations.

The display list processor traverses the display list, applying the required

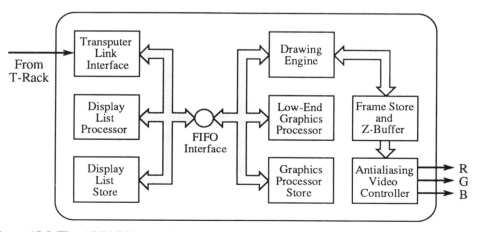

Figure 15.5 The AVIARY graphics subsystem.

transformations to the object descriptions. The transformed primitives are then passed on to a secondary low-end graphics processor which prepares them for scan conversion by a custom drawing engine. Separate eye views may then be extracted from the frame buffer for display on a stereo viewing device.

As well as graphical output, we also consider the use of sound within virtual environments to be essential. It may be used, for example, to relate directional cues corresponding to virtual world events, or to provide audio feedback in response to user interactions. The T-Rack is equipped with a high quality digital to analogue converter which accepts data from an outgoing transputer link, and generates a stereo line signal. This facility was used in a recent research project which modelled the acoustic properties of 3D environments in real time [37]; such modelling techniques should be useful within a VR context.

If the AVIARY system is to provide VR style interfaces for user applications, the machines on which these applications are hosted must be attached to the T-Rack in some way. Several such hosts may be connected to the T-Rack using the external link ports. Alternatively, the T-Rack host may itself be used to run external application programs, with rack access via the host interface transputer (TH, in Fig. 15.4).

6 Summary

In this paper we have highlighted the ways in which some applications are constrained by the inadequacies of interfaces between human beings and computer systems. We have presented AVIARY, a novel model for human–computer interactions, which is underpinned by a coherent philosophy. Our approach provides a generic extensible environment, onto which a range of applications, both existing and anticipated, can be mapped. We intend to evaluate the design by implementing AVIARY on a parallel architecture and applying it to the applications discussed in the paper.

Acknowledgements

It is a pleasure to be able to thank our colleagues, who have generously shared with us their insights and enthusiasm. We are grateful to Jim Garside, Alan Knowles and Pete Jinks of the Department of Computer Science, and to John Churcher of the Department of Psychology.

References

1   Johnson, T.E. 1963. Sketchpad III: A computer program for drawing in three dimensions. *Proc. Spring Joint Computer Conference*, Montvale, NJ.
2   Hubbold, R.J. 1970. TDD – an interactive program for three-dimensional drawing with graphical display and lightpen. *Proc. International Symposium Computer Graphics '70*, Brunel University, UK.
3   Encarnação, J. and Giloi, W. 1972. PRADIS – an advanced programming system for 3D display. *Proc. Spring Joint Computer Conference*, Montvale, NJ, 985–998.
4   Sutherland, I.E. 1968. A head-mounted three-dimensional display. *Proc. Spring Joint Computer Conference*, Washington, DC, 757–764.

5   Lippman, A. 1980. Movie maps: an application of the optical videodisc to computer graphics. *ACM Computer Graphics*, **14** (3): 39–42, July.

6   Lippman, A. 1981. And seeing through your hand. *Proc. SID 22 (2) Computer Graphics*, 103–113.

7   Robertson, G.G., Mackinlay, J.D. and Card, S.K. 1991. Cone trees: Animated 3D visualizations of hierarchical information. *Commun. ACM*, **34** (2): 189–194, February.

8   Airey, J.M., Rohlf, J.H. and Brooks, F.P., Jr. 1990. Towards image realism with interactive update rates in complex virtual building environments. *ACM Computer Graphics*, **24** (2): 41–50, March.

9   Clark, J.H. 1976. Designing surfaces in 3D. *Commun. ACM*, **19** (8): 454–460, August.

10 Parslow, R. 1991. Why is everyone 3D blind? *EUROGRAPHICS '91 Proc.*, August, 367–370.

11 Schmandt, C. 1983. Spatial input/display correspondence in a stereoscopic graphic work station. *ACM Computer Graphics*, **17** (3): 253–261, July.

12 CADCentre Ltd, High Cross, Madingley Road, Cambridge CB3 0HB, UK. *PDMS, Piping Design Management System*.

13 Brodlie, K.W., Carpenter, L., Earnshaw, R.A., Gallop, J.R., Hubbold, R.J., Mumford, A.M., Osland, C.D. and Quarendon, P. (Eds) 1992. *Scientific Visualization: techniques and applications*. Springer-Verlag.

14 Special issue on visualization, May 1991. *IEEE Computer Graphics and Applications*, **11** (3).

15 Feiner, S. and Beshers, C. 1990. Visualizing n-dimensional virtual worlds with n-vision. *ACM Computer Graphics*, **24** (2): 37–38, March.

16 Wang, J-F., Chi, V. and Fuchs, H. 1990. A real-time optical 3D tracker for head-mounted display systems. *ACM Computer Graphics*, **24** (2): 205–215, March.

17 Ware, C. and Osbourne, S. 1990. Exploration and virtual camera control in virtual three dimensional environments. *ACM Computer Graphics*, **24** (2): 175–183, March.

18 Stoops, D., Sachs, E. and Roberts, A. 1991. 3-Draw: A tool for designing 3D shapes. *IEEE Computer Graphics and Applications*, 18–26, November.

19 Kant, I. (Translation by J.M.D Meiklejohn). 1934. *Critique of Pure Reason*. Everyman series. Charles E. Tuttle & Co., Rutland, Vermont, USA.

20 Jefferson, D. and Sowizral, H. 1985. Fast concurrent simulation using the time warp mechanism. *Proc. Distributed Simulation*, 63–69.

21 Sun Microsystems, Mountain View, California, USA. *NeWS Preliminary Technical Overview*, October 1986.

22 Adobe Systems. 1985. *PostScript Language Reference Manual*. Addison-Wesley.

23 Stallman, R.M. 1981. EMACS: The extensible, customizable self-documenting display editor. *SIGPLAN Notices*, **16** (6): 147–156, June.

24 Mayer, N.P. 1991. *WINTERP – The OSF/MOTIF Widget Interpreter*. Hewlett-Packard Laboratories (included in the 'contrib' section of the X11 distribution).

25 Snowdon, D.N. 1991. *MusE: An environment for music*. Master's thesis, Department of Computer Science, University of Manchester.

26 Capon, P.C., Gurd, J.R. and Knowles, A.E. 1986. ParSiFal: a parallel simulation facility. *IEE Colloquium Digest 1986/91*, 2/1–2/3, May.

27 Inmos Limited. 1988. *Transputer Reference Manual*. Prentice Hall. Number 72 TRN 006 04.

28 Murta, A.D. 1991. *Support for Transputer Based Program Development via*

Run-Time Link Reconfiguration. PhD thesis, Department of Computer Science, University of Manchester.

29 Foley, J.D. 1987. Interfaces for advanced computing. *Scientific American*, **257** (4): 82–90, October.

30 Ware, C. and Jessome, D.R. 1988. Using the bat: A six-dimensional mouse for object placement. *IEEE Computer Graphics and Applications*, 65–70, November.

31 Prime, M.J. 1991. *Human factors assessment of input devices for EWS*. Technical Report RAL-91-033, Rutherford Appleton Laboratory, Didcot, April.

32 Polhemus. 3 space isotrak. Polhemus, Colchester, Vermont, USA, 1991.

33 Bolt, R.A. 1980. Put-that-there: Voice and gesture at the graphics interface. *ACM Computer Graphics*, **14** (3): 262–270, July.

34 Yeung, C.-K., 1989. Speakeasy. Project report, Department of Computer Science, University of Manchester.

35 Cheung, H.C. 1989. *A high performance graphics system for transputer arrays*. Master's thesis, Department of Computer Science, University of Manchester.

36 Pountain, D. 1991. ProVision: The packaging of Virtual Reality. *Byte*, 53–64, October.

37 Binns, G. 1991. A virtual sound environment using geometrical ray tracing. Project report, Department of Computer Science, University of Manchester.

Biographies

Dr Adrian West is a Lecturer in Computer Science at the University of Manchester. He has worked in the automated test equipment industry, and on parallel implementations of secure networks. He has published and presented work on the monitoring of parallel systems and the development of high level graphical environments for parallel programming. His current research interests are in programming environments for parallel systems, and the application of VR.

Toby Howard is a Lecturer in Computer Science at the University of Manchester. He has published widely in the field of graphics standards, particularly PHIGS, and his research interests include VR, high-level programming interfaces to graphics systems, electronic typography and publishing, and computer art.

Dr Roger J. Hubbold is a Senior Lecturer in Computer Science at the University of Manchester, and Associate Director, responsible for Visualization, in the Centre for Novel Computing. His primary research interest is software architectures for interactive visualization using parallel computing systems.

Dr Alan Murta is a Lecturer in Computer Science at the University of Manchester. His recent activities have included research into novel connection and communication strategies for transputer based systems. His current interests include the exploitation of parallelism in real-time graphical and acoustic modelling.

Dave Snowdon is a Research Student in the Department of Computer Science at the University of Manchester. In 1990 he obtained a 1st Class Honours degree in Computer Engineering from the University of Manchester, and in 1991 he obtained an MSc following research into an extensible object-oriented environment for the representation and manipulation of music. He is now working on a PhD in VR.

Alex Butler is a Research Associate with the Centre for Novel Computing at the University of Manchester. In 1987 he received a 1st Class Honours degree in Computer Engineering from the University of Manchester, and in 1989 he obtained an MSc by research, studying optical computing and holographic optical interconnects. He is currently completing a PhD thesis on the subject of 'Visualization and Parallelism in Computer Graphics'.

16 Using Gestures to Control a Virtual Arm

Michael J. Papper and Michael A. Gigante
*Royal Melbourne Institute of Technology,
Advanced Computer Graphics Centre*

Abstract

We have defined an extensible set of gestures that prove useful for teleoperation of a generalized human-like robot arm. We describe a useful set of commands, a technique to couple commands and gestures, and a tool to construct a simulated robotic arm.

1 Introduction

In this paper we describe our work on the design of a gesture-controlled simulated arm. This work was divided into three parts:

- specification of a generalized arm useful for teleoperation environments
- design of the interaction with the generalized arm together with a set of gestures to control the interaction
- tools that we built to assist in the creation and simulation of this arm.

We will discuss the technical components of the project: the gesture control/command language, effective gestures for command specification, and the use of limiters to control arm behaviour.

1.1 Motivation

The remote control and operation of robotic devices (teleoperation) is considered to be an important application of virtual reality systems. In these teleoperation environments, robotic manipulators are located at extremely remote (say in space) or hazardous (say nuclear materials handling) environments. The manipulator mimics the actions of the operator. The operator will see either a synthetic image of the remote site, or will see input from cameras at the remote site. In both cases, head-tracked, binocular displays will give the operator an adequate sense of remote presence.

In contrast to teleoperation, where the primary goal is interactive real-time control, conventional six degree of freedom robots are generally pre-programmed either by specialized high level languages or by teach-boxes. There is a considerable wealth of experience with both of these methods.

- High level robot programming languages such as VAL II [1] are well suited for cyclic or repetitive tasks that have complex conditional response. Effective use of high level robot languages require a verification step, typically with a graphical simulator. This is necessary to ensure the robot does not collide with the parts or any fixtures.
- Teach-boxes are direct control devices for the robot manipulator. The operator positions (and orients) the end-effector at positions through the cycle. This is analogous to key frames in computer animation. While the operator can use any available means to move between one 'key frame' and the next, the robot controller will interpolate the path automatically.

    Teach-boxes are in widespread use in the manufacturing industry where the tasks are predominantly fixed cyclic operations with few conditional responses. They are very accessible to production staff who may not be comfortable with programming languages. The teach-box has the additional advantage of providing direct visual feedback to the operator during the programming stage.

Unfortunately, both these methods are inappropriate for teleoperation. In addition to interactive control, we aim to have the manipulator track the movements of the operator as closely as possible. This is actually made difficult by the design of most conventional manipulators which do not mimic the human form. One obvious method of controlling a robot arm is to use inverse kinematics to calculate the intermediate joint angles from the position and orientation of the user's hand, however, there are two problems with this approach:

- there are typically multiple solutions (i.e. different set of joint angles that will result in the end-effector tracking the user's hand). This could cause a problem if the arm is operating in a confined space where some of the solutions could cause collisions or interference.
- there is a portion of the working volume that is inaccessible to the robot end-effector that is reachable for the operator's hand.

These problems reflect the fact that teleoperation was not a design criteria for conventional manipulators. To address these problems, we have proposed that a device more suitable for teleoperation be the basis of our environment.

This manipulator mimics the basic structure of the human arm/hand so that there is a direct mapping between the teleoperation user's arm movements and that of the manipulator. It also has a hand similar to the human form.

The manipulator is both easy and intuitive to operate since it behaves in a very similar way to our own arms. Thus in normal operation, since there is no mental mapping required by the user, there is very low degree of cognitive overhead.

To provide a larger working volume and more effective utilization, we have allowed the arm to operate as either a left or right arm – making it totally ambidextrous. We have also included a few additional degrees of freedom that have proven very useful in conventional manipulators – continuous wrist rotation and telescopic segments. To access these extended capabilities, we have designed a gesture control language.

The performance artist Stelarc has been involved in the design of the gestures and interaction modes. Stelarc was a visiting artist at RMIT during part of 1991.

He has become well known for his performances with a third arm.[1] He intends to use our simulated manipulator in live performances to largely replace his existing device. Stelarc's requirements for the arm's operation are extremely demanding and his feedback as a potential user has been very valuable.

Furthermore, this type of hand and gesture interaction may also be useful for controlling industrial machinery such as an excavator or back-hoe where it could replace the existing multiple joystick controllers.

1.2 Goals

The aim of our project is therefore to design a robotic manipulator with a structure similar to the human arm. This arm should also provide extended modes of operation found useful in conventional robotics. The manipulator should also be able to operate as both left or right-handed.

We also aim to define a set of gestures that prove useful for teleoperation environments using the manipulator. We can define a different set of gestures optimized for different applications. The definition of a 'gesture command language' results in appropriate gestures and ways to communicate them to the user. We hope that these techniques from the gesture command language will also be extensible to other applications.

We do not currently aim to physically build the manipulator, so instead, we are using a *simulated arm* which is displayable with conventional 3D computer graphics techniques. One of the reasons for using a simulated arm is that it allows us to explore which features are necessary for our applications. This would fully specify the requirements for a physical arm, should it be manufactured.

2 Overview of the System

The system is comprised of a number of separate components:

1. Interaction mechanisms and commands
2. Coupling of gestures with manipulator commands
3. Constraints (limitations) on the arm's behaviour and motion
4. An arm editor to build, edit and configure the manipulator

There are two primary interaction modes, one to essentially mirror that of a human arm with minimal need for direct control, and one to access the additional features of the arm. To switch between modes and to control the extra features, a comprehensive set of gestures has been designed.

Our system separates gestures and commands allowing us to re-couple gestures and commands in a simple fashion. In addition, we provide groups of gestures and groups of limiters from which one set can be activated. For example, the same gesture belonging to two different groups can have a different effect depending on which group is activated.

The command set is also extensible by the use of user-defined macros.

Each joint has a set of restricted ranges (constraints) associated with it, these act

---

[1] This device is attached to his body and is operated by electronic sensors attached to his skin above muscle tissue on his stomach and elsewhere.

as limiters on the joint motion. These constraints are based largely on the same limitations on a human arm.

The arm editor is used to construct the virtual arm from a collection of primitives (limb, hand and joint). The association of gestures and commands and the definition of limiters is also provided by the editor. This arm editor is a conventional graphics application – it is not accessible to the user during teleoperation activities.

The design incorporates a pair of DataGloves[2] to track the hand and arm motions as well as to measure hand/finger positions for gesture recognition.

3   Controlling the Simulated Arm

There are two distinct methods to send commands to the simulated arm: via the user's simulating hand or via the user's control hand. At any time the role of the user's arms may be interchanged.

During most of the operation of the system, the simulated arm simply mimics the user's simulating arm. No special actions are required by the operator to control the simulated arm. As such, minimal cognitive effort is required to operate the arm in this phase. Gestures performed with the user's control hand are used to access the interaction modes and extended capabilities. The control hand provides access to added functionality, which we have broken down into interaction modes and extended capabilities.

3.1   Interaction modes

The interaction modes describe the various ways the user can control how the simulated arm behaves. These are modes of operation that are controllable by the user. These modes are now described:

- Disengaging the control hand from gesture interpretation: this is known as a *clutch* action (we use clutch in the sense of an automobile clutch, not as in grasping with the hand). This is useful to avoid inadvertently sending control commands to the system.
- Controlling the coupling of the simulating hand with the simulated arm: thus the user can cleanly start and stop the simulation at any time. This allows the user to rest his or her arm or perform other actions such as using the system's arm editor. This is the same clutch operation described above, except applied to the simulating hand instead of the control hand.
- Locking the arm in fixed positions: positions may be pre-determined, thus the user can force the arm to adopt a useful position (such as hovering over a target) or prevent parts of the arm from moving during precise operations. For example, the arm from the wrist up to the shoulder can be locked in position so the user can rest her arm without fear of disrupting the simulated arm. In fact, the clutch operation may be used to reposition the user's arm to a more comfortable position from which to continue the operation of the simulated arm.
- Using a macro mode, used to encapsulate sets of commands: the user can assign

---

[2] DataGlove is a trademark of VPL Inc.

a group of commands to one command. Then the command can be coupled with a gesture, enabling the user to perform complex commands in a single gesture.

- Fine control: the user can enter a fine-tuning mode where large movements of the simulating hand result in small movements of the teleoperated arm.
- Editing the arm: the current simulated arm's characteristics can be changed at any time during its use. This includes the arm's limiters, size, position, and material properties. Switching to this mode enables the user to interactively re-define the arm.

3.2   Extended capabilities

The extended capabilities are actions that the simulated arm is capable of that a human arm is not (and therefore cannot be simulated using the simulating hand).

These extended capabilities are implemented by coupling commands from the arm editor with gestures, which in effect becomes a way of directly controlling the simulated arm. This mechanism is similar to the previously described macros, except that the capabilities are specifically built in to the system.

Although we use gestures in our system, we are not limited to this type of command interaction, for instance we could activate the commands using any other input mechanism such as voice.

We describe the default set of arm editor commands, coupled to gestures, which constitute the extended capabilities:

- Continuous wrist rotation: this is useful for performing many operations such as winding or threading a screw top lid.
- Limb extension: this feature can be used to position the arm in hard to get at positions, or re-position the hand in space without having to move the simulating hand.
- Ambidextrous arm behaviour: our simulated arm has the capability to behave like a right or left hand, this being accomplished by switching the user's control and simulating hands.

4   Gestures

Gestures have long since been proposed as a means for human–computer interaction, one of the first symbol recognition systems was part of the GRAIL project at the RAND corporation [2]. Such systems are not in widespread use today. In fact there are very few systems that use gesture interaction as the main form of input, generally they form a simple and incomplete subset of the main command set.

Our main concern with gestures is their usability, not with gesture recognition algorithms. We see gesture interaction as a most natural type of interaction well suited for controlling manipulators. We are attempting to define a gesture-based command language for teaching and control of conventional robot hands and manipulators as well as for advanced manipulators, such as our simulated arm.

We have explored using our system for teleoperation by combining different styles of gesture interaction to produce an effective, efficient and concise set of gestures for teleoperation environments. These gestures should also be useful for other applications.

Most gesture implementations recognize symbols that are generated using a 2-dimensional input device such as a light pen, stylus, or mouse. We refer to this type of gesture as *motion gestures*. The Pencept system [3] is used to recognize hand-printed characters that replace keyboard characters. The GRANDMA system [4] recognizes continuous-path gestures generated from a mouse.

The DataGlove has opened up the possibilities for specifying and recognizing various finger positions as gestures – we refer to this type of gesture as *hand* and *state* gestures in this paper to differentiate from the motion gestures.

We have combined different classes of gestures to form a gesture language suitable to control many aspects of our arm and the available interaction modes. We now describe the three types of gestures used with the system:

Hand gestures: Recognition of these gestures is based on the relative positioning (flexure) of the fingers – irrespective of hand orientation. These include the familiar *point*, *shoot* and *OK* gestures.

State gestures: These gestures are specified by the orientation of the hand (relative to some reference frame) and the positioning (flexure) of the fingers. For instance, *palm facing inward*, (relative to the position of the viewer), is a separate gesture from *palm facing outward*. We use the viewer's orientation as the reference frame.

Motion gestures: Recognition is based on a path defined by the hand as it travels through space over time. In our system we only recognize continuous motion gestures that have been projected onto the viewing plane. Thus we only need to deal with two dimensional data, increasing the accuracy of gesture recognition. We plan to extend the feature recognition aspect of the GRANDMA recognition software to function with 3D motion gestures.

Figure 16.1 shows a subset of the more important gestures we are using to control the arm. We will now describe how some of our gestures are used:

- Starting and stopping of the simulation is carried out with a reversible state gesture: palm facing out for stop, facing in for start (or continue).
- The switch between a left-handed and right-handed simulated arm is accomplished using the user's simulating hand together with the control hand: whenever they both reach a position that is bent backwards past vertical, the simulating and control hands switch roles.
- Selecting the part of the arm to lock is carried out by touching the user's arm while holding the control hand in the lock gesture.

We have incorporated a mechanism to allow interactive switching among the coupling of gestures with commands. This increases the number of commands that can be executed while using a small static set of gestures. This is accomplished by allowing different sets of gesture–command couplings to exist, but only one set to be active at one time. This allows the user to be in a mode in which a gesture rotates the arm and then switch modes so that the same gesture extends the arm. A gesture itself can be used to perform the mode switching. This allows us to easily set up different scenarios for testing what gestures are most useful for specific types of operations – in effect we can customize the coupling of gesture and function. The specific coupling we used for an artistic performance is discussed in section 7.

LEFT/RIGHT HAND: Commands for Special Capabilities

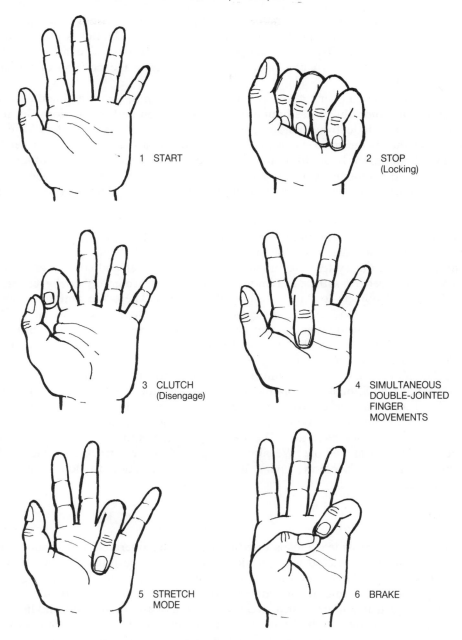

1 START

2 STOP (Locking)

3 CLUTCH (Disengage)

4 SIMULTANEOUS DOUBLE-JOINTED FINGER MOVEMENTS

5 STRETCH MODE

6 BRAKE

Figure 16.1 Some gestures used in our system.

5   Limiters

The current system allows the user to define limitations on ranges motion and the size of each object making up the arm. This simple form of limiter is used to deal with inaccuracies from DataGlove sampling, to generate desired control that the operator chooses for a particular operation, and to define the position of the arm from the hand.

Limiters are defined over the *size* parameters of the limb, joint and hand objects. In addition the joint object has limitations on its position and orientation. Because we provide for ambidextrous hand operation we define two sets of limiters for each object: one that is enforced when in right-handed operation and the other set for left-handed operation. In addition, limiters can be grouped so that any set of limiters can be applied interactively using a hand gesture. At any time, only one set of limiters is functional, the user may switch among the group of limiters to select an active set.

Typical uses of our limiters are to ensure that fingers don't bend backwards, wrists don't over-rotate and limbs are within a range of lengths. The initial settings of the limiters define the behaviour of a typical arm.

The limiters in our system are independent of each other and consequently they are easily enforced or satisfied. Limiter satisfaction is accomplished by changing invalid states of objects to the nearest legal value that keeps the limiter satisfied. At some point we intend to generalize the system to use algebraic constraints. This will enable the user to tie together the behaviour of various objects of the arm. For instance, the elbow bend could be a small fraction of the shoulder bend so that the arm is kept as straight as possible.

The DataGlove only supplies information about the hand, not the rest of the arm. We have additional information about the position (and orientation) of the user's head and thus can approximate the position of the shoulder joint. Currently we do not track the user's elbow, this results in an undetermined mapping from the user's elbow to the simulated arm. We are using heuristics to determine the position of the simulated arm's elbow. We also have provision for a tracking device to be attached to the user's elbow, giving us enough information to deterministically construct the entire arm.

6   Arm Editor

In our system we provide a means to customize the teleoperated arm. Each aspect of the arm can be associated with positioner devices and gestures. The mechanism for this is known as the arm editor. We use a direct manipulation style (non gesture based) application for interaction with the arm editor. It also serves for DataGlove calibration, construction of the arm, and specification of arm parameters and limiters. Different hand gestures can be coupled with commands; and the association between gestures and commands can be edited at run time.

The arm is constructed from *limb* and *hand* primitives connected by *joints*. These are the basic primitives that are used to construct a user-defined arm. The hand and limb primitives are connected together with joints (thus there is a joint between each limb or hand). For instance, an arm can be constructed from two limb primitives (representing the upper arm and the forearm), connected to a joint object (for the elbow). Each object has a number of material parameters, such as colour and texture, as well as parameters to specify its size. The advantage of this specification is that it is extensible, we are not limited to one pre-defined arm type.

We must specify the position of enough primitives so that the system can draw the entire arm. The primitives that we have not specified a position for are positioned using their connecting primitives. For example, the position of the elbow joint may be determined from the position and orientation of the shoulder and the length of the upper arm. We can specify the position and orientation of a joint by associating an input device with that joint.

6.1 Coupling of gestures and arm editor functionality

The coupling of arm editor commands with the control hand's gestures is known as extended capabilities (see section 3.2). The coupling of the simulating hand's position and orientation specify the arm's parameters by default.

The actual coupling of gesture and command (or object parameter) is fairly complex and is accomplished using the arm editor, not a gesture. This is because the specification of the object parameter or command is best done using a direct manipulation interface.

7 The System in Use

7.1 A performance

We have observed the system used for an artistic performance by Stelarc. This type of interaction demands a great deal of functionality to create the effects desired. This application was the primary motivation for providing groups of gestures to switch among several *sets* of gesture couplings.

We could not use a large number of gestures at once in the system because gestures that are too similar are easily confused by the hardware. This is a result of the limited accuracy of the DataGlove.

The ease of binding gestures to commands was very beneficial for choosing the mapping between gesture and command. The artist adopted a trial and error approach to create these mappings.

7.2 Delineating gestures

Some gesture systems, for example SELMA [5], do not explicitly delineate gestures (the system is in a mode in which it is always ready to recognize movements as gestures). The problem in this case is that random movements may be interpreted as gestures. We judged that this was too cumbersome in a simulation environment.

Other systems use an explicit state, such as *button-down*, or a special gesture to delineate the extent of the gesture. We have adopted a variation of both these approaches and have provided a mechanism to enter and exit continuous recognition state.

The clutch mechanism decouples gesture recognition from hand movement upon demand. This feature may be used to allow the operator to rest or to disable gesture recognition during critical operation where the accidental invocation of a command gesture would be undesirable.

8 Conclusions

The command gestures have proved to be useful but must be kept to a small number for technical reasons: the limited accuracy and phase lag of the DataGlove does not allow us to process gestures that do not differ by very noticeable amounts in a short period of time. While the artist Stelarc is willing to learn a large set of gestures for his performance, we believe this is not generally true. This issue is present for all gesture systems and needs further investigation.

During the course of our work on a gesture language for teleoperation we have developed a set of gestures for command interaction with an enhanced robotic manipulator. We have demonstrated that gestures can successfully provide a rich set of control for teleoperation environments.

Acknowledgements

This work was funded in part by a grant from the Victorian Education Foundation.

Additional programming was undertaken by ACGC staff member Craig McNaughton (the arm displays subsystem) and by RMIT Computer Science undergraduate students James Boyle and Dean Hansen (the arm editor and performance software).

References

1   Unimation, *User's Guide to VAL II, Version 2.0.* February 1986.
2   Ellis, T.O. and Sibley, W.L. 1967. On the development of equitable graphic I/O. *IEEE Trans. Human Factors in Electronics*, **8** (1): 15–17, March.
3   Ward, J.R. and Blesser, B. 1985. Interactive recognition of handprinted characters for computer input. *IEEE Computer Graphics and Applications*, 24–37, September.
4   Rubine, D. 1991. Specifying gestures by example. *Computer Graphics (Proc. SIGGRAPH '91)*, **25** (4): 329–338, July.
5   Konneker, L.K. 1984. A graphical interaction technique which uses gestures. *IEEE 1984*, 51–55.

Part 6
Theory and Modelling

17 Toward Three-Dimensional Models of Reality

P. Quarendon
IBM UK Scientific Centre

Abstract

A project is taking place at the IBM UK Scientific Centre which has the aim of creating three-dimensional models from two-dimensional images. These models are intended for use in a variety of graphics applications such as virtual reality environments. This paper discusses some of the issues involved and the methods being adopted. Some initial results are presented, and these show that significant progress toward a simple, easy-to-use method of creating models of real objects and scenes.

1 Motivation

Graphics rendering methods have reached the stage where it is often difficult at first glance to tell computer generated scenes from real ones. While there clearly are many unsolved details remaining, we can now produce acceptable images of artificial virtual worlds and it is now mainly a question of improving the performance before we can produce a convincing real-time illusion. Outside the realm of pure entertainment, the bottleneck and main inhibitor to making use of the technology in useful applications is that of creating the models to inhabit these virtual worlds. As one who has been involved in a small way in such activities, I can confirm the fact that large amounts of effort have to go into creating what appear to the viewer to be disappointingly simple models. It is said that some of the craft in early animations in 'Return of the Last Starfighter' contained 500,000 polygons. Although these were not entered individually, the amount of effort to create realistically complex models is very high.

In entertainment, apart from effects such as metamorphosing real actors into unreal beings and the reverse, it is not usually necessary to model reality closely in the graphics. By contrast, in practical applications this is usually an essential part of the task, although often it is not stated. Most design, for example, has to be fitted into a real environment, and the design can only accurately be judged in its natural context. One is aware, for instance, how different a watch can look on the wrist from its appearance against a matt felt background in a display case.

As an example, one retail chain were discussing the possibility of modelling the inside of their larger stores. These are frequently changed round to keep them interesting and to optimize the sales. However, standard computer-aided design

(CAD) packages do not appear to be very satisfactory for the purpose. As one of the staff put it: 'How do you model a rack of coats on a CAD system?'. A second similar example was a group who specialized in the design of outside auditoria and events. On one occasion they were designing for an arena in what had been a Roman amphitheatre. Attempting to use a standard CAD package, they had managed to approximate the contours and natural features of the site using a large number of spline curves. They started to add audience seating into the model. After a handful of chairs, the system produced a message: 'Model too large'. 'But', they said, 'we still have five thousand to go!'.

In both these examples the models to be handled are structurally complex and would take a great deal of effort to model with realistic detail. But they consist largely, if not entirely, of objects which already exist. In the case of a store design one might be dealing with large numbers of objects, many such as clothes, being very hard to model even individually. In the case of outdoor arena one is dealing with a natural terrain, and naturalized objects which again do not have convenient Euclidean geometries.

It is important that the result is visually convincing, but the packages which tend to be used are trying to do much more than the applications really need. Undoubtedly, the systems would have been quite capable of creating numerical control commands to machine the entire site from blocks of steel. To do this they have rich and high structured internals, such as boundary files, to allow such processes but which are not necessary for simpler tasks.

Virtual reality and other graphics methods are likely to be inhibited in many such practical applications until there are easy methods to capture the complex shapes, textures and colours from the real world and to incorporate these into the virtual world along with new or hypothesized objects.

2   Current Solutions

Computer animations in the film world which imitate reality are created patiently with much measurement, calibration and accurate modelling. CAD techniques are used, but on specialist systems. It is said that 60 programmers were involved in the animations for *Terminator 2*. This degree of effort can seldom be justified for more everyday applications and while, no doubt, modelling systems will improve, hand-building such models is not an attractive option if it can be avoided. It is therefore profitable to look at more automatic methods of building three-dimensional models from real objects.

Existing methods of automatic capture can be divided into two broad classes: active methods and passive methods. In active sensing, the system creates and controls a signal (such as a light beam), which is directed at the object and interprets the signal reflected. Passive sensing relies only on existing illumination.

2.1   Active sensing

By scanning a light beam across an object and observing it from a second known position, the shape can be determined. Methods of this type are now well-developed for industrial applications such as the profiling of turbine blades. They can be made to operate at very high speeds but require an expensive and delicate mechanical scanning system. One example is described by Mundy and Porter [1].

Methods have also been developed which use a static pattern of stripes or spots and so do not require a mechanical scanner. The disadvantage here is that the resulting pattern is ambiguous, and different interpretations give different results. Although Blake *et al.* [2] report an improvement on this system, using two patterns to render the interpretation unambiguous, the system requires accurate set-up and may not be suited to conditions outside a laboratory.

Other reported techniques make use of Moiré fringing or the time-of-flight of laser light to estimate the distance between the sensor and the target. Overviews of such systems are given by Jarvis [3] and Bastustcheck [4].

Active sensing methods give good results. However, the equipment is generally specialized and expensive. Because the illumination has to be controlled, the environment is restricted as is the range of size of objects which can be captured. Also, importantly, the devices do not capture the appearance of the object at the same time as their shape. This would have to be added as a separate step.

2.1.1 CAT reconstruction

In computer-assisted tomography, the effect is of a series of X-rays of the object taken from different angles. The X-rays are attenuated according to the opacity of the material through which they pass. The intensity of a ray which has passed through the object in a particular direction gives the sum of the opacities along the path it has taken. With many views, one can essentially solve a large set of simultaneous equations to find the opacity to X-rays of each elemental volume of the space containing the object. Thresholding will then identify various constituents, for example bone or soft tissue, according to the opacity range in which it falls.

2.2 Passive sensing

Passive methods only require images of the object and so do not require as much special equipment. Only a camera and digitizer are necessary to capture the data and a controlled environment is not needed. The appearance of the object can be captured at the same time as the shape. In theory they are ideal.

2.2.1 Volumetric intersection

If a series of views of an object is taken against a contrasting background, these can be thresholded to identify the profile of the object in each. Considering just one of these images, the object must lie somewhere within the volume of the polygonal pyramid which is formed from all the points in space which project within the profile. An approximation to the object volume can be built by intersecting the pyramidal volumes for all the images. As more images are taken so the accuracy increases. A method of generating a voxel model in this way is reported by Potmesil [5], and a recent report of system generating a polygonal model is by Doi [6].

Although this method has been classified as a passive method, it does rely on being able to separate the background and the object in the images and so relies on highly controlled lighting. Further, because of the method of construction, it cannot reproduce objects with concavities.

2.2.2   Stereo vision

A huge amount of work has been reported aimed at constructing depth maps by matching stereo pairs. Much of the work has been part of the study of the human visual system or in the context of robotics. One review of computational stereo is given by Barnard and Fischler [7]. A number of methods available at the IBM Scientific Centre have been tried, including the Sheffield vision system [8]. None of these seem to work well for the present application. The problem with using the known algorithms for model construction seems to stem from the fact that depth cannot reliably be determined solely by matching pairs of images as there are many potential matches for each pixel or edge element. Other information, such as support from neighbours and limits on the disparity gradient must be used to restrict the search. Even with these, the results are not very reliable and a significant proportion of the features are incorrectly matched. The edge models which result are, in consequence, often erroneous. In the Sheffield system a database of possible models is assumed from which a valid structure can be selected. However, if there is no database of models from which to draw, it is not clear how the various model fragments should best be combined to give a complete three-dimensional whole.

Optic flow methods match images taken successively from a single camera and derive a two-dimensional velocity field which describes the apparent motion. There is typically much less difference between the images than for stereo, and fewer problems of ambiguity arise. However, existing algorithms seem to have been used more to determine camera-motion rather than to build three-dimensional models.

2.2.3   Photogrammetry

Matching stereo images pairs in a photogrammetry machine has been used for many years to find the height of features for map making. Recently, successful photogrammetric matching by automatic means has been reported, for example by Muller [9]. His work uses the Otto-Chau algorithm [10], which searches for the affine transformation which produces the best match between patches in the two images. The method works well in smoothly varying regions, but is a region-growing algorithm and so needs to be seeded with initial depth values to start the process. It does not cope well with discontinuities of depth and usually needs a seed value in each area. For photogrammetry, where there is lots of detail and the depth generally does vary quite smoothly, this is not critical, but for more general scenes some additional method has to be used to generate these seed depths.

While passive methods have all the advantages, there does not appear to be an existing method which can be directly used to create graphics models. The last method does, however, offer some promise.

2.3   Building realistic models

Computer graphics usually relies on texture mapping (see, for instance, Blinn and Newell [11]) to obtain a realistic amount of visual complexity. Geometric models would be too large and inefficient for describing a complete scene in detail. Geometry is usually used only for the basic shapes and images are mapped onto the surfaces to add the necessary small variations in colour and orientation. Some recent work has focused interest on using photographic textures and mapping them onto three-dimensional shapes also captured from the real world. For example, to make realistic animations of facial expressions, Williams [12] has mapped photographs of a face onto a model of a head digitized using a laser scanner. The subject for this work had to have a plaster cast made of her head for the digitization to take place. Braccini *et al.* [13] have used the volumetric intersection method to produce a model of a simple object and then mapped the original images onto the surfaces. Sharma and Scrivener [14] also discuss a similar solution. Kaneda *et al.* [15] have mapped aerial photographs onto digital height maps of terrains to make realistic models to assess environmental impact of proposed developments. They produce exceptionally convincing results.

Apart from some early work by Potmesil [16], there is little evidence of attempts to build graphics models purely using image correspondence.

3   Objectives

At the IBM UK Scientific Centre, a small project is investigating the creation of three-dimensional models for graphics purposes. They are intended for applications such as those cited in the introduction, or as a component of a virtual world. It is not intended necessarily that the models be dimensionally accurate, as they would need to be for industrial mensuration. Accuracy is only needed to the extent that this affects the final appearance on a display. Neither is there any intention of recognizing the object, nor of understanding its structure. For recognition purposes it may be important to identify edges, plane surfaces or other features so that these can be matched against possibilities in a database. The creation of a realistic rendering of a model depends to a considerable extent on accurately reproducing the recognizable features of the object, but one of the aims behind the work is to find the extent to which this can be done without explicitly recognizing and storing them.

The types of manipulation one might like to perform on an object model in a graphics application are:

- To view the object from different viewpoints.
- To combine the object with others in a composite scene. The other objects may be captured from the real world, or generated in a CAD package. Clearly, correct hidden surface removal would be expected as the viewer's position is changed.
- To scale the object. For example, at larger viewing distances a less complex model might be used. Interpolation might be appropriate when a closer viewpoint is chosen.
- To detect collisions between the object and others. This aspect of reality seems vital to easy manipulation. For example, it is convenient when placing two objects in a touching position to use collision detection (and the fact that virtual objects are unbreakable!).
- The model should participate in the lighting algorithm chosen for rendering. Various alternatives are:
  - Ambient light only. The colour and brightness of each surface element is assumed to be constant, independent of both the surface orientation and the position of the viewer. This is the type of assumption made when the output from a previous radiosity calculation is viewed.

— Directional lighting, Lambertian reflection. The brightness of each surface element is related to the surface normal of the element and the direction of the light source only. It is independent of the position of the viewer and of the nature of the surface.

— Directional lighting, general reflection. The brightness of each surface element depends both on the surface normal of the element, the degree of specularity of the surface and other characteristics as well as the viewing position.

- To distort the model, for example by spatial transformation. This can be used to perform limited sorts of animation: for example, to produce realistic flattening at a collision.
- To change object colouration, or other surface characteristics such as texture.

4 Proposed Model

Almost universally in computer graphics, geometry is described by a collection of polygonal faces, often with colours associated with the vertices. While this is a convenient canonical form for computer generated graphics, when capturing data from the real world it is not ideal. Natural objects are not often simply described in polygonal terms. Moreover, man-made objects with regular shapes are usually decorated in complex ways to disguise their simplicity. In a manually entered design the basic shape and the superficial texture can be separated, but in automated capture this is less easy to do. Even with objects generated by CAD systems, one can question the wisdom of reducing all the shape data to hundreds of thousands of polygons when the majority will cover only a pixel or so on the screen, even if they appear at all.

In the present work, objects are defined as three-dimensional fields. These describe the arrangement of matter in space by giving its visual properties at every point in the space. Such a form of model is unusual in computer graphics, but has been used for some time for modelling diffuse objects such as smoke and clouds [17]. There is also a strong relation to the voxel and cuberille models which are used for rendering density distributions from three-dimensional CAT and MRI scans, see for example [18].

The most general form of three-dimensional graphics field is called a texel model. Texels were introduced by Kajiya [19] as a generalization of particle fields to render textures, such as fur, which had previously proved difficult. A texel has the following components:

- A density field. This measures the probability that a ray of light will encounter a surface at every point in space.
- A lighting model field. This specifies how light falling on each point in space will be modified in colour, how it will be reflected and so on.
- A direction field. This gives the principle directions for each point in space, containing a typical surface normal in the vicinity as well as a binormal, giving the principal direction within the surface.

To cope with all aspects of real objects, all these elements can be needed. However, this work is aiming to capture objects automatically and an extremely simplified view has been taken. The model of the scene is reduced to two simple fields:

- A binary field $S(x)$, which takes the value 1 if the point $x = (x, y, z)$ is solid and 0 if it is empty.
- A field $C(x)$, which specifies the colour of light diffused from each point x. Clearly, the value of this field is not relevant if the point is empty.

This restricts the types of object which can be represented and the manipulations which can be performed:

- It does not allow for semi-transparent objects. All points in space are either completely transparent or totally opaque.
- It does not allow for specular reflection. All surfaces will be assumed to have the same lighting model, and to be Lambertian reflectors. Light falling on the surface is assumed to be diffused uniformly in all directions, and so be independent of the direction from which the surface is seen.
- Lighting only consists of direction-less ambient light. Since neither the illumination nor the lighting model depends on direction, the orientation of surfaces in space is unimportant.

These assumptions are not very realistic and in particular few surfaces encountered in practice are pure diffuse reflectors of light. At a later stage it is expected that some extra attributes will be introduced, in particular a surface normal at each point so that non-isotropic reflectivity can be incorporated.

4.1 Representation

The simplest representation would be to sample the two fields and store the values on a regular grid of points. The assumption would be that values between grid points would be obtainable by some interpolation process. This would be very similar to a two-dimensional image, but with shapeless blobs of colour placed regularly in three-dimensional space, rather than on a plane. The field S serves to indicate which grid points have a value and which should be considered empty.

Most grid points will either be empty or will have an irrelevant colour value because they lie inside the object and so cannot be observed. It is therefore more economical to store just grid values which are observable and which are not empty – the surface points – and to suppress the others. This requires a sparse matrix storage method and the most convenient seems to be to use some form of oct-tree.

For instance, the fields S and C can be reduced to a linear representation over a three-dimensional region R by applying the following rules recursively:

- If the field S is 0 throughout R, represent by the indicator value 'empty'.
- Otherwise, represent it by an initial indicator value 'not empty'.
  - If R is smaller than some chosen extent, follow this by the average value of C in the region.
  - Alternatively, divide the region R into eight parts by dividing in half along each of the three coordinate axes. Then represent the fields in the region by concatenating the representations for these eight sub-regions in order.

If the indicators 'empty' and 'not empty' are suitably short, the resulting string is not much longer for a typical object than the sum of the individual surface colour values. Objects in such an oct-tree form could be generated from CAD modellers. A set theoretic modeller, WINSOM [21], written at the IBM UK Scientific Centre for experimental purposes has been adapted to do this. Measurements of models from this source indicate that models are typically between 5 and 20 times the size of a two-dimensional image of the object at the same resolution.

5   Display

Both Blinn [17] and Kajiya [19] give algorithms for displaying fields. Ray-tracing is the favoured method for diffuse fields, but simpler methods, such as scanning the field and using a Z-buffer, can be used if effects such as shadows are not needed. The oct-tree representation of the data seems particularly amenable to fast display, since little unnecessary data is scanned and the transformation to screen coordinates and clipping to the screen edges can be done incrementally, avoiding multiplications.

The representation does, however, have certain disadvantages:

- If the object is enlarged, pixellation may become apparent. This is similar to that observed in enlarging a two-dimensional image.
- Because the voxels have no shape and no direction, edges are often much more jagged than one expects. Unlike a display generated from a geometric model, this jaggedness increases as the object is enlarged.

6   Building Models

The eventual aim is that models are built from images recorded with a standard camcorder, using it in a natural and relatively unrestricted way to capture views of the object from all directions. These images alone are used to construct the three-dimensional model.

For initial experiments a still video camera is being used rather than a camcorder. This has the advantage that a short series of pictures can be taken from individually controlled positions.

6.1   Method
Given a sequence of image frames, the aim is:

1. to find a camera position for each frame and
2. to construct a three-dimensional model which, when rendered onto the given camera positions, most nearly approximates the images.

This is not easy.

However, suppose we were able to obtain a guess at the model after processing some of the images. We might proceed by taking a new image and postulating a camera position for it. We could render the model onto this camera position, and then modify the postulated camera position until the rendered image and the actual image are as close as possible. Having done this, we could modify the model to reconcile the differences between the actual and rendered image before proceeding to the next image in the sequence.

In practice, this has two disadvantages. It would take a very long time to perform the minimization and it is not at all clear how one might sensibly represent the model during the processing. Therefore, the process is divided into two distinct steps, separating the camera position algorithm from that for building the complete model for rendering.

To find the optimum camera positions, the camera motion algorithm builds, not a complete model of the object, but only certain recognizable features in the scene. It is derived from the 'Plessey' egomotion algorithm, developed by Harris *et al.* [21]. This bases its estimates on the position of 'corners'. These are not necessarily real corner points of the object, but are points in the image where the intensity has a strong gradient in two directions. Edge points can also be used, but an advantage of corners is that they can be tracked in whichever direction they move on successive images. The algorithm assumes that these corners are at fixed positions in space, and keeps a list of them.

Given a new image, the algorithm first tries to identify these known corner features within it. It then finds the position and orientation of the camera which minimizes the distances between the pixel positions to which the recorded features project and their actual observed positions. Once the best camera position is determined, the pixel locations of the observed feature are used in a Kalman filter to refine the three-dimensional positions of the features.

Once the camera position is estimated from these selected features, the remaining parts of the model can be filled in. In the Plessey Droid system this was done simply by triangulating the corner points in three dimensions. The purpose in that case was to demonstrate a self-guided vehicle, and this method is satisfactory for tasks such as identifying the road surface. However here, we would like to build a model with the right appearance and there is no reason for edges and surfaces of objects always to follow a triangulation of the corners. Instead we attempt to find the three-dimensional colour field which, when rendered from the computed camera positions, gives the nearest approximation to the observed images. The method is described in detail in Quarendon [22].

7 Results

Figure 17.1 shows a set of 36 pictures. These were taken with an inexpensive still-video camera mounted on a tripod. The object was placed on a turntable and pictures were taken at 10° intervals. The lighting was kept reasonably uniform by pointing the main light-source at the ceiling. The background consisted of an office white-board. The camera placement and orientation was determined simply with a ruler.

This arrangement was used because it is much easier to move the object in a controlled way than to move the camera. However, the algorithm expects the camera to move and not the object. The only difference in the pictures is that the background should move on the pictures if the camera moves, but should remain fixed if the camera is fixed. To disguise the difference, the background (which can be recognized because it is very bright) is made completely featureless by setting all pixels of high enough intensity to a standard value.

The pictures were digitized from the PAL output of the camera and reconstruction

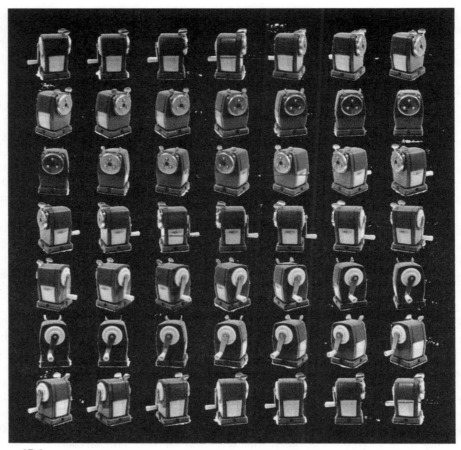

Figure 17.1

was carried out on an IBM 3090. In this case, the measured relative camera positions were used, rather than the output from the camera motion algorithm. The resulting model contains some 35,000 non-empty voxels. Figure 17.2 shows the results of rendering the oct-tree onto the original 36 views, to give images 128 pixels square.

While the overall impression is similar to the original pictures, closer inspection reveals a number of faults:

- there is overall blurring
- the overall contrast is low
- there are areas missing
- there are some unexpected protuberances.

These stem from a number of effects:

- No camera calibration was performed and the other measurements were made by rather rudimentary means.
- The surface of the object is, contrary to the assumptions, fairly shiny and so appears to have different colours at different angles.

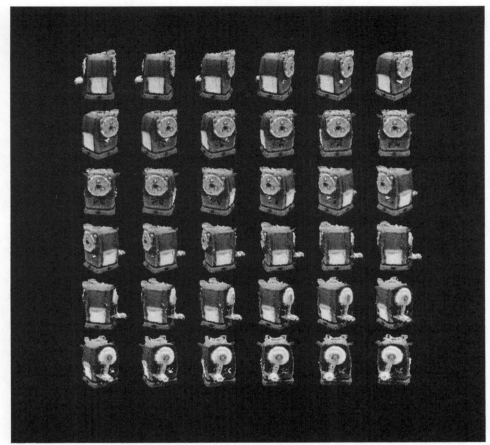

Figure 17.2

- As the object rotates, any shadowing moves across the surface. It should remain stationary if the object is stationary. On the very plain surfaces, this provides the main variation and the algorithm deduces the surface position incorrectly.

8 Conclusions

The possibility of capturing three-dimensional models from two-dimensional images has been discussed. The problems with standard methods of representing 3D models in graphics systems have been outlined, and it was noted that these are particularly acute for objects derived from the real world. Methods of data capture were then reviewed.

A representation suitable for storing data from real objects has been presented and an example shown which uses image matching to build a visual model directly. The results presented show that it does appear possible to construct graphic models in this way.

While the results are far from perfect, it is also possible to improve on the present method. It is intended, for example, to add a surface normal component to the field values. This would turn the volume elements into directional surface elements. Although this greatly increases the amount of information associated with each element, it should improve both the display quality and the results from the model building algorithm.

References

1 Mundy, J.L. and Porter, G.B. 1987. A three-dimensional sensor based on structured light. In T. Kanade, editor, *Three-dimensional Machine Vision*. Kluwer, 3–62.
2 Blake, A., McCowen, D., Lo, H.R. and Konash, D. 1990. Epipolar geometry for trinocular active-range sensors. *Proc. British Machine Vision Conference*, Oxford, UK, 12–25.
3 Jarvis, R.A., 1983. A Laser time-of-flight sensor for robotic vision. *IEEE Trans. PAMI*, **5** (5): 505–512, November.
4 Bastuscheck, C.M. 1989. Techniques for real-time generation of range images. *IEEE Proceedings of CVPR*, 262–289.
5 Potmesil, M. 1987. Generating octree models of 3D objects from their silhouettes in a sequence of images. *Computer Vision, Graphics and Image Processing*, **40**: 1–29.
6 Doi, J., Koeda, K. and Miyake, T. 1990. Three dimensional reconstruction of solid models from multi-directional images and applications to industrial mensuration. *SPIE Volume 1395 Close Range Photogrammetry meets Machine Vision*, 564–571.
7 Barnard, S.T. and Fischler, M.A. 1982. Computational stereo. *Computing Surveys*, **14** (4): 553–572.
8 Pollard, S.B., Pridmore, T.P., Porrill, J., Mayhew, J.E.W. and Frisby, J.P. 1989. Geometric modeling from multiple stereo views. *International Journal of Robotics Research*, **8** (4): 3–31, August.
9 Day, T. and Muller, J.P. 1989. Digital elevation model production by stereo matching SPOT image pairs. *Proc. 4th Alvey Vision Conference*, Manchester, UK, August, 117–122.
10 Otto, G.P. and Chau, T.K.W. 1989. Region-growing algorithm for matching of terrain-images. *Image and Vision Computing*, **7** (2): 83–94, May.
11 Blinn, J. and Newell, M. 1976. Texture and reflection on computer generated images. *Commun. ACM*, **19** (10), October.
12 Williams, L. 1990. Performance driven facial animation. *Computer Graphics*, **24** (4): 207–214, August.
13 Braccini, C., Grattarola, A. and Zappatore, S. 1989. Volumetric and pictorial reconstruction of 3D objects from correspondences in moving 2D views. In *Recent Issues in Pattern Analysis and Recognition*. Springer-Verlag, 249–258.
14 Sharma, A. and Scrivener S.A.R. 1983. Computer vision based models of 3D geometry scene models. *Proc. IT 1990 Conference*, Southampton, UK, March, 71–78.
15 Kaneda, K., Kato, F., Nakamae, E., Nishita, T., Tanaka, H. and Noguchi, T. 1989. Three dimensional terrain modelling and display for environmental assessment. *Computer Graphics*, **23** (3): 207–214, July.
16 Potmesil, M. 1983. Geometry models of solid objects by matching 3D surface segments. *Proc. 8th Joint Conference on Artificial Intelligence*, August, 1089–1093.

17 Blinn, J.F. 1982. Light reflection functions for simulation of clouds and dusty surfaces. *Computer Graphics*, **16** (3): 21–29, July.
18 Chen, L.-S. and Sontag, M.R. 1989. Representation, display, and manipulation of 3D digital scenes and their medical applications. *Computer Vision, Graphics, and Image Processing*, **48**: 190–216.
19 Kajiya, J. 1989. Rendering fur with three-dimensional textures. *Computer Graphics*, **23** (3): 271–280, July.
20 Quarendon, P. 1984. *WINSOM Users' Guide*. IBM UK Scientific Centre Report 124.
21 Harris, C.G. and Pike, J.M. 1987. 3D positional integration from image sequences. *Proc. Third Alvey Vision Conference*, September, 233–236.
22 Quarendon, P. 1993. Creating three dimensional models from sequences of images (in preparation).

Biography

Peter Quarendon has been involved in graphics at IBM for 15 years, originally prototyping and then producing a product, GDDM, to make graphics available on all IBM mainframe terminals. He moved to the IBM UK Scientific Centre in 1983, to carry out research in the scientific uses of computer graphics. He developed WINSOM, intended as an easy-to-use package, for scientific rendering and has been involved in numerous visualization projects. It jointly won the BCS computer applications award in 1989. After a period as manager of the Graphics Applications Research Group, he is now Graphics Research Leader at the Scientific Centre and responsible for technical aspects of the graphics and visualization research.

Part 7
Ethics and Societal Implications

18 Back to the Cave – Cultural Perspectives on Virtual Reality

George Mallen
System Simulation Ltd

Abstract

Two contrasting paradigms for interpreting reality are proposed as a means for understanding the 'virtual reality' phenomenon. The first is a direct descendant from the European 'triumph of reason over nature' school of enlightenment. The second derives from older traditions, that there are myths or 'given' truths which are looked at and interpreted much as an audience looks at and interprets a play in a theatre. An early experiment in the technology of virtual reality, Ecogame, is identified with the first and more recent scene simulators with the second. Finally, the two paradigms are linked together to provide some pointers to more fundamental possibilities.

1 Image and Reality

Regularly, this past winter, there have been small groups of people outside the café next to System Simulation's offices in Covent Garden watching young men in plastic helmets pursue a 'virtual reality' adventure. In the spring, summer and into late autumn this space is usually occupied by tables of relaxed tourists and workers from all around and contributes its own bit to the live buzz of the piazza. Sometimes in June or July a very large television screen is erected nearby and the evening's performance in the Royal Opera House is presented, free and *al fresco*, for public enjoyment and usually to great acclaim. By contrast, the spectators watching the awkward gyrations of the lads in helmets as they tried to shoot the pixellated dangers projected into their hatbands were silent, interested but puzzled. By definition the participants were totally wrapped up in their adventure and oblivious of the audience, unlike Pavarotti. I concluded that 'virtual reality' was not going to catch on as a spectator sport and I notice now, as the warmer weather comes, that the 'virtual reality' machines have been replaced by the more sociable, and probably more profitable but lower tech, tables. Such is economic reality!

So, for a short time, I was an observer of spectators watching participants in a virtual reality adventure. You are now reading about this and adding another layer of interpretation and meaning to the several already involved. Consider also the fact that these events were located in the colonnade on the north side of Covent

Garden Piazza which is an 1890s interpretation of the Inigo Jones colonnade of 1630, which was itself an interpretation of renaissance Italian architecture. What is 'real' in all of this?

In this essay I shall try to answer that question by examining some aspects of the evolution of human cultures and particularly our attitudes to knowledge and reality!

In *Travels in Hyperreality* [1], Umberto Eco sets himself the quest for the 'Absolute Fake'. This takes him to Fortresses of Solitude, Satan's Creches, Enchanted Castles, Monasteries of Salvation and the City of Robots! Lest you think this is a dungeons and dragons scenario it isn't. *Travels in Hyperreality* is a trenchant analysis of US attitudes to imitation, art and culture written in 1975 well before dungeons and dragons became a fad. However it was just about the time computer graphics started down its trail to the glitzy 'realities' of the ad men. Though there is no evidence that Eco was interested in computer graphics at this time, the cultural backcloth that he depicts strongly suggests that US computer graphics is every bit a product of US culture as Disneyland. Could the same urges that led to the creation of Las Vegas, Disneyland and Hearst Castle, as places which are simultaneously real and artificial, be involved in the quest for the computerized virtual reality, as Californian as Hollywood, Eco's 'Absolute Fake'? As a thoroughly European scholar committed to the triumph of reason over ideology and dogma, Eco attributes this Californian predilection for making fake realities to the physical separation of its early European population from their cultural roots. Such brashly Eurocentric theorizing is a bit embarrassing to the British, but it does suggest there may be deeply rooted cultural forces at work which have shaped even the short development of computer graphics.

The hypothesis to be explored in this paper is that two schools of computer graphics have emerged during the past 20 years, and that each is a direct product of the two quite different ways in which we come to 'know' the world in the philosophical sense. The first way is through myth, the second is through reason. These interplay throughout history and in our individual lives. In the rest of the paper, I shall show how they provide a framework for understanding the cultural bases of developments in computer graphics.

2 Two Paradigms for Knowing

Some years ago I saw this startling graffito, neatly felt-tipped in a west London commuter train: 'Reality is an illusion brought on by alcohol deficiency'. Pure genius! This is a succinct encapsulation of one world view, the paradigm in which the individual sits at the centre trying to make sense of the mystery out there. Essentially lonely, this quest for individual understanding is a dominant theme in European civilization. Hegel in his *Lectures on the Philosophy of History* [2] proposes a model for cultural development. Strongly influenced by eighteenth century enlightenment thinkers like Adam Ferguson, he develops the idea that the historically known cultures, the early Egyptian and Asiatic, Greek, Roman and, latterly, Western European, were and are steps on the way to a culture of self-comprehension. In Hegel's view, cultural progress was related to political progress. In early civilizations, Egypt for example, only one person was free, namely the god-king; in Greek and Roman cultures more people were free, namely the aristocracy; in the ultimate civilization every one would be free. This was a very powerful idea shaping

Marx's ideas, and it was an interpretation of Hegel's philosophy of history that led Francis Fukuyama [3] to describe the collapse of communism as the 'end of political history'. This meant for Fukuyama, at least, the triumph of western liberal/capitalistic democracy. Everyone is free, hence the end of Hegel's historical trek!

> With the end of the cold war what we may be witnessing is not just the passing of a particular period of postwar history but the end part of mankind's ideological evolution and the emergence of western liberal democracy as the final form of human government, the result of the unabashed victory of economic and political liberalism.

So our paradigm, from the eighteenth century European enlightenment, is of the evolution of the individual as reasoning and self-conscious, at the centre of an objective reality which his/her reason was actively involved in comprehending leading inevitably to a complete understanding of an ultimately understandable universe.

However, modern Europeans cannot really claim title to this development. The ancient Greeks have a prior claim having established the roots of modern rational, scientific thought. They also established the roots of the second paradigm I want to discuss which is theatre based. At the theatre, cinema or opera, we sit in the audience and watch the action taking place on a stage or screen. In this case we, the audience, are on the outside looking in. The plot, characters and set are carefully designed to deliver the aggregate interpretation of the author, director, actors, set designers and so on. We sit in the stalls, or perhaps the 'gods', and are raised to the heights or cast into the depths according to how we relate to the 'reality' on the stage. Be it theatre in the round, proscenium arch or cinema screen the basic paradigm is that we watch a reality from the outside and try to interpret it.

The roots of this second paradigm lie deep in human consciousness. The ancient Greeks turned their pre-literate myths into literature and drama, a process which took the mythological and religious realities of their society and made them more repeatable and criticizable. The link between the mythic and religious and the performance of rituals and dramas is important. Much of modern anthropology has been concerned with the modes of knowing which exist in pre-literate cultures and how it is that magic can co-exist with commonsense [4]. Such studies seem increasingly relevant today as we see forces of fundamentalist religion emerging to challenge the validity of the 'scientific' model of reality. Drama and theatre in our society are one means of expressing the myth/magic/religious components in our social and psychological make-up. Paradoxically the fruits of the scientific/technological process, the other persuasion, are supplanting the older concept of theatre and replacing it with the 'media'. The possibility, therefore, is that the media men who place their realities before us in such profusion may be latter day John the Baptists preparing the way, for what?

To summarize, I have briefly suggested two ways of knowing the world. The first is the powerful scientific/rational model which is an active, homocentric, consensus seeking quest for understanding of an objective reality. The second places the knower in an audience absorbing another's reality. These two intertwine throughout history. Indeed, they intertwine in most of our lives. We are all, at one time or another, in one or other mode, at one time trying to make sense of what we find ourselves in, at another trying to make sense as audience, of someone else's experiences. Let us now consider how all this is relevant to the development of computer graphics and particularly virtual reality.

3   Two Kinds of Computer Graphics

3.1   The simulation of reality

The convergence of cheap TV tube production and cheap reliable semi-conductor memory in the mid-1970s totally changed the emergent art of computer graphics. Work in the early 1970s had shown the feasibility of generating representations of 3D objects on raster screens and I recall a demonstration in 1973 of the Computer Aided Design Centre's considerable achievement in creating a low resolution, very low number of polygons but, nevertheless, manifestly a recognizable model of a vase to a group at the Royal College of Art. One eminent professor gave vent to a mighty 'Hrrrmph!' and 'Is that all it can do?', and stomped out. Happily others had vision. The steady, gradual development of the techniques and technology over the intervening years can leave us in no doubt that complete visual verisimilitude is possible. That is at the level of the reproduction of the physical optics of scenes and objects. This kind of computer graphics has become a laboratory for testing understanding of physical optics, when originally it was a lab for testing the older subjects of geometry and trigonometry. So in an interesting way the development of computer graphics has recapitulated the development of human knowledge in these areas, from Euclid, through Descartes at least to nineteenth century optics.

This view of computer graphics as simulated optics puts it firmly in context as a branch of engineering, a practical exercise in putting to work a particular set of sub-disciplines of scientific and technical knowledge. This new discipline of visual engineering differs from other engineering disciplines in that, unlike say structural engineering, where the engineer will first use the computer to calculate or also simulate the structure prior to building it, the visual engineer's final product is what appears on the screen. The final test, *à la* Turing, is whether the fake is subjectively distinguishable from the real.

Left to the natural forces of technological development and marginal improvement visual engineering inevitably moved towards 'virtual reality'. The same inevitability, the same technological determinism, that causes racing cars to go faster, computer memory to get bigger and production processes to get more efficient will also cause computer graphics to become more realistic. Let us refer to this branch of computer graphics as SOR, the simulation of reality.

3.2   The simulation of complexity

Another school of computer graphics is concerned with using the computer as a tool to help understand the structure and behaviour of the world around us. In this role the computer graphics screen is a tool, like the telescope or microscope, only it allows the presentation of the unseeable, the very large and the very small and the complexity in between. 'Envisioning', a term which seems to have sneaked into the vocabulary in recent years, describes the use of graphics by, for example, a chemist looking at molecular structures, a corporate planner looking at graphical financial projections, a traffic engineer looking at speeded up traffic patterns. SOC, the simulation of complexity, is still very much in its infancy. Apart from the pre-computer pie charts, bar graphs, and so on, there is no commonly accepted visual vocabulary for displaying complex processes. Perhaps one will emerge, but at the moment the scientist, engineer or designer seeking to explain or understand the theory, structure or design has to create a visual vocabulary to do this. This is an imaginative and, of course, an aesthetic act which emphasizes that the creative process of understanding the world and the creative process of visualizing that understanding are inseparable. At this level science and art are one.

The early forms of computer art were almost entirely explorations of the computer's capacity for generating complexity. Many pieces in the collection of such early material which we house in our offices explore the theme of how complexity grows from the working of simple rules. These generative forms were a long way from representational art, but as we look back to them, through fractals and chaos, we can see that the ideas of generative art anticipated these later developments.

If early forms of computer art were concerned with understanding abstract complexity, early forms of computer game were primarily concerned with education, that is with ways of simplifying complexity to facilitate understanding. Simulating the workings of complex processes and interacting with these was an obvious pedagogical tool.

One project, recalled from 1970, encapsulates many features inviting comparisons with current 'virtual reality' themes. That project, called Ecogame, was commissioned in late 1969 with the brief to create a publicly accessible computer system which would illustrate the way in which computers might be used ten years later, that is, in 1979! The Computer Arts Society carried out this brief, and Ecogame was the theme exhibit at the Computer '70 exhibition at Olympia, London in October 1970. System Simulation Ltd continued the development of the system and Ecogame II featured at the First European Management Forum in Davos in February 1971. Happily, both the European Management Forum and System Simulation Ltd continue to thrive, though EMF changed its name some years ago to become the prestigious World Economic Forum. I am pleased that this year SSL has again provided computing support for its Davos gathering.

Ecogame was designed round a system dynamics [5] type model of a national economy. It is fully described in Mallen [6]. The model ran on a remote time sharing computer to which nine user terminals were connected via 300bd modem lines. A tenth line was connected to a minicomputer which powered an interactive graphics system with refresh display. The nine user terminals were the first Tektronix storage tube displays to be available in Europe. Players of Ecogame selected options from a menu of choices for investment or consumption in the model economy using a joystick controlling crosshairs on the graphics screen – the first GUI? The mini-driven interactive graphics system contained a model of the economic model which was depicted as a diagram of reservoirs and taps and flows of resource. This was used to train the players prior to participation and to replay sessions for debriefing. However, the most important feature of Ecogame was that a measure of 'quality of life' was derived and used to select images from a bank of computer controlled slide projectors reflecting the 'quality of life'. The original implementation at Olympia was inside a blue, translucent, air-conditioned geodesic dome which provided a completely enclosed environment in which the 15 or 16 participants and a few spectators could concentrate on the fake reality of their economic/social game.

The second implementation, in Davos, was different. This was in a large conference room which allowed plenty of space for the nine player stations, the minicomputer and the tower for the slide projectors and, importantly, much more space for an audience. In this configuration Ecogame had become theatre.

As a technological paradigm Ecogame had most of the characteristics of a virtual reality system. Players interacted directly with a model which fed visual results back to provide a continuous dynamic interaction.

As a cultural paradigm, however, it was quite different. It was designed as a group activity, the underlying model was of an economy rather than of a physical world, it was designed for spectators, the visual feedback was not literal but was interpretive (the 700 or so images for the slide projectors had been chosen to represent different kinds of social situation, some were impressionistic), and there was a strong pedagogical intent.

4   An Hypothesis

The suggestion of this paper is that the two types of computer graphics SOC and SOR, are direct manifestations of the two ways of knowing, that of the insider looking out, the subject looking for an objective reality, and that of the outsider looking in, the voyeur of other, given, realities, the rational and the mythic respectively. In the one the computer screen is a window or a viewpoint which is used to look more deeply into reality. In the other the screen itself, or rather the image on the screen, is the reality. There are several kinds of evidence to support this suggestion. First consider the kinds of applications of SOR. Broadly, at the moment, these are things like advertising, special effects for film and television, adventure games and flight simulation. Apart from flight simulation, which has claim to be an application of both SOR and SOC, the others are all concerned with depicting fictions, with adventure games nudging close to mythology. Second consider the debates in the graphics field. In one of the Panel Discussions at Siggraph 90 (Hip, Hype and Hope: The Three Faces of Virtual Worlds) Myron Krueger, a noted pioneer in the field [7], had to force his way to the platform to make some points about the difficulties of getting support for his work, and indicated a schism between what he called the 'West Coast school of virtual reality' and his own kind of work as an artist. His work is concerned with the exploration of forms of interaction, with games, learning and the aesthetic and emotional responses to the systems. In our terms his work is definitely in the SOC camp and the schism he referred to is, I believe, the same one we are suggesting here between SOR and SOC and their attendant world views.

So there is some evidence supporting our suggestion. But it is certainly not enough to give more than mild encouragement that there is something worth further investigation. However, being optimists, let us assume that the suggestion turns out to be substantiated, that there is indeed a definite link between the rational/scientific mode of knowing and the SOC paradigm, and myth/magic mode of knowing and the SOR paradigm. What does this mean?

5   Conclusions

Our conjecture is that the two modes of computer graphics we have distinguished relate closely to the two modes of knowing which underlie human social systems. These modes of knowing are characterized in different ways but broadly are what anthropologists and philosophers refer to as the rational and the mythic, sometimes as the profane and the sacred, sometimes as the commonsensical and the magical. In all societies these co-exist and social evolution seems the result of continuous struggle between them. In Western democratic societies at the end of the twentieth century there is a feeling that, after a period of successful dominance of the rational over the mythic the complexity of problems engendered by its success is stimulating a resurgence of the second mode, manifest through worldwide emergence of fundamentalist religious views.

Virtual reality, the stream of computer graphics development dedicated to the simulation of reality (SOR), has the features of a powerful new medium which, like theatre in ancient Greece and imaginative literature in modern Europe and cinema in America, could project and sustain this revival of the mythic substrate. It is a medium which can present realities unfettered by constraints of practicality and therefore offers a powerful tool to those who would revive tribal consciousnesses and untestable 'truths'.

However, as luck would have it, and rather like the US cavalry emerging from behind the hill in Hollywood's failed attempt to create a mythology for the Euro-American people, computer graphics as simulation of complexity (SOC), offers an antidote to encroaching myths. SOC seeks to increase our rational understanding of the world in ways which are testable, repeatable and therefore consensually acceptable within society in its broadest sense.

But this is not a battle of the Titans from which only one will emerge triumphant. Rather there appears to be a complex symbiosis in which the two ways of knowing feed off each other. The more open the competition becomes the more healthy it becomes to the ultimate benefit of all societies. So the new medium of computer graphics moves to a central position of which its practitioners should be fully aware.

Just as the more general computer metaphor is changing the way we think of our thinking processes [8,9], the narrower computer graphics field will also influence emerging models of intelligence and consciousness. Dennett, drawing on practical work on vision, proposes consciousness as some kind of mediation process selecting from amongst multiple realities each of which is an hypothesis about what is going on 'out there'. I would take this further and suggest the models we have touched on in this essay point to a model of consciousness which is the result of flipping between the two modes of knowing. Each mode will have its own multiple realities but our grasp of what is real is determined by which mode is dominant at the time and, rather as a Necker Cube will flick between its two perspectives, so reality flickers in and out of view between the two modes. My guess is that the roll over between modes is what we perceive as consciousness.

Finally let us return to ancient Greece where the emergence of hero and anti-hero set us off down the road to self-consciousness. Plato proposed the metaphor of mankind sitting in a cave with its back to the opening watching the shadows of the real world on the cave walls and trying to make sense of it.

We need to be aware that, in our modern electronic, networked caves, the flickering shadows are not just projections from the outside world they are also projections, fictions, from an inside world.

References

1   Eco, U. 1987. *Travels in Hyperreality*. Picador.
2   Hegel, G.W.F. 1840. *The Philosophy of History* (Re-published 1956 by Dover, New York).
3   Fukuyama, F. 1989. Witnessing the end of political history. *San Francisco Chronicle*, August 9, 1.
4   Morris, B. 1987. *Anthropological Studies of Religion*. Cambridge University Press.
5   Forrester, J. 1961. *Industrial Dynamics*. MIT Press, MA, USA.
6   Mallen, G.L. 1973. The role of simulation in social education. *Programmed Learning*, July, 248–258.
7   Krueger, M. 1983. *Artificial Reality*. Addison-Wesley.
8   Penrose, R. 1989. *The Emperor's New Mind*. Oxford University Press.
9   Dennett, D. 1991. *Consciousness Explained*. Allen Lane.

Suggested Reading

Barlow *et al.* 1990. *Images and Understanding*. Cambridge.
Tufte, E.R. 1990. *Envisioning Information*. Graphics Press.

Biography

George Mallen is co-founder and Managing Director of System Simulation Ltd, software development company, specializing in multimedia information management systems. He became involved with computers in 1962 working on the development and use of digital simulations of air traffic control systems. His PhD explored the extension of simulation techniques to the study of information flows in organizations and in human learning. In 1977 he founded the Computing Activities Unit in the Department of Design Research at the Royal College of Art, where he was Deputy Head of Department. From 1983 to 1985 he was Head of the Department of Communication and Media at Bournemouth University, and initiated a multi-disciplinary degree course in Communication and Media Production.

19 Ethical Issues in the Application of Virtual Reality to the Treatment of Mental Disorders

L.J. Whalley
Department of Mental Health, University of Aberdeen

Abstract

A second computer revolution is under way. Smaller, more powerful and, possibly, less expensive computing systems will become available for use in medicine. An important advantage of proposed systems is that a part of their computing power can be set aside to make them easier to use. Should patients be allowed directly to interface with advanced computers? Specifically, should the mentally ill be offered assessment and treatment within the context of 'virtual reality' as simulated by computer? These questions are placed in historical context. 'Pseudo-scientific' therapies in psychiatry are briefly discussed as are the electrical treatments of depression and behaviour disorders. The 'punitive' component of some treatments is emphasized and the role of social expectations of the causes and treatment of mental disorders is examined. Ethical issues are considered under the general headings of (a) current principles in the ethical conduct of research on persons with mental incapacity, (b) the application of virtual reality to the assessment and treatment of fears, phobias and stress, and (c) the prosthetic use of advanced computer interfaces in the care of patients with brain injury. It is concluded that discussion of ethical issues in this exciting and potentially rewarding application would be timely and that the means of professional self-regulation should soon be introduced to ensure continuing surveillance of clinical practices.

1 Introduction

The development of advanced computer systems, their subsequent reduction in costs and a renewed interest in making computers easier to use has underpinned much of the current interest in 'virtual reality' systems. Initially, enthusiasm was expressed for improvements in the way computers are used, how they are controlled and eventually for the prospect that interfaces between operator and computer could be made more intuitive or natural. Early examples were provided by flight simulators and later military applications specifically intended to protect a pilot's vision from nuclear flash. Myron Krueger pioneered the development of a computer interface that appeared to surround the operator. In one example of virtual reality, the operator's visual fields are filled by two television screens which portray a graphical representation of reality (generated by sophisticated image processing) presented by a binocular headset. A motion detector picks up head movements and instructs the computer to re-calculate the graphical reality in keeping with the head position. By these means, the phenomenon of parallax is introduced, substantially strengthening the conviction that the observer is situated *within* the computer's graphical world. In another 'virtual reality', the binocular headset is replaced by large projection television screens and the subject views images generated by the computer. The development of the DataGlove (attributed to Zimmerman and Young Harvill) shows how the operator may interact with the computer in an entirely novel way. Special fibre optics are embedded in a glove and detect finger movements. The position of the hand is detected by a separate motion sensor and this information is used by the computer to construct a graphical representation of the glove in the computer-generated virtual reality. Movements of the glove are used by the computer to re-calculate the co-ordinates of its image and by these means, the operator can both visualize the gloved hand and manipulate objects in the computer's synthesized world.

Limitations to this early technology are the time taken by the computer to recalculate movements of the graphically represented objects and the poor quality of the images. Importantly, the paucity of other contextual visual clues (texture, contours, colour hues and shading of natural light) constrain the credibility of the synthesized world. Present technologies are easily recognized for what they are, even by unsophisticated observers, but do not terminally condemn this approach to computer generated reality. Further expected advances in computer design, the application of parallel processing to the problem of visualization and the development of computer systems that mimic the visual neural circuitry of the human brain each point to likely major improvements in this field of study. Probable developments include the inclusion of video material in the graphical world, the introduction of sound and 'sensory feedback' from the DataGlove such that the object to be manipulated feels and weighs as expected. In time, the DataGlove seems likely to be replaced by a BodySuit and the possibility of the 'experience machine' that can provide a wide and complex menu of experiences can be contemplated with confidence. It is in this projected setting that most potential applications of virtual reality to the treatment of clinical problems, to education, leisure and, speculatively, to punishment are proposed. To consider adequately the ethical issues that may arise when this innovative technology is applied to clinical problems it is first necessary to place the proposed application into its historical context. Secondly, it is necessary to set out current thinking on the most appropriate approach to ethical issues in psychiatric research and, finally, the ethics of recent proposals to study or treat the mentally impaired in the setting of virtual reality are discussed.

2   The Ethical Problem of Electrical Treatments in Psychiatry

The application of technological innovation to the treatment of mental disorders has consistently aroused strong feelings. Soon after the scientific discovery of electricity, 'animal magnetism' quickly replaced popular beliefs about the role of the spiritual world in the causes and care of insanity. In the late eighteenth century, doctors wrote about the human body as a kind of machine. Anton Mesmer (1734–1815) used an ingenious system of rods and mirrors to produce amnesia, paralysis or even convulsions to intrigued, naïve audiences. In keeping with his advancing 'scientific' reputation, Mesmer's unsophisticated audiences grew steadily larger. Contemporaneously, he was considered a charlatan or 'pseudo-scientist' by members of the French Academy and pioneers of the humane care of the insane such as Pinel. Yet Mesmer's public demonstrations attracted the interest of men and women of substantial intellect. Hegel and Schopenhauer wrote sensibly and widely about 'animal magnetism' though Mesmer's own pupils were given to exaggerated claims about the discovery. One pupil, an American called Quimby, 'magnetized' a young Mary Baker Eddy who later developed her own 'scientific' religion: Christian Science. Subsequently, less flamboyant medical practitioners applied 'animal magnetism' to everyday clinical problems and in so doing developed hypnosis. Later, neurologists such as Charcot discovered the value of hypnosis in the study of hysteria, observations witnessed by Freud, who later used the insights provided by hypnosis (he was an inexperienced but enthusiastic practitioner) to begin his own studies on the unconscious. The pathway from the application of a scientific discovery led by a largely logical route through the absurd theatre of Mesmer to a reasoned neurological model of the mind. Although such an approach has been roundly (and often fairly) criticized as being too reductionist, too deterministic and too simplistic, it has laid a secure foundation for the modern resurgence of interest in 'biological psychiatry' with its much-praised advances in drug therapy.

Exaggerated uncritical commentaries on medical uses of 'virtual reality' are really not too dissimilar to the extraordinary popular enthusiasms for earlier treatments of the mentally ill. Mesmer's legacy persuades the disinterested observer to inspect carefully the proposal to adapt a new technology to the treatment of disorders whose causes are not understood. Other issues are relevant here. From an historical perspective, novel treatments in psychiatry have reflected the pre-occupations of the age. Computers today are thought in the popular way to be adequate models of how the brain works. Why not use computers to treat mental illness? Encyclopaedias from the 1930s presented the telephone exchange as a model of the brain; why not use electricity (for that was what the brain was thought to use for information processing) to treat mental illness? Like all pseudo-scientific explanations, the acceptability of these ideas was much enhanced by another, older popular belief. In some way, the mentally ill could be held responsible for their illness, they were blameworthy, justifiably ill. Punishment, or more commonly, treatments with a punitive element were frequent. Proposals to use 'virtual reality' systems in the treatment of the mentally ill require care.

Electrical treatments have a long and not entirely distinguished history of use (some would say abuse) in psychiatry. Since antiquity when ancient Romans applied electric eels to the heads of the infirm, the power of electricity has fascinated doctors, many of whom subsequently used it with enthusiasm as a treatment while largely ignorant of any of the physical theory underpinning its use.

Electricity is also used as an aversive stimulus in behaviour therapy. Electrical Aversive Therapy was never popular as a technique but quickly entered public folklore and there is widespread awareness of its use as a treatment. During the 1930s and 1940s aversion therapy was widely employed as a treatment of alcoholism and after a period of disuse it was re-introduced to treat behaviour disorders, most notably, fetishism. The therapist decides on the timing of the noxious (electrical) stimulus and his choice is usually based on one of three models of learning (classical conditioning, avoidance conditioning and punishment training). The current status of electrical aversion therapy in modern psychiatric practice is that it now has a very limited use and is offered judiciously to carefully selected patients often in a forensic setting.

The discovery of electricity has been applied to the care of the mentally ill in other ways. In the late eighteenth century, zoologists observed the frog's muscular responses to the discharge of static electricity and speculated on the role of the phenomena, believing this might provide insights into the nature of life itself. This could even be the 'vital force' that gave passive organic matter its identity and volition. Such ideas were widely read and consumed. Mary Shelley (1818) recognized the public interest in (and fear of) the new technology and allowed electricity to vitalize her monster at the hand of Baron Frankenstein. Technology, in the public imagination, could be a valuable resource (e.g. steam trains, industrial machinery, etc.), but could threaten society and, potentially, wreak havoc upon its inventors and administrators. Over a century later, two Italians, Cerletti and Bini, used electricity to damage selectively the hippocampus in their studies on the pathogenesis of epilepsy. In so doing, they noticed a marked difference between the 'dose' of electricity required to cause a convulsion (epilepsy) and the 'dose' required to kill their experimental dogs. Electroconvulsions were produced in man on the basis of the false assumption that schizophrenia and epilepsy were incompatible. Nevertheless, clinicians soon recognized that electroconvulsive therapy (ECT) was effective in the treatment of depression. In the 1940s and 1950s it was widely administered without anaesthetic. Throughout this time, no controlled studies of the efficacy of ECT were properly conducted, ethics committees did not exist and many practitioners realized that ECT was introduced on the basis of a false assumption (about epilepsy and schizophrenia) and continued to be used in the absence of data on efficacy.

Electroconvulsive therapy (ECT) is a treatment of severe depressive disorders that has remained controversial since its introduction in 1938. It involves the brief application (about 1.5 s) of an electrical current through scalp electrodes to the brain of an anaesthetized and transiently paralysed patient whose respiration is assisted. A grand mal epileptic convulsion follows lasting about 20–50 s and within minutes the patient regains consciousness. About 6–12 treatments spaced at intervals of 2–3 days are usually required to effect recovery. The present status of ECT is that of specific treatment of severe depressive illnesses where other (usually drug) therapies have failed or there is a need to introduce rapidly effective treatment, perhaps because of suicide risk.

A popular view emerged that ECT was a cruel treatment of the mentally ill who were ill-equipped to decide for themselves and, possibly, worthy of a punitive treatment. In many respects the public view was well-founded: ECT *was* over-used, and probably abused. Much of the popular imagination about ECT was well-portrayed in novels such as Ken Kesey's *One flew over the cuckoo's nest* [1]. The informed, scientific view of ECT was hardly better. Garfield [2] cited a report in

Science titled 'Electroshock experiment at Albany violates ethics guidelines' [3] as evidence of 'ECT abuse'. The report, in fact, refers to the study of electroshock in a social learning experiment. The misunderstanding is noteworthy, however, as it points to a widely held belief, among both scientific and lay people, that there is scant difference between ECT and the use of electroshock as a negative re-informer in learning schedules. As will be discussed below, innovative therapeutic technologies are certain to arouse public and scientific concerns and when the potential for punishment is easily identifiable in that technology, its therapeutic component may be replaced by a punitive one. The primitive view that the mentally ill are worthy of a punishment which is visited on them for their past misdeeds remains extant. Some advocates of patients' rights and interests may equate an enthusiastic clinician's use of a new technology with the self-interested need for clinicians to advance their careers, and to profit at their patients' expense. It is in this historical context that technological innovations in therapy for mental disorders should be set.

Jacobs and Kotin [4] describe relevant ethical issues with compelling clarity: patients can be exploited to serve the non-therapeutic interests of the researchers. Career advancement and university funding rely in large part on a record of productivity and innovation. It is not unthinkable that some clinical research could be determined by such unwelcome motivations. There are many pressures especially on ambitious young investigators to take 'short-cuts' in human experimentation [5]. The chance to be first, to establish oneself as an authority seems greatest at the outset: other fields of study soon become crowded and competitive. Clinical studies on 'virtual reality' are in their infancy, and it is probably during this time, when public interest and professional surveillance are low, that the greatest ethical hazards exist.

3 Medical Ethics

Ethical issues in medical research were not widely discussed before the Second World War. After the Western World became aware of the disgraceful conduct of doctors in Germany (and later Japan), interested parties provided much-needed leadership to doctors in ethical matters. The World Medical Association Declaration of Helsinki (1964, and revised in 1975 and 1983) established beyond doubt the responsibilities of doctors to establish and regulate the duties and ethical standards of other doctors. These public concerns in the West were reinforced when a major medical atrocity in the USA was widely reported in the 1950s. In 1932, a group of patients in Tuskegee had been, without their consent, denied treatment so as to serve as a control group in a study of syphilis [6]. In this period of intense public debate, when memories of the Nuremberg trials were fresh, acknowledgement that 'civilized' Western doctors had not been above reproach, served to confirm and strengthen the belief in the USA of the need to replace common law by statute. Well-considered standards are now available to inform the design and conduct of therapeutic and experimental research procedures. Their intention is to protect human subjects from harm and exploitation [7]. These standards contain explicit acknowledgements of the need to protect the autonomy of patients in a research programme [8] and the requirement to meet precise recommendations regarding consent to research [9].

The development and later incorporation into the legal framework of the requirement of employing authorities to introduce institutional review boards (or ethics of research committees) that included well-informed, independent members who displayed an interested concern in the welfare of potential subjects and were capable of advocating the best interests of patients, was a welcome innovation. However, their introduction did not arise in isolation. A great deal of attention was paid in the 20 years that followed the Second World War to the role of society in the pathogenesis of mental illness. Laing [10], Cooper [11] and Szasz [12] reacted intensely to 'establishment psychiatry' and viewed with deep mistrust expressions of concern for the well-being of vulnerable, mentally disordered patients. Of relevance to the present discussion of an innovative technology is the substantial success of the 'anti-psychiatrists' in obtaining political commitments to deinstitutionalization, community care and the removal of harsh, stigmatizing and cruel, physical regimens for psychiatric patients. The medical uses of electricity (ECT and electrical aversion therapy) were much-quoted examples of degrading physical therapies [13, p. 31]. The establishment of ethics of research committees formed part of society's response to concerns about the causes, care and investigation of the mentally incompetent and are only properly understood when viewed in their socio-historical context.

The modern 'consumer' movement has further advanced the need to protect the interests of patients and medical malpractice claims have become commonplace. Litigation suits following the investigation of new treatments are not infrequent and many investigators are circumspect in the advice offered to potential patient subjects of their proposed research. Currently, it is required in many parts of the USA (and is a Good Clinical Practice guideline in the UK) that researchers advise potential subjects (who may be patients) not only of the possible hazards of a research procedure, but of their rights to compensation should adverse events arise. In consequence, current research activity in mental illness is understandably constrained by the need:

1. to work, quite properly, within uniformly accepted ethical guidelines
2. to be sensitive to potential criticism that a proposed novel treatment may be viewed as more punitive than therapeutic
3. to be aware that the investigation of advanced technologies may be equated by disinterested observers with the need to advance the career of the investigator
4. to be aware that the harmful effects of a new treatment may not be manifest for periods of years and that, in the case of the treatment of mental illness, such adverse effects may selectively exaggerate the symptoms or signs of the initial illness.

Recently, the Medical Research Council (MRC) has endorsed the recommendations of its Working Party on the ethical conduct of research on the mentally incapacitated [14]. The declaration of Helsinki (1964) had stated that freely given informed consent should be obtained from those participating in any medical research but that, 'where physical or mental incapacity makes it impossible to obtain informed consent . . . permission from the responsible relative replaces that of the subject in accordance with national legislation'. Additionally, the Committee of Ministers of the Council of Europe issued a recommendation (No. R (90)3) to governments of Member States to adopt legislation or measures to ensure implementation of a set of principles concerning medical research on human beings. The principles accepted by the MRC included:

Principle 4

A legally incapacitated person may only undergo medical research where authorized by Principle 5 and if his legal representative, or an authority or an individual authorized or designated under his national law, consents. If the legally incapacitated person is capable of understanding, his consent is also required and no research may be undertaken if he does not give his consent.

Principle 5

1. A legally incapacitated person may not undergo medical research unless it is expected to produce a direct and significant benefit to his health.
2. However, by way of exception, national law may authorize research involving a legally incapacitated person which is not of direct benefit to his health when that person offers no objection, provided that the research is to the benefit of persons in the same category and that the same scientific results cannot be obtained by research on persons who do not belong to this category.

In July 1990 the European Commission issued guidelines, prepared by the Committee for Proprietary Medicinal Products, on Good Clinical Practice for Trials on Medicinal Products in the European Community (the 'Good Clinical Practice' guidelines). These guidelines do not yet have statutory force in the UK, but it is proposed to require all member states to make them part of national law and it appears likely that they will represent national law by 1992. The guidelines cover a number of issues from ethics committees to consent in trials of medicinal products which, though not of direct relevance to the present discussion of virtual reality, do convey a sense of the importance now attached to this area. Paragraph 1.13 states:

If the subject is incapable of giving personal consent (e.g. unconsciousness or severe mental illness or disability), the inclusion of such patients may be acceptable if the ethics committee is, in principle, in agreement and if the investigator is of the opinion that participation will promote the welfare and interest of the subject. The agreement of a legally valid representative that participation will promote the welfare interest of the subject should also be recorded by a dated signature. If neither signed informed consent nor witnessed signed verbal consent are possible, this fact must be documented with reasons by the investigator.

Paragraph 1.14 states:

Consent must always be given by the signature of the subject in a non-therapeutic study, ie, when there is no direct clinical benefit to the subject.

The Royal College of Physicians' (RCP) 1990 report, *Research Involving Patients*, also emphasizes that, with some exceptions such as observational research which carries no risk and is not intrusive, patients should know that they are taking part in research and that research should only be carried out with their consent. The RCP report also emphasizes that many mentally handicapped and mentally ill patients will be able to give consent. It continues:

> A strong ethical case can be made out for non-therapeutic research (involving only minimal risk) in mentally handicapped patients because only through better understanding of their condition can care for such patients be improved. We think that the best guidance under these circumstances might be that there should be agreement by the close relatives or guardians and that the mentally handicapped individual seems to agree to the procedure.

This report, together with the RCP's 1990 *Guidelines on the Practice of Ethics Committees in Medical Research Involving Human Subjects*, recommends that the considerations quoted above in relation to mentally handicapped adults are relevant to therapeutic and non-therapeutic research involving mentally ill patients who cannot give consent or whose consent is in doubt. The RCP's reports emphasize, however, that no patient who refuses or resists should be included in research.

The Royal College of Psychiatrists' (RCPsych) 1990 *Guidelines for Ethics of Research Committees on Psychiatric Research Involving Human Subjects* puts the case for psychiatric research as follows:

> Research is as essential in psychiatry as in any other branch of medicine. While there are ethical problems in carrying out research, it is unethical for the profession to fail to do research because this deprives present and future patients of the possibility of more informed and better treatment as well as the (more distant) prospect of prevention of psychiatric disorder.

The RCPsych Guidelines emphasize that 'The majority of psychiatric patients are as capable of giving consent as are other patients'. On the question of 'incompetent' patients, they point out that many suffer from conditions, such as mental handicap and dementia, in which advances are most needed and which cannot be obtained by studying other patients. The Guidelines recommend a 'common sense' approach to research in such circumstances. They do not distinguish explicitly between therapeutic and non-therapeutic research but emphasize that the Local Ethics of Research Committees (LREC) should decide in the usual way whether the research is acceptable in terms of the balance of benefits, discomfort and risks, and suggest that in most cases the research worker should discuss the research with one or more close relatives. If there is no relative, or the patient expresses the wish that his relatives should not be consulted (confidentiality may be an important issue in this and other contexts), they recommend consulting an independent person approved by the LREC who knows the patient well and will protect his interests. Whatever the views of third parties, the Guidelines state that no research should proceed if the patient refuses, or appears to refuse, either in words or actions.

4 Fears, Phobias and Stress

Applications of virtual reality to the treatment of fears and phobias and in the investigation of stress responses in disorders such as hypertension or ischaemic coronary artery disease are the likeliest first targets for medical researchers.

Complaints about unwanted anxiety, its interference in daily life and unpleasant bodily feelings that accompany anxiety are amongst the most common grounds for requests for medical intervention. Although studies of human emotions have, historically, been largely introspective ('I can observe my own pain and pleasures but I cannot observe yours, only infer what you may feel') the twentieth century has seen considerable interest in 'methodological behaviourism'. Pioneered by Watson (1913), psychology was reconstrued as a 'purely objective, experimental branch of natural science' and considerable therapeutic success followed implementation of his argument in the treatment of anxiety and, specifically, phobias. The simplistic views propounded by Watson did not go unchallenged (see Gray [15]) but the benefits of 'behaviour therapy' became one of the lasting achievements of twentieth century psychology. Systematic behaviour therapy programmes rely upon careful manipulation of the patient's environment and meticulous observation of the patient's responses to change. Target symptoms include generalized anxiety, pain (especially head and neck). Eventually a patient may learn to control the bodily consequences of unpleasant feelings by learning to observe these carefully and employ a learnt relaxation procedure. More active programmes may link learnt relaxation procedure with the request to imagine scenes depicting the patient in an anxiety-provoking situation [16]. These procedures are exhaustively elaborated upon [17], and are often available as quasi-automated programmes, usually based on tape-recordings but sometimes video material is used. Recently, virtual reality has been proposed as a more appropriate – and possibly more effective – modality within which to work.

Not surprisingly, since the proposed 'virtual reality' technology remains largely at the prototype stage – images are cartoon-like and carry little conviction – no attempt has been described that links physiological correlates of anxiety to the generation of artificial reality ('psycho-physiological interactive virtual reality') but there is considerable potential. Given the success of behaviour therapy using more limited devices that rely upon the use of imagination or the deliberate, premeditated exposure to a fear-provoking stimulus, the opportunities provided by 'virtual reality' systems may be irresistible to potential therapists or researchers.

The ethical issues involved when using 'virtual reality' systems to conduct behaviour therapy focus largely upon their potential for abuse. Most anxious patients remain capable of informed decisions about the potential benefits to themselves of taking part, no hazards seem likely to be encountered and most independent disinterested but knowledgeable observers would agree that the application of virtual reality in this way represents a logical extension of over 50 years careful clinical work in behaviour therapy. But what threat would the very existence of the technology pose for the non-consenting individual, perhaps someone regarded by society as deserving punishment or 'encouragement' to disclose information when under interrogation? The potential for abuse is certainly present and more self-evidently so as devices reconstruct reality with increasing verisimilitude. Perhaps, an authoritarian government would invest heavily in improved technology and, encouraged by therapeutic success, seek to develop methods of modification of social behaviour towards the goals of socially acceptable behaviour. These matters have previously been widely discussed [18], and it is clear that the extent of the aversive or negative stimuli used to model or shape behaviour has greatly influenced views about the ethical issues involved. The conduct of behavioural therapies in the absence of facilities that allow the patient to develop a trusting relationship with the therapist and thereby have useful opportunities to assign meanings to the treatment is thought to be, at one level, an example of poor clinical practice and at another level an example of procedures that are difficult to justify in the care of that group of patients whose difficulties may be linked to their failure to establish basic, trusting relationships. The admired, supreme efficiencies of a 'virtual reality' system which follows the rules of therapy set out by a guiding behaviour therapist may prove an inadequate substitute for interpersonal experience. The implicit ethical issue then becomes apparent; can a patient even when just moderately impaired by inappropriate anxiety truly give informed consent to such procedures? Human experiences determine much of mental life, perceptions give rise to feelings, thinking and imaginings, and in turn meanings are attributed to each of these aspects of mental life. Behaviourists have not addressed this problem, language has been seen only as response to mental events occurring in a setting of consciousness [19]. The problem becomes more complex when the phenomenon of 'transpositional learning' is introduced. Subjects (including animals) appear able to recognize relationships between stimuli or objects and distinguish these from the absolute qualities of the objects. Experiments that require exact discrimination between patterns of stimuli are not readily explained in behaviourist terms and become especially difficult to account for when relationships between verbal stimuli demand previous detection and evaluation by experimental subjects. The attribution of meaning by patients to behavioural therapeutic paradigms presented in a 'virtual reality' designed by behaviourists raises the possibility that vulnerable subjects may experience largely unexpected hazards from ill-judged exposure to 'virtual reality' systems, no matter how well-intended.

5 Innovative Psychotherapies

Corsini [20] has collated systematic descriptions of 66 varieties of psychotherapy. Many seek to place those patients' experiences that are the focus of distress into a context conducive to change, by bringing issues into the 'here and now'. Making past experiences come alive again so that attendant emotions may be relived, modified or replaced poses technical problems for many psychotherapists who aim to facilitate change by such means. Could 'virtual reality' systems be useful for such therapists and their patient and would their use be welcome?

An example clinical problem might be presented by a daughter who continues to grieve for her deceased father while other close family members successfully resolve their feelings. The therapist might consider re-uniting father and daughter in 'virtual reality' with the assistance of personal reminiscences and family mementos such as home-video or photographs. Such an experience might be harmful. It may so strongly re-awaken dependency needs that the patient's pathological grief remains unresolved. She may indeed prefer her experiences in 'virtual reality' with her deceased father to her misery in the world shared with her friends and relatives.

The problem, common to many psychotherapies, of pathological dependency on the psychotherapeutic milieu, can be skilfully resolved by the psychotherapist leading, explaining and encouraging the patient to move by safe steps into an emotionally independent and more secure future. 'Virtual reality' in this setting may seem hardly more than an unhealthy pre-occupation with the memorabilia of another's life, comparable to a widow's wish to change nothing after her husband's death, leaving clothes untouched, continuing to set a table for dinner on (his) return from work.

Common sense suggests that the widow is exercising her own free will; her life is not constrained by her behaviour and she may indeed derive substantial comfort from the proximity of the deceased possessions, the re-enactment of old repertoires. 'Free Will' is sometimes illusory, a contrived rationalization of unwanted, unnecessary behaviour to support a complex web of self-deception.

Suppose the 'virtual reality' system became commercially available as a home-based entertainment. Technological progress might lead quickly to its use as a family archive from which familiar people and places might be recalled and re-engaged at will. These advances might allow us to experience whatever we wished, avoid anxiety and distress without recourse to mind altering drugs, alcohol or strenuous exercise. Once in 'virtual reality' our motivation to change may reduce or even disappear. It is clear that for many people the experience per se is simply not enough. We want to achieve, to succeed, we want to learn from experience. The grieving widow who resolves her grief, and later draws upon the experience to help her daughter come to terms with the loss of her child, has opinions, values and possible solutions taken from a real world. Likewise, achievement of mastery over unpleasant internal feelings that threaten the integrity of the self is a matter that gives rise to understandable pride not simply in the acquisition but more so in the effort expended (and its attendant failures) through which mastery was obtained.

Concern about 'Free Will' in virtual reality used as a therapeutic medium also arises in a different way. Each of us has an idea of how we would ideally wish to be, what sort of person we would hope others would find on making our acquaintance. A patient who chose to remain in virtual reality for prolonged periods is not accessible to appraisal. Is he worth getting to know? Warm, generous, witty? Patients tormented by unpleasant feelings may understand the barrier too well. The preference for 'virtual reality' experiences to a shared world becomes an effective means of social withdrawal. Used to an extreme, it is a form of suicide. The way we are is important to us, it helps motivates us to change. How does a therapist feel viewing a patient trapped by pictures unconcerned by what is happening to their own private selves?

There is a single compelling reason to regard the therapeutic application of 'virtual reality' systems with some circumspection. The experiences offered in 'virtual reality' no matter how life-like, how compellingly vivid, rich in detail, are fundamentally pre-fabricated. They are man-made. The simulated world of virtual reality is skin-deep, as meaningful as man can construct. The social realities of interpersonal contact can be simulated but not experienced to the same extent. Many on occasion may be content to confine their social contacts in this way, preferring superficial, transient relationships to which they have no lasting personal commitment, and from which they do not seek any deeper significance. The broad aims of psychotherapists are to encourage personal development and fulfilment, to allow individual responsibilities to be defined and accepted and, potentially, to assist individuals to move to full independence, integrated within society's expectations and norms. 'Virtual reality' devices do not well prepare a patient to address such an agenda. Experience with computer games and their fascination for youngsters, suggest quite the opposite; that fantasies will be exploited, that 'omnipotence of thought' will be allowed to range at will. If patients have problems in reality, surely it is appropriate if not mandatory that those problems are resolved in contact with a shared world

– something a 'virtual reality' system cannot do for us. Psychotherapy teaches us that things other than our experiences concern us. These matters may motivate us, determine our values and greatly influence our choices about the person we wish to be.

6   Rehabilitation after Brain Injury

Each year, most large towns in the Western world are faced with the need to respond to young people aged 15–50 years with brain injuries. Common causes include head trauma, cerebrovascular disease and medical accidents. Many survive to enter rehabilitation programmes that provide the opportunity to re-learn skills, recognize deficits and continuously inform the patient and carers about progress. The work is intense and often effective but it demands high-order therapeutic skills from multiple disciplines. Not surprisingly such programmes are expensive and sadly unavailable to many.

'Virtual reality' systems potentially offer the opportunity to enrich the experiences of disabled patients, allowing those, say, with motor deficits, to extend their awareness of themselves and, to a lesser extent, provide indicators of performance in a neutral, non-critical setting. In this context, the 'virtual reality system' acts as a true user-friendly interface with an advanced computer dedicated to advise and assist patients and therapists alike to maintain progress in rehabilitation. Examples may include a supportive role to meet memory deficits, impaired visuo-motor performance or reduced vigilance. Assisted in this way, a brain-damaged patient may be spared their intense emotional responses to failure. All that might be required would be the ability to indicate an intention and, possibly, to contribute to its enactment. In this setting 'virtual reality' systems might be regarded as prosthetic devices whose intervention could be appropriately reduced as the patient progressed. Limitations to their use might arise if the patient preferred (as discussed above) simulated experiences to a shared world and if the time spent in virtual reality was to the exclusion of therapist intervention. Skilled, motivated therapists require to interact with patients in order to sustain their work.

A separate but important problem in the application of virtual reality systems to the care of the brain injured arises when the interface between advanced computing system and surviving brain tissue becomes direct. Already, the feasibility of 'silicon-neurone' connections has been demonstrated and it is clearly only a matter of time before novel methods of interface between computer and organism are attempted. Their consequences for the brain injured and those mentally handicapped from birth are outside the scope of this review.

7   Conclusions

The potential value of 'virtual reality' systems to the problems of treatment and causation in psychiatry is about to be explored. Reduced computer size, lower costs and considerable increases in sheer computing power are likely to make advanced computer systems available in many clinical situations. Patient reactions to the technology involved will vary substantially but it is clear that considerable care will be required in the selection and training of patients with mental illness. From an historical perspective, medicine does not have an impressive record of achievement in the application of new technologies to psychiatry while other disciplines seem often to have fared better.

When sufficient computing power is applied to the problem of 'virtual reality', when efficient acceptable interfaces are available, the shared, sensible world will be largely indistinguishable from that simulated by computer. The promised development of a whole body DataSuit seems likely to prompt the neurologist to seek to restore motor experience to the stroke victim, albeit in an illusory manner. Soon, some psychiatrists, psychotherapists and clinical psychologists will wish to explore 'virtual reality' with their patients. Anxiety, phobias and stress control seem possible targets that could be fruitfully explored. Neuropsychologists may wish to go a little further and use the opportunity of ease of access to advanced computing power to gain a better understanding of complex brain disorders such as schizophrenia. Direct interfacing between the schizophrenic patient and the computing system may become feasible and lead – speculatively – to the development of computer-generated models of brain function and its disorders, especially those of language.

However, considerable caution should be exercised before patients are introduced to 'virtual reality', specifically those whose judgement or insight may be impaired. 'Virtual reality' may have the capacity to distort reality testing in those for whom it is already impaired, limit freedom of choice in those who do not understand their basic freedoms and, worst of all, become a playground for another example of medical paternalism let loose.

An early scenario might be an experiment conducted with a patient suffering irreversible brain disease and confined to bed. The responsible clinician wishing to reduce psychotropic drug administration offers 'virtual reality' experiences to allow the patient to escape from the confines of his bed. Available to him are the desirable experiences of others, presented as a menu to the afflicted patient. Soon, the patient prefers 'virtual reality' to the world he has shared with his carers. But his 'virtual reality' is fundamentally distinct from our own. We do things, have experiences because we want to have them. 'We win some, we lose some', profit from the experience and shape our future choices. We exercise our free will, when we better inform ourselves of our limitations and choose advisedly what task, within our resources and attributes, we are best equipped to face. 'Virtual reality' seems likely to encourage infantile thinking, 'omnipotence of thought' in those whose maturational tasks include satisfactory resolution of their problems in shared realities, the acquisition of effective means of 'reality testing'. Vulnerable, brain-damaged patients should not be exposed to 'virtual reality' until the impact of its experience can be properly understood.

Experiences offered in 'virtual reality' are restricted to what man can design and are much more limited than the choice available to an individual going about a daily routine. These constraints placed on choice offer potential uses in education, for example, or in the treatment of subjects with problems of impulse control or socially unacceptable behaviour. Limitation of choice does, however, carry a considerable responsibility and, importantly, sizeable potential for abuse. The distinction between a 'virtual reality' system designed to treat a variety of phobias with interactive physiological biofeedback, and a possible instrument of torture may be clear in the mind of its designer but the capacity of the first to serve effectively as the second is self-evident.

'Virtual reality' systems require professional self-regulation. Abuse by ambitious, enthusiastic experimentalists seems likely. Amongst the 66 varieties of psychotherapy cited above, many on inspection seem as pseudo-scientific as Mesmer's 'animal magnetism'. It is only a matter of time before the ethical issues discussed above are brought just as forcibly to our attention. It is now timely to discuss and resolve those ethical issues that may arise from the application of 'virtual reality' to the problems of mental illness.

References

1   Kesey, K. 1962. *One flew over the cuckoo's nest*. Viking Press.
2   Garfield, E. 1980. ECT abuse. *Current Contents* (April). Reprinted in: *Essays of an Information Scientist*, Vol. 4. ISI Press, Philadelphia.
3   Smith, R.J. 1977. Electroshock experiment at Albany violates ethics guidelines. *Science*, **198**: 383–386.
4   Jacobs, L. and Kotin, J. 1972. Fantasies of psychiatric research. *Am. J. Psychiatry*, **128**: 1074–1080.
5   Beecher, H.K. 1988. Ethics and clinical research. *N. Eng. J. Med.* **274**: 1354–1360.
6   Brandt, A.M. 1978. *Racism and research: the case of the Tuskegee syphylis study*. Hastings Center Report, **8** (6): 21–29.
7   Tancredi, L.R. and Maxfield, C.T. 1983. Regulation of psychiatric research. *Int. J. Law Psychiatry*, **6**: 17–38.
8   Stanley, B.H. and Stanley, M. 1981. Psychiatric patients in research: protecting their autonomy. *Comp. Psychiatry*, **22** (4): 420–427.
9   Applebaum, P.S. and Roth, L.H. 1982. Competency to consent to research. *Arch. Gen. Psychiatry*, **39**: 951–958.
10 Laing, R.D. 1980. *The divided self*. London, Tavistock.
11 Cooper, D. 1967. *Psychiatry and antipsychiatry*. London, Tavistock.
12 Szasz, T.S. 1974. *The Myth of Mental Illness*. Harper and Row.
13. Szasz, T.S. 1971. *The Manufacture of Madness*. Routledge & Kegan Paul.
14 The Ethical Conduct of Research on the Mentally Incapacitated. Working Party on Research on the Mentally Incapacitated. London: Medical Research Council, December 1991.
15 Gray, J.A. 1987. *The Psychology of Fear and Stress*. Cambridge University Press.
16 Wolpe, J. 1958. *Psychotherapy by reciprocal inhibition*, Stanford U.P. Palo Alto.
17 Rimm and Masters 1979. *Behavior Therapy: Techniques and Empirical Findings* R & M (eds) 2nd Edn, Academic Press, London.
18 Bandura, A. 1989. *Principles of behavior modification*. Holt, Rinehart and Winston.
19 Dollard, J. and Miller, N.E. 1950. *Personality and Psychotherapy: An analysis in terms of learning, thinking and culture*. McGraw-Hill, New York.
20 Corsini, R.J. 1981. *Handbook of Innovative Psychotherapies*. John Wiley.

Further Reading

Callan, J.P. Electroconvulsive therapy. *J. Amer. Med. Assoc.* 1979; **242**: 545–546.

Crisp, A.H. *Anorexia Nervosa: let me be.* London, Toronto, Sydney; Academic Press. New York: San Francisco; Grune & Stratton, 1980.

Fink, M. Myths of 'shock therapy'. *Am. J. Psychiatry*, 1977; **134**: 991–996.

Friedberg, J. *Shock treatment is not good for your brain.* San Francisco, Glide Publications, 1976, 176.

Friedhoff, M.R. and Benson, W. *The second complete revolution visualization.* New York: W.H. Freeman and Company, 1988.

Guntrip, H. *Schizoid phenomena object-relations and the self.* London: The Hogarth Press, 1968.

Hamilton, V. and Vernon, M.D. *The development of cognitive processes.* London: New York: San Francisco: Academic Press, 1976.

Meichenbaum, D. *Cognitive-behaviour modification: an integrative approach.* New York and London: Plenum Press.

National Institute of Mental Health (NIMH). Approaching the 21st Century: opportunities for NIMH neuroscience research. The National Advisory Mental Health Council Report to Congress on the Decade of the Brain. DHSS Publication No. (ADM) 88–1580. January 1988.

Nozick, R. *Anarchy, State, and Utopia.* New York: Basic Books Inc., Publishers, 1974.

Popper, K.R. and Eccles, J.C. *The self and its brain.* New York, London, Heidelberg, Berlin: Springer-Verlag, 1977.

Regestein, O.R., Murawski, B.J. and Engle, R.P. A case of prolonged, reversible dementia associated with abuse of electroconvulsive therapy. *J. Nerv. Ment. Dis.*, 1975; **161**: 200–203.

Scheflin, A.W. and Opton, E.M. *The mind manipulators.* New York, Paddington Press, 1978, 354–402.

Siris, S.G., Docherty, J.P., McGlashan, T.H. Intrapsychic structural effects of psychiatric research. *Am. J. Psychiatry* 1979; **136**: 1567–1571.

Skinner, B.F. *Beyond freedom and dignity.* New York, Alfred A. Knopf, 1972.

Slawson, P.F. Psychiatric malpractice: the California experience. *Am. J. Psychiatry*, 1979; **136**: 650–654.

Steir, C. *Blue jolts: true stories from the cuckoo's nest.* Washington: New Republic Books, 1978; 245.

Terwilliger, R.F. *Meaning and mind.* New York, Oxford University Press, 1968.

Biography

Professor Lawrence J. Whalley received his training at the Universities of Newcastle-upon-Tyne, Oxford and Edinburgh. He graduated MD from Newcastle in 1976 and joined the staff of the Medical Research Council (MRC) in 1977. His first studies were in alcoholism and later he worked extensively in psychoneuroendocrinology with a special interest in the biological sub-classification of major mental disorders. In 1986 he joined the staff of the University of Edinburgh and established a research programme in dementia funded by MRC and the SHHD. He became Professor of Mental Health at the University of Aberdeen in 1992. Whalley contributes regularly to medical journals and is an enthusiastic teacher in clinical medicine.

Bibliography

Acknowledgements

This bibliography is derived from a public domain, online bibliography available on the archive site for the Usenet news group sci.virtual-worlds.
   It was assembled by the collective efforts of a number of people, including:

- Merideth Bricken, HITL, University of Washington
- Bob Jacobson, HITL, University of Washington
- Mark deLoura, HITL, University of Washington
- Wanda Pierce, McGill University
- Huw Jones, Middlesex University
- Terese McAleese, ACGC, Royal Melbourne Institute of Technology
- Andrew Cassin, ACGC, Royal Melbourne Institute of Technology
- Robert Webb, ACGC, Royal Melbourne Institute of Technology
- Karen Paik, ACGC, Royal Melbourne Institute of Technology

It is provided in the belief that this bibliography is a valuable resource for the Virtual Reality community.
   The bibliography includes most conferences and workshops, journal articles and press references.
   The online version is available on the Internet via anonymous FTP to the host –
      milton.u.washington.edu
in the directory –
      public/virtual-worlds/citations

Adams, C. If looks could kill: The eyes have it. *Military and Aerospace Electronics*, pages 35–37, Mar. 1990.

Am. Assoc. for Advancement of Science Annual Meeting. *Virtual Concepts for Crew Member/Computer Integration*, May 29 1985.

Amburn, Col. P. Mission planning and debriefing using helmet mounted display systems. In *Proceedings of the 1992 EFDPMA Conference on Virtual Reality*, 1992.

Amburn, P., Grant, E., and Whitted, T. Managing geometric complexity with enhanced procedural models. In *SIGGRAPH Proceedings*, volume 20, pages 189–195, August 18–22 1986.

Andrew, I. Cyberzone – virtual reality comes to the tv screen. In *Virtual Reality 91: Impacts and Applications*, pages 35–39, 1991.

Applewhite, H.L. Position tracking in virtual reality. In *Proceedings of Virtual Reality '91, 2nd Annual Conference on Virtual Reality, Artificial Reality and Cyberspace*, page 1, 1991.

Arnold, B., Powers, T. and Frankel, A.D. The computer graphics virtual device interface. *IEEE Computer Graphics and Applications*, 6 (8), pages 33–41, 1986.

Ashby, W.R. *An Introduction to Cybernetics*. John Wiley and Sons, New York, 1963.

Attneave, F. Representation of physical space coding processes in human memory. Winstone, Washington DC, 1972.

Aviles, W. Telerobotic remote presence. In *Proc. Human-Machine Interfaces for Teleoperators and Virtual Environments*, page 38, Mar. 1990.

Backman, D., Jacobson, S., Iversen, E., Davis, C. and Biggers, K. Issues in the design of high dexterity, force reflective teleoperators. In *Proc. Human-Machine Interfaces for Teleoperators and Virtual Environments*, page 39, Mar. 1990.

Badler, N.I., Webber, B.L., Kalita, J. and Esakov, J. Animation from instructions. In N. Badler, B. Barsky, and D. Zeltzer, editors, *Making Them Move: Mechanics, Control and Animation of Articulated Figures*, pages 51–93. Morgan Kaufmann, San Mateo, CA, 1991.

Baraff, D. and Badler, N.I. *Handwaving in Computer Graphics: Efficient Methods for Interactive Input Using a Six-Axis Digitizer.* Department of Computer and Information Science, Univ. of Penn., Philadelphia, PA, 1986.

Barlow, J.P. Being in nothingness. *Microtimes*, pages 97–98, 104, 110, Jan. 22 1989.

Barlow, J.P. Life in the data cloud. *Mondo 2000*, pages 44–51, summer 1990.

Bates, J. Oz project: Overview and schedule, 1989.

Beauchamp, R.G. James Burke on the computer age. *Microtimes*, pages 84, 86, 97–99, May 1988.

Beaudan, E. Cockpits of the future. *American Way*, pages 35–36, 38, Oct. 15 1987.

Beck, S. Virtual light and cybervideo. *Mondo 2000*, pages 64–64, summer 1990.

Bejczy, A.K. and Dotson, R.S. Manual control of manipulator forces and torques using graphic display. In *IEEE Proceedings, Intl. Conf. Cybernetics and Society*, pages 691–698, 1982.

Bejczy, A.K. and Salisbury, J.K. Jr. Controlling remote manipulators through kinesthetic coupling. *Computers in Mechanical Engineering*, pages 48–60, July 1983. (Keywords: force feedback).

Benedikt, M., (editor) *Cyberspace: First Steps*, MIT Press, Cambridge, MA, 1991.

Benzon, B. The visual mind and the Macintosh. *BYTE*, pages 113–130, Jan. 1985.

Bergman, L., Fuchs, H., Grant, E. and Spach, S. Image rendering by adaptive refinement. *ACM SIGGRAPH*, 20 (4): 29–37, August 18–22 1986.

Beyers, D. 'Super Cockpit' plans to be unveiled March 31. *Air Force Times*, page 32, Mar. 16 1987.

Birt, J. and Furness, T. Visually-coupled systems. *Air University Review*, 20 (3): 28–40, April 1974.

Bishop, G. and Fuchs, H. The self-tracker: A smart optical sensor on silicon. In *Conference on Advanced Research in VLSI*, pages 65–73. MIT, 1984.

Blake, A. 'Supercockpit' appears right on target. *Albuquerque Journal*, page B1, June 29 1987.

Blake, A. When looks can kill. *Boston Globe*, pages 55–56, June 15 1987.

Blauert, J. The telepräsenz-consortium: Structures and intentions. In *Proc. Human-Machine Interfaces for Teleoperators and Virtual Environments*, page 59, Mar. 1990.

Bodisco, A. Sense8 plans affordable vr now. *Mondo 2000*, page 54, summer 1990.

Boff, K.R., Kaufman, L. and Thomas, J.P, editors. *Handbook of Perception and Human Performance*, volume I & II. Wiley Interscience, 1986.

Bolt, R.A. "Put-that-there": Voice and gesture at the graphics interface. *Computer Graphics*, 14 (3): 262–270, July 1980.

Boy, G.A. Interface to real and virtual worlds. In *Advanced Interaction Media: in Proceedings of Informatique '92*, pages 551–568, 1992.

Brand, S. *The Media Lab – inventing the future at MIT*. Viking-Penguin Books, 1987.

Brand, S. Sticking your head in cyberspace. *Whole Earth Review*, pages 84–87, Summer 1989. (Keywords: dataglove, virtual reality).

Brand, S. Social and cultural implications of virtual reality: Part two. *Cyberthon*, October 1990.

Branwyn, G. Virtual reality. *The Futurist*, page 45, May–June 1990.

Breen, P. The need for establishing vr requirements. In *Proceedings of the 1992 EFDPMA Conference on Virtual Reality*, 1992.

Brett, C., Pieper, S. and Zeltzer, D. Putting it all together: An integrated package for viewing and editing 3D microworlds. In *Proc. 4th Usenix Computer Graphics Workshop*, Cambridge, MA, October 8–9 1987.

Brian, Hoey, and Captain. Cockpits of the future. *Airman*, XXIX (10): 9–13, October 1985.

Bricken, M. Cyberspace: A mind-blowing trip into artificial reality. *ACADS Quarterly*, (61): 20–23, September 1989.

Bricken, M. Designing virtual worlds: The vs-x. In *Siggraph 91 Virtual Interface Technology (Virtual Reality) course notes*, pages 80–82, 1991.

Bricken, W. Cyberspace 1999. *Mondo 2000*, pages 56–75, Summer 1990.

Bricken, W. Virtual environment operating system: Preliminary functional architecture (tr-hitl-m-90-2). Technical report, Human Interface Technology Laboratory, University of Washington, 1990.

Bricken, W. Virtual reality: Directions of growth. In *Virtual Reality 91: Impacts and Applications*, pages 1–6, 1991.

Bricken, W. Training in virtual reality. In *Virtual Reality 91: Impacts and Applications*, page 46, 1991.

Bricken, W. A formal foundation for cyberspace. In *Proceedings of Virtual Reality '91, 2nd Annual Conference on Virtual Reality, Artificial Reality and Cyberspace*, page 9, 1991.

Bricken, W. Coordination of multiple participants in virtual space: *SIGGRAPH Course Notes*, pages 54–58, 1991.

Bricken, W. Human interface technology laboratory research agenda. *Siggraph 91*, pages 59–63, 1991.

Bricken, W. Virtual reality: Directions of growth. *Siggraph 91*, pages 64–79, 1991.

Brindle, J. and Furness, T. Visually coupled systems in advanced air force applications. In *National Aerospace Electronics Conference*, Dayton, OH, May 1974.

Brody, F. How virtual is reality? In *Virtual Reality 91: Impacts and Applications*, pages 18–20, 1991.

Brooks, F. Virtual reality at work. In *Proc. Human-Machine Interfaces for Teleoperators and Virtual Environments*, pages 45–46, March 1990.

Brooks, F.P. *Grasping Reality Through Illusion – Interactive Graphics Serving Science*. ACM SIGCHI, 1988.

Brooks, F.P. Jnr. Walkthrough p a dynamic graphics system for simulating virtual building. *Proceedings 1986 Workshop on Interactive 3D Graphics*, pages 9–22, 1986.

Brooks, F.P. Jnr. Virtual reality at work. In T.B. Sheridan et al., (eds). *Proceedings of the Engineering Foundation Conference, Human-Machine Interfaces for Teleoperators and Virtual Environments*, NASA, 1990.

Brooks, F.P. Jnr, Aiery, J.M. and Rohlf, J.H. Towards image realism with interactive update rates in complex virtual building environments. *ACM Computer Graphics*, pages 41–50, 1990.

Brooks, F.P. Jnr and Batter, J.J. Grope-1. In *IFIPS Proc 71*, page 759, 1972.

Brooks, M. The dataglove as a man-machine interface for robotics. *The Second IARP Workshop on Medical and Healthcare Robotics*, pages 213–225, September 5–7 1989. (Keywords: neural net, kohonen net).

Brosselin, S. Le pilote que voit l'invisible. *Science et Vie*, (832), January 1987.

Brown, D.A., Teams disagree on training system for army LHX helicopter program. *Aviation Week and Space Technology*, pages 60–61, Jan. 15 1990.

Brown, D.J., Cobb, S.V., Eastgate, R.M., Gibson, I. and Smith, P.A. Research applications of virtual reality. *Interactive Learning International (UK)*, pages 161–163.

Brozan, N. From citibank millions for schools. *The New York Times*, Wed., May 16 1990.

Buckwalter, L. Military avionics. *Avionics*, 10 (5): 15–26, May 1986.

Burdea, G., Ahuang, J., Roskos, E., Silver, D. and Langrana, N. Direct-drive force feedback control for the dataglove. In *Proceedings of the European Robotics and Intelligent Systems Conference*. Kluwer Academic Publishers, Corfu, Greece, 1991.

Burdea, G., Roskos, E., Silver, D., Thibaud, F. and Wolpov, R. A distributed virtual environment with dextrous force feedback. In *Proceedings Informatique '92: Interface to Real and Virtual Worlds*, pages 255–265.

Burdea, G., Ahuang, J., Roskos, E., Silver, D. and Langrana, N. A portable dextrous master with force feedback. *Presence: Teleoperators and Virtual Environments*, 1992.

Burgess, P. Head of VPL research virtually makes his own worlds. *Mac WEEK*, pages 38–39, Aug. 2 1988.

Burton, R.P. and Sutherland, I.E. Twinkle box: A three-dimensional computer input device. *Proc. of the National Computer Conference*, pages 513–520, 1974.

Buxton, B. Smoke and mirrors. *Byte*, pages 205–210, July 1990. (Keywords: user interface).

Buxton, W. and Meyers, B.A. *A Study in Two-Handed Input*. ACM SIGCHI, 1986.

Callahan, M.A. A 3-D display head-set for personalized computing. M.s. thesis, MIT Dept. of Architecture, June 1983.

Carollo, J.T., editor. *Helmet-mounted Displays*, volume 1116 of *Proc. SPIE*, 1989.

Carroll, J.M. Evaluation, description and invention: Paradigms for human-computer interaction. Technical report RC 13926 (No. 62583), User Interface Institute, IBM T.J. Watson Research Center, Yorktown Heights, NY, August 1988. (Keywords: user interface).

Carroll, J.M. and Campbell, R.L. Artifacts as psychological theories: The case of human-computer interaction. Technical Report RC 13454 (No. 60225), IBM Research Division, T.J. Watson Research Center, Yorktown Heights, NY, 1988. (Keywords: user interface).

Caruso, D. Coupling people machines. *San Francisco Examiner*, Aug. 20 1989.

Caruso, D. Virtual reality, get real. *Media Letter 1* (3), 1990.

Cassidy, R. Scientific visualization: A new computer research tool. *R and D Magazine*, pages 50–56, 58, 60, April 1990.

Chan, K. and Hoeltzel, D.A. *A Knowledge-Based User Interface for the Interactive Design of Three-Dimensional Objects*. AI EDAM, 1988.

Chandler, D.L. Robot stand-ins reach out and touch. *The Boston Globe*, pages

35–36, Dec. 13, 1990. (Keywords: telepresence, telemanipulation, undersea robots).

Chin, K.P. and Sheridan, T.B. Work with computers: Organizational, management, stress and health aspects. In M.J. Smith and G. Salvendy, editors, *Proceedings of HCI '89, Boston*, pages 505–511, Amsterdam, 1989. Elsevier Science Publishers B.V.

Chung, J.C., Harris, M.R., Brooks, F.P., Fuchs, H., Kelley, M.T., Hughes, J.W., Ouh-young, M., Cheung, C., Holloway, R.L. and Pique, M. Exploring virtual worlds with head-mounted displays. In Woodrow E. Robbins and Scott S. Fisher, editors, *Three-dimensional Visualization and Display Technologies*, volume 1083 of *Proc. SPIE*, pages 42–52, January 1989.

Churbuck, D. The ultimate computer game. *Forbes*, pages 154–155, 158, Feb. 5 1990.

Clapp, G.A. and Sworder, D.D. Teleoperator response characteristics. In *IEEE Conference on Systems, Man and Cybernetics, Proceedings Cat No 90CH2930-6*, pages 463–5.

Clapp, R.E. Aerial image display systems in simulation. In *Simulators IV, Proceedings of SCS Simulators Conf.*, pages 223–228, 1987.

Clark, J. Designing surfaces in 3-D. *Communications of ACM*, 19 (8): 454–460, August 1976.

Clarkson, M.A. An easier interface. *BYTE*, pages 277–282, February 1991.

Cohen, E., Namir, L. and Schlesinger, I.M. *A New Dictionary of Sign Language*. Mouton, The Hague, 1977.

Comeau, C. and Bryan, J. Headsight television system provides remote surveillance. *Electronics*, Nov 1961.

Coull, T.B. Texture-based virtual reality on a desktop computer using world toolkit. In *Proceedings of Virtual Reality '91, 2nd Annual Conference on Virtual Reality, Artificial Reality and Cyberspace*, page 37, 1991.

Coursey, D. Intel micro 200: A computing revolution in the making. *MIS Week*, page 89, Mar. 5 1990.

Cutkosky, M. and Howe, R. Human grasp choice and robotic grasp analysis: in *Dextrous robot hands*. Springer Verlag, pages 5–31, 1990.

Cutt, P. The sense of touch in Virtual reality. In *Proceedings of Virtual Reality 1991, 2nd Annual Conference on Virtual Reality, Artificial Reality and Cyberspace*, page 43, 1991.

Davidson, A. Re: Research topics in VR. sci.virtual-worlds, July 1991. Description of the 3dm three-dimensional modeller created by Jeff Butterworth, Andrew Davidson, Stene Hench and Marc Olano.

Davis, S. After the beep. *San Francisco Examiner*, page D20, Sun., Feb. 11 1990.

Daviss, B. Grand illusions. *Discover*, pages 37–41, June 1990. (Keywords: virtual reality, dataglove).

De Gennaro, S. Watch what you say, your computer might be listening! In *Proc. Human-Machine Interfaces for Teleoperators and Virtual Environments*, pages 15–16, March 1990.

Delany, S.R. *Babel-17*. Ace Books, Inc, 1966.

Delp, D. and Delp, S. Understanding human movement with computer graphics. *SOMA Engineering for the Human Body*, 3 (3): 17–25, 1989. (Keywords: surgical simulation, kinematics, tendons).

Delp, S., Loan, P., Hoy, M., Zajac, F., Fisher, S. and Rosen, J. An interactive graphics-based model of the lower extremity to study orthopaedic surgical procedures. *IEEE Transactions on Biomedical Engineering*, 37 (8), August 1990. (Special issue on interaction with and visualization of biomedical data).

Dewitt, E. (mis)adventures in cyberspace. *Time*, pages 74–5, Sept. 1990.

Ditlea, S. Datasuit. *Omni*, page 22, September 1988.

Ditlea, S. Inside artificial reality. *PC Computing*, pages 90–91, 93–95, 98–99, 101, November 1989.

Dockerty, J. and Littman, D. Intelligent virtual reality as a universal interface for the handicapped. In *Proceedings Informatique '92: Interface to Real and Virtual Worlds*, pages 515–522, 1992.

Dowding, T.J. A self-contained interactive motorskill trainer. In *Proceedings of Virtual Reality '91, 2nd Annual Conference on Virtual Reality, Artificial Reality and Cyberspace*, page 44, 1991.

Duffy, R.B. PC mind control. *PC Computing*, pages 155–156, November 1989.

Durlach, N. Human-machine interface hardware: The next decade. In *Proc. Human-Machine Interfaces for Teleoperators and Virtual Environments*, page 73, March 1990.

Economy, R. Putting the reality in vr. In *Proceedings of the 1992 EFDPMA Conference on Virtual Reality*, 1992.

Eglowstein, H. Reach out and touch your data. *Byte*, pages 283–290, July 1990. (Keywords: dataglove, dhm, powerglove, whole-hand input).

Ehrlich, S.F. Social and psychological factors influencing the design of office communications systems. In *CHI + GI Conference*. ACM Document ACM-0-89791-213-6/87/0004/0323, 1987.

Ellis, S. Pictorial communication: Pictures and the synthetic universe. In *Spatial Displays and Spatial Instruments Conf.*, Asilomar, CA, August 1987.

Ellis, S. Varieties of virtualization. In *Proc. Engineering Foundation Workshop on Human-Machine Interfaces for Teleoperators and Virtual Environments*, page 14, Mar. 4–9 1990.

Ellis, S. Virtual environments presented via head-mounted, computer-driven displays. In *Proceedings of the 1992 EFDPMA Conference on Virtual Reality*, 1992.

Ellis, S., Grunwald, A., Smith, S. and Tyler, M. Enhancement of man-machine communication: The human use of inhuman beings. In *Proceedings of IEEE Compcon*, Spring 1988.

Ellis, S., Kim, W.S., Tyler, M., McGreevy, M. and Stark, L. Visual enhancements for perspective displays: Perspective parameters. In *IEEE Proceedings Intl. Conf. on Systems, Man, and Cybernetics*, pages 815–818, November 1985.

Elmer-Dewitt, P. Through the 3-D looking glass. *Time*, pages 65–66, May 1 1989.

Enbar, G. Human operator tracking performance with a vibrotactile display. In *Proc. Human-Machine Interfaces for Teleoperators and Virtual Environments*, page 76, March 1990.

Endo, T. and Ishii, H. NTT human interface laboratories. In *Proc. CHI'90 (Seattle)*, pages 81–82, Apr. 1–5 1990.

Endsley, M. Objective evaluation of situation awareness for dynamic decision makers in teleoperators. In *Proc. Human-Machine Interfaces for Teleoperators and Virtual Environments*, page 65, March 1990.

England, R.D., Edgar, G.K. and Carr, K.T. Human factors in virtual worlds: Enabling interaction and performance. *IEEE Colloquium on Using Virtual Worlds, Digest 093*, pages 4/1–5, 1992.

Erickson, T.D. and Mercurio, P.J. Interactive scientific visualization: An assessment of a virtual reality system. In *Proceedings of the 3rd IFIP Conf. on Human–Computer Interaction*, August 1990.

Esposito, C. Aerospace applications of vr-ongoing research and anticipated applications of vr at Boeing. In *Proceedings of the 1992 EFDPMA Conference on Virtual Reality*, 1992.

Fahlén, L. Issues in telepresence. In Björn Pehrson and Yngve Sundblad, editors, *Proceedings of 2nd MultiG Workshop*, pages 31–41, June 1991.

Fahlén, L. The MultiG TelePresence system. In Yngve Sundblad, editor, *Proceedings of the 3rd MultiG Workshop*, pages 33–57, December 1991.

Fahlén, L. The SICS telepresence system. In *Proceedings of the First COST #229, WG.5 Workshop, Telepresence – A New Concept for Teleconferencing*. Linköping University, October 1991.

Fairchild, K. and Gullichsen, E. From modern alchemy to a new renaissance. *ACM-SIGCHI Mixed Mode Workshop*, December 1986.

Farmer, F.R. Cyberspace: Getting there from here. *Journal of Computer Game Design*, Oct 1988.

Feiner, S. and Deshers, C. Visualizing n-dimensional virtual worlds with n-vision. *ACM Computer Graphics 24 (2)*, page 37–38, 1990.

Feldman, T. (Ed.). Virtual reality '91: Impacts and applications. In *Proceedings SPIE 726 Cambridge Symposium on Optical and Optoelectronic Engineering*, 1986.

Fischler, M.A. and Barnard, S.T. Computational stereo. *Computing Surveys*, pages 553–572, Dec. 1982.

Fisher, S.S. Implementing and interacting with realtime microworlds. In *ACM SIGGRAPH '89 Course Notes No. 29*, July 31 1979. (Keywords: NASA).

Fisher, S.S. Viewpoint dependent imaging: An interactive stereoscopic display. In *Processing and Display of Three-Dimensional Data*, volume 367 of *Proc. SPIE*, pages 41–45, 1982.

Fisher, S.S. Telepresence master-glove controller for dexterous robotic end-effectors. In *Intelligent Robots and Computer Vision*, volume 726 of *Proc. SPIE*, pages 396–401, 1986.

Fisher, S.S. Virtual environments: Personal simulations and telepresence. *Virtual Reality: Theory Practice and Promise*, pages 101–110, 1991.

Fisher, S.S. and Tazelaar, J.M. Living in a virtual world. *Byte*, pages 215–221, July 1990. (Keywords: virtual reality, heads-up displays, stereo).

Fisher, S.S., McGreevy, M., Humphries, J. and Robinett, W. Virtual environment display system. In *Proc. 1986 ACM Workshop on Interactive Graphics*, pages 77–87, Chapel Hill, NC, October 23–24 1986.

Fisher, S.S., McGreevy, M., Humphries, J. and Robinett, W. Virtual workstation: A multimodal, stereoscopic display environment. In *Intelligent Robots and Computer Vision*, volume 726 of *Proc. SPIE*, pages 517–522, 1986.

Fisher, S.S., McGreevy, M., Humphries, J. and Robinett, W. Virtual interface environment for telepresence applications. In *Proceedings ANS International Topical Meeting on Remote Systems and Robotics in Hostile Environments*, 1987.

Fisher, S.S., Wenzel, Coler, C. and McGreevy, M.W. Virtual interface environment workstations. In *Proceedings of the Human Factors Society, 32nd Annual Meeting, Anaheim*, pages 82–90, 1988.

Fisher,S.S., Jacoby, R., Byrson, S., Stone, P., McDowall, I., Bolas, M., Dasaro, D., Wenzel, E. and Coler, C.D. The Ames virtual environment workstation: Implementation issues and requirements. In *Proc. Human-Machine Interfaces for Teleoperators and Virtual Environments*, pages 20–24, March 1990.

Fitts, P.M. The information capacity of the human motor system in controlling amplitude of movement. *Journal of Experimental Psychology*, 47 (6): 381–391, 1954.

Flogiston Corp. Flogiston flyer two: Virtual realities-active and passive, 1990.

Foley, J.D. Interfaces for advanced computing. *Scientific American*, 257 (4): 126–135, October 1987.

Foley, J.D., van Dam, A., Feiner, S.K. and Hughes, J.F. *Computer Graphics: Principles and Practice*. Addison-Wesley, second edition, 1990.

Freiherr, G. Building a way to see. *Computer Graphics World*, pages 42–48, July 1989.

Freiherr, G. Invasion of the spacebots. *Air and Space Smithsonian*, pages 73–75, 78–81, March 1990.

Fuchs, H., Abram, G.D. and Grant, E.D. Near-real-time shaded display of rigid objects. *ACM Computer Graphics*, 10 (3): 65–72, July 1983.

Fuchs, H., Kedem, Z.M. and Naylor, B.F. On visible surface generation by *a priori* tree structures, *SIGGRAPH 80*, 124–133, 1980.

Fuchs, H., Levoy, M. and Pizer, S.M. Interactive visualization of 3-D medical data. *IEEE Computer*, pages 46–50, August 1989.

Fulghum. New helmet could replace head-up display. *Navy Times*, pages 31–39, Jan. 18 1988.

Furness, T. The application of head-mounted displays to airborne reconnaissance and weapon delivery. In *Proceedings, Symposium for Image Display and Recording*, Wright-Patterson AFB, OH, April 1969. U.S. Air Force Avionics Laboratory. Technical Report TR-69-241.

Furness, T. Helmet-mounted displays and their aerospace applications. In *National Aerospace Electronics Conference*, Dayton, OH, May 1969.

Furness, T. The use of visually-coupled systems in high vibration and buffeting environments. In *Symposium on Aeromedical Considerations of Low Level Flight and Long Duration Missions, 19th Meeting of Air Standardization Coordination Committee (Working Party 61)*, Canberra, Australia, November 1978.

Furness, T. Visually-coupled information systems. In *ARPA Conference on Biocybernetic Applications for Military Systems*, Chicago, IL, April 5–7 1978.

Furness, T. The effects of whole-body vibration on the perception of target imagery presented on a helmet-mounted display. In *United Kingdom Informal Group on Human Response to Vibration*, Farnborough, England, September 1979. Royal Aircraft Establishment.

Furness, T. Helmet-display reading performance during whole-body vibration. In *52nd Annual Meeting of Aerospace Medical Association*, San Antonio, TX, May 4–7 1981.

Furness, T. Virtual panoramic display for the LHX. *Army Aviation*, pages 63–66, June 30 1985.

Furness, T. Fantastic voyage. *Popular Mechanics*, December 1986.

Furness, T. The super cockpit and its human factors challenges. In *Proceedings of Human Factors Society Symposium*, November 1986.

Furness, T. Designing in virtual space. In W.B. Rouse and K.R. Boff, editors, *System Design*. North Holland, 1987.

Furness, T. Harnessing virtual space. In *SID International Symposium*, pages 4–7, May 1988.

Furness, T. 'Super Cockpit' amplifies pilot's senses and actions. *Government Computer News*, pages 76–77, August 15 1988.

Furness, T. Creating better virtual worlds. In *Proc. Human-Machine Interfaces for Teleoperators and Virtual Environments*, pages 48–51, March 1990.

Furness, T. Experiences in virtual space. In *Human-Machine Interfaces for Teleoperators and Virtual Environments*, 1990.

Furness, T. Designing in virtual space. In *Siggraph 91 Virtual Interface Technology (Virtual Reality) course notes*, pages 28–44, July 1991.

Furness, T. Harnessing virtual space. In *Siggraph 91 Virtual Interface Technology (Virtual Reality) course notes*, pages 3–6, July 1991.

Furness, T. and Kocian, D. Putting humans into virtual space. In *Proceedings of Society for Computer Simulation Aerospace Conference*, January 1986.

Furness, T., Task, H. and Verona, R. Current status and performance of helmet-mounted displays. In *Symposium on Night Vision Devices and Displays*, Ft. Belvoir, VG, November 1974. U.S. Army Night Vision Laboratory.

Furness, T. and Kocian, D.F. Putting humans into virtual space. In *Siggraph 91 Virtual Interface Technology (Virtual Reality) course notes*, pages 13–27, July 1991.

Gaffney, T. Pilots will see hear touch cockpit inside special helmet. *Dayton Daily News and Journal Herald*, March 6 1987.

Gaillard, J.-P. Operator's distance estimation to supervise satellite grasping. In John Patrick and Keith D. Duncan, editors, *Training, Human Decision Making and Control*, pages 383–393. North-Holland, 1988.

Gaines, M. Super cockpit. *Flight International*, 131 (4052): 29–30, 32, 34, March 7 1987.

Ganapathy, S.K. Machine perception and its role in virtual environments. In *Human-Machine Interfaces for Teleoperators and Virtual Environments*, Santa Barbara, CA, March 1990.

Gaver, W. Auditory icons: Using sound in computer interfaces. *Human Computer Interactions*, 2: 167–177, 1986.

Gehring, B. and Gehring Research Corporation. The focal point 3-D audio system.

Geschwind, D.M. Adapting traditional media for virtual reality environments. In *Proceedings of Virtual Reality '91, 2nd Annual Conference on Virtual Reality, Artificial Reality and Cyberspace*, page 51, 1991.

Gibbons, A. Surgery in space. *Technology Review*, pages 9–10, April 1989.

Gibson, W. *Neuromancer*. Ace Books, 1984.

Gibson, W. *Count Zero*. Ace Books, 1986.

Ginsberg, C.M. and Maxwell, D. Graphical marionette. In *Proc. ACM SIG-GRAPH/SIGART Workshop on Motion*, pages 172–179, Toronto, Canada, April 1983.

Glenn, S. Real fun, virtually: Virtual experience amusements and products in public space entertainment. In *Proceedings of Virtual Reality '91, 2nd Annual Conference on Virtual Reality, Artificial Reality and Cyberspace*, page 62, 1991.

Goldfeather, J., Molnar, S., Turk, G. and Fuchs, H. Near real-time CSG rendering using tree normalization and geometric pruning. Technical Report TR88-006, UNC at Chapel Hill, 1988.

Good, M. and Wixon, D. Interface style an eclecticism: moving beyond categorical approaches. 1: 571–575, October 1987.

Grantham, C. Visual analysis of organizational functioning. In *Proceedings of the 1992 EFDPMA Conference on Virtual Reality*, 1992.

Grantham, C.E. Visual thinking in organizational analysis. In *Proceedings of Virtual Reality '91, 2nd Annual Conference on Virtual Reality, Artificial Reality and Cyberspace*, page 70, 1991.

Graphics CiS, Salem, New Hampshire. *Geometry Ball Series Technical Specifications*, January 1990.

Gregory, W. Virtual cockpit's panoramic display afford advanced mission capabilities. *Aviation Week and Space Technology*, 122 (2): 143, 146, 151–152, Jan. 14 1985.

Grimes, G.J. Digital data entry glove interface device, *US Patent 4414537*, November 8, 1983.

Grimes, G.J. An adaptive subdivision method for surface-fitting from sampled data. *IEEE Computer Graphics and Applications*, 11 (11): 81–83, November 1991.

Grimsdale, C. dVS: Distributed virtual environment system. In *Proc. Computer Graphics 91*, pages 163–170, London, 1991.

Grimsdale, C. A parallel vision for virtual reality. In *Virtual Reality 91: Impacts and Applications*, pages 12–17, 1991.

Grimsdale,C. Virtual reality – key technologies, problems and emerging solutions. In *Virtual Reality International 92: Impacts and Applications*, pages 14–22, 1992.

Grimsdale, C. and Ghee, S. Virtual realities – artificial environments. In *Proc. Computer Graphics 90*, pages 1–8, London, 1990.

Grunwald, A. and Ellis, S. Spatial orientation by familiarity cues. In John Patrick and Keith D. Duncan, editors, *Training, Human Decision Making and Control*, pages 257–279. Elsevier Science Publishers B.V., 1988.

Gullichsen, E. Artificial realities through cyber-quantum technology. In *USICON Eighty-Seven 2nd Annual User-System Interface Conference, Lockheed Austin Division*, pages 153–161, Austin TX, February 1987.

Gullichsen, E. Abstract: The building blocks of virtual reality. In *Virtual Reality 91: Impacts and Applications*, page 7, 1992.

Hägglund, P. Användning av datahandsken för navigering i en enkel 3d-miljö. Technical Report TRITA-NA-P8913, NADA, IPLab, 1989. In Swedish.

Hagsand, O. Consistency and concurrency control in distributed virtual worlds. In Björn Pehrson and Yngve Sundblad, editors, *Proceedings of 2nd MultiG Workshop*, pages 43–56, June 1991.

Haines, R.G. Human aspects in computing in design and use of interactive systems and work with terminals. In *4th International Conference on HCI*, pages 625–629, Elsevier, Netherlands, 1991.

Hall, M.R. and Miller, J.W. Head-mounted electocular display: A new display concept for specialized environments. *Aerospace Medicine*, pages 316–318, April 1963.

Hampden-Turner, C. *Maps of the Mind*. Collier Books, 1981.

Hand Holder. Hand holder. *Popular Science*, page 72, December 1989.

Hanson, D.P. and Robb, R.A. Analyze: A software system for interactive display and quantitative analysis of multidimensional medical images, 1989.

Hapgood, F. and Hapgood, F. The lab that is putting a new face on the computer. *Smithsonian*, pages 70–79, June 1990.

Harvey, D. VCASS: A second look at the super cockpit. *Rotor and Wing International*, 21: 32–33, 63, Jan. 8 1987.

Heim, M. The erotic ontology of cyberspace. In Benedikt, M., editor, *Cyberspace: First Steps*, MIT Press, Cambridge, MA, 1991.

Heim, M. The metaphysics of virtual reality. *Virtual Reality: Theory, Practice and Promise*, pages 27–34, Meckler, 1991.

Heinlein, R.A. Waldo. *Astounding Science-Fiction*, 29 (6): 9–53, August 1942 (Keywords: teleoperation).

Helsel, S.K. and Roth, J.P. (eds). *Virtual Reality: Theory, Practice and Promise*. Meckler, 1991.

Henderson, D.A. Jr. and Card, S.K. Rooms: The use of multiple virtual workspace to reduce space contention in a window-based graphics user interface. *ACM Transactions on Graphics*, 5 (3), 1986.

Henderson, J. *Virtual Reality: Theory, Practice and Promise*, pages 65–73. Meckler, 1991.

Henderson, J.V. Cyberspace representation of Vietnam war trauma. In *Proceedings of Virtual Reality '91, 2nd Annual Conference on Virtual Reality, Artificial Reality and Cyberspace*, pages 77–103, 1991.

Hiltz, S.R. Collaborative learning in a virtual classroom: Highlights of findings. In *Proceedings of the Conference on Computer-supported Cooperative Work*, Portland OR, Sept. 26–29 1988. Sponsored by ACM SIGCHI and SIGOIS.

Hirose, M. Artificial reality and man-machines interface. *Journal of Inst. Elec. Eng. Jpn*, 111 (10): 831–834, 1991.

Hochberg, J. Representation of motion and space in video and cinematic displays. In K. Boff, L. Kaufman, and J. Thomas, editors, *Handbook of Perception and Human Performance*, volume I, pages 1–5. John Wiley and Sons, NY, 1986.

Hochberg, J.E. *Perception*. Prentice-Hall, Inc, 2nd edition, 1978.

Holloway, R.L. Head-mounted display technical report. Technical Report TR87-015, UNC at Chapel Hill, June 1987.

Hon, D. An evolution of synthetic reality and tactile interfaces. In *Proceedings of Virtual Reality '91, 2nd Annual Conference on Virtual Reality, Artificial Reality and Cyberspace*, pages 104–108, 1991.

Hosni, Y.A., Hamid, T.S. and Okraski, A.E. Hypermedia based applications for space shuttle processing. *Comput. Ind. Eng.(UK)*, 21: 241–5, 1992.

Howard, E. Enhancing pilot situation awareness (sa) in air combat. In *Proceedings of the 1992 EFDPMA Conference on Virtual Reality*, 1992.

Hubley, C. Establishing design principles for vr technology. In *Proceedings of the 1992 EFDPMA Conference on Virtual Reality*, 1992.

Human Interface Technology Laboratory, University of Washington. Mission statement and prospectus, November 1989.

Human Interface Technology Laboratory. An invitation to join the human interface technology laboratory's virtual worlds consortium. In *Laboratory Information Package*. April 1990.

Human Interface Technology Laboratory, University of Washington. Research project descriptions 1–9. In *Laboratory Information Package*, pages 1–9. April 1990.

Huntley, J.S. and Partridge, M. Fluxbase: A Virtual Exhibit. In *Virtual Reality: Theory, Practice and Promise*, pages 75–93. Meckler, 1991.

Inamura, K., Michitaka, H., Myoi, T. and Amari, H. Development of visual 3D virtual environment for control software. In *Proc. Human-Machine Interfaces for Teleoperators and Virtual Environments*, page 66, March 1990.

Iwata, H. Artificial reality with force-feedback: Development of desktop virtual space with compact master manipulator. *Computer Graphics*, 24 (4): 165–170, August 1990.

Jää-Aro, K-M. Tankathon – a process plant simulation. Technical report, 1991.

Jää-Aro, K-M. The X-ray factory – some experiments with three-dimensional, iconic, control displays. In *Proceedings of the First COST #229, WG.5 Workshop, Telepresence – A New Concept for Teleconferencing*, October 1991.

Jää-Aro, K-M. The X-ray factory – some experiments with three-dimensional, iconic, control displays. In Yngve Sundblad, editor, *Proceedings of the 3rd MultiG Workshop*, pages 59–67, December 1991.

Jabaz, A. Mini screen is a real eye opener. *The Sunday Times (London)*, 598 (8): 1, May 28 1989.

Jacob, R.J.K. What you look at is what you get: Eye movement-based interaction techniques. In *Proc. CHI'90 (Seattle)*, pages 11–18, Apr. 1–5 1990.

Jacobsen, R. Televirtuality: Networked experience. In *Virtual Reality International 92: Impacts and Applications*, pages 44–52, 1992.

Jacobsen, S.C., Iversen, E.K., Knuthi, D.G., Johnson, R.T. and Biggers, K.B. Design of the Utah/MIT dextrous hand. In *IEEE Conf. on Robotics and Automation*, 1986.

Jacobson, R. Designing the information environment. *BYTE*, 1991.

Jacobson, R. Televirtuality: Status of projects around the world. In *Proceedings of the 1992 EFDPMA Conference on Virtual Reality*, 1992.

Jacobus, H. Implementation issues for a 6 degree of freedom force reflecting hand controller with cueing of modes. In *Proc. Human-Machine Interfaces for Teleoperators and Virtual Environments*, page 68, March 1990.

Jenkins, J. Virtual reality II: Virtual environments. *PC AI*, pages 42–43, Nov./Dec. 1989.

Jernstedt, G.C. Computer enhanced collaborative learning: A new technology for education. *T.H.E. Journal*, May 1983.

Johnsen, E.G. and Corliss, W.R. *Human Factors Applications in Teleoperator Design and Operation*. Wiley-Interscience, 1971.

Johnson, D.W. and Johnson, R.T. Interdependence and interpersonal attraction among heterogeneous individuals: A theoretical formulation and a meta-analysis of the research. *Review of Educational Research*, Spring 1983.

Johnson, D.W. and Johnson, R.T. Internal dynamics of cooperative learning groups. In R. Slavin, S. Sharon, S. Kagan, R. Lazarowitz, C. Webb, and R. Schmuck, editors, *Learning to Cooperate, Cooperating To Learn*. Plenum Press, New York, 1985.

Johnson, D.W. and Johnson, R.T. *Learning from Colleagues: Cooperation Among Adults*. Cooperative Learning Center, University of Minnesota, June, 1987.

Johnson, D.W. and Johnson, R.T. Social skills for successful group work. *Educational Leadership*, Dec./Jan. 1989/1990.

Kalawsky, R.S. From visually coupled systems to virtual reality: an aerospace perspective. In *Computer Graphics '91, Blenheim Online*, 1991.

Kalawsky, R.S. Reality of virtual reality. In *IEEE Colloquium on Real World Visualisation: Virtual World – Virtual Reality, London*, 1991.

Kalawsky, R.S. State of virtual reality in the UK. In *IEEE Colloquium on Real World Visualisation: Virtual World – Virtual Reality, London*, 1991.

Kalawsky, R. Beyond the super cockpit. In *Virtual Reality International 92: Impacts and Applications*, pages 69–77, 1992.

Kalawsky, R.S. *Beyond the Super Cockpit, Virtual Reality '92*. Meckler, 1992.

Kama, W.N. and DuMars, R.C. Remote viewing: A comparison of direct viewing 2-D and 3-D television. Technical Report TR AMRL-TDR-64-15, Wright-Patterson AFB, OH, February 1964.

Kaneda, K., Ishida, S. and Nakamae, E. Pan focused stereoscopic display using a series of optical microscope images. In Patrikalakis, N., (editor), *Scientific Visualization of Physical Phenomena*, Springer-Verlag, Tokyo, 609–622, 1991.

Karon, P. Pocket sized portable will smash miniaturization barriers. *PC WEEK*, 6 (28), July 17 1989.

Karr, B. Effective human interface design in virtual reality. In *Virtual Reality 91: Impacts and Applications*, pages 8–11, 1991.

Kegan, R.G. Donkey Kong, Pac Man and the meaning of life: Reflections in river city. In *Papers and Proceedings of a Symp. held at Harvard Grad. School of Education*, Cambridge, MA, May 22–24 1983.

Keller, J.D. A computer uses an eye for its hearing aid. *The Wall Street Journal*, page B1, Mar. 4 1990.

Kiesler, S., Siegel, J. and McGuire, T.W. Social psychological aspects of computer-mediated communications. *American Psychologist*, October 1984.

Kilpatrick, P.J. *The Use of Kinesthetic Supplement in an Interactive System*. PhD dissertation, Computer Science Department, University of North Carolina at Chapel Hill, 1976. (Keywords: force feedback, force reflection).

Kim, W.S., Tendick, F. and Stark, L.W. Visual enhancements in pick-and-place tasks: Human operators controlling a simulated cylindrical manipulator. *IEEE Journal of Robotics and Automation*, RA-3 (5): 418–425, October 1987.

Kim, W.S., Liu, A., Matsunaga, K. and Stark, L. A helmet-mounted display for telerobotics, 1988 *IEEE COMPCON 88*, Feb 29 – Mar. 3, 1988.

Kinnucan, P. The whirling world of 3-D work stations. *Computer Graphics Review*, pages 20–23, 26, 28–30, 32, January 1989.

Klein, S. The Intel 80860 super chip. *Computer Graphics Review*, pages 6–8, April 1989.

Knowlton, K.C. Computer displays optically superimposed on input devices. *The Bell System Technical Journal*, 56 (3): 367–383, March 1977.

Kocien, D.F. VCASS: An approach to visual simulation. In *Proceedings, IMAGE Conference*, Williams AFB, AZ, 1977.

Kolberg, R. Japanese build powerful new computer. *UPI Wire Service*, May 3 1990.

Konneker, L.K. A graphical interaction technique which uses gestures. *IEEE 1984*, pages 51–55, 1984.

Koved, L. Interactive simulation in a multi-person virtual world. In *Proceedings of the 1992 EFDPMA Conference on Virtual Reality*, 1992.

Koved, L. and Selker, T. Room with a view (RWAV): A metaphor for interactive computing. Technical report, IBM Research Division, T.J. Watson Research Center, Yorktown Heights, NY, 10598, USA, 1990.

Kramer, J. The talking glove in action. *Communications of the ACM*, page 515, Apr. 1989.

Kramer, J. and Leifer, L. The talking glove: An expressive and receptive 'verbal' communication aid for the deaf, deaf-blind, and non-vocal. Technical report, Stanford University, Department of Electrical Engineering, 1989. (Keywords: ASL).

Krueger, M. The emperor's new reality. In *Virtual Reality International 92: Impacts and Applications*, pages 53–64, 1992.

Krueger, M., Gionfriddo, T. and Hinrichsen, K. Videoplace – an artificial reality. In *Proceedings of the Association for Computing Machinery CHI Symposium*, pages 35–40, April 1985.

Krueger, M.W. Videoplace – a report from the artificial reality laboratory. *Leonardo*, 18 (3), Oct. 1985.

Krueger, M.W. Videoplace – an artificial reality. In *ACM Conference on Human Factors in Computing Systems*, Apr. 1985.

Krueger, M.W. Artificial Reality: Past and Future. In *Virtual Reality: Theory, Practice and Promise*, pages 19–25. Meckler, 1991.

Krueger, M.W. *Artificial Reality*. Addison-Wesley, 1982.

Krueger, M.W. *Artificial Reality II*. Addison-Wesley, 1991.

Kuntz, L.A., White, K., Shuman, D., Krantz, J. and Woods, C. Destabilizing effects of visual environment motions simulating eye movements or head movements. In *Proc. Human-Machine Interfaces for Teleoperators and Virtual Environments*, page 78, March 1990.

Lackner, J.R. *Intersensory Coordination, Human-Machine Interfaces for Teleoperators and Virtual Environments*. Santa Barbara, Cal, Mar. 1990.

Lapham, L.H. The feely is here. *The Saturday Evening Post*, pages 28–29, April 18 1964. (Keywords: mort heilig, sensorama, virtual reality).

Lasko-Harvill, A., Blanchard, C., Smithers, W., Harvill, Y. and Coffman, A. From dataglove to datasuit. *IEEE Compcon*, pages 536–538, Spring 1988.

Latta, J.N. When will reality meet the marketplace? In *Proceedings of Virtual Reality '91, 2nd Annual Conference on Virtual Reality, Artificial Reality and Cyberspace*, page 109, 1991.

Latta, J. Virtual reality – are there real applications? In *Proceedings of the 1992 EFDPMA Conference on Virtual Reality*, 1992.

Laurel, B. On dramatic interaction. *Verbum 3.3*, pages 6–7, 1989.

Laurel, B. *Towards the Design of a Computer-Based Interactive Fantasy System*. PhD thesis, Ohio State University, 1990.

Laurel, B. *The Art of Human Computer Interface Design*. Addison-Wesley, 1990.

Laurel, B. *Computers as Theatre*. Addison-Wesley, 1991.

Laurel, B. Virtual Reality Design: A Personal View. In *Virtual Reality: Theory, Practice and Promise*, pages 95–99. Meckler, 1991.

Laurel, B.K. Interface as mimesis. In D.A. Norman and S.W. Draper, editors, *User Centred System Design*, pages 67–85. Lawrence Erlbaum Associates, Inc., Hillside, NJ, 1986. (Keywords: human-computer interface user).

Lederman, S.J. and Klatzky, R.L. Hand movements: A window into haptic object recognition. *Cognitive Psychology*, 19 (3): 342–368, 1987.

Lederman, S.J. and Taylor, M.M. Fingertip force, surface geometry, and the perception of roughness by active touch. *Perception and Psychophysics*, 12 (5): 401–408, 1972.

Lee, P., Zhao Wei, J. and Badler, N. Strength-guided motion. *Computer Graphics*, 22 (4), August 1990. Proc. ACM SIGGRAPH '90.

Leibs, S. They do it with mirrors. *Informationweek*, pages 30–31, Feb. 12 1990.

Lenat, D., Borning, A., McDonald, D., Taylor, C. and Weyer, S. Knoesphere: Building expert systems with encyclopedic knowledge. In *Proceedings, International Congress for Artificial Intelligence*, pages 167–169, Karlsruhe, Germany, 1984.

Lerner, E. Toward the omnipotent pilot. *Aerospace America*, 24 (10): 18–22, October 1986.

Lerner, E. Helping pilots handle the supercockpit. *Aerospace America*, 25 (2): 29–31, February 1987.

Levy, S. Out on a sim. *Macworld*, pages 51–53, Apr. 1990.

Lewandowski, R.J., editor. *Helmet-Mounted Displays II*, volume 1290 of *Proc. SPIE*, 1990.

Lewis, J.B. The realities of building virtual realities. In *Proceedings of Virtual Reality '91, 2nd Annual Conference on Virtual Reality, Artificial Reality and Cyberspace*, pages 142–147, 1991.

Lewis, J.B., Koved, L. and Ling, D.T. Dialogue structures for virtual worlds. In *CHI '91, ACM*, 1991.

Lewis, P. Put on your data gloves and goggles and step inside. *The New York Times*, page 8, 20 May 1990.

Ling, D.T. Beyond visualization – virtual worlds for data understanding. Research

Report RC 15479 68850, IBM Research Division, Yorktown Heights, February 9 1990. (Keywords: dataglove, leep optics, head-mounted display).

Linköping University. *Proceedings of the First COST #229, WG.5 Workshop, Telepresence – A New Concept for Teleconferencing*, October 1991.

Lippman, A. And seeing through your hand. In *Proceedings, SID*, volume 22, pages 103–107, 1981.

Lipton, L. Sensorama. *Popular Photography*, July 1964.

Lynch, J. Press release: Sense8 corporation formed, Dec. 20 1989.

Machover, C. Seeing the future in 3-D stereoscopic viewing. *Computer Graphics Review*, pages 60, 62–63, August 1989.

Mackinlay, J.D., Card, S.K. and Robertson, G. Rapid controlled movement through a virtual 3-D workspace. *Computer Graphics*, 24 (4): 171–176, 1990.

Marcus, B.A. and Curchill, P.J. Sensing human hand motions for controlling dexterous robots. In *The Second Annual Space Operations Automation and Robotics Workshop, held at Wright State University*. Sponsored by NASA and the USAF, July 20–23 1988.

Maretka, V. Helmet helps pilots see at high speeds. *Current Science*, 72 (5): 13, Oct. 31 1986.

Mase, E. and Pentland, A.K. Lipreading: Automation visual recognition of spoken words. Technical Report Tech. Report 117, MIT Media Lab Vision Science, Cambridge, MA, 1989.

Mase, K., Watanabe, Y. and Suenaga, Y., A real-time head motion detection system, *SPIE Workshop on Sensing and Teconstruction of 3D Objects and Scenes*, Vol. 1290, pages 262–269, 1989.

Mattoon, J. Building a framework for future vr systems. In *Proceedings of the 1992 EFDPMA Conference on Virtual Reality*, 1992.

McCluskey, J. Educational applications of virtual reality: Medium or myth? In *Proceedings of Virtual Reality '91, 2nd Annual Conference on Virtual Reality, Artificial Reality and Cyberspace*, pages 148–153, 1991.

McCormick, G., DeFanti, T. and Brown, M. Visualization in scientific computing. *Computer Graphics*, 21 (6), 1987.

McGreevy, M. The history of NASA's virtual workstation. NASA Award Nomination, September 1989.

McGreevy, M. NASA's virtual workstation. Submitted to the Congressional Record, Apr. 13 1989.

McGreevy, M. Personal simulators and planetary exploration. Keynote Speech at CHI '89, May 1989.

McGreevy, M. *Virtual Workstation Overview, FY88*. NASA Ames Research Center, CA, 1989.

McGreevy, M.W. The Exploration Metaphor. In *Human-Machine Interfaces for Teleoperators and Virtual Environments*. Santa Barbara, Cal, Mar. 1990.

McGreevy, M.W. Virtual reality and planetary exploration. In *29th AAS Goddard Memorial Symposium*, Washington, DC, Mar. 1991.

McGuinness, B. Human factors in virtual worlds: Information structures and representation. *IEEE Colloquium on Using Virtual Worlds, Digest 093*, pages 3/1–3, 1992.

McKellar, C. and Harriss, P. Realtime lighting for virtual worlds. In *Virtual Reality International 92: Impacts and Applications*, pages 37–43, 1992.

McKenna, A.M., Pieper, S. and Zeltzer, D. Control of a virtual actor: The roach. In *Proc. 1990 Symposium on Interactive 3D Graphics*, pages 165–174, Snowbird, UT, 1990.

McKenna, M. and Zeltzer, D. Dynamic simulation of autonomous legged locomotion. *Computer Graphics*, 24 (4): 29–38, August 1990.

McKenna, M., Atherton, D. and Sabistion, B. Grinning evil death. *Computer Animation*, 1990.

McKim, R.H. *Thinking Visually*. Wadsworth, Inc., 1980.

McKinney, B.C. The Virtual World of HDTV. In *Virtual Reality: Theory, Practice and Promise*, pages 41–49. Meckler, 1991.

McPartlin, J.P. The incredible shrinking chip. *Informationweek*, page 26, Apr. 23 1990.

McShane, J. Pilot of the future . . . ET. *Daily Mirror*, page 3, Jan. 26 1985.

Mills, R.B. CRTs give new look to cockpit of the future. *Machine Design*, pages 34–40, June 6 1985.

Minsky, M. Telepresence. *Omni*, pages 45–50, June 1980. (Keywords: telemanipulation).

Minsky, M., Ouh-Young, M., Steele, O. Jr., Brooks, F.P. and Behensky, M. Feeling and seeing: Issues in force display. *Computer Graphics*, 24 (2): 235–243, March 1990. (Keywords: force-feedback).

MIT Press. *Proceedings of a Symposium on Large-Scale Calculating Machinery*, volume 7 of *The Charles Babbage Institute Reprint Series for the History of Computing*, Cambridge, MA (1985), January 1947.

Miyashita, T., Uchida, T. and Nagata, S. Stereoscopic display using double guest–host liquid crystal cells. *SID International Symposium Digest of Technical Papers*, pages 387–390, May 1987.

Mohl, R. The interactive movie map: Surrogate travel with the aid of dynamic aerial overviews. *MIDCON/80 Conf.*, November 1980.

Molyneau, M. Is it live or is it cyberspace. *Video Games and Computer Entertainment*, pages 57–58, 61–62, 64, January 1990.

Morrison, T.R. The resiliency of families. In *Meeting of the College of Family Physicians and Surgeons of Canada*, Quebec City Canada, May 12 1981.

Moshell, M., Moshell, M., Dunn-Roberts, R. and Glodiez, B. SIMNET and Ender's Game: Military training in cyberspace. In *Proc. Human-Machine Interfaces for Teleoperators and Virtual Environments*, March 1990.

Moshell, M., Hughes, C., Blau, B., Li, X. and Dunn-Roberts, R. Network virtual environments for simulation and training. In *Sim Tec 1991 Conference, Society for Computer Simulation*, 1991.

Nash, J. Bridging the real and unreal. *Computerworld*, page 20, 12 March 1990.

National Institute of Mental Health. The US department of health and human services. *Television Behavior*, 1982.

Negroponte, N. Media room. In *Soc. for Information Display*, volume 22, pages 109–113, 1981.

Nelson, T.H. How many ds in reality. In *Proceedings of Virtual Reality '91, 2nd Annual Conference on Virtual Reality, Artificial Reality and Cyberspace*, pages 154–174, 1991.

Neugebauer, J. Industrial applications of virtual reality: Robot application planning. In *Virtual Reality International 92: Impacts and Applications*, pages 92–102, 1992.

Noll, A.M. Man-machine tactile communication. *SID Journal*, July/August 1972.

Nordwall, B. Adv. cockpit development signals wide industry involvement. *Aviation Week and Space Technology*, 126 (16): 72–73, 77, April 20 1987.

NTT Human Interface Laboratories. Visual media laboratory 1989 annual report, 1989.

NTT Human Interface Laboratories. Visual perception laboratory: Activity overview, 1989.

Okoshi, T. *Three-Dimensional Imaging Techniques*. Academic Press, 1976.

Ouh-Young, M. *Force Display in Molecular Docking*. PhD thesis (tr90-004), Department of Computer Science, University of North Carolina at Chapel Hill, February 1990. (Keywords: force feedback).

Ouh-Young, M., Pique, M., Hughes, J., Srinivasan, N. and Brooks, F.P. Jr. Using a telemanipulator for force display in molecular docking. *IEEE pub CH 2555-1/88*, pages 1824–9, 1986.

Pentland, A. and Mase, K. Automatic lipreading by computer. In *Proc. Symposium on Advanced Image Understanding*, pages 65–70, 1989.

Pepper, R.L., Cole, R.E. and Spain, E.H. The influence of camera separation and head movement on perceptual performance under direct and tv-displayed conditions. In *Proceedings, SID*, volume 24, pages 73–80, 1983.

Pereira, J. Nintendo looks at MIT for brain-teasing video games. *The Wall Street Journal*, page B1, May 15 1990.

Perlin, K. An image synthesizer. *Computer Graphics*, 19 (3): 287–296, July 1985.

Peterson, I. Artificial reality. *Science News*, 127: 396–397, June 22 1985. (Short article about Myron Krueger's Videoplace).

Peterson, I. Computer at your fingertips. *Science News*, 133 (22): 351, May 28 1988. (Short article about Myron Krueger's Videodesk).

Phillips, R., Jacobson, J., McCammon, I. and Biggers, K. Design of tactile sensing systems for dextrous manipulators. IEEE Control Systems Mag., 8 (1): 3–13, February 1988.

Piantanida, T. Virtual perception program at sri international. In *Proceedings of Virtual Reality '91, 2nd Annual Conference on Virtual Reality, Artificial Reality and Cyberspace*, pages 175–179, 1991.

Pieper, S. More than skin deep: Physical modeling of facial tissue. Ms thesis, MIT, Cambridge MA, February 1989.

Pischel, E.F. and Pearson, J.J. Image processing and display in three dimensions. In *Digital Image Processing*, volume 528 of *Proc. SPIE*, pages 23–28, 1985.

Plimpton, J. Virtual reality in Japan. In *Proceedings of Virtual Reality '91, 2nd Annual Conference on Virtual Reality, Artificial Reality and Cyberspace*, pages 180–189, 1991.

Poe, R. Manipulating reality. *Success*, page 80, March 1990.

Pollack, A. For artificial reality wear a computer. *New York Times*, pages A1, D5, Apr. 10 1989.

Pollack, A. What is artificial reality? *The New York Times*, page 1, 10 April 1989.

Pomfret, J. Darth vision. *The Fort Wayne News-Sentinel*, page D6, June 9 1986.

Porter, S. and Emmett, A. Virtual reality. *Computer Graphics World*, 15 (3): 42–54, 1992.

Posnick-Goodwin, S. Dreaming. *Peninsula*, July 1988.

Pountain, R. Provision: The packaging of virtual reality. *Byte*, pages 53–64, Oct. 1991.

Queau, P. The virtues and the vertigo of the virtual. *J. of Visualization and Computer Animation*, 2 (3): 114–115, 1991.

Raab, F.H., Blood, E.B., Steiner, T.O. and Jones, R.J. Magnetic position and orientation tracking system (polhemus device). *IEEE Transactions on Aerospace and Electronic Systems*, AESE-15 (5): 709–718, September 1979.

Reinhart, W.F., Beaton, R.J. and Snyder, H.L. Comparison of depth cues for relative depth judgments. In John O. Merritt and Scott S. Fisher, editors, *Stereoscopic Displays and Applications*, volume 1256 of *Proc. SPIE*, pages 12–21, 1990.

Rheingold, H. What's the Big Deal about Cyberspace? In *The Art of Human Computer Interface Design*. Addison-Wesley, 1990.

Rheingold, H. Teledildonics. *Mondo 2000*, pages 52–54, Summer 1990.

Rheingold, H. *Virtual Reality*. Secker and Warburg, 1991.

Ridsdale, G., Hewitt, S. and Calvert, T.W. The interactive specification of human animation. In *Proc. Graphics Interface '86*, pages 121–130, May 26–30 1986.

Riel, M. Education and ecstasy: Computer chronicles of students writing together. *The Quarterly Newsletter of the Laboratory of Comparative Human Cognition*, July 1983.

Ritman, E.L., Robb, R.A., Hoffman, E.A., Sinak, L.J. and Harris, L.D. High-speed three-dimensional X-ray computed tomography: The dynamic spatial reconstructor. *Mayo Clinic Proceedings*, 71 (3): 308–319, March 1983.

Ritman, E.L., Sinak, L.J., Hoffman, E.A., Julsrud, P.R., Mair, D.D., Seward, J.B., Hagler, D.J., Harris, L.D. and Robb, R.A. The dynamic spatial reconstructor: Investigating congenital heart disease in four dimensions. *Cardiovascular and Interventional Radiology*, 71 (1): 125–139, July 1984.

Robert, I. Psychological and pedagogical issues in using virtual reality systems. In *Virtual Reality International 92: Impacts and Applications*, pages 7–13, 1992.

Robinett, W. Head-mounted display project. In *Imagina '91 INA*, pages 5.5–5.6, 1991.

Robinson, R. Opus I. 14: 233–234, January 1989.

Roese, J.A. and Mcleary, L.E. Stereoscopic computer graphics for simulation and modeling (piezo electro optic shutter stereoscopic viewer). In *Proceedings, SIGGRAPH*, volume 13, pages 41–44, 1979.

Rogore, M. Now 'artificial reality'. *Newsweek*, pages 56–57, 9 Feb. 1987.

Rohan, T. Plane research fallout. *Industry Week*, 230 (7): 37, Sept. 29 1986.

Rolfe, J.M. and Staples, K.J, editors. *Flight Simulation*. Cambridge University Press, Cambridge, 1986.

Root, R.W. Design of a multimedia vehicle for social browsing. In *Proc. of Conference on Computer-Supported Cooperative Work*, Portland, OR, Sept. 26–29 1988. Sponsored by ACM SIGCHI and SIGOIS.

Roscoe, S.N. Judgments of size and distance with imaging displays. *Human Factors*, 26: 617–629, 1984.

Roscoe, S.N. The trouble with HUDs and HMDs. *Human Factors Society Bulletin*, 30 (7): 1–3, July 1987.

Roskos, E. Towards a distributed object-oriented virtual environment. Report to the National Science Foundation, NSF Grant CCR89–09197, 1991.

Roskos, E. and Zuang, J. *Real-Time Software for the VPL Dataglove*. Center for Computer Aids for Industrial Productivity, Rutgers University, 1990.

Rubine, D. Integrating gesture recognition and direct manipulation. In *Summer 1991 USENIX Conference*, pages 291–298, 1991.

Russo, M.A. The design and implementation of a three degree of freedom force output joystick. Ms thesis, MIT, Cambridge, MA, May 1990.

Saffo, P. Desperately seeking cyberspace. *Personal Computing*, pages 247–248, May 1989.

Saffo, P. Virtual reality is almost real. *Personal Computing*, pages 99–102, June 1990.

Satava, Col. R. Telepresence surgery. In *Proceedings of the 1992 EFDPMA Conference on Virtual Reality*, 1992.

Scheinin, R. The artificial realist. *San Jose Mercury News*, pages C1–2, Jan. 30 1990.

Schmandt, C. Interactive three-dimensional computer space. In *Processing and Display of Three-Dimensional Data*, volume 367 of *Proc. SPIE*, pages 155–159, 1982.

Schmandt, C. Spatial input/display correspondence in a stereoscopic computer graphic workstation. *ACM Computer Graphics*, 17 (3): 253–261, July 1983.

Shaw, J. Virtual reality: A new medium for the artist? In *Virtual Reality International 92: Impacts and Applications*, pages 65–68, 1992.

Sheff, D. The virtual realities of Timothy Leary. *Upside*, pages 66–68, 70, 72–76, 79, April 1990.

Sheridan, T.B. Merging mind and machine. *Technology Review*, pages 33–40, October 1989. (Keywords: teleoperation, telerobots).

Sheridan, T.B. Applications focus: Telepresence. In *Virtual Reality 1991*, 1991.

Sims, K. and Zeltzer, D. A figure editor and gait controller for task level animation. *Course Notes, Synthetic Actors: The Impact of Robotics and Artificial Intelligence on Computer Animation*, August 2 1988.

Singer, J., Behrend, S.D. and Rochelle, J. Children's collaborative use of a computer microworld. In *Proc. of Conf. on Computer-Supported Cooperative Work*, Portland, OR, Sept. 26–29 1988. Sponsored by ACM SIGCHI and SIGOIS.

Slater, M. and Davison, A. Liberation from flatland: 3D interaction based on the desktop bat. *Eurographics 1991*, pages 209–221, 1991.

Slavin, R.E., Madden, N.A. and Stevens, R.J. Cooperative learning models for the 3 Rs. *Educational Leadership*, Dec./Jan. 1989/1990.

Slocum, G. and Furness, T. Airborne multisensor design. In *National Aerospace Electronics Conference*, Dayton, OH, May 1969.

Smith, B. The use of animation to analyze and present information about complex systems. In *Proceedings of Virtual Reality '91, 2nd Annual Conference on Virtual Reality, Artificial Reality and Cyberspace*, pages 190–199, 1991.

Smith, B. The flowsheet: Animation used to analyse and present information about complex systems. In *Proceedings of the 1992 EFDPMA Conference on Virtual Reality*, 1992.

Smith, D. Envisioning new applications. In *Proceedings of the 1992 EFDPMA Conference on Virtual Reality*, 1992.

Smith, J. Exploring future business environments. *The Deeper News*, 1 (3): 2–7, 9–14, June 1989.

Smith, M.J. Tactile interface for three-dimensional computer-simulated environments: Experimentation and the design of a brake-motor device. Ms thesis, mechanical engineering, MIT, 1988.

Smith, R.B. The alternate reality kit: An animated environment for creating interactive simulations. In *IEEE Workshop on Visual Languages*, pages 99–106, Dallas TX, 1986.

Smith, R.B. Experiences with the alternative reality kit: An example of the tension between literalism and magic. In *CHI 1987*, page 67, 1987.

Smith, S., Bergeron, R.D. and Grinstein, G.G. Stereophonic and surface sound generation for exploratory data analysis. In *Proc. CHI'90 (Seattle)*, pages 125–132, April 1990.

Spain, E.H., Cole, R.E. and Pepper, R.L. Visual performance and fatigue with stereoscopic television displays. In *Proceedings of the 1984 National Topical Meeting on Robotics and Remote Handling in Hostile Environments*, pages 61–67, April 1984.

Spring, M.B. Informating with virtual reality. *Virtual Reality: Theory, Practice and Promise*, pages 3–17, 1991.

Stark, L. Telerobotics: Display, control and communication problems. *IEEE Journal of Robotics and Automation*, 3 (1): 67–75, February 1987.

Starker, I. and Bolt, R.A. A gaze-responsive self-disclosing display. In *Proc. of CHI'90 (Seattle)*, pages 3–10, Apr. 1–5 1990.

Starks, M. Stereoscopic video and the quest for virtual reality. In *Proceedings of Virtual Reality '91, 2nd Annual Conference on Virtual Reality, Artificial Reality and Cyberspace*, pages 200–225, 1991.

Stereoscopic and multiplanar computer graphics. *Tutorial, SIGGRAPH 1988 15th Conference on Computer Graphics*, 1988.

Stewart, D. Through the looking-glass into an artificial world – via computer. *Smithsonian*, 21 (10): 36–45, January 1991. Popular overview of state-of-the-art in virtual realities.

Stewart, M.K. Visualization resources and strategies for remote subsea exploration. Patrikalakis, N. (editor) *Scientific Visualization of Physical Phenomena*, Springer Verlag, Tokyo, 85–109, 1991.

Stone, R. A virtual environment demonstrator for remote driving applications. In *Proc. Human-Machine Interfaces for Teleoperators and Virtual Environments*, page 77, March 1990.

Stone, R.J. Advanced human-system interfaces for telerobotics using virtual reality and telepresence technologies. In *Fifth International Conference on Advanced Robotics*, 1991.

Stone, R.J. Human factors requirements for telerobotic command and control: The European Space Agency experimental programme. In *Proc. Human-Machine Interfaces for Teleoperators and Virtual Environments*, page 76, March 1990.

Stone, R.J. Virtual reality – the serious side: Where next, and how? In *Virtual Reality 91: Impacts and Applications*, pages 21–25, 1991.

Stone, R.J. Virtual reality and telepresence: A UK initiative. In *Virtual Reality 91: Impacts and Applications*, pages 40–45, 1991.

Stone, R. Virtual reality in perspective. In *Virtual Reality International 92: Impacts and Applications*, pages 7–13, 1992.

Stone, R. New developments in telepresence. In *Virtual Reality International 92: Impacts and Applications*, pages 103–116, 1992.

Stone, R.J. and Dalton, D.G. Virtual reality and telepresence: Creating visual worlds from non-visual sensors. In *ORIA 1991: Telerobotics in Hostile Environments*, 1991.

Stoppi, J. Virtual and real-time interactive spatial modelling. In *Virtual Reality International 92: Impacts and Applications*, pages 23–30, 1992.

Stratton, R. Imagenation 'virtual reality' for entertainment. *Mondo 2000*, page 63, 1990.

Stuart, R. Virtual reality at nynex. In *Proceedings of Virtual Reality '91, 2nd Annual Conference on Virtual Reality, Artificial Reality and Cyberspace*, pages 226–232, 1991.

Stuart, R. Virtual reality: Directions in research and development. *Interactive Learning International*, pages 95–100, 1992.

Sturman, D., Zeltzer, D. and Pieper, S. Hands-on interaction with virtual environments. In *Proc. UIST '89: ACM SIGGRAPH/SIGCHI Symposium on*

User Interface Software and Technology, pages 19–24, Williamsburg, VA, Nov. 13–15 1989.

Sturman, D., Zeltzer, D. and Pieper, S. The use of constraints in the bolio system (course notes, implementing and interacting with realtime microworlds). In *ACM SIGGRAPH 89*, Boston, MA, July 31 1989.

Sturman, D.J. *Whole-hand Input*. Thesis proposal, MIT, 1991.

Sutherland, I. *Sketchpad, A Man-Machine Graphical Communication System*. PhD thesis, MIT, January 1963.

Sutherland, I. The ultimate display. In *Proceedings IFIP Congress*, pages 506–508, 1965.

Sutherland, I. A head-mounted three dimensional display. In *Proc. Fall Joint Computer Conference*, pages 757–764, 1968.

Tachi, S. Tele-existence and/or cybernetic interface studies in Japan. In *Proc. Human-Machine Interfaces for Teleoperators and Virtual Environments*, pages 40–41, March 1990.

Tait, A. Desktop virtual reality. *IEEE Colloquium on Using Virtual Worlds*, pages 5/1–5, 1992.

Tait, A. Authoring virtual worlds on the desktop. In *Virtual Reality International 92: Impacts and Applications*, pages 31–36, 1992.

Teitel, M., Blanchard, C., Burgess, S., Harvill, Y., Lanier, J., Lasko, A. and Oberman, M. Reality built for two: A virtual reality tool. In *Proc. Human-Machine Interfaces for Teleoperators and Virtual Environments*, March 1990.

Tello, E.R. Between man and machine. *BYTE*, pages 288–292, September 1988.

Theasby, P. Virtual reality and simulation. In *Virtual Reality International 92: Impacts and Applications*, pages 78–91, 1992.

Thomas, W. Hyperwebs. *Mondo 2000*, pages 68–69, 1990.

Thompson, S. Driving through a virtual world. *Autoweek*, 37 (28): 31–36, July 13 1987.

Thompson, S.L. The big picture. *Air and Space Smithsonian*, pages 4–83, May 1987.

Thompson, S. A new era for man and machine. *The Washington Post*, page B3, May 10 1987.

Thurman, R. Simulation and training based technology. In *Proceedings of the 1992 EFDPMA Conference on Virtual Reality*, 1992.

Traub, D.C. Simulated world as classroom: The potential for designed learning within virtual environments. In *Virtual Reality: Theory, Practice and Promise*, pages 111–121, Mechler, 1991.

Turner, R., Balaguer, F., Gobbetti, E. and Thalmann, D. Physically-based interactive camera motion control using 3D input devices. In Patrikalakis, N. (editor) *Scientific Visualization of Physical Phenomena*, Springer Verlag, Tokyo, pages 135–145, 1991.

Turvey, M.T., Fitch, H.L. and Tuller, B. The problems of degrees of freedom and context-conditioned variability. In J.A.S. Kelso, editor, *Human Motor Behavior*, pages 239–252. Lawrence Erlbaum Associates, Hillsdale, New Jersey, 1982.

Tutorial, virtual interface technology (virtual reality). *SIGGRAPH 1991 18th Conference on Computer Graphics*, 1991.

Underwood, D. VCASS: Beauty (and combat effectiveness) is in the eye of the beholder. *Rotor and Wing International*, 20 (3): 72–73, 107, February 1986.

Uttal, W.R. *The Perception of Dotted Forms*. Lawrence Erlbaum Associates, 1987.

Vickers, D. Head-mounted display terminal. In *Proc. IEEE Int. Computer Group Conference*, pages 102–109, 1970.

Vickers, D.L. Sorcerer's apprentice: Headmounted display and wand in remotely manned systems. In E. Heer, editor, *Exploration and Operation in Space*. Caltech, 1973.

VoiceMED. Kurzwiel AI newsletter, Summer 1989.

Vondruska, T. WPAFB premier generator of research. *The Daily Gazette*, page 17a, April 22 1987.

VPL Research Inc. *DataGlove Gesture Editor Software for the Apple Macintosh, Operation Manual*, March 1989.

VPL Research Inc. *RB2Swivel User Interface Documentation*, January 1989.

VPL Research Inc. *Reality Built for Two: RB2 Operation Manual*, January 1990.

VPL Reserarch Inc. *Body Electric Manual*, February 1991.

Vygotsky, L.S. *Mind in Society*. Harvard University Press, Cambridge, 1978.

Waldern, J.D. Virtuality – the world's first production virtual reality workstation. In *Virtual Reality 91: Impacts and Applications*, pages 26–34, 1991.

Waldern, J.D. Virtual reality – the serious side. In *Proceedings of the 1992 EFDPMA Conference on Virtual Reality*, 1992.

Walker, J. Through the looking glass. International paper, Autodesk, 1988.

Walker, J., Beard, D. and Toki, O. Fingerpointing and eyetrackers for task analysis of medical image information systems. Technical Report TR 90-015, Univ. of N. Carolina, Computer Science Dept., 1990.

Walser, R. Doing it directly – the experimental design of cyberspace. In *Proc. 1990 SPIE/SPSE Symposium on Electronic Imaging Science and Technology*, February 1990.

Walser, R. Elements of a cyberspace playhouse. In *Virtual Reality: Theory, Practice and Promise*, pages 51–64, Meckler 1991.

Walser, R. The emerging technologies of cyberspace. In *Virtual Reality: Theory, Practice and Promise*, pages 35–40, Meckler 1991.

Walser, R. On the road to Cyberia. (Excerpts From A Proposal Draft For Autodesk Research Lab), November 1988.

Walser, R. Construction in cyberspace – developing a next generation programming environment for virtual reality. In *Proceedings of the 1992 EFDPMA Conference on Virtual Reality*, 1992.

Ware, C. Using the hand position for virtual object placement. *The Visual Computer*, 6: 245–253, 1990. (Keywords: bat, polhemus, user interface, input device, virtual environments, 3D interaction).

Ware, C. and Jessome, D.R. Using the bat, a six-dimensional mouse for object placement. *IEEE Computer Graphics and Applications*, pages 65–70, November 1988.

Ware, C. and Osborne, S. Exploration and virtual camera control in virtual three dimensional environments. *Computer Graphics*, 24 (2): 175–183, March 1990.

Watanabe, Y. and Suenaga, Y. Synchronized acquisition of three-dimensional range and color data and its applications, in Patrikalakis, N. (editor), *Scientific Visualization of Physical Phenomena*, Springer Verlag, New York, 1991.

Weiner, E. New heights for cockpit electronics. *Seattle Post-Intelligencer*, Feb. 20 1990.

Weintraub, J. Virtual reality I: Virtual life. *PC AI*, page 41, Nov./Dec. 1989.

Wenzel, E., Wightman, F. and Foster, S. A virtual display system for displaying three dimensional acoustic information. In *Proceedings of the Human Factors Society – 32nd Annual Meeting*, pages 86–90, 1988.

Wenzel, E.M. and Foster, S.H. Realtime digital synthesis of virtual acoustic environments. *Computer Graphics*, pages 139–142, 1990.

Wenzel, E.M., Wightman, F.L. and Foster, S.H. Development of three-dimensional auditory display system. In *CHI 1988*, 1988.

Wenzel, E.M., Stone, P.K., Fisher, S.S. and Foster, S.H. A system for three-dimensional acoustic 'visualization' in a virtual environment workstation. In *IEEE Conference on Visualization*, pages 329–337, 1990.

Wexelbat, A. Near term commercialization of vr technology – the 5 and 10 year picture. In *Proceedings of the 1992 EFDPMA Conference on Virtual Reality*, 1992.

Whalley, S. Applications of visualization within British Telecom. In *IEEE Colloquium on using Virtual Worlds*, pages 6/1–3, 1992.

Wickens, C.D. Three-dimensional stereoscopic display implementation: Guidelines derived from human visual capabilities. In John O. Merritt and Scott S. Fisher, editors, *Stereoscopic Displays and Applications*, volume 1256 of *Proc. SPIE*, pages 2–11, 1990.

Wickens, C.D., Todd, S. and Seidler, K. Three-dimensional displays: Perception, implementation, and applications. Technical Report CSERIAC SOAR 89-001, AFAAMRL, Wright-Patterson AFB, Ohio, 1989.

Wilhelms, M.M. and Skinner, R. Dynamic animation: Interaction and control. *The Visual Computer*, 4 (6): 283–295, December 1988.

Wilke, J. This device has people staring into space. *The Wall Street Journal*, page 1, December 7 1989.

Williams, W.J. *Voice of the Whirlwind*. Tom Doherty Associates, Inc, 1987. ISBN 0-812-555785-9.

Wise, S.A., Rosen, J., Fisher, S., Glass K. and Wong, Y. Initial experience with the dataglove, a semi-automated system for quantification of hand function. In *RESNA 10th Annual Conf.*, pages 259–260, San Jose CA, 1987.

Wolfe, A. Off the shelf visualization. *Computer Graphics World*, pages 50–54, July 1989.

Won, K-Y and Nam Y-H. VR = AI + CHI. *Korean Inf. Sci. Soc. Rev.*, pages 71–76, 1991.

Yager, S., Johnson, D.W. and Johnson, R.T. Oral discussion group-to-individual transfer and achievement in cooperative learning groups. *Journal of Educational Psychology*, 1985.

Yeh, Y-Y. and Silverstein, L.D. Using electronic stereoscopic color displays: Limits of fusion and depth discrimination. In Woodrow E. Robbins and Scott S. Fisher, editors, *Three-Dimensional Visualization and Display Technologies*, volume 1083 of *Proc. SPIE*, pages 196–204, 1989.

Young, J. A new generation of virtual worlds – the structure of cyberspace. In *Proceedings of the 1992 EFDPMA Conference on Virtual Reality*, 1992.

Zachary, G.P. Artificial reality. *The Wall Street Journal*, pages A1, A12, Jan 23 1990.

Zachmann, W.F. Adventures in cyberspace. *PC Magazine*, pages 83–84, May 30 1989.

Zeltzer, D. Knowledge-based animation. In *Proc. ACM SIGGRAPH/SIGART Workshop on Motion*, pages 187–192, Toronto, Canada, April 1983.

Zeltzer, D. Towards an integrated view of 3-D computer animation. *The Visual Computer*, 1 (4): 249–259, December 1985. Reprinted with revisions from Proc. Graphics Interface 85.

Zeltzer, D. Motor problem solving for three dimensional computer animation. *Proc. L'Imaginaire Numérique*, May 14–16 1987.

Zeltzer, D. Task level graphical simulation: Abstraction, representation and control.

In N. Badler, B. Barsky, and D. Zeltzer, editors, *Making Them Move: Mechanics, Control and Animation of Articulated Figures*, pages 3–33. Morgan Kaufmann, San Mateo, CA, 1991.

Zeltzer, D. and Johnson, M.B. Motor planning: An architecture for specifying and controlling the behavior of virtual actors. *The Journal of Visualization and Computer Animation*, 2 (2).

Zeltzer, D., Pieper, S. and Sturman, D. An integrated graphical simulation platform. In *Proc. Graphics Interface '89*, pages 266–274, London, Ontario, June 1989.

Zimmerman, T.G., Lanier, J., Blanchard, C., Bryson, S. and Harvill, Y. A hand gesture interface device. *ACM SIGCHI/GI*, pages 189–192, 1987.

Zintz, W. Neural wire-tapping. *UNIXWORLD*, VII (8): 160, August 1990. Article on current research on neural implants.

Zyda, M. Educational and technological foundations for the construction of a 3D virtual world. In *Proceedings of the 1992 EFDPMA Conference on Virtual Reality*, 1992.

Appendix: Overview of Virtual Reality Software Suppliers

Craig McNaughton

Royal Melbourne Institute of Technology
Advanced Computer Graphics Centre

Abstract

In this paper, we identify a number of suppliers of software designed to support the development of virtual environments. We also provide an overview of the most popular, readily available software 'toolkits'.

Our review is, by necessity, limited by the availability of information about the software toolkits and is also limited by our personal access to the software. Nevertheless, it is hoped that this information will be useful to potential developers of virtual environment applications.

1 Introduction

In recent years, many software packages have been written to build and manage virtual environments. As well as commercial software packages, many universities are distributing toolkits that have grown out of research projects. We have provided a list (see section 3) of the known software (at the time of writing) that relates to virtual environments. Three of these packages, VPL's Body Electric, Sense8's WorldToolKit, and the MR toolkit from the University of Alberta will be covered in greater detail in the following sections.

2 Reviews

2.1 VPL

VPL, the manufacturers of the well known DataGlove and EyePhone, also provide a series of software packages for designing and investigating virtual environments. These packages consist of the following:

- *Body Electric* A data flow network manager for obtaining and manipulating data from various sources, including DataGloves and positional sensors
- *Swivel 3D* A 3D modelling package with links to Body Electric
- *Isaac* A 3D rendering package (for SGI machines) which takes Swivel models, modified by Body Electric data, and renders them in real time.

These three packages combine to give a complete virtual environment development system. A user designs a virtual environment in Swivel, which creates a 'tree'. This tree is modified by data from the Body Electric, and finally passed on to Isaac for rendering.

The original versions of Swivel 3D and Body Electric only ran on the Macintosh platform, but versions have recently been released to run on SGI machines as well.

2.1.1   Body electric
This data flow network package provides a link between physical devices and objects and features in the virtual environment. Raw data modules can take data from a variety of places, including VPL DataGlove and DataSuit, and Polhemus 3Space trackers as well as traditional mouse and keyboard inputs. There are also a number of raw data inputs that provide data from such things as clocks and random number generators. Data from these raw inputs can then be sent through a network of 'massage' modules, which can process the data in a variety of ways. There are mathematical massage modules, logical massage modules and filter modules, to mention just a few.

2.1.2   Swivel 3D
Swivel 3D provides a complete 3D modeller. It allows for the design of polygonal objects. It includes support for colouring and lighting, and well as a number of rendering styles, including fast wireframe and hidden line modes for previewing. Objects in Swivel can be named, and it is these names that are used as links by Body Electric for changing objects in the scene.

2.1.3   Isaac
Running on SGI machines, Isaac takes the 3D database that can be exported from Swivel, and renders it in real time. It can run either in stand-alone mode, where interaction is controlled by mouse and keyboard, or it can run in conjunction with the Body Electric, communicating via Ethernet. When communicating with Body Electric, the data values are used to modify the appropriately named objects in the database. Isaac provides support for PAL and NTSC video.

2.2   Sense8
The WorldToolKit from Sense8 Corporation is a complete Virtual Environment library, providing over 230 functions for handling all facets of interaction with virtual environments. It is distributed as a library of C functions, callable from user programs. Organized in an object-orientated framework, the library provides objects for most things that would be required for simple environments. It runs on several platforms, including SGI graphics workstations for high performance applications and IBM compatible PCs, for more budget applications.

It has built in support for a variety of positional sensors, including the Polhemus 3Space, and the Ascension Bird tracker. Also supported are the SpaceBall and the Fake Space Labs BOOM positional sensor. Adding user defined devices is fairly easy, provided the devices can be handled within the framework of the WorldToolKit device structure.

WorldToolKit provides little in the way of modelling tools, but compensates for this by importing DXF files from many popular CAD packages. It also defines a neutral ASCII file format and can read and write its own custom format. The only modelling tools provided in the toolkit are for simple terrain creation. Flat and random terrain objects can be created, or height data can be read from a file to create terrains.

The world or 'universe' is constructed as two differing types of objects. The universe object (of which there can be only one), provides a static background for the environment. Into this universe, dynamic objects can be placed. Much preprocessing is done on the static universe, so in general, this will be rendered at higher quality than the dynamic objects. The class of dynamic objects contains such things as polygonal models, light sources, and viewpoints.

The main strengths of the WorldToolKit lie in rendering and interaction. For interaction, you can add as many sensors as the hardware supports (e.g. mouse, SpaceBall, Polhemus), and these sensors can be attached to one or more of the dynamic objects in the 'universe'. So to create a head tracked view of the universe, a position sensor could be opened and attached to a dynamic viewpoint in the scene. During the main processing loop, the position and orientation of the viewpoint would automatically be updated to reflect the position and orientation of the sensor.

As the environment can only consist of one universe at a time, the toolkit provides 'portals' for transferring between universes. A portal is merely a polygon in the scene. When the viewpoint passes through the portal, the current universe is removed, and the universe that the portal links to is loaded from disk and becomes active.

Interactions are controlled by user supplied callback functions. To assist the functions, the toolkit provides many support routines. Both objects and individual polygons can be picked, based on screen coordinates of sensors. Collision detection routines are also provided, both fast bounding box tests, and slower accurate tests.

Dynamic objects can also be set in predefined animation sequences, where the model for the object cycles through a set of predefined objects at a given rate.

Rendering is done either in software, or if available, passed on to graphics hardware. In the case of an SGI VGX machine, or with special graphics hardware in a '486 PC, texture mapping is supported. Timing statistics can be obtained, and these can be used to control adaptive resolution for the images, and adaptive level of detail of the dynamic objects in the universe.

2.3 MR

In contrast to the other virtual environment software examined here, MR (or Minimal Reality to give it its full title) is not a complete library for virtual environments. What MR does provide is a low level library for communicating with the devices commonly used in VR, e.g. DataGloves and EyePhones. MR also provides support for distributed computation.

MR consists of three levels of libraries. At the lowest level are the device drivers. These communicate directly with the EyePhones and DataGloves. The drivers get the raw data from these devices and can optionally perform filtering on this raw data to account for noise in these readings. There is also a Kalmann predictive filter available, which attempts to compensate for the phase lag of the Polhemus sensors.

Sitting above the device drivers are libraries for each individual device. In the case of the DataGloves, this library provides calibration facilities and gesture recognition. The gestures can be recognized from a number of tables, providing a large range of functions available at gesture command. The DataGlove library also provides routines for rendering simple imagery of the hand.

Atop the individual device libraries lies the top level toolkit library. This contains routines for such things as setting up units for the virtual environment and for setting up both mono and stereo viewpoints prior to rendering the scene.

The original MR toolkit assumed that a distributed computing environment was being used, and relied very heavily on having a master process with many slaves for things such as rendering. It also assumed that two workstations were being used to generate the twin views required for a stereo head-mounted display.

MR makes no effort to provide any modelling capabilities, or any world database management or world interactions. Support for user supplied rendering routines is present in the form of routines to set up the viewing projections and for rendering hand imagery.

An adaptation of MR called MRx (Minimal Reality Extensions) removes some of the restrictions on the computing environment that MR imposed. An entire system can be run on a single processor, and one machine can generate both stereo views.

The main differences between MR and MRx can be summarized as follows:

- MR provides full distributed support, but enforces a distributed environment. MRx can run as a single process.
- MRx provides more gesture support routines, with the ability to produce imagery of gestures as a guide to users.
- MRx currently only runs on SGI workstations.
- MRx supports fingertip position and direction calculation from current hand data.

MR currently runs on both SGI workstations and under PHIGS. A licence to run MR is available free of charge on application to the University of Alberta.

MRx is currently under development at the Advanced Computer Graphics Centre of the Royal Melbourne Institute of Technology and will hopefully be available through the University of Alberta in the near future.

3   Software Suppliers

Supplier	VPL Research Inc.
Software	Body Electric, RB2 Swivel, Isaac
Platform	Mac, SGI
Summary	Full suit of virtual environment development and interaction applications.
Contact	VPL Research Inc.
	3977 East Bayshore Road
	Palo Alto, CA 94303
	(415) 988 2250 (Voice)
	(415) 988 2557 (FAX)
Supplier	University of Washington

Software	VEOS (Virtual Environment Operating Shell)
Platform	Unix
Summary	Virtual environment database and interaction handler. *Research Software*.
Contact	Human Interface Technology Laboratory
	FJ-15, University of Washington
	Seattle
	Washington 98195
	email veos-support@hitl.washington.edu

Supplier	University of Alberta
Software	MR (Minimal Reality Toolkit)
Platform	Unix, SGI or PHIGS graphics support
Summary	Lower level VR device support. *Research Software*
Contact	Department of Computer Science
	615 General Service Building
	University of Alberta
	Edmonton,
	Alberta,
	Canada T6G 2H1

Supplier	Virtus Corporation
Software	Virtus Walkthrough
Platform	Mac
Summary	3D walkthrough software
Contact	Virtus Corporation
	117 Edinburgh South
	Suite 204
	Cary, North Carolina 27511
	(919) 467-9700 (voice)

Supplier	Sense8 Corporation
Software	WorldToolKit Library
Platform	PC, SGI
Summary	Virtual environment interaction and rendering library.
Contact	Sense8 Corporation
	1001 Bridgeway, No. 477
	Sausalito, CA 94965
	(415) 331-6318 (voice)
	(415) 331-9148 (FAX)

Supplier	Swedish Institute of Computer Science
Software	SICS Telepresence
Platform	SUN, SGI, IBM RS6000
Summary	Complete virtual environment design and interaction library. *Research Software*

Contact   Lennart Fahlen, DS Labs
                     Swedish Institute of Computer Science, Stockholm

Index